D0049841

American Sportsmen
and the Origins of Conservation

Third, Revised and Expanded, Edition

American Sportsmen
and the
Origins of Conservation

Third, Revised and Expanded, Edition

John F. Reiger

Oregon State University Press
Corvallis

Front cover photograph: President Benjamin Harrison (on right) in his duck blind (1891).
Back cover photograph: Gifford Pinchot fly-fishing.

The paper in this book meets the guidelines for permanence and durability of the Committee on Production Guidelines for Book Longevity of the Council on Library Resources and the minimum requirements of the American National Standard for Permanence of Paper for Printed Library Materials Z39.48-1984.

Library of Congress Cataloging-in-Publication Data
Reiger, John F.
  American sportsmen and the origins of conservation / John F. Reiger.—3rd rev. & expanded ed.
    p. cm.
Includes bibliographical references and index.
  ISBN 0-87071-487-2 (alk. paper)
  1. Wildlife conservation—United States—History. 2. Nature conservation—United States—History. I. Title.
  QL84.2 .R43 2000
  333.95'416'0973--dc21
                                                                00-011078

OREGON STATE UNIVERSITY

Oregon State University Press
101 Waldo Hall
Corvallis OR 97331-6407
541-737-3166 • fax 541-737-3170
http://osu.orst.edu/dept/press

To Andrea—for always being there.

He was always to be seen in serene afternoons haunting the river, and almost rustling with the sedge. . . . His fishing was not a sport, nor solely a means of subsistence, but a sort of solemn sacrament and withdrawal from the world, just as the aged read their Bibles.

HENRY DAVID THOREAU DESCRIBING A LOCAL ANGLER.
From *A Week on the Concord and Merrimac Rivers* (1849)

Some of our newspapers [erroneously] reported that the President intended to hunt in the Park. A woman in Vermont wrote me, to protest against the hunting, and hoped I would teach the President to love the animals as much as I did—as if he did not love them much more, because his love is founded upon knowledge, and because they had been a part of his life.

JOHN BURROUGHS COMMENTING ON HIS TRIP
THROUGH YELLOWSTONE NATIONAL PARK IN 1903
WITH THEODORE ROOSEVELT.
From *Camping and Tramping with Roosevelt* (1907)

Contents

Preface to the Third, Revised and Expanded, Edition

Since its original publication in 1975, *American Sportsmen and the Origins of Conservation* has continued to generate debate. Given the wealth of original sources supporting the thesis, many readers have found the book convincing. But for others, the interpretation that hunters and anglers cherished wildlife and habitat, and organized the first movement to preserve them for future generations, has seemed strange, even illogical.

This last reaction is a natural one for Americans growing up in urban or suburban settings, who lack personal experience with the sporting traditions of the rod and the gun. Most of us go through our daily routines assuming that water comes from the tap and meat from the supermarket—instead of the land[1]—and we fail to see the appeal of catching or "bagging" our own food. The "blood sports" of fishing and hunting, particularly the latter, may seem like barbaric holdovers from an earlier age that should be replaced with more enlightened, humane pursuits.

Reinforcing this viewpoint is the growing animal-rights movement. Aside from its obvious humane appeal, the animals-rights crusade also attracts Americans unhappy with decreasing populations of many wildlife species and the deterioration of the environment generally. Factors like ballooning numbers of human beings, continuous "development" and its resulting habitat loss, and the invasion of alien species that soon dominate an ecosystem—the most common causes for wildlife decline—are generalized, amorphous phenomena that seem incapable of being controlled, while hunters and fishermen are specific, high-profile groups that can be focused on and attacked.

In the Introduction of the first edition, the author noted the inconsistency of those who profess animal rights, but fail to give fishes the same consideration for humane treatment as more appealing animals like "innocent" deer and "comical" bears. Hunters presumably try for a quick, clean kill, with as little suffering of the animal or bird as possible. In contrast, the angler values most those species that struggle the longest to escape the inexorable pressure of line and rod. Obviously, sailfish, smallmouth bass, and other "sensate beings"—to use a phrase favored by animal-rights advocates—find the experience of being hooked an unpleasant one, as demonstrated by their continual leaps for freedom. The angler, of course, can respond that he or she practices "catch-and-release" fishing, and never actually kills the catch. But the reality is that a certain percentage of game fish die after being released, the best efforts at revival notwithstanding.

In the quarter century since this book first appeared, animal-rights proponents have come to see the inconsistency in their earlier position of accepting angling, but condemning hunting. For them, whether or not the catch is released is irrelevant, for they increasingly condemn the humans who obtain pleasure from the discomfort of a fellow creature. Indeed, the writer has been told on more than one occasion in recent years that any fishing which does not have the procurement of food as its objective and which does not involve the quick capture and death of the fish is more immoral than hunting, assuming, of course, that the hunter eats the kill.

Despite this condemnation of sport fishing by an ever-larger number of animal-rights supporters, sport hunting remains their chief target. Their crusading zeal has even penetrated the field of historical scholarship, formerly considered off-limits for those advocating a particular ideological position. An example is historian Thomas R. Dunlap's proclamation in the Preface of his *Saving America's Wildlife* (1988): "A significant minority among us grants animals rights and *seeks* [emphasis added] to have society do the same. We 'instinctively' draw back from cruelty and pain."[2] Because sport hunting always involves—at least as far as animal-rights advocates are concerned—a certain amount of cruelty and pain, historians who espouse an animal-rights doctrine "draw back" as scholars and have difficulty examining hunting in detail, with scholarly detachment. In another work Dunlap goes so far as to label hunters a "despised minority," whose days, he hopes, are numbered.[3]

That hunter-conservationists of the latter part of the nineteenth century were part of a separate culture, or subculture, is a concept that has escaped many academic historians who have seen hunting either as a minor avocation fraught with whimsy or as one that merits attack from an animal-rights point of view. According to Yellowstone National Park historian Paul Schullery: "Perhaps one reason that scholars occasionally have difficulty developing a scholarly perspective on the history of hunting is that so few have taken the subject on as a field of study." Like some other avocations, including fishing, "hunting seems to have been viewed not as an element of culture but as a vacation from it, a sort of analysis-exempt aspect of daily life." The result is a "view [that] trivializes something of great significance."[4]

The good news is that other scholars have been able to view the historical record objectively, regardless of their individual predilections; they do not "read the present backwards" and impose their own values on the past. In fact, I have been gratified by the generally positive response to the book from my colleagues in the historical profession.

There is evidence that the general public may also be gaining a more sophisticated understanding of hunting and fishing from the often-attacked medium of television. Every weekend, hundreds of thousands of viewers across the country tune into programs on spring largemouth-bass fishing, fall duck hunting, etc., that stress the conservation message. Rarely have I seen a program in recent years that does not include something on the aesthetics of sport and the need to accept responsibility for conserving game and habitat. While outdoor writers have also played a role in improving, through education, the image of hunters and anglers,[5] there are few things as persuasive as the visual impact of television.

What is particularly interesting about the appeal of these programs is that they represent the latest example of a continuing democratization of these activities and the principles on which they are based. As will be shown, sport hunting and fishing in Europe, and later America, were originally reserved for elite members of society. What I have called "the code of the sportsman," which regulated behavior in the field and the taking of game to ensure its survival into the future, began as an aristocratic set of rules in Europe, particularly England, and was later adopted by the American upper classes, at least partly to separate themselves from the "common" hunter and fisherman. Thus, the conservation creed that evolved out of the code of the sportsman also had its origins in an elite world view, at least before 1901, when the main time period covered by this book ends. But the twentieth century witnessed a continuous "trickling down" of these conservation principles, to the point where they are now part of the thinking of millions of contemporary hunters and anglers.

Even in southern, Appalachian Ohio, where the writer has taught "American Environmental History" for ten years at Ohio University, my students tell me that a change seems to be taking place in the attitudes of poor rural folk toward game. In the past every smallmouth bass caught would end up being eaten; increasingly, all but the very largest are returned, to keep the stream from being "fished out."

Similarly, people living back in a valley used to shoot white-tailed deer anytime they had a taste for venison, but they now tend to see such practices as unethical, and wait for deer season to open before doing their hunting. Neither they nor the bass fishermen probably realize how much their thinking derives from what was originally the world view of a relatively small, elite group of Americans.

Before proceeding with the book, some comments should be made concerning its origins. Research began in 1967, when, with the help of James B. Trefethen of the Wildlife Management Institute, I discovered the main body of the papers of George Bird Grinnell, a central figure in the first conservation movement. Located at that time at the Connecticut Audubon Society in Fairfield, the collection begins in the 1880s and includes copies of thousands of letters, many of them to prominent individuals. Grinnell had willed these papers to a personal friend, John P. Holman, who was a later editor of *Forest and Stream,* the newspaper Grinnell edited for over thirty years, and the President of Connecticut Audubon. A smaller collection of papers, relating primarily to Grinnell's work in Plains Indian ethnography and his Western travels, he willed to Frederick Webb Hodge, curator of the Southwest Museum near Los Angeles. It was a privilege to be able to interview Holman about his friendship with Grinnell, and to be the first academic historian to research the main collection, as it is one of the most significant sources of unpublished materials pertaining to early conservation.

After completing my Northwestern University Ph.D. dissertation on Grinnell in 1970 and becoming a history professor at the University of Miami (Florida), I continued to work in the Grinnell papers and expand my research to include all of conservation history. In 1975 Winchester Press in New York published, in hardback, the first edition of *American Sportsmen and the Origins of Conservation.* Small, but important, additions to the text, like clarifying when the *original* American Forestry Association actually began, were made in 1986, when the University of Oklahoma Press published a revised edition.

Earlier, I had given up my professorship at the University of Miami to do full-time environmental education and advocacy work at the Connecticut Audubon Society, an organization I had learned about while working in the Grinnell papers. After becoming Executive Director of the Society in 1983, I discovered that the collection, which had been the genesis of this book, was in danger of being lost to posterity; for example, a few years earlier, a board member of the Society had, on his own initiative, taken all thirty-eight letterbooks of copied outgoing letters to the curb, to be taken to the city dump. Only the timely intervention of a staff member saved the papers. As Executive Director, I arranged for the transfer in 1984 of the entire collection to Yale University.

In 1988 I completed a five-year term at Connecticut Audubon[6] and resumed my academic career on the Chillicothe campus of Ohio University. There, and at the main campus in Athens, I utilized the book in my classes and discovered that other scholars teaching "environmental history"—the history of human interaction with the natural world—also used it. Some of them were kind enough to suggest ways in which *American Sportsmen* could be improved, which brings me to the reasons for this third, revised and expanded, edition published by Oregon State University Press.

In 1975, in the first edition, I noted that the study was originally going to be much longer, but that it had been kept deliberately short so that its thesis was not sidetracked by lengthy discussion of topics like commercial hunting and fishing and destructive logging practices. Both the "Picture Album" and "Selected Bibliography" were intended, therefore, to illustrate ideas pertaining to subjects only briefly presented in the text. But as other environmental historians pointed out, the antecedents of the sportsmen's conservation movement that came into being in the 1870s needed greater coverage; could my thesis be pushed farther back into the past? This edition's new first chapter, "Precursors of Conservation: American Sportsmen Before the Civil War," will, I hope, answer that question.

Another issue that had to be addressed was whether or not the code of the sportsman and the sportsman-conservationist ideal continued to have an influence after 1901. I have already dealt with that question to some degree in this Preface, and will do so in greater detail in the new "Epilogue: Aldo Leopold and the Continuing Tradition of the Sportsman-Conservationist Ideal."

An additional problem that had to be dealt with was the large number of new publications on conservation history that have appeared since 1975. I have added these works, often with accompanying comments, to the new "Annotated Bibliography."

Finally, the reader should be advised that I have made a tremendous number of additions and revisions throughout the book. Most of the time, these changes were made only to clarify, or expand, a particular point; an example is the greater development of the discussion on angling and fish conservation in the third chapter, "Conservation Begins with Wildlife." I have not, however, altered my conclusions regarding the importance of sportsmen in the making of American conservation.

During the work on this third edition, I have, of course, acquired many obligations. Ohio University gave me a sabbatical at a key juncture in my research for the new first chapter, as well as a grant toward the cost of preparing the manuscript. Thomas L. Altherr and Char Miller were kind enough to read, and comment on, the new sections of the book. Other individuals who offered their help, and who have not already been thanked in earlier editions, are Nina Leopold Bradley, Robert A. McCabe, Marie McCabe, Dennis Deane, Polly Burroughs, Paul Schullery, Joseph A. Miller, Harold K. Steen, Warder H. Cadbury, Richard P. Harmond, Jerold Pepper, George M. Luer, William G. Tapply, Marcy Culpin, Betsy Mendelsohn, Sarah E. Broadbent, F. Richard Vaughan, M.L. Biscotti, J. Kenneth Callahan, Dennis Fowler, and Brandi Betts. Warren Slesinger, Jo Alexander, Mary Braun, Paul Merchant, and Tom Booth of Oregon State University Press provided excellent advice about the revision process. Particularly helpful was my research assistant, Pamela Kraft, who provided leads and keyed numerous revisions of the manuscript. Finally, there is Andrea, my wife, whose essential contribution is recorded on the dedication page.

Notes

1. This idea is suggested by philosopher and scientist, Aldo Leopold. See his *A Sand County Almanac* (New York, 1966), 6; this edition is an enlarged version of the book published in 1949, including essays that first appeared in *Round River* (1953).
2. Thomas R. Dunlap, *Saving America's Wildlife* (Princeton, New Jersey, 1988), x.
3. Dunlap, "Sport Hunting and Conservation, 1880-1920," *Environmental Review*, XII (Spring, 1988), 58. Despite its general title, this article is essentially a critique of *American Sportsmen and the Origins of Conservation*. For my response, see "John F. Reiger's Commentary on Thomas R. Dunlap's Article, 'Sport Hunting and Conservation, 1880-1920'," *Environmental Review*, XII (Fall, 1988), 94-96. In 1991, 14.1 million Americans sixteen years old and older participated in hunting; U.S. Department of the Interior, Fish and Wildlife Service, and U.S. Department of Commerce, Bureau of the Census, *1991 National Survey of Fishing, Hunting, and Wildlife-Associated Recreation* (Washington, D.C., 1993), 4 and 32.

4. Paul Schullery, "Theodore Roosevelt: The Scandal of the Hunter as Nature Lover," in Natalie A. Naylor, *et al.*, eds., *Theodore Roosevelt: Many-Sided American* (Interlaken, New York, 1992), 229 (Note #1).

5. Examples are: George Reiger, Conservation Editor of *Field & Stream;* Chris Madson, Editor of *Wyoming Wildlife* and Conservation Editor of *Wildfowl* magazine; and Jim Posewitz, founder of Orion—The Hunters Institute and author of *Beyond Fair Chase: The Ethic and Tradition of Hunting* (Billings, Montana, 1994).

6. For a discussion of how my experience at Connecticut Audubon shows how historical perspective can help resolve present-day environmental issues, see the second essay in John F. Reiger, *"Gifford Pinchot with Rod and Reel"/ "Trading Places: From Historian to Environmental Activist"—Two Essays in Conservation History* (Milford, Pennsylvania, 1994).

Introduction

Ever since the first decade of the twentieth century, when President Theodore Roosevelt and his Chief Forester, Gifford Pinchot, made "conservation" a household word, the term has received a variety of definitions, and every group from the Sierra Club to the United States Army Corps of Engineers has claimed to be its one true representative. During the latter 1960s, the public discovered the word "ecology" and began to use it as if it were a more fashionable version of the older term. Though both words entered the American vocabulary in the late nineteenth century and are now used interchangeably, even by some historians,[1] they have in reality very different meanings.

As a discipline, ecology is "the study of the interrelationships of organisms to one another and to the environment."[2] Because this book deals with the nineteenth century, its human subjects cannot be called "ecologists." Even though many of them possessed an ecological orientation—perceiving the interrelatedness of wildlife and their habitats—they studied organisms (like birds) or environments (like forests), but rarely both simultaneously. Not until the twentieth century did ecology become a recognized science in the United States.

"Conservationist," not "ecologist," is the more precise term for the American pioneer of environmental concern. Long before 1907, when Gifford Pinchot claims to have been the first to perceive the interrelationship of all resource use,[3] an influential segment of the American population had come to understand that renewable resources like wildlife and forests could be utilized indefinitely as long as a certain amount of "capital" was maintained. Even nonrenewable resources like coal and oil could be made to last infinitely longer if managed on an efficient basis. Historically, conservation has not been a science like ecology, but a reform movement using political and legal methods to obtain what the Theodore Roosevelt administration called the "wise use" of resources.

The confusion between ecology and conservation is only one of many ambiguities surrounding the origins of American concern for the environment. There may, in fact, be no aspect of United States history more in need of revision than the historiography[4] of conservation.

One of the most important misconceptions is that no conservation movement existed until the twentieth century. Despite the publication of a number of books and essays purporting to treat the "origins" of the crusade, academic historians invariably begin their works at the close of the nineteenth century, with perhaps a passing nod to a few "prophets" like George Perkins Marsh and John Wesley Powell. Conversely, this volume commences several decades earlier, and shows that the movement originated in the 1870s. The work ends in 1901, when most historians of conservation are just "getting into" their studies. The first years of the twentieth century have been chosen as the closing period because with the ascendancy of Theodore Roosevelt to the Presidency, a movement that began a generation before flowered into a developed federal program of resource management.

Another widely believed myth of conservation historiography is the result of historians examining only the most available sources. Accepting at face value the political rhetoric of the Roosevelt administration, scholars through the 1950s pictured conservation as a movement of "the people" against the monopolistic control of resources by "special interests."[5] According to this thesis, conservation was an integral part of the early twentieth-century reform movement known as "Progressivism."

The problems with this interpretation are immense. First is the fundamental question of whether there was really a Progressive *movement* at all, or simply a myriad of diverse reform efforts later consolidated by historians under one all-encompassing label.[6] Even if we accept the existence of Progressivism as a unified movement, another impasse materializes when we try to bring conservation within its fold. Though historians of Progressivism and conservation have described them as undifferentiated "middle-class" causes, this study will show that conservation, at least, began as an effort of the upper classes. If this is true, then how could conservation simply be one component of the larger, Progressive, supposedly middle-class, phenomenon? Of course, if conservation is to be seen as a democratic movement of the people against economic elites, then one must conclude that its base was middle class, since that socioeconomic group presumably makes up the majority of Americans.

One historian who has challenged the simplistic interpretation of conservation as the fulfillment of democracy is Samuel P. Hays. In *Conservation and the Gospel of Efficiency* (1959), he shows that the goals of leading conservationists commonly clashed with "grass-roots" democratic impulses. More often than not, "the people," particularly in the West, opposed efforts aimed at keeping them from exploiting resources in the traditionally wasteful manner. While Hays's thesis has received widespread acceptance by historians, the notion it set out to destroy is still firmly embedded in the popular mind. Perhaps part of the reason is that he insists, like those before him, that conservation was a middle-class movement, despite the conspicuous roles played by upper-class individuals like Roosevelt and Pinchot.

There are, however, other, more significant, problems with the Hays interpretation. Though his book begins only with the last decade of the nineteenth-century, he argues that the conservation movement started as the result of efforts by a small corps of engineers and physiographic specialists in the federal government. He ignores all nongovernment conservation efforts before the 1890s, and wildlife, the first "resource" to galvanize conservationists into action, is barely even mentioned. During the Roosevelt Presidency, in the years from 1901 to 1909, a federal bureaucracy dealing with environmental issues emerged, and the engineers, geologists, and other "experts" Hays singles out were indeed important *by that time,* but they were not the group that originated the movement in the 1870s.

American sportsmen, those who hunted and fished for pleasure rather than commerce or necessity, were the real vanguard of conservation. Long before the period Hays and other historians choose to begin their works, sportsmen had initiated an environmental movement composed of thousands across the country.

With the establishment in the early 1870s of national newspapers like *American Sportsman, Forest and Stream,* and *Field and Stream,*[7] sport hunters and fishermen acquired a means of communicating with each other, and a rapid growth of group identity was the result. Increasingly, they looked upon themselves as members of a fraternity with a well-defined code of conduct and thinking. To obtain membership in this order of "true sportsmen," one had to practice proper etiquette in the field, give game a sporting chance, and possess an aesthetic appreciation of the whole environmental context of sport that included a commitment to its perpetuation.

The most obvious manifestation of this increasing self-awareness was the rapid growth of sportsmen's clubs and associations. While a desire for comradery was the underlying reason for their creation, one need only look at the names and constitutions of these organizations to understand that subjects like "game protection" and "fish culture" were major concerns of the members.

This early emphasis on the preservation and management of wildlife contains key implications for the historiography of conservation. Accepting the opinions expressed by Roosevelt and Pinchot in their autobiographies, historians have concluded that concern for the forests was the genesis of American conservation. Yet this work will show that the first challenge to the myth of inexhaustibility[8] that succeeded in arousing a substantial segment of the public was not the dwindling forests, but the disappearance, in region after region, of game fishes, birds, and mammals.

While in the beginning, sportsmen as a group concerned themselves more with wildlife than woodlands, individual hunters and fishermen were among the most important pioneers of American forestry. Giants of forest conservation like Bernhard E. Fernow, Joseph T. Rothrock, and Gifford Pinchot were sportsmen long before they began their efforts to have the United States adopt a program of scientific timber management.

Regardless of which of the three main areas of early conservation we pick—wildlife, timberlands, or national parks—sportsmen led the way. During the 1870s and 1880s, local and state associations forced one legislature after another to pass laws limiting and regulating the take of wildlife by market men and sportsmen alike. And in this same period, outdoor journals, particularly *Forest and Stream,* anticipated the later muckrakers in exposing the federal government's shameful neglect of Yellowstone National Park, the nation's first such preserve.

Finally, in 1887, Theodore Roosevelt, George Bird Grinnell, and other prominent sportsmen founded the Boone and Crockett Club, named after two of America's most famous hunters. Though almost ignored by academic historians, it, and not the Sierra Club, was the first private organization to deal effectively with conservation issues of national scope. The Boone and Crockett played an all-important role in the creation and administration of the first national parks, forest reserves, and wildlife refuges. In addition, "those Halcyon Days," as Roosevelt called the early Boone and Crockett period,[9] were the formative years of his development as the future leader of the conservation movement. But before the reader can fully understand why Roosevelt, Grinnell, and other sportsmen acted as they did, we need to go back into the decades before the Civil War to examine the origins of their thinking.

1

Precursors of Conservation: American Sportsmen Before the Civil War

The preservation of game is. . . associated in the popular mind with ideas of aristocracy—peculiar privileges to the rich—and oppression towards the poor. What wonder, then, that men, forgetful of the future, surrendering themselves to the present, mingle with the throng of destructives who seem bent on the extermination of the game, rather than attempt the difficult, and unpopular, and thankless office of conservators!

WILLIAM ELLIOTT
Carolina Sports By Land and Water (1846)

On August 29, 1787, a twenty-year-old future president of the United States, John Quincy Adams, went hunting near Newburyport, Massachusetts. In his diary that evening he recorded his thoughts on the experience:

> Rain'd in the fore part of the day, but cleared up in the afternoon. I went with my gun down upon the marshes, but had no sport. Game laws are said to be directly opposed to the liberties of the subject; I am well persuaded that they may be carried too far, and that they really are in most parts of Europe. But it is equally certain that where there are none, there is never any game; so that the difference between the country where laws of this kind exist and. . . where they are unknown must be that in the former very few individuals will enjoy the privilege of hunting and eating venison, and in the latter this privilege will be enjoy'd by nobody.[1]

Even before he began his long political career, Adams saw that the essential problem in trying to preserve and manage, i.e., "conserve," natural resources like white-tailed deer for future generations meant that the present generation had to have restrictions imposed on it from above, and restrictions on local authority smacked of the same Old World tyranny America had just thrown off.

He would be reminded of this dilemma again shortly after leaving the White House, when his successor, Andrew Jackson, attacked him for establishing a 30,000-acre live-oak reservation on Santa Rosa Island in Pensacola Bay, Florida. Adams had hoped to conserve the trees as a future source of hulls and masts for ships of the United States Navy. But when the spokesman for the common man became president, Jackson viewed the project as a federal infringement on the "rights" of local people to use the timber in any way they saw fit. As a future chief of the United States Forest Service, William B. Greeley, observed: "One can readily imagine the language of Old Hickory's followers in denouncing the 'New England aristocrat' for locking up lands that belonged to the people." The Jacksonians got their way, and the reservation was abandoned.[2]

In later years, many other hunters—and fishermen as well—would join John Quincy Adams in the realization that if wildlife, forests, and other natural resources were to be saved, concepts and practices already developed in aristocratic societies on the other side of the Atlantic would have to be adopted. As will be shown, a conservation *movement* began after the Civil War through the efforts of self-styled "sportsmen," individuals of the upper classes who hunted and fished primarily for recreation, rather than for commerce or necessity. These sportsmen-conservationists differentiated themselves from countless other American males who hunted and fished by their class consciousness and world view. Both of these led them to found national newspapers emphasizing conservation issues, to establish organizations for protecting wildlife, including fishes, and to lobby state legislatures, and finally Congress, for the passage of laws that would force all other hunters and fishermen to accept the "code of the sportsman" as the only correct way to pursue game.

As will also be shown, the development of this self-imposed code meant that a sportsman should adopt a kind of contract with his quarry. Eventually, this one-sided "agreement" would mean that game should not be killed in the breeding season or sold for profit; that it should be taken only in reasonable numbers, without waste; and that it should be pursued only by means of sporting methods. The individual fish, bird, or mammal was to have a "fair chance" of escape, even though its capture was made more doubtful as a result; sportsmen came to condemn fishing for trout with worms instead of artificial flies, shooting at bobwhite quail on the ground before they could take flight, or hunting white-tailed deer on snowshoes when the animals were mired down in deep snow. In other words, a "true sportsman" of the upper classes came to see himself as superior to the great majority of hunters and fishermen at least partly because of the generous spirit he supposedly manifested toward the game.

While there has been a small, but increasing, amount of scholarship on the conservation interests of sportsmen since the Civil War, historians have written relatively little about their concerns in the decades before 1861.[3] But a study of works by William Elliott, Henry William Herbert, and others in the earlier period show that some sport hunters and fishermen advocated what later came to be called conservation long before the movement coalesced in the 1870s. Although not as numerous nor as organized as their later comrades, they helped to provide the philosophical foundation, and inspiration, for national conservation leaders like George Bird Grinnell and Theodore Roosevelt.

Both in books and magazine articles, early sportsmen continually pushed for the adoption of an Old World-derived code of conduct in the field. They emphasized that sportsmen should be "gentlemen," suggesting that they were members of the upper classes who should have nothing in common with the lower-class "market" (commercial), or "pot" (meat), hunter and fisherman. The first group presumably killed without restraint, because the more game they took, the more money they made; the second group supposedly killed simply to fill stomachs, without any appreciation of the aesthetics of sport and the rules for giving game a fair chance of escape. Sportsmen, too, ate what they bagged, believing that wildlife should never be wasted, but they demanded that it must be taken in an appropriate way, meaning that the experience and skill of the sportsman should be challenged before being able to make a kill.

This tradition of self-imposed restraints extends down to the present time. At first, the rules were entirely voluntary, but they soon became formalized in law. The myriad do's and don'ts a hunter or fisherman was to follow in the field had been developing in Europe for centuries, but the country that seems to have played the leading role in introducing the code of the sportsman to the United States was Great Britain.

An illustration of this point is *The Sportsman's Companion; or, An Essay on Shooting*, published in New York City in 1783, just as the new nation was winning its independence from Great Britain. Not another reprint of an English book on field sports, it described actual hunting trips near New York. As a result, it has been called "the oldest American shooting book."[4] Its anonymous author was probably a British army officer stationed in the city during the Revolution.[5] Whoever he was, he chose to remain hidden behind the phrase "By a Gentleman."

The references to the "code" in *The Sportsman's Companion* are not extensive, but they are still significant in a work of the eighteenth century. For instance, the author showed an empathy for, and responsibility to, the bobwhite quail he pursued, using the phrase "poor Quail" for one bird that had been hit and flown on, only to be discovered later on the ground by the pointer dogs, still alive and badly wounded. He told the reader that just because a flying bird failed to drop immediately when the hunter shot does not necessarily mean he missed. A sportsman should "have an eye to the flight of the game and mark them in [where they landed] as close as possible."[6] One's responsibility to the quarry meant that they had to be followed up and added to the bag, rather than to allow them to suffer a lingering death.

Another example of this responsibility to the game is his implicit request that the reader go shooting only during the "proper season for poults,"[7] a term then used for game birds, particularly grouse and quail, as distinct from nongame. The author hunted near New York City, and New York had one of the first sportsmen-sponsored closed-season laws in the American colonies. Passed in 1708, it protected, at least on paper, wild turkeys, bobwhite quail, ruffed grouse, and heath hens in the breeding season.[8] The last-named species was an eastern race of the prairie chicken (*Tympanuchus cupido*),[9] now extinct.

Thus, even as early as the beginning of the eighteenth century, some hunters showed a concern about declining populations of their favorite game.[10] But it would not be until well after the Civil War that sportsmen began to grapple successfully with the problem of enforcement, as they came to realize that wildlife conservation had to be taken out of local hands and given over to state, and sometimes even federal, authorities.

Other manifestations in *The Sportsman's Companion* of an evolving responsibility to the game, and acceptance of its inherent "rights," appear in a conversation between "Mr. Aimwell" and "Squire Jollyman," who "spend the morning on the Moor for Grouse [heath hens], and the afternoon . . . on the Stubble for Partridge [bobwhite quail]." When "Jol" fails to drop a grouse with his shot, "Aim," who is apparently a better marksman, tells him: " 'We can't always hit—if we did, God help the poor Grouse!' " Jol's response is part compliment, part embryonic conservationist sentiment, and part rationalization of his miss: " 'If we all fired like you, Sir, there would be none left to breed. . . .' " Aim reveals the same thinking later in the day when he observes: " 'They are Partridge to be sure—I see them gather, Sir—we may kill many—what the deuce, four brace [8]? That's [already] too many—I think it's time to return home . . . for tea.' "[11]

While *The Sportsman's Companion* of 1783 may have been the oldest American shooting book, it would be followed by more extensive works in the years before the Civil War. What has been called "the second book on American shooting,"[12] and the first comprehensive treatise, is *The American Shooter's Manual,* published in Philadelphia in 1827. "By a Gentleman of Philadelphia County," who, in reality, was "Dr." Jesse Y. Kester,[13] the work's subtitle illustrates some important aspects of the sportsman's world view by promising *Such Plain And Simple Rules As Are Necessary To Introduce The Inexperienced Into A Full Knowledge Of All That Relates to The Dog, And The Correct Use Of The Gun; Also A Description Of The Game Of This Country.* It is clear, then, that sportsmen wanted everyone to adhere to strict "rules" when pursuing game; hunting was not simply a matter of going out and killing wildlife. The older, "seasoned" sportsman also had a duty to bring up the young tyro in the proper etiquette and responsibilities of the sport and the care of the hunting dogs, considered so essential to finding game and—in bird shooting in particular—recovering wounded wildfowl that otherwise might escape to die a protracted death. Here was that paradoxical thinking that the hunter owed the hunted a quick, humane death if at all possible. And finally, the last section of the subtitle notes the necessity of the accomplished sportsman becoming something of a naturalist, because the best hunters are those who "know" the game and its habits.

While seeking to provide "a treatise . . . better adapted to our own country . . . than the British publications which are occasionally imported," Kester nevertheless begins *The American Shooter's Manual* with an attack on the lawlessness of his countrymen. He believed he was "living in a country destitute of game laws and almost without any legal restrictions in regard to its [game] destruction. . . ." Every male in the country seemed to be a hunter, but only a tiny number "will be found entitled to the appellation of sportsmen; they [most hunters] are . . . generally game killers, and nothing more." The chief purpose of his book, Kester asserted, "is . . . to diffuse throughout the community a taste for genteel and sportsman-like shooting, and to abolish that abominable poaching, game destroying, habit of ground shooting, trapping, and snaring, which prevails throughout our country in the neighborhood of all cities and large towns."[14]

Because a sense of fair play must always be central to the sport, Kester wanted "the art of shooting flying" to become the standard technique, rather than the loathsome practice of firing at birds sitting or standing, when there was neither the opportunity for escape nor for the sportsman to test his skill as a wing shot. In giving out his lessons for how the young novice could become a good shot, Kester attacked the custom of practicing one's shooting skills on nongame birds, in particular swallows. No sportsman in the making should endeavor to become skilled with a gun by "destroying those useful, amusing and agreeable creatures. . . ."[15] Kester believed, therefore, that a real sportsman should enter into a kind of contract with a game bird by giving it the "right" to escape by flying, even when he could easily shoot it when immobile. In doing so, he took the chance that he would misjudge its distance, speed, or height, all of which would result in a miss. And nongame birds, like swallows, should never be shot, because they possess both utilitarian and aesthetic attributes. One wonders how many Americans in the 1820s appreciated swallows for their insectivorous habits, much less for their aesthetic appeal!

In the "Game" section of his book, Kester listed the different species that qualify under this category. It is also at the start of this section that he lamented that "game of any kind in the United States is less abundant than formerly, owing to the increase of population and the extension of our settlements. . . ." Hard winters and "vermin" like hawks and foxes also had a deleterious impact, but neither did as much harm as "the sneaking pot-hunting shooter, who, at one fell sweep, will destroy a whole covey [of bobwhite quail on the ground]; a practice disgraceful to those who pursue it, but which is not so much followed as formerly." Still, quail continued to be "lured to certain doom by our qualified poachers," who used unfair methods and "who only shoot for the market or the pot."[16]

Other species, too, were in jeopardy from "common" shooters who possessed no empathy for their quarry. Woodcock (*Scolopax minor*), for example, were hunted much too early, before the birds were grown enough to be able to fly well and, thus, have a fair chance to escape. They were also too small to be fit for the table. Although many shooters began hunting them as early as June 1st, they should wait, Kester urged, at least until July 1st, but preferably until September or October.[17]

Finally, the "rail," meaning in this case the sora rail (*Porzana carolina*), was another species that was pursued sooner than it should have been, when it was, according to Kester, "very poor [to eat] and totally worthless." The problem was "the great increase of shooters, many of whom not having a due regard for their reputation as sportsmen, shamefully commence slaughtering and harassing them before they are fit for any purpose whatever."[18] Again, Kester tried to get the reader to accept the standards of his elite class, but the common folk continued to manifest little or no appreciation for sport and the inherent responsibilities of hunters to the pursued species, which sportsmen had elevated to the status of "game."

While Kester's *American Shooter's Manual* is a well-known classic, the sporting literature is extensive enough that even relatively obscure books contain the same advocacy of higher standards for those aspiring to become "sportsmen." An example of such a work is *Essays on Various Subjects, Written for the Amusement of Everybody* by "One Who is Considered Nobody." Published in New York City in 1835, the book's anonymous author was really John Davis.[19] As with Jesse Kester, there is virtually nothing known about Davis, except that internal evidence in his book indicates that he may have been a British immigrant to the United States, and that he did most of his hunting near New York City. One thing is sure: Davis was thoroughly imbued with the code of the sportsman. In fact, he began his book by differentiating between what he called the "true sportsman" and pretenders to that title.

Despite the obvious class-consciousness of early sporting literature, Davis claimed that "the true sportsman is confined to no particular rank in society. . . ." The important point was that "he hunts [not for the market] like the vagabond [hunter], because he is averse to all regular employment; nor like the dandy [hunter], because he wishes to be fashionable. . . ." Unlike the two pretender groups, the hunter who had earned the title of "true sportsman" was one who hunted only "because he has an innate and ardent love of healthful exercise, and the most exhilarating of all amusements, the sports of the field."[20]

Among the many other attributes of the true sportsman was that "*he does nothing at random*," Davis emphasized, for he knows the habits and haunts of the game so well that "he is always to be seen hunting in the right place, according not only to the season, but to the peculiar state of the weather and the hour of the day. . . ." When his dogs pointed the game he "knew" was there, "he does not run himself out of breath to get ahead of his companion, but walks cooly up to his dogs; and when the birds spring, singles out his victim with deliberate and *deadly* precision."[21] By not "flock shooting," he exhibits his skill as a wing shot by killing single birds "cleanly," rather than having two or three flutter down, crippled, with only one or two pellets in each and none in a vital spot.[22]

According to Davis, once the true sportsman humanely killed his bird, dead in the air, he "does not tumble it carelessly into his pocket or game-bag, but not unfrequently devotes a moment to admire the beauties of its plumage, which, in accordance with the suggestions of good taste, he endeavors to preserve unruffled."[23] Many of those specimens would end up mounted ("stuffed") in "cabinets of curiosity" or other interior settings.

In the section of his book entitled "Hints to Young Sportsmen," Davis revealed that the concept of game conservation as a natural outgrowth of the code of the sportsman was beginning to gain a secure foothold by the 1830s. He hunted in the vicinity of New York City, and in addition to the already mentioned 1708 law—"the first closed season . . . on game birds in the country"—other regulations followed in later years that gave paper protection to deer and several kinds of game birds.[24] Usually never more than countywide in coverage and without wardens to enforce them, these laws proved ineffectual.

Still, they were a beginning, and might be enforced through "peer pressure": "We take it for granted," Davis asserted, "that the readers of this essay are *gentlemen;* it is, therefore, unnecessary to use argument for the purpose of convincing them that shooting game before the time specified by law is unbecoming [to] the character of a true sportsman." In fact, "anyone who *constantly* does that is to all intents and purposes a *poacher,* and is guilty of a crime, which, by the jurisprudence of hunters, should consign him to the contempt of the whole community."[25] In other words, sportsmen were to take the lead not only in the passage of game laws, which formalized the code of the sportsman and the "contract" between hunter and hunted, but in seeing to it that shooters who broke the code and contract were condemned by the sporting fraternity.

Even when it was legal to hunt some species, it may not have been ethical, and Davis believed that the true sportsman should wait "until the young of the latest broods are able to take care of themselves." This "can never be the case when the anxiety of the parent for their preservation is evinced by her throwing herself in the way of the sportsman for the purpose of drawing his attention from her offspring."[26] Again, we have the seemingly paradoxical empathy and protective sentiment for the prey, but it is only a paradox if we forget that sport hunting *was* a game, with definite rules and respect for the species pursued. The animal or bird lost the game if it was "bagged," but the shooter lost the game, or at least that round, if the quarry outwitted him or he missed the shot. This sense of fair play, with the chance to "lose," seems to have been what John Davis was trying to inculcate in his readers. Of course, for the contemporary reader who considers killing under any circumstances to be wrong, such arguments must seem self-serving and fatuous.

By the 1840s, we can see an increase in sporting books with similar sentiments to the ones already described. In them, it is possible to discern a continuing refinement of basic principles, one of which was the need to acquire natural history knowledge if one expected to become a "true sportsman." A book that exhibits the integration of sport and ornithology is *The Birds of Long Island,* written by J. P. Giraud, Jr., and published in New York City in 1844. As with virtually all the early ornithologists, he was a hunter and believed that the shooting of birds was a prerequisite to their study.[27]

Giraud told his readers not to be dismayed by "the large scope . . . our Zoology embraces, [which] deters many persons from making collections, as they despair [of] ever being able to complete them." But, he urged, one should begin with the birds of his own immediate region and then gradually branch out. By "pursuing this plan, they would be enabled to obtain such species of birds as visit their section, and also have an opportunity of studying their habits, which affords greater pleasure than labeling a dried skin received from a distance." Giraud believed that from these collections, "interesting facts would be acquired relative to the migration and habits of many species of which at present we know but little; and it is highly probable that new species would be discovered even in those sections supposed to be thoroughly explored. . . ."[28]

It is obvious that Giraud loved the birds, even when he was shooting them, for he stated his belief "that those who pass through life without stopping to admire the beauty, organization, melody, or habits of Birds, rob themselves of a very great share of the pleasures of existence." And "the place to study Ornithology is in the open air, while rambling through the woods and fields, following the water-courses; and by frequenting the sea-shore and interior lakes. . . ." He had contempt for the "closet Naturalists, who study altogether from dried specimens" collected by others, and who "are merely theorists."[29]

Giraud considered himself a naturalist above all else, but his "favorite amusement . . . [was] water fowl shooting in the celebrated [Great] South Bay" of Long Island, and he adhered to the code of the sportsman when describing the hunting of the "classic" game birds. For example, he attacked as "unsportsmanlike" the use of nets for catching bobwhite quail, and the practice of shooting ruffed grouse out of trees.[30]

Given his fascination with birds, it is to be expected that Giraud would have exhibited compassion for them. An example can be found in his description of the clapper rail (*Rallus longirostris*), an inhabitant of the salt marshes that flies weakly and would rather run through the grass to escape if given the chance. During very high tides, the secretive birds are pushed out of their hiding places. Seizing the opportunity, hunters in skiffs approached the "poor" rails, which were forced to "collect on the drifting grass and sea-weed. Becoming bewildered with the scene, and not knowing whither to go, . . . [they allowed] the boat to approach within a few yards." After being fired on, the survivors moved to another mass of drifting grass, and the scene was repeated. Because the clapper rail flies so feebly, "the sportsman, after pursuing it for a few hours, becomes wearied of this unexciting sport, and returns to shore with little to boast of save numbers."[31] Giraud disdained hunting that gave the quarry little chance to escape and, thus, seemed to break the contract between hunter and hunted.[32]

An illustration of how discerning early sportsmen were regarding the behavior and habits of different species is Giraud's observations about the solitary sandpiper (*Tringa solitaria*). Although small, it was not size that made sport hunters uninterested in it as game. Rather, it is because the bird flies only a short distance when flushed and is far too trusting, exhibiting none of the qualities that make "wing shooting" a challenge. "Not being considered game by sportsmen," he observed, "the Solitary Tatler [Sandpiper] becomes quite familiar."[33]

It is evident that Giraud wanted his readers to follow the code of the sportsman as well as to learn the identity and habits of birds they encountered in the field. Like all true sportsmen, he had contempt for the market gunner. For instance, the legal hunting season for woodcock began on July 1st and closed on February 1st, in order that the species could exercise its right to breed unmolested. Giraud claimed that "sportsmen generally observe this law, but those persons who shoot [for the market] to gratify the palate of the epicure commence previous to the first of July, or as soon as their dogs can find a bird to point, notwithstanding [that] a fine is imposed for every bird found in their possession, when out of season." As with so many of the earliest conservation laws, which had to do with wildlife, not forests, this New York City ordinance was written by sportsmen and directed against the hated market hunter. It stated that "No person shall bring into any market or sell or offer or expose for sale any Woodcock, in any market or other place in the city of New York, between the first day of February and the first day of July in any year, under the penalty of ten dollars for each offense."[34]

As in the case of the 1708 law to protect game birds, sport hunters in the New York City area continued to be in the forefront of American wildlife-conservation efforts. Why this was true is not entirely clear. One reason may have been because the British cultural model of the "sportsman" took root there earlier than elsewhere. By 1840, the city was also the leading port of the United States and the nucleus of a growing publishing industry; this dynamic milieu probably made New York sportsmen more receptive than their counterparts in other regions to new ideas like human responsibility for the future of wildlife. Finally, this largest of all American urban areas, with its burgeoning, hungry population, may have been fertile ground for early conservation sentiment simply because of the sport hunter's dismay at the sheer volume of wildlife sent to city markets by a legion of commercial hunters, who competed directly with sportsmen for the dwindling supply of game.

Of all the species pursued by New York market gunners, none received more attention than the brant (*Branta bernicla*), a small black-and-white goose of saltwater bays and inlets. Feeding on eelgrass (*Zostera marina*), an underwater plant that gave it a delicious flavor, it was in great demand. Having no code of the sportsman to restrain them, commercial hunters, of course, killed as many birds as they could, for more birds meant more money. To illustrate the point, Giraud cited two brothers who leased Fire Island Bar in Great South Bay, Long Island for $120 a year and made several hundred dollars from the waterfowl, mainly brant, that they sent to New York City.[35] Remembering that these are 1844 dollar values, it is easy to see why market hunters would fight sportsmen every step of the way in their efforts to conserve the birds by limiting the number taken.

One of those conservation efforts was to outlaw shooting from a "battery," which was a coffin-like box that the gunner would lie in on his back. Anchored in the brants' feeding area some distance from shore, and equipped with a coaming and canvas-and-wooden "wings" extending out from the box to keep water from sloshing in, the battery was almost invisible to low-flying waterfowl as they approached the huge flock of wooden decoys surrounding the hidden hunter. When the shooter sat up, the birds were often very close, and as Giraud observed, "great havoc is made in this way, particularly among young [unsuspicious] birds." From the beginning of their use, batteries were "objected to by many, they supposing it to be too destructive, as well as the means of driving from the bay those which escape." The market shooter, on the other hand, argued "that they have a right to secure them in any way that fancy dictates" since brant supposedly stayed only a few days in one area.[36]

Sportsmen, naturally, disagreed, and in order to end this unfair practice on the waters of Long Island, a law was passed in New York in 1838 making the use of batteries illegal. "For a short time it was respected," Giraud reported, "but the gunners who depend on Water Fowl shooting for a great part of their living considered it such an invasion of their rights that they defied it; at first shooting with masks, at the same time threatening to shoot the informer, should one be found." Apparently, they became so hostile that sportsmen were thoroughly intimidated. The market hunters "finally laid aside their masks, and the law became a dead letter and has since been repealed."[37]

Sportsmen lost this particular battle, but they would eventually win the war. Not only were unsportsmanlike methods like battery-shooting finally made illegal, but the sale of game was itself outlawed. In 1911 New York was the first state to prohibit the sale of native game, to be followed by the whole country after the passage of the Migratory Bird Treaty Act in 1918.

Because hunters tended to be particularly outspoken and "visible" in the decades before the Civil War, it is easy to forget that anglers, too, had deep concerns over dwindling fish stocks and loss of habitat. The very first sportsmen's clubs or associations seem to have been for fishing, rather than hunting. The earliest was the Schuylkill Fishing Company, organized in 1732 by anglers in Philadelphia.[38] Other clubs soon followed, and laws as well. One of the earliest game-protection statutes in America was a 1734 New York City ordinance that limited fishing in "Fresh Water Pond" to " 'angling with angle-rod, hook, and line.' "[39]

This disdain for commercial net fishermen continued to grow into the next century, as demonstrated by the actions of avid sportsman Daniel Webster, who believed that hunting and fishing should be conducted according to ethical rules of conduct. In 1822 he briefly served in the Massachusetts House of Representatives. In a speech made later, he recalled that " 'it has so happened that all the public services which I have rendered in the world in my day . . . have been connected with the General Government. I think I ought to make an exception. I was ten days a member of the Massachusetts Legislature, and I turned my thoughts to the search of some good object in which I could be useful in that position, and, after much reflection, I introduced a bill, which, with the general consent of both houses of the Massachusetts Legislature, passed into . . . law, . . . which enacts that no man in the State shall catch [brook] trout [*Salvelinus fontinalis*] in any other manner than with the ordinary hook and line.' "[40] A leading authority on the history of angling believes that this law against netting "was the first measure in the interests of fishing as a sport enacted in Massachusetts, and it is possible that it was the first general protective measure applying specifically to any game fish passed by an American legislature."[41]

That sportsmen's dislike for commercial fishermen and their netting was already widespread by the 1820s is further demonstrated by the writings of George Gibson. Born in Pennsylvania about 1775, he was a prominent military officer who did much of his angling near Carlisle, in the eastern part of the state. Though it would focus mainly on horse racing, a new periodical, *American Turf Register and Sporting Magazine*, also wanted fishing and hunting material, and in 1829 its editor asked Gibson to characterize his local angling.[42]

His letter to the editor, which fly-fishing historian Paul Schullery believes may have been "the earliest firsthand 'article' about local trout-fishing experiences to appear in an American magazine,"[43] is particularly noteworthy because of its author's concern for fish conservation. Gibson tells the periodical's readers that " 'although I commenced *wetting* flies in times long gone by, my experience extends only to Cumberland county; but [brook] trout were formerly found in all the limestone springs in the state. Owing, however, to the *villainous* [emphasis added] practice of netting them, they are extinct in some streams, and scarce in others.' "[44]

The best sport, Gibson believed, could be found on Big Spring, west of Carlisle. Even though it is only about five miles long, " 'a law of the state makes it penal to net in this stream, and forbids the taking of trout between the months of July and April.' " At the time, it was " 'the only spring branch in the state protected by law'," but " 'the good effects of which [are] . . . so apparent that it is hoped other streams will receive . . . like protection.' "[45]

For some streams, Gibson felt protection could not come too soon. For example, the Letort " 'formerly afforded excellent sport, but owing to the infamous practice of *netting* and setting *night* [*trot*] *lines*, the fish have been much lessened in numbers and size.' "[46]

Gibson continued to write letters to the editor of *American Turf Register*, and in one of them, published in 1830, he described what he admired most in a fishing companion, " 'one of the best fly-fishers of the age.' " It was the " 'one trait in his character decidedly sportsman[like]—*he never sold a trout in his life. . . .*' "[47]

In summing up the significance of Gibson's letters, Schullery points out that "maybe the most important thing . . . is that he wasn't alone. He described many fishing companions, making it clear that fly-fishing was a long-established and honored use of the stream, practiced by a sizeable brotherhood of sportsmen (he never mentions women)." But there was something else in those letters. As Schullery observes, Gibson "detested all the threats to his beloved trout, whether pollution, or netting or other commercial fishing."[48] Undoubtedly, his viewpoint reflected the feelings of many in the "brotherhood of sportsmen."

This concern about commercial fishermen using unfair methods to catch too many fish was not restricted to the East. In 1830 the Cincinnati Angling Club was organized.[49] Composed of twenty-five leading citizens of the state, including the Governor, it waged a running battle with the commercial netters of the Great and Little Miami Rivers. In 1834 the Secretary of the Club complained that " 'it is useless to disguise the fact, for the members know and lament it, that the bass of the Miamies are becoming scarcer every year, diminished no doubt by the unhallowed depredations of the piratical seine-fishers, those pests of the waters, who set at defiance all rules of the science of our noble art [of angling]. A remedy for this evil is loudly called for. Nothing short of legislative enactment of the severest penalties can put it down.' "[50] Perhaps because the Club was not successful in its efforts to stop the netters, it became "dormant" by 1854 and only had four members in 1869.[51]

Like those who emphasized hunting in their writings, sportsmen who wrote mainly about angling manifested all the same concerns for their favorite quarry. One early example is Jerome V.C. Smith, a medical doctor from Boston. In his *Natural History of the Fishes of Massachusetts, Embracing a Practical Essay on Angling* (1833), he protested not only commercial fishing, but dams and water pollution! One "distinguished individual who occasionally indulges in angling as a relief from the cares of an arduous profession and a public life"—probably Daniel

Webster—got the Massachusetts legislature to pass a law "imposing a penalty of fifty cents for each [brook] trout taken in any other way except with the rod and line." But the "disregarded" law had no impact, and Smith lamented that "factories and saw-mills have done their part towards the work of extermination [of trout through pollution], and the destructive *net* bids fair to do the rest."[52]

Another early example of the concerned angler is John J. Brown, a prominent New York City fishing-tackle dealer, who, in 1845, published *The American Angler's Guide*, "the first useful American fishing manual."[53] In a later edition of that popular work, he asked his fellow fishermen if they thought their sport would last, and answers his own question by declaring:

> You who have trod the mossy bank in pursuit of [brook] trout, and warred against the swift current when the striped basse [*Morone saxatilis*] was the object of your sport, will answer emphatically *no*. You are painfully assured that the well-known haunts wherein in happy boyhood you took many a "silver side" are deserted, and the overarching banks of your favorite streams conceal your spotted friends no longer. You know that at your basse grounds you take few and still fewer fish, and that some of your former places are now never visited by the sought-for game. It is the commonest complaint of the old anglers that fishing nowadays is uncertain; that it is much more difficult to take a mess of fish; there are too many after them; in short, that "times are not as they used to be," and so also says the gunner of his favorite sort of game.[54]

"The causes" of the decline in fish populations, Brown observed, "are easily seen, and almost as easily remedied, if those interested in the preservation of our game would unite their efforts to do so." One cause, he believed, was the fact that "the haunts of our favorite fish are *netted* by mercenary fishermen, who, in season or out of season, take large and small (for all is fish that comes to their net) to the nearest city, where they get extravagant prices for their unhallowed spoil." To avoid confrontations with sport fishermen, the market men did most of their netting at night, for "night is the time to cover their dark deeds."[55]

In Brown's estimation another reason for the diminution of the angler's quarry "is the indiscriminate taking of fish at spawning time by boys and (what is worse) ignorant men, and also by market fishermen, who take them in great numbers from their icy retreat and spawning grounds in tide waters." Even some calling themselves "anglers" (sport fishermen) were guilty of "wanton waste." "Angling not for the pleasure of fishing, but to see how many they can take," these pseudo-sportsmen "leave them [their catches] to gasp and die by the stream side." Combining all these causes together, Brown concluded, "and you have reasons enough for the depopulation of all the waters in creation."[56]

Like other early sportsmen-conservationists, Brown did more than complain; he also proposed remedies. One of the simplest was the suggestion that anglers protect their ponds and streams by driving stakes into the bottom. Then, when the commercial fishermen came in the night to raid these waters, their nets would be torn up and the market men discouraged from returning. "Were a few anglers in the vicinity of water netted by poachers to club together to protect it," Brown argued, "and see that the ground [fishing area] was properly staked, the ponds and streams could in a measure be preserved from the depredations of such barbarians."[57]

One way for anglers to improve their lot, Brown decided, was for them to realize that "in regard . . . to the protection of game, we have the same interest with the fowler [wildfowl hunter] . . . as there are many who pursue fish and fowl, and . . . concert of action among them could not fail to be effectual." The two groups should unite to pass "strong laws against taking or vending [peddling] game out of season, strictly enforced by the rigorous prosecution of all offenders. . . ." Most of all, "sporting clubs should be formed in the different cities, towns, and districts of [the] country, which might be benefited by such laws; and vigilance committees formed to correspond with and visit the sporting grounds, and see that every violation of the statutes is thoroughly dealt with." Through such a course of action, Brown affirmed, "our game grounds could be preserved, our pleasures greatly increased, and a stock of nature's 'best gift, our ever new delight,' preserved to future generations."[58]

Like many other sport fishermen before the Civil War, Brown also advocated the adoption of a wide-scale fish-culture program. "This is a subject of great importance," he observed, "not only to the angler, but to those who own farms or property in the country. In Germany and France, the renting of fish ponds is a source of large income to the owners of the land, and an acre of water is considered of equal value to an acre of soil." In America, by contrast, "few lovers of the beautiful in nature ever think of improving, enlarging, or adorning a natural water spot, and making it joyous and lively with the finny brood." While "the rearing and breeding of various kinds of cattle and feathered creatures for food is an object of interest and study with the farmer, . . . the propagation, naturalization, or transportation of the scaly tribe seems to be with most tenants or owners of land beneath or beyond their notice."[59]

Americans should change their habits of thinking, Brown argued, for "as an article of food, the fish is given to us [by God], without doubt, to gratify our varied tastes; in some seasons, particularly in the early spring and summer, when other meats are out of season . . . , [fish] is more tasteful, healthful, and desirable than any other palate delicacy." Adding, of course, to the appeal of fish is "the pleasure, excitement, and vigor embraced in his piscatorial capture. . . ."[60]

Unfortunately, as early as 1832, according to Brown, an angler-fish-culture enthusiast, "Captain" Henry Robinson of Newburgh, New York, "brought some six or seven dozen carp from France, and put them into a pond, supplied by springs of clear and pure water, on his farm, where they increased to a surprising degree." This "public-spirited gentleman" then compounded his error by planting them in the Hudson River, where they "have increased so much that they are often taken by the fishermen in their nets," and by giving them to his many friends, "who have distributed them about in various parts of the country."[61]

According to scholars who have studied exotic wildlife introductions, the carp was not successfully transplanted to America until the United States Fish Commission performed that "service" in the 1870s.[62] But as Brown's statements reveal, it was established in the Hudson River drainage, and probably other regions as well, by the 1840s when Brown's book appeared. One wonders if Captain Robinson knew that his carp from France were originally from Asia, being brought to Europe so long ago that Aristotle mentions the species in 350 B.C.[63] The carp is an excellent example of what usually happens when an alien species, which did not evolve in an ecosystem, is introduced into that ecosystem. Because of its feeding habits on the bottom, which uproot plants and keep them from growing back by reducing water clarity, this "living pollution" has degraded aquatic habitats all over North America.

Though Brown erred in his positive appraisal of the carp, he was not always wrong. "There is hardly a doubt," he predicted, "that our elegant striped basse of the salt water, which goes up into . . . freshwater streams to spawn, could be domesticated, and made a tenant of freshwater ponds that are supplied with . . . springs."[64] In 1879 and 1882 this excellent game and food fish would be introduced by angler-ichthyologists to the Pacific coast and established by 1883, and later to landlocked, freshwater environments, particularly in the South. Though transplanted widely, it is native to the Atlantic and Gulf coasts of North America, and unlike the carp, it does not seem to damage ecosystems.

Along with John J. Brown, another sporting writer living in the New York City area, who will be discussed in detail later, also called for the restoration of game fish to waters depleted by dams and pollution. Henry William Herbert, or, as he would be better known, "Frank Forester," wanted to extend the range of game fishes like the Atlantic salmon [*Salmo salar*], which he thought could be stocked in the Great Lakes.[65] Though this idea proved impractical, the coho salmon [*Oncorhynchus kisutch*] of the Pacific coast was established in the Great Lakes in the second half of the twentieth century, providing an immense sport fishery. Like so many anglers and hunters, Herbert hated the American obsession with "progress" that was causing such rapid destruction of the natural world. For example, in *Frank Forester's Fish and Fishing of the United States and British Provinces of North America* (1849), he exclaimed: "Modern improvements—heavens! How I loathe that word!"[66]

Though it has been overlooked by most scholars, the fish-culture movement was, in fact, the very first environmental crusade to capture the imagination of a significant segment of the American public. Sportsmen, and increasingly nonsportsmen as well, were becoming alarmed over the disappearance of both game and food fishes; the brook trout had all but vanished in many waters, and the Atlantic salmon and American shad runs that had once made New England's Connecticut River famous, providing both recreation and a cheap source of protein, had been reduced or eliminated by nets, pollution, and especially dams. Though earlier sportsmen-sponsored efforts to establish state-run fish-culture programs in Connecticut and Massachusetts had failed, largely because of questions over funding and state authority,[67] the fishermen of Vermont were determined to try again. Consequently, the State commissioned George Perkins Marsh to find out the reasons for fish decline, and study the feasibility of establishing a state-run fish-culture program to restore Vermont's depleted waters. His *Report, Made Under Authority of the Legislature of Vermont on the Artificial Propagation of Fish,* appeared in 1857. It antedates by seven years the publication of his classic *Man and Nature* (1864), which has been called the "fountainhead of the conservation movement"[68] because it was the first book to recognize the full significance of the human species as an environmental agent, the first to realize the appalling losses caused by destruction of natural resources, and the first to propose a remedy for the future.

Marsh was born in Woodstock, Vermont, on March 15, 1801. His father was the town's leading lawyer and United States District Attorney for Vermont. A lonely boy, he sought refuge from his loneliness in the outdoors, and developed a deep love for nature in general and fishing in particular. As he wrote his friend, the scientist Spencer Fullerton Baird, many years later: "I had in my boyhood a good fishhook acquaintance with the piscatory population."[69]

Like many other students of "natural history" in the nineteenth century, Marsh did not want simply to "dabble" in the subject, or to relate to nature merely as a spectator. He felt compelled to hunt down ("collect"), study, and if possible, understand the objects of his affection. This affinity for collecting all sorts of natural history specimens would stay with him his whole life. It was a major reason why he became a proponent of the establishment of the Smithsonian Institution while serving as a Whig Congressman, and why he became one of its regents in 1847. It was also why he sent the Smithsonian numerous specimens, from beetles and fishes to snakes and birds, while he was Minister to Turkey.[70]

Marsh's well-known interest in science was one reason why he received his appointment from the Governor as Fish Commissioner of Vermont, which led to his 1857 *Report*. A bigger reason was the intercession of the well-born George Franklin Edmunds, who had married Marsh's niece, and who was, at the time, the Speaker of the Vermont legislature.[71]

Edmunds was one of the best-known sportsmen of his day. In angling circles, especially among those who pursued the "king" of game fishes, the Atlantic salmon, he had few peers. As a "keen sports fisherman," he hoped to restore the salmon and other species to waters "that had once teemed with fish," but which were now "barren."[72] The appointment of his friend and relative to Fish Commissioner was also an opportunity for Edmunds to follow up successfully on earlier, but abortive, efforts in Connecticut and Massachusetts to establish fish-culture programs.

Like all of Marsh's work, the *Report* was a model of scholarly thoroughness. Fish were important to the state of Vermont, he asserted, not only as a source of food, but to preserve the sport of angling. Perhaps with a nod to the sportsmen-supporters of his study, many of whom were both hunters and fishermen, Marsh argued that "the chase is a healthful and invigorating recreation, and its effects on the character of the sportsman, the hardy physical habits, the quickness of eye, hand, and general movement, the dexterity of the arts of pursuit and destruction, . . . the courage and self-reliance, the half-military spirit, in short, which it infuses, are important elements of prosperity and strength in the bodily and mental constitution of a people. . . ." And though "it must be admitted that angling and other modes of fishing are under few circumstances attended with as great moral and physical benefits as the pursuit of the larger quadrupeds, . . . they are nevertheless analogous in their nature and influences, and as a means of innocent and healthful recreation at least, they deserve to be promoted rather than discouraged by public and even legislative patronage."[73]

Marsh concluded that the claims of serious declines in trout, salmon, and other fishes were accurate. "The diminution of the fish is generally ascribed mainly to the improvidence of fishermen in taking them at the spawning season, or in greater numbers at other times than the natural increase can supply." Furthermore, "the erection of sawmills, factories and other industrial establishments on all our considerable streams has tended to destroy or drive away fish, partly by the obstruction which dams present to their migration, and partly by filling the water with sawdust, vegetable and mineral . . . matter from factories, and other refuse which render it less suitable as habitation for aquatic life."[74]

But Marsh believed that these were only the most obvious reasons for fish decline; "it is . . . probable that other . . . more obscure causes have had a very important influence in producing the same result." Through cultivation of the soil and the cutting down of forests, runoff and erosion had increased, water clarity had declined, and water temperatures had risen. "Many brooks and rivulets, which once flowed with a clear, gentle, and equable stream through the year, are now dry or nearly so in the summer, but turbid with mud and swollen to the size of a river after heavy rains or sudden thaws." These "inundations . . . destroy or sweep down fish and their eggs, and fill the water with mud and other impurities," and "the mechanical violence of the current . . . continually changes the beds and banks of the streams, and thus renders it difficult and often impossible for fish to fulfill that law of their nature which impels them annually to return to their breeding place to deposit their spawn."[75]

Marsh also knew, as does every fly-fisher, that fishes require a healthy, diverse population of insect life. After all, one of the keys to success in fly-fishing is matching the "fly" with the insect the quarry is feeding on at the time the angler is "on the stream," and then presenting the fly in such a way that it acts like the insect in question. "Forests and streams flowing through them," Marsh observed, "are inhabited by . . . a greater . . . abundance of . . . insects than open grounds and unshaded waters. The young of fish feed in an important measure on the larvae of species which, like the mosquito, pass one stage of their existence in the water, [and] another on the land or in the air."[76] When these insects are no longer available to young fishes, they starve.

Marsh went on to give one example after another of how overfishing, agriculture, and industrialization had altered, and damaged, the ecology of Vermont's aquatic environments, and he thought that these examples "might be indefinitely multiplied. . . ." It was "enough to say that *improvements* have produced an almost total change in all the external conditions of piscatorial life, whether as respects reproduction, nutriment, or causes of destruction, and we must of course expect that the number of our fish will be greatly affected by these revolutions."[77]

It is obvious that Marsh possessed a real ecological understanding of why fishes had declined in the Connecticut River and other major streams in Vermont, though he was probably not completely unique in this knowledge. He had, after all, based his conclusions to some degree on angling literature, which was full of detailed complaints about why fishing had worsened, as well as on interviews with the fishermen themselves.

In the end, Marsh was not very sanguine about solutions to the problems he had so thoroughly detailed. Anticipating his later *Man and Nature,* he probed European history for possible models of mutually beneficial human interaction with wildlife—mammals and birds as well as fishes—that the people of Vermont might emulate. There were, however, few positive examples. While the "magnificent" game bird, the capercaillie (*Tetrao urogallus*), had recently been reintroduced to Scotland, presumably by sportsmen, the "wild ox"— probably the European bison (*Bison bonasus*)—"exists only in the parks [hunting preserves] of one or two great landed proprietors. . . ."[78] Indeed, Marsh seemed to suggest that aristocratic hunters were the only significant segment of the European population to have shown real concern for wildlife. An example was the fox, which "has been preserved from extirpation only by a public opinion . . . [that] exempts him from ordinary agents of destruction . . . [by sparing] him as the object of a manly sport."[79]

Marsh noted that, like Europe, where "large quadrupeds" that used to be abundant were "now only known by history and tradition," Vermont, too, had lost "the moose, the deer, the catamount [mountain lion], the wolf, the lynx, the beaver, the vast flocks of [passenger] pigeons and waterfowl, and other birds of passage, which have so important a relation to the nutrition and . . . sports of our fathers. . . ."[80] Yet, even though "we must, with respect to our land animals, be content to accept nature in the shorn and crippled condition to which human progress has reduced her, we may still do something to recover at least a share of the abundance which, in a more primitive state, the watery kingdom afforded."[81] For example, he joined his relative, George Franklin Edmunds, in advocating the restoration of the Atlantic salmon, "which formerly furnished so acceptable a luxury to the rich, and so cheap a nutrient to the poor . . . , but which now [is] . . . almost as . . . extinct as the game that once enlivened our forests."[82]

The one example of human-wildlife interaction from the past that Marsh believed Vermonters could most benefit from was the long history of European fish culture. As he pointed out, "the luxurious and extravagant habits of imperial Rome first introduced the artificial breeding, or at least feeding and fattening of fish, in both salt and freshwater ponds." But "with the overthrow of that empire, its civilization and its industry, this practice was discontinued and the art forgotten." Eventually, however, "it was revived in the middle ages by the religious observances of the Papal church, which, by determining that fish and certain favorite species of waterfowl were not *flesh*, and accordingly not forbidden food at seasons of fasting and mortification, ingeniously contrived to reconcile the indulgence of the palate with the discipline of Lent." Soon, "to every favorably situated monastic establishment was attached a fish-pond, which not only supplied the tables of the professed during the prescribed fasts, but often yielded a considerable revenue from the sale of fish to worldly penitents." Later, "the success of the monks led to the extension of this branch of industry, and large ponds were constructed by laymen, so that in the sixteenth century fish-ponds were an appurtenance of most great estates, whether lay or ecclesiastical."[83]

What European history also showed, according to Marsh, is that even in countries where "the preservation of land and aquatic game has been an object of legislation for centuries," game protectors have depended more "upon guards and enclosures than upon the terror of the law, for the protection of the objects of the chase or the fishery."[84] In the late 1850s, when Marsh was writing these words, he saw little hope for *"general"* legislation to support fish culture in Vermont: "it is believed that our main reliance in this, as in all other matters of economical interest, must be upon the enterprise and ingenuity of private citizens, and . . . our legislative action should be limited to . . . further protective laws as private establishments may require, and (which is earnestly recommended) the granting of liberal premiums [subsidies] for judicious and successful private efforts in the restoration and improvement of the fisheries."[85]

To do more at this early date would have been impractical, Marsh concluded, for it was "not clear that the Legislature possesses *all* the power required for the complete protection even of an experimental public fish-breeding establishment, and the State . . . at present has title to no suitable localities for such a purpose." In addition, "the habits of our people are so adverse to the restraints of game-laws, which have been found peculiarly obnoxious in all countries that have adopted them, that any *general* legislation of this character would probably be found an inadequate safeguard." Finally, Marsh advised that Atlantic salmon and American shad runs in the Connecticut River could be restored only if cooperative action was taken by every state through which the river passed, but "the difficulties of a cooperation with other States by concurrent legislation seem, for the present at least, insuperable."[86]

Though Marsh's recommendations in his 1857 *Report* were limited, he earnestly hoped that the Vermont legislature would act on his proposals for state support, both legislative and financial, of private efforts in behalf of fish culture. But after thanking him for the study, and paying him $100 for it, the legislature concluded that "in the present state of information" nothing else could be done.[87] This result was almost inevitable, given Marsh's own advise against establishing a state-run program, but he was, nevertheless, disappointed at the lack of interest in backing private endeavors in fish culture.

Despite the legislature's response, or lack of it, Marsh's *Report* "was one of the most influential, thoughtful, and prophetic studies ever written on the subject."[88] Sponsored by sportsmen, who provided Marsh with much of his information, the study documented the fact that elite hunters and fishermen, in Europe as well as the United States, had long been the chief advocates of what would later be called wildlife "conservation."

The *Report* was also a neat summation of the sportsmen's frustrating position in the period before the Civil War. They knew, in detail, what the problems were and how to solve them, but the hostility of the general public to "game laws" and the lack of legal precedents for any legislation that had more than local coverage meant that hunters, as well as anglers, were stymied in their attempts at game protection.

The *Report* had other results as well. "Clearly foreshadowing his later geographical work," according to biographer David Lowenthal, "the fish report was an exercise in miniature for *Man and Nature*."[89] Including sections on the "Destruction of Fish," "Introduction and Breeding of Fish," and "Extirpation of Aquatic Animals"—as well as whole chapters on "The Woods" and "The Waters"—the 1864 volume was, as Lowenthal stated, a massive extension of the 1857 *Report*.

In the earlier work, for example, Marsh pointed out that the aristocratic monopoly in Europe over game and hunting had benefited the fox. In a much more detailed discussion in *Man and Nature,* entitled "Royal Forests and Game Laws," he showed that the nobles' control of hunting came at a terrible price to the peasantry of countries like England and France. The "poaching" of a deer or wild boar could result in the death penalty, and whole villages were razed to the ground, and the people removed, to provide forest habitat for game. But as unfair as these practices were, they did preserve the forest and the wildlife in it, including all the nongame species. Nevertheless, "in the popular mind, the forest was associated with all the abuses of feudalism, and the evils the peasantry had suffered from the legislation which protected both it and the game it sheltered blinded them to the *still greater physical mischiefs which its destruction was to entail upon them* [emphasis added]."[90] The challenge, then, on both sides of the Atlantic would be to preserve the natural world, and the rights of "the people," both at the same time.

Finally, Marsh's 1857 *Report* was significant because it impressed Spencer Fullerton Baird, probably the leading authority in the mid-nineteenth century on North American vertebrate zoology, who credited the Vermonter "with the first important contribution toward the restoration of salmon in the United States."[91] As will be discussed in Chapter Three, Baird's initiative in 1871 helped create the United States Commission of Fish and Fisheries. By trying to extend federal jurisdiction over the protection and management of fish stocks, Baird hoped to overcome the questions Marsh and others had raised in the prewar years about local versus state and regional authority on natural resource issues.

Though Marsh's 1857 *Report* would prove to be a pivotal work in the early literature of conservation, we should remember that his study actually appeared rather late in the ante-bellum period. As noted earlier in this chapter, sportsmen, particularly hunters, had been pushing for legislation to protect game long before they sponsored Marsh's fish-culture research. The writings of John Davis, J.P. Giraud, Jr., and others made it clear that the Northeast, especially the New York City area, was a concentration point for early sporting literature and conservation activity, at least partly because many Americans adopting the British pattern for sport lived in the region.

But this elite model was not exclusive to the Northeast, as the writings of William Elliott prove. Published first in 1846, his *Carolina Sports By Land and Water* gives insight into the thinking of the South Carolina slave-owning class regarding hunting and fishing. Born into a leading family in Beaufort in 1788, Elliott became a successful planter, politician, and poet. In addition to his colorful narrative, which includes everything from riding after hounds pursuing a bobcat to being towed in a boat by a harpooned manta ray, Elliott exhorted the reader to adopt a conservation creed. He worried that "there are causes in operation which have destroyed, and are yet destroying, the game to that extent that in another generation, this manly pastime [of hunting] will no longer be within our reach." Even though he was a "sportsman," he could not "regret the destruction of the forests, *when the subsistence of man is the purpose. It is the order of events that the hunter should give place to the husbandman*"; and he would "not complain of it." But, Elliott affirmed, "it is the wanton, the uncalled-for destruction of forests and . . . game that I reprehend."[92]

What is so remarkable about Elliott's conservation message is the detail he provided regarding land uses in South Carolina in this period, and how they impacted wildlife. Showing sympathy for the hunted, he observed that "undoubtedly, the most obvious cause of the disappearance of . . . deer and other game is the destruction of the forests—that of the river swamps especially. . . ." For "in their original state," these forests were virtually impenetrable to the hunter on horseback, and the deer had a refuge to which they could always escape. "These lands, being cleared and cultivated, no longer afford them refuge." A similar situation had developed in regard to the upland areas that used to be heavily wooded, but had now been cleared for cotton. The game's "feeding and hiding places" were "more contracted," and "they can [now] more easily be hemmed in and destroyed."[93]

As if these problems were not bad enough, wildlife also had to contend with increased herds of cattle, whose "trampling and cropping of . . . shrubs and undergrowth" eliminated vegetation. Damage caused by livestock, combined with "the practice of burning the woods in spring to give these cattle more luxuriant pasturage," meant that there was little wildlife habitat left.[94]

Like all good sportsmen, Elliott hated the market gunners who never gave their prey a chance to escape and never knew when to stop killing. The demand for game from the growing cities and many wealthy epicures "has called into being a race of professional hunters, who, settling themselves wherever the game is abundant, and cultivating merely corn enough to sustain themselves, their horse and a couple of hounds, devote their days and nights to hunting."[95]

Apparently, the appeal of such a life was great. Besides "the freedom from restraint" was the money that could be made, which was "greater than accrue[d] from the cultivation of the soil." And like the market hunters of Long Island who continued to use batteries after they were illegal, the South Carolina "professional" hunters continued to practice any method, legal or not, that would bring them large kills and big profits.[96]

One such prohibited practice was "fire hunting," where hunters used a light at night to stun and confuse deer and other wildlife, making them easy targets. As with the use of batteries, sportsmen considered fire hunting too lethal and a breaking of the contract between hunter and hunted. Despite their success in making it illegal, Elliott complained that "it is too much to expect of this class of men [the professional gunners] to refrain from 'fire hunting,' though forbidden by law."[97]

The problem was in catching the offenders and the reluctance of many Carolinians to turn informer, unless, of course, the fire hunting was done on their own land. As a result, "in a few years the game is destroyed or driven off." Then, the market hunter "follows them [the game] to their new retreats, pitches his tent, or builds his cabin . . . , and recommences his career of destruction."[98]

As an elite sportsman, Elliott shared a common frustration experienced by the members of his class, regardless of where in the United States they lived. Although their sporting code and conservation impulse sprang from European roots, particularly Great Britain, sportsmen in America were powerless to keep the game strictly for themselves, as had traditionally been done in England. "The right to hunt wild animals," Elliott lamented, "is held by the great body of the people, whether landholders or otherwise, as one of their franchises, which they will indulge in at discretion and to all limitations on which they submit with the worst possible grace!"[99]

The sentiment seemed to be that the game was the property of whoever was able to kill it—"irrespective of any conflicting right in the owner of the soil." So intense was this feeling by the common people "that some overseers refused to accept a place (otherwise desirable) if they are restricted in the right to hunt." Because wealthy planters such as Elliott often left their low-lying plantations for up to half a year to escape the heat, mosquitoes, and yellow fever outbreaks, overseers wielded great power as to how the owner's land and everything on it were to be treated. Once, after returning to his plantation, Elliott found that his overseer had killed off all the game. This forced him to draw up a clause in the overseer's annual contract that restricted his hunting. But "having made his [Elliott's] own grounds, by this restriction, a *preserve* [emphasis in original], they [the hunting grounds] were only the more harassed, on this account, by the unrestricted in the neighborhood—who took a malicious pleasure in destroying the game which a proprietor had presumed to keep for himself."[100]

Thus, no matter what Elliott tried to do to preserve and manage—i.e., to "conserve"—his lands for the benefit of himself and the wildlife, the common people and their "rights" complicated his plans. The landowner may have thought he owned the land, but unless he enclosed it, Elliott complained, "it is his neighbors', or anybody's." It was apparently impossible to obtain redress in the courts, even when a neighbor drove his cattle onto one's land, browsing on, and trampling under, all the vegetation, thereby making the game preserve worthless.[101]

Like the sportsmen after the Civil War who would make the American conservation movement, Elliott understood that a revolution in thinking and law would have to take place before there was any hope of saving wildlife for the future. The central problem, he knew, would long continue to be the common people's "deep disgust at the tyranny of the English game laws" which seemed "to be the sorest and best remembered of their griefs. . . ." As a result, he lamented, "the preservation of game is . . . associated in the popular mind with ideas of aristocracy—peculiar privileges to the rich—and oppression towards the poor." It is no "wonder, then, that men, forgetful of the future, surrendering themselves to the present, mingle with the throng of destructives who seem bent on the extermination of the game, rather than attempt the difficult, . . . unpopular, and thankless office of conservators!"[102]

Remembering that William Elliott was writing in the 1840s makes his call for wildlife "preserves" and "conservators" all the more striking. His thinking, however, was not unique, but rather a further refinement of a European, elite, sporting code still in the process of being adapted to the United States, and not yet fully adopted by American gentlemen hunters. Probably no one would do more to speed up the acceptance of that code by this group than the extraordinary sporting writer Henry William Herbert, better known under his pen name of "Frank Forester."

Landing in New York City in the spring of 1831, the twenty-four-year old Herbert had been born into the British nobility, was a graduate of Eton and Cambridge, and had seemingly been destined for a life of public service until he committed some grave, but unknown, offense against his class that forced his family to banish him to America. From the time he arrived, Herbert struggled to build a literary career that would make him so famous that his family would take him back. Failing to make his mark as quickly as he had hoped, but still believing that the authorship of historical novels and other "serious literature" was his destiny, Herbert hesitantly turned to writing about hunting and fishing only after his sportsman friend, William T. Porter, editor of *American Turf Register and Sporting Magazine,* encouraged him to deal with the subjects he knew best. Believing that to write about "field sports" would lessen his stature as an author, Herbert insisted on having a pen name, and he accepted Porter's suggestion of "Frank Forester."[103] Ironically, it would be under that name, and for his writing on sport, that Herbert would become well known in America and England. Despite this recognition, he did not return home, but continued to live, unhappily, near New York City until his suicide on May 17, 1858.

The formal start of "Forester's" career began in the spring of 1839 with the publication of the first installment of a serialized story, "A Week in the Woodlands; or Scenes on the Road, in the Field, and Round the Fire. . . ." Other Frank Forester accounts soon followed, and the readers of sporting newspapers were quick to express their appreciation.[104]

By the time Herbert began to write under his pen name, the basic outlines of the appropriate world view all "true sportsmen" were supposed to possess had already been sketched out in the sporting press. In a 1986 study, "Antebellum American Sporting Magazines and the Development of a Sportsmen's Ethic," historian Donald W. Klinko analyzed the contents of *American Turf Register and Sporting Magazine* (1829-1844), originally established in Baltimore by John

S. Skinner and later taken over by Porter in New York, and *The Spirit of the Times* (1831-1861), founded by Porter in that same city. Much of the material in these early periodicals consisted of letters and articles sent to the editor from subscribers, and Klinko found that by the 1830s those contributions included "proposals for revision of game laws, diatribes against market hunters and commercial fishermen, schemes for fish and wildlife propagation, and general expressions of concern about game habitat destruction."[105]

We have already discussed George Gibson's letters of 1829 and 1830 in *American Turf Register* attacking commercial fishermen and defining sportsmanship. And as early as the April, 1830, issue, a letter to the editor from a Philadelphia sportsman in the same magazine complained that "real sportsmen" have trouble getting other hunters to obey the game laws. " 'I am,' " he asserted, " 'by no means an advocate for European game laws, but [I] do think that some legislative restrictions more than we have at present are absolutely necessary to prevent the total annihilation of every variety of game in the settled part of our states, and that at no distant period.' "[106]

Because many subscribers to *American Turf Register* were from the South, that region supplied its share of letters and articles complaining about the decline of game. In the March, 1836, issue "G.T.N." of Virginia disapproved of the destruction of woodlands for agriculture: " 'I must premise that in this section of the state, where much of the native forest has been cut down, and the lands cleared, in consequence of their being particularly adapted to that curse of the Ancient Dominion [of Virginia], *tobacco*, the deer have become very scarce, having sought a more quiet asylum among the mountains, where they abound in immense numbers.' "[107] In addition to habitat destruction and its impact on deer, G.T.N. was also concerned about the decline of turkeys due to the use of unsporting methods in hunting them. While calling them in with a "yelper" and flushing them from cover with dogs were legitimate techniques, driving them into pens and shooting them over bait from a blind were not. " 'These [last] two methods,' " he warned, " 'are very destructive to the game, and should be discountenanced by all who are fond of turkey hunting, except where they are very plenty.' "[108]

"The West" of the 1830s was also a region that interested the readers and editors of *American Turf Register*. Gideon Smith, who was then editor, discovered an anti-sportsman article in the *Wisconsin Territorial Gazette* of July 2, 1837. Though Wisconsin would not become a state until 1848 and was still very much the "frontier," sportsmen had apparently managed to pass a game law in the territory. It was this legislation, and the supposed class discrimination behind it, that caused the Wisconsin resident to attack sport hunters. He mocked the use of sportsmen's terms like "bagged" and "poaching," and bragged that even though a friend had killed a deer recently in violation of the "game laws," the " 'venison . . . proved delicious, though, in sportsmen's tongue [jargon], it was not killed . . . according to . . . [the] "rules and regulations". . . .' "[109]

The anger of the editor of *American Turf Register* is shown by his long, heated response to the Westerner. Smith began by reminding his readers of " 'how often do we meet with such sneers . . . at "game laws"!' " But if it had not been " 'for game laws in England, there would long since have been *no game* in that country.' " And the same was true, he asserted, " 'in the whole of the thickly settled part of our country, [where] all kinds of game are rapidly disappearing.' " The wildlife still so plentiful in Wisconsin had once been equally abundant in the East, " 'and would have remained so to this day had there been wholesome game laws *in force.*' " By "wholesome," Smith did not mean " 'laws that authorize one class of citizens to take game and prohibit another,' " as in England, but " 'laws that will effectually prohibit the taking and even . . . molestation of any kind of game *out of season;* that is, when birds, etc. are breeding and rearing their young, and when they are in bad condition [for eating]. If we had such laws in full and efficient force heretofore, we should now have abundance of all kinds of game.' " Sounding very much like the later conservationists of the Progressive era, Smith concluded that " 'we are all apt to look upon laws that are calculated to restrain us in heedless *wastefulness* [emphasis added] as evils, whereas they are intended and ought to be looked upon as blessings.' "[110]

Like the *American Turf Register and Sporting Magazine, The Spirit of the Times* also carried fishing and hunting material. But editor William Porter would go even farther in *The Spirit,* founded in New York City in 1831, in devoting "significant attention to field sports."[111] According to Donald Klinko, "its wide circulation and more diverse audience (compared to the *American Turf Register*'s genteel and well-to-do readership) also suggests that a broader spectrum of American readers were becoming receptive to the idea of conservation."[112]

An example of Porter's thinking can be found in his editorial of February 20, 1836, entitled "Club for the Preservation of Game." A group of New Jersey sportsmen had just formed the "Trenton Club" to preserve bobwhite quail hunting in their area by propagating them.

Live birds would be purchased and released to restock the hunting grounds. Unfortunately, a bounty would also be placed on hawks under the misguided notion—shared by virtually all "animal-lovers," sportsmen and nonsportsmen alike—that eliminating the top of the food chain (other than humans) would provide *permanent* quail abundance. Still, Porter applauded the creation of the sportsmen's club and its objectives, and declared that " 'the example of the Trenton Club is worthy of all praise, and we trust will be generally emulated at the North. The Sportsmen of Long Island and New York we particularly enjoin to 'Go and do likewise.' "[113]

While the *American Turf Register* continually evaluated current game laws, contributors to *The Spirit* decided on "more immediate, practical solutions." William P. Hawes, a prominent New York attorney and sporting writer, who wrote under the pen name of "J. Cypress, Jr.," published an article on July 1, 1837, describing his "defense" of "an avid sportsman desirous of seeing the game law enforced."[114] The statute in question prohibited anyone from possessing or consuming game birds except during the hunting season. Hawes's "client" deliberately entrapped the proprietor of a local restaurant by telling the police ahead of time that he was going to be there at a specific time illegally dining on woodcock. When the police arrived they found the illegal woodcock and subsequently eight more as well, recently killed by unprincipled market hunters who cared nothing about the rights of game to breed unmolested. The sportsman-activist was fined five dollars for eating one woodcock, but the restaurant's proprietor had to endure a fine of forty dollars for eight birds, a hefty sum in 1837. Hawes concluded his article with the suggestion that this "direct-action" approach to poorly enforced game laws should be a model for sportsmen to use everywhere.[115]

While fishing and hunting may not have been the exclusive, or even primary, concerns of the eclectic *American Turf Register* and *The Spirit of the Times,* they received enough attention to show that Donald Klinko is right in chiding environmental historians, including the author, for understating the significance of these early periodicals. They helped publicize the sportsmen's "ethic"—Klinko feels that "the word 'code' may imply a body of rules more fixed and well defined than was the case for the American sportsman of the 1830s"—and they provided the model for post-Civil War journalism. Finally, they remind us that we may have given Henry William Herbert too much credit as an innovative thinker. By the time he metamorphosed into "Frank Forester" and began writing for *American Turf Register* in 1839, sportsmen across the country had been exposed for a decade to letters and articles that, in Klinko's words, "promoted an aesthetic sense of nature, a non-exploitive use of—or appreciation of—the natural world which translated into preservationist sentiments."[116]

Though Herbert may not have been quite as much of a "pioneer" in introducing the code of the sportsman (or its antecedents) and conservation activism as we formerly thought, there is no denying that once he joined the cause, the volume and popularity of his writings would eventually make Frank Forester an influential force for conservation.[117] Of his many articles and books, probably none reflect his thinking better than *Frank Forester's Field Sports of the United States and British Provinces of North America*, a synthesis of earlier writings and published in two volumes in 1848, first in London and later in New York.[118]

In the very first sentence of his work, Forester told the reader that his expectation for *Field Sports* was that it would "tend, in some small degree, to avert the impending doom which seems to have gone forth from the democracy of the land [i.e., the 'common people'] against game of all sorts." And since "no one abler, or elder, seemed willing to stand forth," Herbert felt compelled, despite his "imperfections," to offer himself "as the champion of American Sport and Sportsmanship. . . ."[119] Thus, he hoped to lead a revolution in thinking that would result in the adoption of what I have called the "code of the sportsman" by the "average" hunter, who would then join sportsmen in their efforts to conserve game.

Quoting from an earlier article he had published in *The Spirit of the Times*, Herbert's "Introductory Observations" in *Field Sports* included his view that " 'there is, perhaps, . . . no country in the world which presents to the sportsman so long a catalogue of the choicest game, whether of fur, fin, or feather, as the United States. . .' "; furthermore, " 'there is none, probably, which counts more numerous, or more ardent, devotees' "; and " 'there is none . . . in which the wide-spread passion for the chase can be indulged, under so few restrictions, and at expense so trifling.' " But " 'all this, notwithstanding, it is to be regretted greatly that there is no country in which the nomenclature of these . . . roving denizens of wood . . . and water is so confused and unscientific; none,' " too, " 'in which their habits are so little known, and their seasons so little regarded' "; and " 'none in which the gentle craft of Venerie[120] [hunting game or "the chase"] is so often degraded into mere pot-hunting. . . .' " Consequently, " 'the game that swarmed of yore in all the fields and forests, in all the lakes, rivers, bays, and creeks of its [America's] vast territory are in peril of becoming speedily extinct.' "[121]

In case the reader was too ignorant to know what Herbert was talking about, he provided examples of disappearing wildlife: the heath hen, wild turkey, snowshoe hare [*Lepus americanus*], and white-tailed deer. And for the casual observer who thought that human activities like farming *always* reduced wildlife populations, Herbert had an answer: "It has been alleged," he wrote, "that the increase of population, the spread of cultivation, and the transfiguration of the woods and wastes into corn-lands and pastures are in themselves an all-sufficient and irremediable cause for the disappearance of all the various kinds of game, the extinction of which the sportsman and . . . naturalist alike deplore." But the reality "with regard to very many kinds of game [is that] . . . the very converse of the proposition is true." In fact, many of the "best" game species "prefer the vicinity of cultivated regions on account of the [plentiful] . . . and choicer quality of . . . food, and are found nowhere in such abundance as in those localities which afford the combination of rough, wild lying-ground ['cover'] with highly cultivated land on which to feed at morn and dewy eve."[122]

In other words, Herbert understood that large game populations could be maintained in settled country if humans protected wildlife when it was mating and raising its young, and later hunted it only by sporting methods that ensured the survival of breeding stock. Consequently, he claimed that it was neither settlement nor hunting, *per se,* that was the problem, but rather "the reckless and ignorant, if not wanton, destruction of these animals by the rural population."[123]

As Herbert pointed out, the decline of the heath hen was a good example. Its destruction, which by that time was "total on Long Island, and all but total in New Jersey and the Pennsylvania oak-barrens," was "ascribable to the brutal and wholly wanton havoc committed among them by the charcoal-burners, who frequent those wooded districts." In addition to cutting down trees to make charcoal fuel for sale by partially burning the wood, these humble individuals were supposedly "destroying the parent birds [of the heath hen] at all seasons, even while hatching and hovering [keeping together] their broods, shooting the half-fledged *cheepers* [original emphasis] in whole hatchings [on the ground] at a shot, and trapping them in deep snows— [and] with a degree of wantonness equally barbarous and unmeaning, [they] steal or break all the eggs which they can find."[124] If this were not enough, the rural folk in the North, like those in South Carolina, burned the forest land each spring during the nesting season, apparently to improve the pasturage for their grazing animals.[125]

To prove that it was human ignorance and "wantonness" that were the causes of wildlife decreases, and not settlement of the country *per se*, all one had to do, Herbert observed, was to look at Martha's Vineyard. There, on that bucolic island off the Massachusetts coast, the heath hen prospered in his time because the residents "take an honorable pride in preserving it, and neither kill it themselves nor allow visitors to do so, except in the proper seasons, and under restrictions as to numbers." Initially, when the sportsmen-sponsored program to save the bird began on the island, "the prohibition to kill [any heath hens] was absolute" for five years, "and the fine so heavy, and so rigorously enforced—backed as it was by public opinion—that the desired end was gained."[126] In the end, of course, this eastern subspecies of the prairie chicken died out even on Martha's Vineyard. The habitat and, consequently, the gene pool, were just too small, and the last one, an old male, was spotted near West Tisbury a final time on March 11, 1932.[127]

To contemporary readers with more democratic sensibilities, Herbert's class consciousness probably seems arrogant, but without a certain *noblesse oblige*, which sprang from his aristocratic background, he might have lacked the confidence, and zeal, to show the American "people" the error of their ways. As will be shown, George Bird Grinnell, Theodore Roosevelt, and other patrician hunters possessing the same confidence and zeal would play a leading role in the conservation movement after the Civil War.

It is understandable why individuals from a privileged background would be the first, as a self-conscious group, to argue for what later came to be called "conservation." In England, which the sportsmen used as their example, the game and its habitat had originally been the exclusive property of the monarch, and later, the wealthy landowners of the upper tiers of British society. But in America, it became increasingly obvious to the educated hunter that the English system could not be transferred, unchanged, across the Atlantic. In a democratic society the same kind of exclusive control over wildlife was impossible. What had to percolate downwards, crossing class lines on the way, was the sportsmen's acceptance of a proprietary interest in game. Only when the American people "realized" that wildlife belonged to them and their descendants would they begin to take responsibility for it.[128]

As Herbert suggested, the survival of the heath hen on Martha's Vineyard in his own day was the model to follow. At first, there would be no hunting at all, to allow a species to become reestablished. Only after it was reproducing well enough to allow some hunting would a short season, with strict bag limits, be allowed. And, as the Martha's Vineyard case revealed, the support of the rural population was key to the effort's success. Those familiar with the dramatic successes in American wildlife conservation in recent decades know that this is exactly how game species have been restored. Examples include white-tailed deer, wild turkeys, and the giant race of the Canada goose.

Herbert, then, was advocating in the 1840s a rudimentary form of what would later be called "the conservation of renewable natural resources." As biologist Aldo Leopold argued in his *Game Management* (1933), "crops" of white-tailed deer, cottontail rabbits, ring-necked pheasants (introduced into the United States by sportsmen in the 1880s), and other game species all could be "harvested" year after year without any diminution in their total numbers as long as enough breeding stock survived at the end of each hunting season, and the habitat remained healthy and sufficient. What is remarkable about the history of the heath hen on Martha's Vineyard is not so much that it disappeared eventually, but that it survived in its confined habitat for over eighty years from the time Herbert recorded the effort to conserve it.

While he was optimistic about the heath hen's future on its island retreat, Herbert could not say the same for other wildlife, and he summarized the reasons for his concern in *Field Sports*. First was the "incomprehensible characteristic"—at least to an Englishman—"of the people of the United States to disregard and violate all laws, even laws of their own making." Second was "the apathy of the rural population with respect to game, and the error into which they have fallen of regarding all game laws as passed to their detriment and for the pleasure of the dwellers in cities," i.e., gentlemen hunters. Third was "the dishonest gluttony of all classes in the cities, with the exception of a few sportsmen," who consumed game all year long, thereby providing an incentive for market hunters to kill it out of season. The fourth, and final, reason for dwindling wildlife in America was the "want of union among themselves of genuine sportsmen."[129]

Given these trends, it was not enough that individual sportsmen continued to be the chief architects of wildlife legislation in the United States. Their lack of organization fragmented their efforts. And laws meant little if the rural population saw them as nothing more than an effort to transplant "feudal rights, individual privileges, and nominal distinctions," which in turn caused resentment of the wealthy urbanites who wanted to hunt on the farmer's land. Herbert urged that sportsmen join together to convince the farmers that this legislation was important, and for the common good. "I believe," he wrote, "that if they [rural people] could now be brought as a body to understand that the provisions of these laws are not arbitrary and intended to suit [only] the wishes of [the upper] classes, they might be induced to lend their hand to the good work of game-preservation."[130]

The difference between Herbert and his fellow sportsmen, and other Americans who were disenchanted with the march of "progress," was that sportsmen began to unite and take direct legislative action. They were not isolated individuals, as exemplified by their contemporary, Henry David Thoreau, who protested on his own and whose impact for environmental good, *during his lifetime*, was limited.

In passing, it should be pointed out that Thoreau, who is usually depicted as anti-hunting by historians, was, at worst, ambivalent on the subject; sometimes he criticized it, but many times he praised it. For example, in the "Higher Laws" section of *Walden* (1854), he fondly recalled how each of his boyhood contemporaries had his own "hunting and fishing grounds [that] were not limited like the preserves of an English nobleman, but were more boundless even than those of a savage." In the end, Thoreau mused, "perhaps the hunter is the greatest friend of the animals hunted, not excepting the Humane Society." There was never any ambivalence in his mind about fishing— he loved to fish his whole life.[131]

Unlike Thoreau, sportsmen were part of an elite subculture with a world view that required them to assume the leading role in enacting, and enforcing, wildlife laws in the United States. For Herbert, the means to these ends would be the New York Sportsmen's Club, established on May 20, 1844.[132] Another association with a similar name, the "New York Sporting Club," had been created as early as 1806 to enforce the code of the sportsman by seeing to it that the game laws were obeyed and the game preserved. What connection it had, if any, to the latter organization is unknown.

In addition to Frank Forester, the later group would come to include a number of upper-class hunters and anglers who were well-known for their sporting books, Charles E. Whitehead, Genio C. Scott, and Robert Barnwell Roosevelt, uncle of Theodore, among them. The organization immediately demonstrated its commitment by getting through the New York legislature a game law that Herbert wrote to prohibit summer woodcock hunting. Although the law applied to only two counties north of New York City, it was a beginning; Herbert triumphantly notified the readers of *Field Sports* that "there is no more *summer Cock-shooting* . . . in Orange or Rockland—the first two counties of America in which I ever pulled a trigger. Bravo. . . ! Who will be . . . next to follow the glorious example? Long Island, Westchester, Putnam, Duchess [counties]—and last, not least—New Jersey, the eyes of men are upon you!"[133]

According to a leader of the post-Civil War generation of sportsmen-conservationists, George Bird Grinnell, the New York Association for the Protection of Game, the later name of the New York Sportsmen's Club, "gradually built up, first among residents of New York City and later in other communities, a spirit for game protection. . . ." The organization's seal, which displayed a flying woodcock, long a species of special concern to gentleman hunters, bore the inscription: *Non nobis solum*—"Not for ourselves alone." Here, "perhaps for the first time," claimed Grinnell, was the concrete expression of an "ideal now accepted by all sportsmen that the gunners of one generation are, in fact, trustees of the game, to hold and use it for their time and to hand it down to those who are to follow."[134]

By the start of the 1850s, the leadership of a small percentage of American hunters calling themselves "sportsmen" had made it clear, through literary protests and legislative campaigns, that they possessed a blueprint for what they thought should be the proper relationship between people and wildlife. As the decade progressed, more books and articles appeared that would help to solidify sportsmen's attitudes and convince them that they were the only group capable of saving the country's game.

Of the books that appeared during the 1850s, several were influential advocates of the code of the sportsman in all its varied aspects: Elisha J. Lewis's *Hints to Sportsmen* (1851), later expanded and retitled *The American Sportsman* (1855); John Krider's *Krider's Sporting Anecdotes* (1853); Henry William Herbert's first American edition of *Frank Forester's Fish and Fishing* . . . (1850) and his *Complete Manual for Young Sportsmen* (1856); and Samuel H. Hammond's *Wild Northern Scenes; or Sporting Adventures with the Rifle and the Rod* (1857).[135] In these works the authors made the usual requests that market hunting and fishing cease, that game be allowed to breed unmolested and then only taken by "fair means" and with restraint, that nongame be protected at all times, and that wild lands be preserved for the survival of wildlife and the enjoyment of sportsmen.

Particularly noteworthy in regard to this last demand was Samuel Hammond's call for setting aside "a circle of a hundred miles in diameter" in New York State's Adirondack Mountains, "a forest forever." He conceived the proposal while on a hunting and fishing trip to the region, and it should be noted that he included two game fishes, brook trout and lake trout (*Salvelinus namaycush*), among the wildlife he wanted to preserve within the great circle. If he had his way, Hammond told his readers, he would not only "consecrate these old forests," but "these rivers and lakes"—and all their inhabitants— as well. That he had respect, and even affection, for the game fish he pursued is shown by the paragraph preceding his call for a great Adirondack preserve. Quoting, approvingly, "The Doctor," who was one of Hammond's companions on a fly-fishing excursion after brook trout, the author described the group's decision to stop angling: " 'We've got eight, and I bar any more fishing. The [self-imposed] law has reached its limit. No wanton waste of the good things of God, you know.' "[136]

Among the periodicals carrying hunting and fishing material, and upholding the code of the sportsman, none would be as important in the 1850s as William T. Porter's *The Spirit of the Times*. It would "provide," in the words of one historian, "the best documentation of the genesis of the American conservation movement,"[137] i.e., that it began with sportsmen. During the decade, letters, articles, or editorials appeared on the need to curtail bobwhite-quail hunting for a year in the East, and feeding them whenever possible, because of the large numbers killed from severe winter weather; on the reasons for the decline of fish populations and what could be done about it, including the adoption of fish-culture programs; on how commercial hide hunters were exterminating white-tailed deer by killing without limit and using unsporting methods like hunting them when they were mired down in deep snow; and on the need to follow the code of the sportsman through self-restraint, which included protection for nongame birds.[138]

Porter would be particularly active in encouraging the efforts of the New York Sportsmen's Club to end the sale of game, out of season, in New York markets and restaurants—some of it killed from as far away as Indiana and Illinois. In February, 1853, for example, he urged the Club to " 'take this matter in hand'," and they did so under the capable leadership of the organization's Secretary, the prominent attorney Charles E. Whitehead. Despite the "ineffective and vaguely worded statutes" with which he had to work, Whitehead successfully prosecuted, in 1858, a New York City *restaurateur* for selling woodcock out of season.[139]

With *The Spirit* acting as the group's mouthpiece, the New York Sportsmen's Club successfully fostered the idea of a "sportsmen's convention" that met in Geneva, New York on November 15, 1859, " 'for the purpose of discussing and devising means for united action throughout the State for a revision of the present senseless and inefficient Game and Fish Laws.' "[140] Letters from the participants in the Geneva meeting poured into the periodical's offices with suggestions on how the law could be improved. The Sportsmen's Club, led by Whitehead, drew up a bill with all the suggested revisions, and offered it to the legislature. With *The Spirit* and so many sportsmen pushing for its passage, "An Act for the Preservation of Moose, Wild Deer, Birds and Fish" became law in the summer of 1860. Soon, Whitehead and the Club went to work enforcing it and won several cases against individuals selling game out of season in the New York City markets.[141]

The Spirit's editors not only reported these successes, but encouraged sportsmen in other parts of the country to follow New York's example. Actually, the periodical's editors had, for several years, been reporting on the success sportsmen were having in other states in organizing themselves and passing and enforcing new game laws. They were learning how to "become a thundering chorus . . . voicing facts, figures and implied threats of political ruin in the ears of state legislators." Some states where sportsmen had successfully joined together politically in the 1850s to get new legislation passed, with greater promise of enforcement, were Maryland, Wisconsin, Ohio, Massachusetts, Maine, Pennsylvania, Alabama, and Virginia.[142]

Given all these developments, one can only wonder what might have happened in American conservation history if the Civil War and its aftermath had not intervened. By the start of the 1860s, sportsmen were easily the largest, most influential, and best-organized segment of the nation to be concerned about nonutilitarian environmental issues. They had begun to think in more expansive terms than their predecessors about the problem of declining wildlife. Concern increased for fishes and nongame, as well as for game birds and mammals, and the realization started to take hold that the preservation of habitat was more important than saving individual animals. Finally, sportsmen also began to go beyond the local region in conceptualizing their goals.

But just as sport hunters and fishermen were coming together to form a united front, the nation was breaking apart. When the South seceded, a movement that had been building for decades began to dissipate rapidly.

What happened to *The Spirit of the Times* is symbolic of what happened to the conservation cause as a whole. The New York-based weekly relied too heavily on subscribers and contributors from the South. Horse racing had always been the periodical's primary subject, and for most of March, 1861, the editors continued to report on races in the South as if seven states there had not already seceded! There was no way, however, to ignore the start of the bombardment on Fort Sumter on April 12th. The paper sputtered along until June 22, 1861, when it published its last issue.[143]

But the efforts of ante-bellum sportsmen, including *The Spirit*'s editors, were not in vain. It is clear that even though pre-Civil War sport hunters and fishermen lacked the same degree of organization, journalistic support, and legislative success they would be able to muster in the postwar period, they had served a crucial function in providing the philosophical foundation, and model for legislative action, for those coming later.

2

Makers of Conservation:
American Sportsmen After the Civil War

A Weekly Journal Devoted to Field and Aquatic Sports, Practical Natural History, Fish Culture, the Protection of Game, Preservation of Forests, and the Inculcation in Men and Women of a Healthy Interest in Outdoor Recreation and Study.

Subtitle of the first issue of *Forest and Stream,*
August 14, 1873

The appearance of a new monthly newspaper, the *American Sportsman,* in October, 1871, marks a watershed in environmental history. Though we should not forget that other publications, especially *The Spirit of the Times,* had "shown the way," this was the country's first national periodical to make the interrelated subjects of hunting, fishing, natural history, and conservation its *primary* concerns.[1] The welcome reception the journal received proves that a segment of the American public was ready for its teachings.

One reason for the enthusiastic response was the fact that the horror of the Civil War and its aftermath were rapidly receding, and some Americans were ready, once again, to indulge themselves in reading about their favorite recreations. Another reason can be found in changing attitudes regarding hunting and fishing. Many Americans before the Civil War, particularly in the North, seemed to view these activities as acceptable only when necessary or helpful to the maintenance of a livelihood; one pursued game because he depended on it for food or money. If hunting and fishing were spoken of as "sports" at all, they were often lumped together with diversions typified by chance and a purse, like horse racing, boxing, and cock fighting. An individual who acquired a taste for either to the point of practicing it as sport might find his "practical" neighbors regarding him as frivolous, or worse. The editor of one of the later outdoor journals went so far as to claim that "a man who went 'gunnin or fishin' [before the war] lost caste among respectable people just about in the same way that one did who got drunk."[2] (In this period "gunner" and "gunning" were synonyms for "hunter" and "hunting.")

But as we have seen, not all Americans regarded these activities in utilitarian terms. For a minority who looked to the British Isles for their example, "correct" hunting and fishing increasingly became a chief means of distinguishing the "gentleman" in an America best known for its Philistinism and commercialism. Across the Atlantic, the accepted ways of taking game were the products of traditions that preceded even the appearance of Izaak Walton's *The Compleat Angler; or, The Contemplative Man's Recreation* in 1653.[3] Whether fly-fishing for trout in an English stream or grouse shooting on a Scottish moor, an aristocrat took his sport seriously. To be fully accepted by his peers, he had to have a knowledge of the quarry and its habitat; a familiarity with the rods, guns, or dogs necessary to its pursuit; a skill to cast or shoot with precision and coolness that often takes years to acquire; and a "social sense" of the many do's and don'ts involved.

Henry William Herbert ("Frank Forester") and the others who helped introduce, and adapt, this "code of the sportsman" to the United States did much more than simply outline the basics of sporting etiquette; they also lamented the commercial destruction of game and habitat and demanded that sportsmen join together to preserve the entire context of their recreation, which would come to include nongame wildlife as well. The notion that there was only one correct way to take wildlife and that all other methods were "common," or even immoral, was a potential reservoir of reform that would play a key role in the making of the conservation movement.

What post-Civil War sportsmen and their journals had to fight was nothing less than the national myth of progress. An incredible rapidity of physical change, probably unexcelled in world history, was already the single most dramatic fact of the American experience. This impermanence had long been glorified as the essence of "progress"— that indefinable but inevitable something that was the trademark of the United States. In the words of one observer of the 1830s, "Americans *love* their country, not . . . *as it is*, but *as it will be*. . . . They live in the future, and *make* their country as they go on."[4] The truth of those statements is shown by the fact that from 1607 to 1907— scarcely more than four lifetimes by present expectations[5]—America would be changed from a couple of wilderness settlements into the most powerful economy on earth.

By the 1870s, the country was well on its way to achieving that 1907 status. In fact, no period of American history, except perhaps our own, saw more physical change than the last generation of the nineteenth century. Rapid industrialization and urbanization, development of mass-production techniques and communication systems, and the building of a national railroad network all combined to effect speedy and dramatic alterations of the natural environment.

Particularly disconcerting to sportsmen were the obvious changes in what were once thought to be inexhaustible wildlife populations. Previously undeveloped regions, teeming with animals, birds, and fish, were made readily accessible to all, and improved guns, ammunition, and fishing gear, which the average man could afford, were produced in huge quantities. Hunting and fishing now became not only more practical, but also more profitable.

When *American Sportsman* came into being, the systematic, commercial exploitation of American animal life was everywhere evident. The nation's industry was on the move, and any natural thing that could be converted to cash was utilized. The taste buds of the American people also had to be satisfied, because it was now fashionable to eat wild game like canvasback duck and striped bass (*Morone saxatilis*). Though long in existence, the commercial hunter and fisherman were entering their "golden era." They killed big game for hides, waterfowl for flesh, wading birds for plumage, and ocean fishes for oil and fertilizer. Quick money, sometimes large amounts, could be made by men like the plume hunters who shot the snowy egret almost into extinction.

What is ironic about this dismal situation is that the same economic developments that made wildlife more accessible to the market hunter and fisherman also brought it closer to the sportsman. Indeed, a major reason for the rapid increase in the ranks of the latter group was because of improvements in transportation and equipment. An outdoorsman could now travel to his hunting and fishing spots in greater comfort and enjoy better sport when he arrived—that is, if market men had not already preceded him.

From at least the time of Frank Forester and Elisha Lewis in the 1850s, sportsmen continually complained of arriving on their favorite grounds only to find that all the game had been killed or driven out by commercial hunters and fishermen. Until sportsmen finally defeated the market men after the passage of the Migratory Bird Treaty Act in 1918, and closed off the sale of game for all except some food fishes, this controversy between the two groups frequently approached a state of war. There were, in fact, some fatalities as a result of the conflict.[6] Sportsmen of the late nineteenth-century would be little less than flabbergasted to discover that historians of today lump them together with commercial gunners and fishermen.

With the appearance of national periodicals like *American Sportsman* (1871), *Forest and Stream* (1873), *Field and Stream* (1874), and *American Angler* (1881), a new impetus was given to the sportsmen's struggle against commercial exploitation of wildlife. While the nation as a whole remained indifferent, these journals, in issue after issue, poured forth a steady stream of propaganda against the market men. Besides enumerating specific offenses, the main technique used was to teach the American public the ethics and responsibilities of sportsmanship.

A typical example of this approach is "What Constitutes A True Sportsman," an editorial in the November, 1872, issue of *American Sportsman*. In order to define "a *genuine* sportsman," says editor Wilbur F. Parker,[7] one need only refer to Frank Forester, the "prince" of sporting writers:

> It is not the mere killing of numbers, much less in the mere killing at all; it is not in the value of the things killed, though it is not sportsmanship, but butchery and wanton cruelty to kill animals which are valueless [as food] and out of season; it is not in the inevitable certainty of success—for certainty destroys the excitement, which is the soul of sport—but it is in the vigor, science [correct technique], and manhood displayed—in the difficulties to be overcome, in the pleasurable anxiety for success, and the uncertainty of it, and lastly in the true spirit, the style, the dash, the handsome way of doing what is to be done, and above all, in the unalterable *love of fair play,* that first thought of the genuine sportsman, that true sportsmanship consists.[8]

But as complex as this definition is, the editor knows it is not complete. Thus, he cites two other unidentified writers. According to the first, "The pastimes of stream and woodland, champaign [flat, open country] and valley are the characteristic exercises of many of the noblest properties of man's nature," and "they call into exertion courage, perseverance, sagacity, strength, activity, [and] caution." In addition, "they are the wholesome machinery of excitement; of hope and fear, and joy and sorrow, regret and rejoicing; they are at once the appetite and the food of manhood. . . . *Instead of being antagonist[ic] meanings, the sportsman and the gentleman are [becoming] . . . synonymous terms.*"[9]

The second of these anonymous authorities, author of "a late and valued sporting work," explains that a true sportsman only "pursues his game for pleasure" and "makes no [financial] profit of his success, giving to his friends more than he retains, shoots invariably upon the wing and never takes a mean advantage of bird or man. It is his pride to kill what he does kill elegantly, scientifically, and mercifully. Quantity is not his ambition; he never slays more than he can use; he never inflicts unnecessary pang or fires an [unnecessary] . . . shot." Nor does he look upon his quarry "as representing so much money value, . . . to be converted into it as soon as possible."[10]

No one will ever know what percentage of sportsmen adhered faithfully to every one of these precepts. But it is known that sportsmen of the 1870s confirmed, both in their writings and in their public actions, a belief in all of these principles. And though they are barely even an adequate outline of the code of the sportsman, they at least illustrate that "sport" was more than noncommercial hunting and fishing. It was, in fact, a "world view," even a religion.

Other *American Sportsman* editorials explaining the fine points of this "religion" have titles like "Shooting—Its Pleasures and Benefits"; "Influence of Field Sports on Character"; "Sporting Nomenclature"; "The Pre-Eminence of Field Sports"; and "The Passion of Sport." In addition to the ideas already cited, these didactic pieces explain how sport hunting and fishing inculcate appreciation of nature and knowledge of "the various habits of animals," improve physical health and mental alertness, and assure righteousness by removing one "from the noise and dirt and moral degradation incident to large towns."[11]

With the appearance of *Forest and Stream* and *Field and Stream* later in the 1870s and *American Angler* in the early 1880s, Americans now had three more national newspapers to consolidate their ranks. While all followed the journalistic precedents set by *American Sportsman*, *Forest and Stream* proved to be the most innovative of the three and had the greatest impact.

Making its debut in New York on August 14, 1873, the weekly's course was determined by its wellborn editor, Charles Hallock, who "should . . . have credit for . . . establishing the policy of *Forest and Stream*."[12] That policy is suggested by the paper's subtitle: "A Weekly Journal Devoted to Field and Aquatic Sports, Practical Natural History, Fish Culture, The Protection of Game, Preservation of Forests, and the Inculcation in Men and Women of a Healthy Interest in Outdoor Recreation and Study." Looking over these topics, it is not difficult to see that Hallock's thinking was far ahead of his time. Less than ten years after the Civil War, he was calling for protection of watersheds and scientific management of forests; establishment of uniform game laws dictated by geography, habitat, and migration patterns, rather than judicial accident; creation of a science and industry of fish culture that would develop new strains of game fish and restock depleted waters; abatement of water pollution; and experimentation into methods for domesticating and "farming" fur-bearing animals.[13]

Like the editors of the other leading outdoor journals, Hallock, and later George Bird Grinnell, used *Forest and Stream* as a vehicle for importing the British concept of sportsmanship. For example, a regular column in the early years was "Sporting News From Abroad," which reported the experiences and viewpoints of aristocratic sportsmen. Other early features that reflect the English influence are "Woodland, Lawn and Garden," which related the advances of English landscape architecture, and "Athletic Pastimes," which kept track of competition, mainly between Ivy League colleges, in such games as polo and cricket. Although the names of the columns changed from time to time, and some eventually went out of existence, the standpoint they represent remained the same.

Why Hallock and Grinnell sought to emulate the English model is not certain, but their outlook may have been a manifestation of the new self-consciousness and Anglophilia that were sweeping the upper classes in the postwar era.[14] What is known—as will be shown—is that what I have called the code of the sportsman became part of the thinking of many wellborn hunters and fishermen. When the moral element in their code was fused with their dissatisfaction over dwindling game and habitat, an important impetus to the conservation movement was born.

For now, all that Hallock could do was to remind the American public week after week of what rapid industrialization was doing to the natural environment. The blind worship of PROGRESS, the nation's secular religion, was at the root of the problem. Men must be taught to "enjoy the present earth and the present life, so that there shall be less necessity to look for the promised creation of 'a new heaven and a new earth.' "[15] Ultimately, it might even be possible "to restore the original Eden which was made perfect for our first parents."[16]

To work toward this goal, hunters and fishermen, the largest category of persons involved with the outdoors on a nonutilitarian basis, would be consolidated into a force for good. *Forest and Stream*'s first issue announced: "It is the aim of this paper to become a medium of useful and reliable information between gentlemen sportsmen from one end of the country to the other. . . ."[17] From the beginning, Hallock made it clear that his periodical was only for the "true sportsman" and not for those who would debase sport. In this second group were men who killed merely for the fun of killing, without appreciation and understanding of the quarry or its natural surroundings; the "pot-hunter," who committed such offenses as shooting grouse in trees or bobwhite quail on the ground; the "meat hunter," who took wildlife only to fill his stomach and knew nothing of the subtleties of sport; the poacher, who killed without regard to season or sex, often trespassing in the process; and worst of all, the market man, who destroyed everything from trout to elk for the money they would bring.

To ensure that none of these individuals would think that *Forest and Stream* was for them, Hallock declared that his weekly "will pander to no depraved tastes, nor pervert the legitimate sports of land and water to those base uses which always tend to make them unpopular with the virtuous and good."[18] Herein lies the underlying thrust of *Forest and Stream:* Hallock sought to define, and ultimately to "legitimize," the proper mode for pursuing field sports and the enjoyment of their natural surroundings. While his immediate purpose was to bring together those already in the true sportsman category— by giving them their own vehicle of communication—he also hoped to set an example so compelling as to cause the ignorant and unethical to give up their ways and join the ranks of the initiate.

Less than seven years after Hallock began *Forest and Stream,* his natural history editor and business partner, George Bird Grinnell, bought him out and became the owner and editor-in-chief of the newspaper.[19] It was a monumental event in the history of conservation. From an old and wealthy Eastern family, Grinnell was already well-known in both scientific and sporting circles.[20] Controlling *Forest and Stream* until 1911, he would pour forth a continual stream of editorials, which, when combined with his private efforts, made his influence on conservation incalculably great.

Upon assuming his new post on January 1, 1880, Grinnell lauded the accomplishments of the weekly and implied that he would follow Hallock's precedents: "It only remains now for it [the paper] to hold its vantage ground and signal success which continue to follow it."[21] Retaining the same subtitle and most of the columns, he continued to emphasize that "sportsmanship" was the chief ingredient of hunting and fishing. Its essence, he maintained, was a concern, not for the size of the bag, but whether the game was taken in season, by legal methods, and with the idea of noncommercial use.[22] He asked his fellow outdoorsmen to join him in scorning the "pot-hunter" and "trout hog," those unprincipled enough to shoot ducks on the water and catch trout on the spawning nests. But he thought they were no worse than the so-called "honorable sportsman," who shoots ducks in the correct manner but leaves them in the cattails to rot, or catches trout also in "a perfectly scientific way," all of which, however, happen to be fingerlings.[23]

Grinnell went to the heart of what was troubling him in "The Corruption of Sport." He lamented that America was in the "money-making stage" of her history, when "the mighty dollar is the controlling agency in every branch of social and public life." Perhaps, he continued, "this generalization may sufficiently account for the mercenary element of so many forms of alleged sport" in which the "sordid clutching after purses, gate money, entrance fee or prize" seemed the main attraction.[24] Even competition in rifle and trapshooting was being prostituted in this way. He asked that all competitors contend only for "well earned and respected superiority in quick sight and steady aim, [and] not for a paltry sum of money."[25] Only then would these last preserves of men of quality be kept from being "cast into a disrepute which will bar gentlemen from enjoying in them and reaping their benefits."[26]

Like Hallock before him, Grinnell was clearly attempting to define, and ultimately to legitimize, the proper mode for pursuing field sports and the enjoyment of their natural settings. Both men seemed to feel that an older, more refined way of life was passing out of existence under the assault of rapid industrialization and its accompanying Philistinism, and that "correct" hunting and fishing were two of the ways of differentiating the gentleman.

Hallock and Grinnell came from old family, highly educated, monied backgrounds, and they shared a contempt for what they thought America was becoming—a society of Philistines, noted only for their pursuit of material success. Indeed, the two men seem to be prime candidates for what historian Richard Hofstadter calls the "status revolution."[27] One might surmise that they felt threatened by the challenge presented to their class values by the "new men": the Vanderbilts, Rockefellers, Harrimans, and their lesser-known peers. According to Hofstadter, the recently acquired fortunes of these individuals gave them so much power and prestige that they were supplanting the older elite in basic decision-making. In addition, their wealth enabled them to assume without difficulty the life style of the upper class: landed estates, art collections, and opera tickets could all be easily purchased. But, as has been illustrated, the understanding and appreciation of field sports and their outdoor surroundings could not be bought—one almost had to be "bred" to them. Perhaps Hallock and Grinnell were subconsciously attempting to keep at least one representative element of the older elite's world free from the encroachment of the *nouveaux riches.* In a sense, the preservation of genuine field sports and their natural settings was also the retention of the life style and environment of an otherwise vanishing order.

At first glance, it would seem that the backgrounds of Hallock and Grinnell fit the requirements of the "status revolution" thesis. But when analyzed, their attitudes are more representative of the revision to Hofstadter's theory offered by a number of historians. One of these is George M. Fredrickson. In describing jurist Oliver Wendell Holmes, Jr., he suggests that Holmes was concerned, not with status anxieties, but "with the fact that so many of his fellow Brahmins had retained their status at the price of joining the Gilded Age[28] as successful businessmen, thereby denying themselves the possibility of being a noncommercial aristocracy."[29] Grinnell's father, interestingly enough, seems to fit this generalization perfectly; after the Civil War bankrupted the family's textile firm, he went to work for none other than Commodore Vanderbilt, recouped his fortune, and made another in the process.[30]

Perhaps the younger Grinnell's disdain for business in his early adult years and his flight from a career in his father's company[31] show that he was trying to "rise above" his father's surrender to the new commercial order. In any case, it will be shown that he possessed no status anxieties in regard to the men of new wealth. Instead, he thoroughly absorbed the ideology of the business world, thereby fulfilling the second part of Fredrickson's analysis: "It would seem in fact that the 'mugwumps' [the name Hofstadter gives to the old elite] acted as spokesmen for a large segment of that [business] community, articulating the prevailing attitude of businessmen toward government, education, philanthropy, etc."[32] Grinnell later applied these conceptions to natural resources, discovering that they could be "managed" like a firm. In fact, his successful handling of *Forest and Stream* and the companies inherited from his father show that he was, himself, a consummate businessman.[33] As will be made clear, what threatened Grinnell, Hallock, and others of their class was not one particular group of individuals, but rather the whole, multifaceted trend toward commercialism and Philistinism that was accompanying the rapid industrialization of American society.

Whether or not the wellborn sportsman resented the new plutocracy, there is little doubt that he and his less privileged fellows deeply regretted the loss of "their" hunting and fishing grounds to the insatiable appetite of commerce. While most other Americans, including farmers and ranchers, seemed to see land only as a commodity of capitalism, sportsmen viewed it as the necessary context of their sport.

Every hunter and angler had his own favorite microcosm composed of woodlots, swamps, ponds, and other topographical features. On a larger scale the little world of the sportsman might be a whole geographical entity like the Adirondacks in New York State or Currituck Sound in North Carolina. But whatever and wherever his "territory," it was part of the fiber of every sportsman's existence. While in its midst, he watched the change of seasons, shared the joys of friends, made discoveries about nature and himself, and experienced other sensations too mystical to put into words. Then, as now, many walked onto old hunting and fishing grounds with some of the same emotions felt by a devout Christian entering the door of his or her church. If that statement sounds like an exaggeration, one need only read the works of John Krider, Samuel H. Hammond, Thaddeus Norris, or Henry Van Dyke.

In their love for the outdoors, sporting authors of the nineteenth century were, of course, influenced by the same Romantic movement that touched every major American writer from Thomas Jefferson to Walt Whitman. Sportsmen, too, paid tribute to nature and derived inspiration from wild grandeur. Even when it came to basic guidebooks, hunting and angling locations were continually rated in terms of their picturesque qualities.

But despite these similarities, there were significant differences between the Romantic movement and the sporting tradition as they evolved in the United States. For one thing, the Romantic movement in the arts originated in Germany and France late in the eighteenth century, while the American sporting tradition originated in the British Isles and dates back at least to Izaak Walton in the seventeenth century—indeed, many would take it back to the medieval world.

Another difference is that Romantics often seemed content merely to stroll through a "sylvan glade" and contemplate the "beauty" around them, while sportsmen wished to involve themselves personally in the rhythms of nature by pursuing and capturing a momentary fragment of that beauty in the form of a ruffed grouse or brook trout [*Salvelinus fontinalis*]. This is precisely the idea expressed by a later sportsman, Aldo Leopold, who, in a period before the rise of "birding" (bird watching) as a popular avocation, described what he thought were the "four categories of outdoors men," defined by "four diverse habits of the human eye." His vast experience with others in the field had taught him that "the deer hunter habitually watches the next bend; the duck hunter watches the skyline; the [upland] bird hunter watches the dog; the non-hunter does not watch."[34] Leopold probably would have agreed with the conclusion that Romantics appeared to be little more than spectators, while sportsmen were participants.

This is undoubtedly one reason why the latter group often combined serious scientific inquiry with their love of nature, while Romantics were usually little more than dilettantes in science and sometimes—as in the cases of Ralph Waldo Emerson and John Muir—even hostile to it because "close study . . . jeopardized the divine mystery and beauty of nature."[35]

Another example of the spectator-versus-participant analogy is the fact that most Romantics only had eyes for the "beautiful" and "scenic" in nature. Like their modern counterparts, they had little use for "ugly" topography like inland swamp and coastal marsh.[36] To the sportsman, however, so-called wastelands were frequently the repositories of fond memories and keen anticipations. Indeed, the word "swamp" is still a synonym for worthless land, a place often considered to be fit only for dumping garbage. As their financial support proves, twentieth-century waterfowl hunters have had a very different notion of its value.[37]

The despair felt by early sportsmen at the loss of precious hunting and fishing grounds and their denizens constitutes one of the basic themes in sport history. Its most common form was a nostalgia for the past, when game was still abundant and its habitat unmarred by "improvements." This continuous wail, which I call the "good-old-days lament," is evident even in the antebellum period, as we saw in the writings of John J. Brown and William Elliott.

By the 1860s, Robert Barnwell Roosevelt, well-known sportsman and the uncle of Theodore Roosevelt, complained that "streams in the neighborhood of New York [City] that formerly were alive with trout are now totally deserted. The Bronx, famous alike for its historical associations and its once excellent fishing, does not now seem to hold a solitary trout, or indeed fish of any kind. The shad that a few years ago swarmed up the Hudson River in numbers incomputable have become scarce. . . ." And "on every portion of our sea-coast, in spite of replenishment from the mighty ocean, the same diminution is visible, while many of our confined inland waters are absolutely depopulated."[38]

In this period the West, of course, was the most dramatic example of rapid environmental change, and America's well-known narrative historian, Francis Parkman, introduced the 1872 edition of his classic, *The Oregon Trail* (1847), with a lament for the hunting grounds of his youth. Where once he had joyfully pursued the buffalo,[39] one now heard "the disenchanting screech of the locomotive" and found hotels, gambling houses, and even "woman's rights"! For Parkman, much of the West had already passed under the rule of "triumphant commonplace."[40]

By the time the national outdoor journals appeared, the good-old-days lament was a well-established characteristic of the "sporting mind." Most issues of the "big four" newspapers contain evidence of its strength. In early 1875, for example, William F. Parker, editor of *American Sportsman,* rhetorically asked his fellow Americans what they had to brag about as the nation's centennial approached: "Shall we boast that where the deer, the buffalo, the salmon, and the feathered game . . . were once plentiful . . . , we may now tramp for many a long summer day and not find a specimen? Shall we take credit for our predatory instinct that as individuals we have wasted natural gifts not exceeded in any other part of the world, and that as a nation we have been so intent on multiplying the almighty dollar that we have given over our streams to pollution, our fish to destruction, and our land and water to the poacher and exterminator," or "that with our immense domain and our boundless endowments we are now poorer in this particular of national wealth than the thickly settled countries of Europe . . . ?"[41]

One of the more ironic examples of the good-old-days lament appeared in the same periodical in October, 1876. The Reverend William H. H. Murray, whose *Adventures in the Wilderness* (1869) is credited with "opening up" the Adirondacks as a fashionable resort,[42] now complains that nonsporting tourists have overrun the region. Because of the need to supply the new hotels with trout and venison, the game had all but vanished. The territory Murray had glorified only a few years before was now "worthless" for sportsmen: "The trout are entirely gone, practically so, and the deer are going as fast as stupid greed [market hunting] can destroy them."[43]

One last example of the good-old-days lament is from an 1882 editorial in *American Field,* the same journal as *Field and Stream* but with a new title.[44] Like all such material in the sporting journals, the piece is unsigned, but is presumably by the paper's editor, Nicholas Rowe. Describing the Long Island (New York) of his youth, he recalls that:

> Not longer than twenty-five years ago, and even less, large bags of quails, woodcocks, ruffed grouse and water fowls could be made; and very fair deer hunting could be had. Then more birds could have been brought to bag in one day than in a week now. . . . To the young generation of sportsmen who live in the vicinity of Long Island, these statements must seem almost incredible; but there are numbers [of hunters] living who can substantiate them. We have shot from one end of Long Island to the other, and as we look back through the vista of years, memory fondly brings back some of the happiest days of our life, and we almost feel like a boy again. Of all the shooting we have had, those days spent on Long Island are the greenest in our memory. Whether July woodcock shooting, or in August basking in the hot sun on Moriches or Shinnecock bay shooting bay [shore] birds, or in September on Mountauk [*sic*] Point shooting plovers, or on the North Side [Shore] shooting Fall woodcocks, or in the brown October days quail and ruffed grouse shooting, or in November duck shooting, we enjoyed ourselves as only one can who delights in the sports of the field. We have always thought Long Island possessed a charm for sportsmen such as no other place that we have seen . . . , and it to be deeply regretted that its glory has departed.[45]

Almost everywhere in the sporting literature of the postwar generation, one will find similar protests. And what is notable for our story is that sportsmen did more than lament—they also acted.

For most, the first step was to join with their brothers and form a club or association. Though these organizations can be found as early as the eighteenth century,[46] they were few and far between until the 1870s.[47] Then, with the establishment of the national sporting journals, a movement began that immediately resulted in the formation of scores of new associations across the nation. Before long, this "club movement"—the term the sportsmen themselves used—engendered not only many local clubs but state and national organizations as well.

As noted conservationist John B. Burnham pointed out later: "All at once, in the winter of 1874-75, . . . it seemed to penetrate the consciousness of the readers of those . . . journals that they had a responsibility for the game, a feeling that was accentuated by the disappearance or decrease of the game in many parts of the country. At any rate, for the first time they not only realized but assumed their responsibility, and in that winter of 1874-75 nearly 100 sportsmen's organizations were organized all over the country, ten or twelve state associations and one national association."[48]

The incredible growth of the club movement after this initial spurt of activity is documented in Charles Hallock's *American Club List and Sportsman's Glossary,* published in 1878. *Forest and Stream*'s editor enumerated thirty-four organizations "devoted chiefly to the pleasure of angling and the protection and propagation of fish," among them the Illinois State Fish Culturists' Association and the American Fish Cultural Association,[49] of which Hallock was a prominent member. Most were in the Northeast, but a number of states outside that region, including California, had at least one club. Separated by Hallock from these associations are what he calls the "Sportsmen's Clubs," those "organized either for field shooting, or for shooting and fishing combined," as well as "the preservation of game and the observance and enforcement of laws governing close[d] seasons." These now numbered 308, more than a threefold increase since 1874-75. Virtually every settled portion of the United States was represented, though the Northeast was again most prominent.[50]

Some of the clubs' names are especially interesting. Two were named for John James Audubon, five for Frank Forester, two for Hallock himself, and eight for *Forest and Stream.*[51] The latter two groups reveal the influence Hallock's paper had already wielded in its efforts to get readers to form associations.

It should also be mentioned that these 308 do not include a long list of what Hallock calls "Guns Clubs"—those that, "technically speaking," are devoted mainly to trapshooting—even though "many Gun Clubs also engage largely in Field Shooting." Neither does it include the angling clubs mentioned above, even though many combined hunting as well, nor fourteen fox-hunting associations concerned with riding to the hounds.[52]

Because all of the 308 associations, and the thirty-four angling clubs as well, claimed to be committed to the perpetuation of wildlife and their habitats, the editors of the "big four" newspapers performed a real environmental service by fostering what they called the "club idea." While only a small minority of these organizations had an important influence on conservation, the general effect of the movement was to increase sportsmen's awareness—and the nation's as well—of the damage being done by American economic growth.

On a more concrete level these associations also acted as centers for discussion and, in many cases, as lobbies for better enforcement of already existing laws and passage of new ones.[53] Except for sportsmen, only a tiny number of Americans had any real interest in conservation before the turn of the century. As we will see later, historians have given these individuals labels like "nature lover," "expert," "scientist," "naturalist," or "preservationist," when many could be categorized as "sportsman" just as easily.

To see how fashionable the club idea had become by the 1870s, the reader need only leaf through the sportsmen's journals, the main vehicle of communication for what they called the "fraternity." In an age that historians claim was devoid of environmental consciousness outside a few "prophets" like John Wesley Powell and John Muir, one is surprised to find organizations cropping up everywhere whose avowed purpose is the preservation of wildlife and natural areas. Typical is an entry in the *American Sportsman* issue of October 25, 1873. Under the heading of "New Sportsmen's Associations," correspondent Frederick W. Jones informs the editor that "An association of gentlemen has been formed in Orange Co., N.Y., under the name of the Summit Lake Association for the purpose of propagating fish and game of various kinds." After giving the acreage controlled by the club, Jones, its president, adds: "We have the lake well stocked with black bass, obtained from Seth Green [the noted fish culturist]. . . ."[54] Another example of an entry under this heading, taken from an issue in the following month, is a letter from a correspondent in Missouri Valley, Iowa, who tells the editor that "at a meeting of the sportsmen of our town on Tuesday evening, December 2d, 1873, a sportsman's club was formed for the purpose of enforcing the game laws, the protection of game, and elevating the standard of . . . sportsmen, to be known as the Missouri Valley Sportsman Club."[55]

By the following year, the paper's editor, Wilbur F. Parker, could already report a "marked and radical . . . change in popular feeling" that "has brought field sports up from being deemed a pursuit for loafers only, to their present estimation as a matter of manly honor and credit to men of the highest rank and position. The asceticism and puritanic[al] condemnation of everything which does not directly tend to the accumulation of the almighty dollar, has fortunately for our good sense and physical improvement given way to a more liberal sentiment." Now, "a professional man who desires a few days' recreation with rod or gun [a]mid the haunts of Nature, is no longer obliged to steal away 'like a thief in the night,' but can go forth openly, and on his return proclaim his success with a flourish of trumpets, if so inclined, without suffering either in purse or reputation thereby. A few years since, a sportsmen's club was a thing unknown;[56] now they may be counted by scores, and exist in almost every important city in the Union, encouraging and fostering a true sportsmanlike spirit. . . ."[57] At last, "the sportsmen of America are . . . roused to the importance of banding themselves together for the purpose of checking and controlling the wanton and wasteful destruction of nature's best gifts intended for the heritage of universal man, and not for the benefit of the reckless and greedy few. . . ."[58]

As Parker believed, this was only the beginning. With the steady encouragement of the sporting journals, the coming years would witness the establishment of an increasing number of local, state, and national associations, and together they would exert a massive influence on both the attitudes of the general public and the history of conservation.

From what has already been said, it is obvious the author feels that the importance—and often even the existence—of these early organizations has been overlooked by academic historians. If this is true, then it can only follow that they have also ignored the individual hunter and fisherman, despite the fact that hunting or fishing was an important part of individual lives.

In the early part of the century purely recreational angling and gunning, even for juveniles, had still been frowned upon in the North outside of elite sportsmen circles, but the same "thaw" in the compulsive practicality of Americans that helped sportsmen benefited boys everywhere; more time now could be taken up by hunting and fishing without fear of censure or punishment. In the South youngsters escaped for the most part the puritanical heritage of their Northern counterparts. Although fishing was never as popular there as in the North, hunting, even for recreation, always seems to have been a central part of the socialization process for males.

Because academic historians, including those writing biographies, have considered these activities of little significance, it is often extremely difficult to discover whether or not a particular individual who helped increase American environmental awareness—and who is not already well known as a sportsman—ever hunted or fished in his youth. The author has made an attempt to track down this information, and I have found that an extraordinarily large number of these men were gunners or anglers some time during their lives. Many, like John F. Lacey and Gifford Pinchot, retained throughout their years the love for sport first acquired in boyhood, while others, like George Perkins Marsh and Robert Underwood Johnson, were extremely fond of angling or hunting in youth, but later discontinued these activities or channeled their enthusiasm for them into "scientific collecting."

Why they no longer pursued them, as "sports," is hard to say. Certainly they had little social pressure on them to give up these avocations because they were allegedly unethical, as is the case today. Possibly the press of business—of achieving status in their chosen fields—simply left them with little time for purely recreational pursuits. Still, this does not explain why others, like George Bird Grinnell and Theodore Roosevelt, managed to combine active careers with an outdoor life. For many, the vitality of the sporting tradition was such that it counterbalanced cultural pressures to give up the "innocent" pursuits of childhood for the "practical" endeavors of adulthood. But others, like Spencer Fullerton Baird and William Temple Hornaday, had to camouflage their old love for the pursuit of wildlife by calling it "collecting," despite the fact that the same techniques were used and the same pleasure experienced when a capture was made (as the photograph of Hornaday in the "Picture Album" of this book attests). Even though some gave up their youthful interest in hunting or fishing, or chose to systematize it in the name of science, most looked back on their early experience as gunners or anglers with the deepest affection. One can only assume that it played an important part in fashioning these individuals' love for the natural world and the desire to see it preserved. And this is just as true for those individuals whom historians have pigeonholed as "preservationists" (persons supposedly concerned only with preserving natural areas and wildlife *untouched*), as it is for those they have categorized as "conservationists" (persons supposedly concerned only with the *utilization* of resources). Given in alphabetical order, the following list of seventy-six names is representative of Americans whose hunting or fishing experiences seemed to have shaped, at least to a degree, their desire to preserve some aspect of the natural world:

John Quincy Adams
Stephen H. Ainsworth
Joel A. Allen
George S. Anderson
Chester A. Arthur
John James Audubon
Spencer Fullerton Baird
Albert Bierstadt
William H. Brewer
William Brewster
John J. Brown
John Burroughs
George Catlin
Frank M. Chapman
Galen Clark
Grover Cleveland
DeWitt Clinton
James Fenimore Cooper
Charles B. Cory
Elliott Coues
Samuel S. Cox
William Dutcher
George F. Edmunds
Daniel G. Elliot
William Elliott
Barton Warren Evermann
Bernhard E. Fernow
Edward H. Forbush
"Frank Forester"
Theodatus Garlick
George Brown Goode
Madison Grant
Seth Green
George Bird Grinnell
Charles Hallock
Samuel H. Hammond
William C. Harris
Benjamin Harrison

Joel T. Headley
Cornelius Hedges
William T. Hornaday
Emerson Hough
Washington Irving
William H. Jackson
Robert Underwood Johnson
David Starr Jordan
Clarence King
John F. Lacey
Charles Lanman
Elisha J. Lewis
William Ludlow
George Perkins Marsh
Fred Mather
C. Hart Merriam
Thomas Moran
William H. H. Murray
Thaddeus Norris
Frederick Law Olmsted
Wilbur F. Parker
Francis Parkman
William Hallett Phillips
Gifford Pinchot
Robert Ridgway
Robert Barnwell Roosevelt
Theodore Roosevelt
Joseph T. Rothrock
Nicholas Rowe
Carl A. Schenck
Ernest Thompson Seton
George Oliver Shields
Livingston Stone
Henry David Thoreau
Henry Van Dyke
George G. Vest
Daniel Webster
Alexander Wilson[59]

The primary interests of nineteenth-century "environmentalists" were "nature appreciation," wildlife, parks, and forests, and whether in artistic, literary, legislative, or scientific form, all of the individuals listed made a contribution to one or more of these subject areas. While this compilation is not all-inclusive—it could have been much longer— the list does contain a fair number of better-known individuals from a wide variety of fields. And what is most interesting is that not only did all these men pursue hunting or fishing at one time, but the majority retained that interest throughout much of their lives.

Though most of those enumerated fit the definition of "sportsman," historians have habitually labeled them as "nature lovers," "nature writers," "naturalists," "scientists," or "experts." Yet the main thing these diverse individuals had in common was a shared experience as anglers or hunters. Surely that personal involvement with the rhythms of nature on a nonutilitarian basis—unlike farmers and ranchers, for example—must have played a crucial part in the fashioning of their love and concern for the outdoors. How many know that forestry pioneer John Quincy Adams ruminated on the difficulty of achieving wildlife conservation in a democratic society while out hunting one evening in 1787; that scientist Spencer Fullerton Baird loved wildfowl hunting in his youth to the point of envying wealthy sportsmen-naturalists who were able to spend all their time shooting; that artists Albert Bierstadt and Thomas Moran were accomplished sportsmen; that author and artist Charles Lanman loved angling; that one of the greatest moments in the lives of photographer William H. Jackson and explorer-scientist Clarence King was the shooting of a grizzly bear in the Great West; that the favorite pastime of "nature writers" John Burroughs and Henry Van Dyke was fishing; that on October 23, 1873, ornithologist Elliott Coues told the readers of *Forest and Stream* that he had long thought of starting a hunting, fishing, and natural history periodical like theirs; that ornithologists William Brewster, Charles B. Cory, and Daniel G. Elliot also loved bird hunting; that the man who some have claimed conceived the idea of Yellowstone National Park, Cornelius Hedges, was an avid trout angler; that the two leading Congressional defenders of the Yellowstone preserve, George G. Vest and Samuel S. Cox, were passionate, self-proclaimed "sportsmen"; that editor Robert Underwood Johnson and scholar George Perkins Marsh considered their youthful angling excursions among the most cherished experiences of boyhood; that artist George Catlin, perhaps the first American to conceive of the idea of a national park, hunted buffalo for sport; that John James Audubon—like Louis Agassiz Fuertes, Lynn Bogue Hunt, and many other bird painters of a later day—loved hunting the birds he illustrated; that Congressman John F. Lacey, who was responsible for drafting much of the key legislation of early conservation, stated publicly that his commitment was based on the code of the sportsman; that C. Hart Merriam, mammalogist and founder of what became the United States Fish and Wildlife Service, was a hunter and active member of the League of American Sportsmen; that Galen Clark, who was a key figure in the early history of what became Yosemite National Park, explored the area while on hunting trips; that ichthyologists Barton Warren Evermann, George Brown Goode, Seth Green, David Starr Jordan, Fred Mather, Thaddeus Norris, and Livingston Stone were all enthusiastic anglers before and after they became "scientists"; that Gifford Pinchot believed that a fishing trip to the Adirondacks in his youth had much to do with his later decision to become a forester; that Joseph T. Rothrock, pioneer in forestry at the state level, was a frequent contributor to sportsmen's periodicals on the subject of hunting; that Samuel H. Hammond, perhaps the first individual to make a specific recommendation for the creation of an Adirondack preserve, did so in a work relating his hunting and fishing adventures in that wilderness region; that zoo director William T. Hornaday, often quoted by historians for his attacks on hunters, was an avid hunter himself; that "preservationist" Frederick Law Olmsted belonged to a fox-hunting club; that Theodore Roosevelt claimed that he would never have become President if it had not been for his experiences in the West, which began with a buffalo hunt; that on a trip to Maine's Mt. Katahdin region, Henry David Thoreau became so excited by the prospect of angling for trout that he was unable to sleep and arose before anyone else in camp in order to get a jump on the fish; that Grover Cleveland wrote a philosophical book on the joys of hunting and fishing; that the only bill angler Daniel Webster introduced in his one term as a Massachusetts state legislator was an act to preserve trout; or that William Dutcher, founder of what later evolved into the National Audubon Society, was a bird hunter?

The author could provide numerous other examples of the same theme. The point is that hunting or fishing for pleasure was almost universal among early proponents of greater environmental appreciation in the United States, regardless of whether they eventually gave up these avocations, became full-fledged sportsmen in adulthood, or channeled their enthusiasm for field sports into "collecting"; men like John Muir and Franklin B. Hough, who never seem to have had any interest in these activities, or were even hostile to them, are clearly the exception. For most, the pursuit of wildlife seems to have provided that crucial first contact with the natural world that spawned a commitment to its perpetuation. Instead of ignoring hunting and fishing and those who made them a cherished recreation, or trivializing them with self-righteous disdain, historians would do well to acknowledge and investigate the role played by sport in inspiring environmental appreciation and reforms.

Flawed analysis, based partly on the inability of scholars to differentiate among the many groups and categories of hunters and fishermen, continues to muddy their understanding of the contributions of sportsmen to conservation. For example, one historian argues that "because a great number of Americans of the late nineteenth and early twentieth centuries enjoyed recreational hunting and fishing, it is difficult to substantiate the claim that these activities fostered an organized desire for wildlife protection."[60] Why is it so difficult? Substantiation for an organized, sportsmen-led, wildlife-conservation movement is the documented existence of an organized, sportsmen-led, wildlife-conservation movement! The great majority of individuals who pursued wildlife in this period simply hunted and fished, without ever taking any action in behalf of their quarry. The fact that only a minority of Americans were the upper-middle and upper-class "gentleman sportsmen" who founded conservation associations and worked for state, and later national, wildlife legislation does not take away from their key contributions to the making of the first conservation movement. This is especially true given the repeated assertations of Theodore Roosevelt, George Bird Grinnell, Iowa Congressman John F. Lacey, and so many other pioneers of conservation that their love for wildlife began with hunting or fishing and their internalization of the code of the sportsman.

Though this study focuses on American men who were, by the usual definitions of sociological class theory,[61] at least upper-middle class and often upper class in background, recent scholarship has shown that similarly placed women in the socio-economic order also had a part to play in the early conservation movement. Because fishing and hunting, particularly the latter, tended to be a male bastion and because women could not vote or participate directly in political life, they almost never had a leadership role. Still, "the conservation movement gained much from women's widespread presence," and "environmentalism would have been far less effective had it not been for the thousands of women who supported it."[62] One area of early conservation where women did lead, as will be shown in a future chapter, was in the efforts of the Audubon societies to protect nongame birds.

What is also interesting about these recent works in women's history is the presentation of evidence for a greater amount of hunting by females than previously thought. While it had long been known that the "gentle art" of angling could be considered, in some circumstances, a legitimate pursuit for Victorian ladies (as the photograph of a woman angler in the "Picture Album" of this book illustrates), hunting was another matter. But at least in the American West, women did engage in this "manly" pursuit.[63] In passing, it should be noted that, today, women are the fastest growing segment of America's 14 million hunters, increasing from 4 percent in the late 1980s to nearly 11 percent by 1999.[64] One woman scholar even argues that the female of our species was always as drawn to hunting as the male—until her urge to hunt was suppressed through male domination.[65] With this increase in women's participation in hunting, there is a corresponding increase in membership in conservation organizations like Ducks Unlimited and the National Wild Turkey Federation.[66] Given the important role of their male counterparts in the past, could we expect otherwise?

3

Conservation Begins With Wildlife

Why shall not we, the people, demand of our representatives at
Boston, at Albany, at Lansing and Springfield and . . .
[Sacramento] and all other seats of legislation, the due protection of
our, the people's, interests, by the conservation of our game and fish?
Laws prohibiting the destruction of game in its breeding season and
of fish on their spawning grounds are not for the advantage of any
narrow class or clique. They are for the good of us, the people. Take
this broad, tenable ground: the greatest good to the greatest number.

GEORGE BIRD GRINNELL'S EDITORIAL,
"We, the People," in *Forest and Stream,* January 26, 1882

I f the reader were to pick up virtually any work on the history of
conservation, he or she would find the same matter-of-fact
statement that concern for the nation's forests initiated American
conservation. First asserted by Theodore Roosevelt and Gifford Pinchot
and later reaffirmed by forestry spokesmen and their supporters, the
claim has now achieved a kind of sacrosanct quality that makes it almost
unassailable. Even the title of what was, for many years, the only
scholarly history journal to emphasize conservation, *Forest History,*
suggests the strength of what is, in fact, an erroneous assumption.

Roosevelt and Pinchot were actually late-comers to conservation.
This statement may sound incredible today, but it is nevertheless true.
By 1901, when these two dynamic men teamed up to make
"conservation" a household word, a less dramatic, but still influential,
movement had already been in existence for a quarter of a century.
From the 1870s on, sportsmen had been working for the restriction
of commercial hunting and fishing, the adoption of a national fish-
culture program that included efforts to control water pollution, the
establishment of adequately protected game preserves, and the passage
of new game laws and the better enforcement of old ones. As it turned
out, individual sportsmen would also pioneer in forest preservation
and management, but the bulk of outdoorsmen were concerned first
with "wildlife," including mammals, birds, *and* fishes.

Because Roosevelt and Pinchot were both extremely proud men, it is only natural that they tended to "forget" what had occurred before *they* arrived on the national scene.[1] Even though Roosevelt's administration established five national parks, eighteen national monuments, and fifty-one national wildlife refuges, its focal point was the forests, as the most all-inclusive, "practical" issue in conservation. In a nation overwhelmingly utilitarian in its outlook, the only political approach they could take was to claim that the forests were being preserved and managed in order to protect watersheds and ensure a never-ending supply of building materials. To do anything else would have been to court political defeat for their whole conservation program, particularly in the fiercely democratic West where the administration's new forests were set aside.

In 1913 the former president related the frustrations he had experienced in office to his cousin Nicholas: "Whenever as President he sought to withdraw lands on the public domain . . . , he was met by prompt and vigorous opposition from the lobbyists of . . . the lumber, mining and grazing interests, . . . [and] these lobbyists brought pressure to bear on state and local politicians, and saw to it that public opposition was loud and effective."[2] Yet Roosevelt knew that while vast tracts of timberland were being preserved—he set aside a total of 148 million acres—the big game he cherished so much would also find relief from uncontrolled hunting and habitat destruction, and he was right. Outside of Yellowstone and Glacier National Parks, the majority of Western woodland mammals south of Canada still live in the "national forests," as the forest reserves were called after 1907.

Following in the tradition of Samuel P. Hays, most historians have stressed the utilitarian objectives of Roosevelt and Pinchot and ignored the aesthetic side of their personalities. For example, Roosevelt wrote to ornithologist, Frank M. Chapman, in 1899: " 'How immensely it would add to our forests if the great Logcock [ivory-billed woodpecker] were still found among them! The destruction of the Wild Pigeon and the Carolina Paroquet [parakeet] has meant a loss as severe as if the Catskills [New York mountain range] or the Palisades [Hudson River cliffs] were taken away. When I hear of the destruction of a species, I feel just as if the works of some great writer had perished, as if we had lost all instead of only part of Polybius or Livy.' "[3] To preserve the species, at least in museums, Chapman had "collected" one of the last ivory-bills in Florida in 1890 (see the photograph in the "Picture Album" of this book), and later worked with Roosevelt to establish the national wildlife refuge system to save egrets, ibises, and other nongame species threatened with extinction.[4]

Another example of Roosevelt's concern for the total environment—for aesthetic as well as utilitarian conservation—is his statement in 1903 regarding the need to protect the giant sequoias of California: " 'There is nothing more practical in the end than the preservation of beauty, than the preservation of anything that appeals to the higher emotions of mankind.' "[5] As in the case of the national forests, where he set aside many millions of acres despite the howls of protest from Western Congressmen, Roosevelt translated his love of beauty into concrete achievement.

Welcoming the legislative leadership of Iowa Congressman John F. Lacey, who was responsible for a number of the key laws of early conservation and who publicly stated that his commitment was based on the code of the sportsman,[6] Roosevelt signed the Antiquities Act on June 8, 1906. Designed originally to protect spectacular archaeological sites, like Colorado's Mesa Verde and New Mexico's Chaco Canyon, from being damaged by looters seeking valuable artifacts to sell, the law quickly became an opportunity for Roosevelt to save other places that appealed to his aesthetic sensibilities. Applying the "object of scientific interest" clause of the Antiquities Act in the broadest possible fashion, he proclaimed the Grand Canyon National Monument in Arizona in 1908 and the Mount Olympus National Monument in Washington in 1909.[7] Both would become the cores of great national parks.

The main reason Roosevelt established the Grand Canyon National Monument, aside from the fact that he "was awestruck by the sight of the gorge," was his desire "to preserve the character of the Grand Canyon from the intrusion of the cable car" by putting "limits on all growth there."[8] As we will see, he first learned the importance of keeping natural areas natural in 1890, when he joined George Bird Grinnell's crusade to exclude railroads and other forms of destructive human activity from Yellowstone National Park.

During the same fight, Roosevelt worked to protect the bison and other big-game species being killed by commercial hunters. This would again be a prime reason for his setting aside Mount Olympus National Monument, which, in addition to its beauty, contained a threatened herd of a subspecies of elk, named the "Roosevelt elk" in 1897 by prominent mammologist and sportsman, C. Hart Merriam.[9] At the time, Merriam thought the animal he discovered was a full species, and as an admirer of Roosevelt's books on natural history and hunting, he believed that " 'it is fitting that the noblest deer of America should perpetuate the name of one who, in the midst of a busy public career, has found time to study our larger animals in their native haunts and has written the best accounts we have ever had of their habits *and chase* [emphasis added].' "[10]

Just as Theodore Roosevelt's aesthetic side and concern for wildlife have been understated by historians, Gifford Pinchot, too, has been misinterpreted by scholars, who have, invariably, only quoted his pronouncements regarding the purpose of the national forests and the United States Forest Service, made in the public arena where political realities prevailed.[11] A big-game hunter as a young man and an ardent angler his whole life, Pinchot knew George Bird Grinnell before the forester began to work closely with Theodore Roosevelt. In fact, Pinchot seems to have relied on Grinnell for information on where to hunt in the 1890s, and even employed Grinnell's own hunting guide in Montana.[12] An analysis by the author of Pinchot's writings on angling, particularly his *Just Fishing Talk* (1936), now considered a classic in sporting literature, shows that he was a "nature lover" from an early age, who manifested a rare sensitivity about the natural world and who wanted to understand it for its own sake.[13] In his private life he was anything but what historians have made him out to be: the short-sighted utilitarian who was the perfect foil to the far-sighted, aesthetic philosopher John Muir.

Just as scholars have trivialized, or condemned, hunting, they have also trivialized fishing. Even Pinchot's biographers have virtually ignored the centrality of angling in Pinchot's life, when, in fact, it is a "window to the inner man."[14]

Simply put, Pinchot compartmentalized his feelings about nature. Like his remark to a friend—"as soon as this present political fight we're in is over, we're going fishing"[15]—he made a clear separation between work (or duty) and "re-creation." The compartmentalization of his personality is revealed in Nicholas Roosevelt's observation that Pinchot "was tough and shrewd in attaining his [political] ends, yet gentle and sensitive to beauty."[16]

The careers of philosopher John Muir and journalist George Bird Grinnell were not dependent on making politically appealing public statements and developing politically acceptable agendas. In one sense, they could "afford" to make declarations based on pure principle and ignore the need for political expediency. American politicians, including Roosevelt and Pinchot, have never enjoyed this freedom.

Like Roosevelt, Pinchot seems genuinely to have believed that it would not only be more politically expedient to make the forests the centerpiece of their conservation program, but that this strategy would also adequately protect the big game that both men cherished. At the beginning of Roosevelt's administration, on November 11, 1901, less than two months after William McKinley died, Pinchot wrote the President that nothing should be done to arouse public opposition to the extension of the forest-reserve system, "which is the prime necessity for the preservation *alike* [emphasis added] of forests, streams, and game."[17]

Historians have tended to follow the Roosevelt-Pinchot "line" in considering timberlands first in importance and wildlife second. As we have seen, these two men had to take that approach—regardless of their personal feelings—but historians have followed them simply because they have not considered animals, birds, and fishes as anything but minor subjects in the history of conservation. Not understanding that wildlife is an index to environmental quality and that in many areas it is worth more economically, as a recreational resource, than the value of potential board feet of lumber, most scholars have been taken in by the same "practical-mindedness" that has always plagued American attempts to develop a holistic natural resource policy.

This is undoubtedly a major reason for their habitual tendency to look upon wildlife as an issue that hardly even competes with the "important" resources like forests and minerals. A major result of this tunnel vision is that they have overlooked the massive efforts of sportsmen to conserve wildlife long before Roosevelt and Pinchot appeared on the national scene.

It is not difficult to prove that in the minds of a substantial segment of the American people, wildlife preceded forests as the most important environmental issue. In the 1870s, as discussed in Chapter Two, hundreds of sportsmen's organizations—including state and national associations—were formed across the country with the express purpose of preserving and propagating game. In addition, several national periodicals with the same objectives came into existence. Where in regard to the forests was there a comparable movement in the decade of the 1870s? The answer is nowhere. There were no forestry clubs scattered all over the nation; no forestry journals appealing to a national audience; and before the 1880s, no more than a scattering of individual forest proponents, many of whom were sportsmen like Charles Hallock and George Bird Grinnell. Only one organization existing in the 1870s might, at first glance, seem to be an exception to the above statements;

this was the *original* American Forestry Association, established in 1875 by John A. Warder. But historians admit that it never showed any life, and the group "did not survive beyond 1882," when it merged with the new American Forestry Congress.[18] In 1889 this more active organization changed its name to the American Forestry Association and was incorporated under that name in 1897.[19]

Of all the conservation efforts relating to wildlife, probably the most popular for sportsmen and nonsportsmen alike was fish culture. As discussed in Chapter One, sportsmen like John J. Brown and Frank Forester had called for the restoration of game fishes to waters depleted by dams and pollution at least as early as the 1840s. And well-known angler George Franklin Edmunds had arranged for his relative, George Perkins Marsh, to do his important study of fish decline in Vermont with a view towards replenishment. After the initial protests, other sportsmen like Robert Barnwell Roosevelt and Genio C. Scott joined the cause. Their works, and the volumes of the national sporting periodicals, are replete with protests against the dumping of sawdust, mine wastes, factory chemicals, and other pollutants into the country's waterways; demands for fish ladders at dams so that migratory fishes could pass around these obstructions; and attacks on commercial fishermen whose nets, it seemed, were staked across every important river, lake, and sound in the nation.[20]

Typical of this literature is *The American Angler's Book: Embracing the Natural History of Sporting Fish, and the Art of Taking Them, With Instructions in Fly-Fishing, Fly-Making, and Rod-Making, and Directions for Fish-Breeding . . . ,* written by Thaddeus Norris and published in Philadelphia in 1864. This influential volume by "Uncle Thad," as Norris was called by his many admirers in the "sporting fraternity," has been described as the American equivalent of Izaak Walton's *The Compleat Angler; or, the Contemplative Man's Recreation* (1653). Unlike some earlier writers, Norris did not slavishly follow English angling tradition when describing how to become an expert fly-fisher; his book was, in fact, " 'the first comprehensive work by an American' " on this subject.[21]

At the beginning of Uncle Thad's chapter on "Fish-Breeding" (he would publish an entire book on the subject four years later) is a section called "Remarks on Fish-ponds and the Manner of Producing and Rearing Fish in a Natural Way." He believed that

> all "*true-hearted* anglers". . . , who have witnessed the ruthless
> and indiscriminate destruction of game fish, will take an interest

in the plans proposed and the means now happily adopted for their increase. Many a fly-fisher who travels a long way to enjoy his favorite sport is shocked at witnessing the willful extermination of [Atlantic] salmon and [brook] trout—the former by spearing, netting, and erecting high dams without providing for their free passage up and down—the latter by snaring them [as they lie stationary] on their spawning beds, catching them in seines and eel weirs [traps], and drawing off millponds. On trout streams there are still other agencies at work: the coal mine poisoning the brook with sulphur; the sawmill filling it with slabs and sawdust; the factory with its dyestuff; and the tannery fouling the clear stream, covering the bottom of the pools and the spawn[ing] beds with its bleached bark, and killing the fish by hundreds with the obnoxious discharge of its lime vat. Any law against such vandalism in the United States is seldom or . . . feebly enforced. . . . If . . . legislators have not the independence to pass laws for a more thorough protection of trout, or officials do not enforce those that are passed, the fly-fisher at no distant day will have to go hundreds of miles farther than he does now to find them.[22]

In addition to protective legislation, fish culture was necessary, Norris argued, for "restocking impoverished and exhausted waters." To guide the reader, he provided the specifics of how to create fishponds, and how to stock them and produce "the young fish in the natural way," as well as the techniques "of hatching the eggs and rearing the young fish to a certain age by artificial means."[23]

As with every other nineteenth-century conservation issue, American pioneers in fish culture modeled their first efforts on English or Continental precedents. France, in particular, had long devoted herself to this subject, and early American fish culturists like Theodatus Garlick and Seth Green studied French discoveries in order to adapt them to the United States. By the late 1860s, there may have been as many as thirty private hatcheries in operation in the United States, and American culturists were making discoveries of their own. One state after another established fish commissions to study and perfect methods of propagation, and the movement was in full swing. While it touched the entire country, enthusiasm for the subject was particularly strong in the Eastern and Middle Atlantic regions, where every state except Delaware had a fish commission by 1871.[24]

As we saw in the discussion of the "precursors of conservation" in the ante-bellum period, New York sportsmen had played a leading role. They would increase those efforts after the Civil War. The New

York Sportsmen's Club—later called the New York Association for the Protection of Game—had been established in 1844 by Frank Forester (Henry William Herbert) and other "leading, socially prominent citizens" to "assure future generations the enjoyment of hunting by restricting poachers, who trespassed and took game illegally, and market hunters, who hunted and sold game commercially." Finding that individual efforts at legislative redress of these problems were ineffective, "the group organized to increase its strength" and "proceeded from the revolutionary principle that game was not held in individual possession" by the landowner, as in English law, "but in trust for the benefit of all."[25]

Soon, fishes would be added to the list of "game" species that the Association felt needed protection. One of the group's postwar leaders was Robert Barnwell Roosevelt, the uncle of Theodore, who would become a key figure in the history of American fish conservation and culture. In the same year the Civil War ended, 1865, he published *Superior Fishing: The Striped Bass, Trout, and Black Bass of the Northern States,* in which he reminded the reader that in order to become a "true sportsman," one had to do much much more than simply catch fish or shoot birds and animals. To "entitle him to full fellowship with the fraternity," a man "must have higher aspirations and nobler gifts; he must look beyond the mere result to the mode of effecting it, regarding, perhaps, the means more than the end." He must never take "any unfair trick or mean advantage . . . , even to fill a vacant creel [fish basket] or pocket [game bag]; he must never slay [shoot on the ground] the crouching bevy [of bobwhite quail], huddled in terror before his pointer's nose; he must never resort to the grapple [snagging hook] or the noose [snare], no matter how provokingly the wary [brook] trout, lying motionless in the clear water, may disdain his choicest flies." Indeed, Roosevelt warned that when a fisherman gives in to temptation and uses natural bait for game species that will take the artificial fly, like black bass and brook trout, he is "at great risk to his reputation." And he who engages in this easier, less "scientific" method of catching game fish "never experiences the higher pleasures of his pursuit—his enjoyment in making ["tying"] a neat and killing fly, his satisfaction at its success, his delight in putting [casting] it properly upon the water, and his gratification when with it and his frail tackle he shall have overcome the fierce and stubborn prey." Only then, claimed Roosevelt, will he be a "true sportsman" and know "SUPERIOR FISHING."[26]

As in the case of Thaddeus Norris and every other sportsman writer in this period, Roosevelt's love for angling extended to his quarry. Like their mammal and bird equivalents, fishes that had been "honored" with the title of *game* were, by definition, warier, faster, stronger, and generally more difficult to catch—more "sporting"—than other species. Anyone who has experienced the "fight" of a game fish like the smallmouth bass or Atlantic salmon, as it strips line off the reel and leaps repeatedly to gain its freedom, can perhaps appreciate how sportsmen like Norris and Roosevelt could admire their prey and feel responsibility—however paradoxical to the nonangler—for its welfare. As the history of wildlife conservation proves, this concern by sportsmen for fishes, as well as for mammals and birds, went well beyond a selfish desire to perpetuate fishing and hunting in their own lifetimes. It was for future generations, yet unborn, that they wanted to preserve both the wildlife and the "sacred games"[27] in which they were pursued.

Demonstrations of these points are found in Roosevelt's chapter on the "Protection of Fish" in *Superior Fishing*. After listing the sources of fish destruction, including both commercial fishermen *and* pseudo-sportsmen, who kill "without mercy" far more brook trout than they can use, he demanded that "the real sportsmen take the matter in hand." After all, it was the "sportsmen [who] have the greatest stake, for if they would retain for their old age and leave to their children the best preserver of health, a love of field sports, they must protect game birds [like woodcock, which he loved to hunt] and fish."[28]

Where legislation did not exist, Roosevelt called for the passage of laws against netting, trapping, snaring, and spearing of fishes, as well as against taking them during the spawning season. Where laws were already in place, they needed to be enforced, for "perfect statutes will not answer if they are not carried out, and the first duty of sportsmen's clubs and of individual sportsmen, a duty to humanity, to themselves, and to their *fellow creatures* [emphasis added], is to enforce the game laws." And "by game laws are not meant those barbarous statutes of England that made it more criminal in a poor man to slay a hare than a human being—statutes that are deservedly odious to free men, and which by no possibility could be introduced into the New World—but provisions for the protection and preservation of the wild inhabitants of our woods and waters, *a common heritage of beauty and sustenance, and the property of our citizens indiscriminately* [emphasis added]."[29]

Though Roosevelt believed that "the first necessity . . . is that proper and uniform enactments should be passed in every portion of our extensive nationality"—unless states had similar dates for closed seasons, "fish will be killed in one and sold in the other"—he reminded his sportsmen readers of their responsibility as models of behavior for all other hunters and fishermen. Sportsmen "should discourage, by their conversation and example, all infringement of the law or any cruel or wasteful prosecution of what should be sport." But "if they find a man who destroys for the purpose of destroying, they should not only shun but expose him," for "the man who kills an animal, bird, or fish, knowing that it must be left to spoil, justifies the charge of cruelty against our class, and deserves the scorn and condemnation of all right-thinking men."[30]

Roosevelt thought, therefore, that sportsmen should be ready at all times to take action if need be—"if they meet with [a] . . . palpable infraction of the law, they should enforce punishment." According to him, gentlemen hunters and fishermen possessed a kind of *noblesse oblige* to the American people to care for *their* wildlife and preserve it for the future. This revolutionary idea of a public trust inherent in what I have called the code of the sportsmen can be found in Roosevelt's declaration that "wanton injury to public property, in game, should be punished precisely as [a] similar injury to public property in grounds or buildings, by incarcerating the offender in prison." In fact, "of the two," he thought "the latter is less injurious in its ultimate results." After all, "a building may be replaced, but who can restore life to the fish that bears a thousand underdeveloped young in its bosom, or can give back to the starving fawn the mother that has been slain at its side?"[31]

The most fundamental part of the code of the sportsman, and the legislation that sprang from it, was the right of fish and deer to breed unmolested. For the poor "poaching criminal" or "wealthy cockney" (an individual only interested in the quantity of game killed and the chance to brag about his success) who violated this cardinal rule, "mere pecuniary fines are an insufficient punishment," Roosevelt asserted. The first type of violator he felt was "the meanest of offenders," because he "laughs at any attempt to collect penalties that are not enforced by imprisonment," while the second type "is willing to run the risk of [a] fine if he can, by taking . . . advantage of honest [ethical] sportsmen, [to] have the chance of boasting of his wonderful prowess and success." The only "cure," Roosevelt concluded, for "the recklessness of the former" and "the ardor of the latter" was "a few months in jail."[32]

Roosevelt knew that for some species of fishes, particularly the Atlantic salmon, it was not enough to pass vigorously enforced laws with stiff penalties. "If we would have salmon at our own doors," and not have to go to Canada for them, "we . . . must restock the Hudson, . . . Connecticut, and . . . numerous other rivers that were once frequented by them." By means of fish culture and "by decent care and treatment" of those species, like brook trout and black bass, that "are still with us," Americans could, Roosevelt believed, have these "seductive little beauties . . . preserved through endless time in undiminished abundance. . . ."[33]

Like all sportsmen-activists, who wanted to solve environmental problems and not simply write about them, Roosevelt used utilitarian arguments as well as aesthetic ones in making his case for conservation. "The subject of the protection of fish demands," he affirmed, "the consideration of every political economist, as well as . . . every sportsman in our country, or we shall soon be reduced to the condition of France, and forced to repopulate our deserted streams and lakes and furnish to the people, with great labor and at high price, one of their chief articles of food." Continuing on this tack, he pointed to the fact that "fish must always constitute a considerable portion of the diet of the poor, and . . . whatever serves for food to the people, above all to the lower class, deserves the attention of the statesman, and any practice that will tend to diminish its price demands the assistance of the philanthropist."[34]

Though it is obvious that the first, and most important, reason Roosevelt wanted to preserve fishes was to "angle" for them, he was enough of a realist to know that he had to couch his advocacy in pragmatic terms if he expected to gain political support in the mass democracy of the United States. But like his more famous nephew, Theodore, he also stressed the humanitarian side of the argument because he had internalized the implicit responsibilities, and obligations, of his class. He was a member of a group of Americans who have been called "patricians," the old upper class, and like their namesakes in ancient Rome, they had been "socialized" from early childhood to believe in themselves as leaders, and as stewards of the well-being of those beneath them on the socio-economic ladder.

After the Civil War, elite anglers would play an ever-larger leadership role in fish conservation and restoration. The New York Sportsmen's Club (which did not change its name to the New York Association for the Protection of Game until 1874) "prodded the legislature to act,"[35] and in 1868 that body created the New York State Fisheries

Commission. Robert Roosevelt, who had joined the Club in 1864, personally presented the bill to the legislature, and he was appointed one of the first Commissioners. The other two were former governor and "ardent sportsman"[36] Horatio Seymour, and the " 'father of fish culture in America,' "[37] Seth Green. The last individual was "the exception to the rule," because even though he was "an accomplished sports angler,"[38] he was not from a privileged background. Instead, this former commercial fisherman was a self-taught, "gifted experimenter, who, more than any other person, made fish culture a practical industry in the United States."[39]

Despite the fact that all three men were avid anglers and most interested in game species, they decided to adopt the humanitarian philosophy expressed by Roosevelt in 1865 in *Superior Fishing*. They would concentrate their first efforts on propagating a food fish, the anadromous American shad, which, before its massive decline at the hands of commercial netters, had filled the Hudson River with legions of fish pressing upstream to spawn. If the species could once again become " 'ordinarily abundant, a fish of the people,' " the Commissioners believed that it would sell " 'at retail for five or ten cents a pound,' " and " 'no cheaper or better food can be imagined.' "[40]

In the same period that sportsmen in New York were creating a fish commission and pushing for the restoration of food *and* game fishes— brook trout, Atlantic salmon, and other "sporting fish"[41] were added to the list of hatchery-bred species—their counterparts in the New England states were doing the same. Between 1864 and 1867, all four states with shoreline on the Connecticut River appointed fish commissions " 'to investigate the whole subject [of fisheries] and especially the construction of fishways ["ladders"] over dams on the Connecticut River.' "[42]

In a 1991 analysis of these early efforts at fish restoration that focuses on Theodore Lyman, the head of the Massachusetts Commission on Inland Fisheries, one scholar demonstrates how the role of sportsmen in the history of conservation can be misinterpreted. In "The Early Making of an Environmental Consciousness: Fish, Fisheries Commissions, and the Connecticut River," historian John T. Cumbler notes, in passing, that Lyman was an angler and "like the commission members from the other states of New England, . . . upper class" in background.[43] While I have argued that an acceptance of the code of the sportsman and the obligations to "the people" inherent in upper-class socio-economic status are what drove these men to create, and lead, the fish commissions, Cumbler overlooks these key aspects of the subject. Because the commissioners of New England, like those of New York, concentrated their first efforts on the restoration of the American shad, a food fish, Cumbler interprets this to mean that the *main* motivation driving them was the same "gospel of [scientific] efficiency" that historian Samuel Hays claims produced the first conservation movement. Once again, scholars have trivialized the meaning of angling to men like Lyman and Roosevelt, and later Pinchot, and ignored the importance of their membership in an elite subculture. Compounding his error, Cumbler cites Hays's 1987 study *Beauty, Health, and Permanence: Environmental Politics in the United States, 1955-1985* to support his conclusion that "Lyman's conservation vision was concerned about restoring and protecting fish for food" and *not* angling. According to the Hays-Cumbler thesis, Lyman was typical of fish conservationists before World War II, for it was supposedly not until "after 1940" that Americans became "interested in protecting fish and the fishing environment for pleasure and recreation."[44] Only someone who has never examined the vast literature on angling and fish culture in the latter part of the nineteenth century could come to such a conclusion.

One issue relating to concern over declining fish stocks in the period after the Civil War would have long-term consequences. By the late 1860s, New England's coastal hook-and-line fishermen, who included both sportsmen and "meat fishermen,"[45] had become so incensed by what appeared to be a diminishing supply of fish that they petitioned the legislatures of Connecticut, Rhode Island, and Massachusetts to put a stop to the ravages of commercial netters and trappers. Although the controversy went back at least to 1856, when a petition was sent to the Rhode Island legislature, it did not pick up steam until 1866, when the commissioners of fisheries of the New England states met in Boston to develop methods "for restoring [Atlantic] salmon and increasing the number of [American] shad in the different rivers of the States."[46] Soon, concern spread to other inshore, saltwater fishes like striped bass, tautog, and scup (porgy).[47]

To catch these and other species, a small number of commercial fishermen operated fixed nets, "traps," or "weirs" that extended out from shore as much as a thousand feet and caught huge amounts of fish, particularly in spring and early summer. Those devices built of brush or boards were called weirs, while those made of nets stretched around posts were called traps, "fykes," or "pounds," depending on their form (for an illustration of one type, see the "Picture Album" in this book).

The clamor against these contrivances continued, and from Massachusetts alone, petitions and protests signed by almost 11,000 people poured into the legislature in early 1870.[48] Like the market hunters who claimed that bison and passenger pigeons were without limit, the commercial netters and trappers asserted that saltwater fishes were "inexhaustible."[49] And the prominence of sport fishermen in the "anti-trap coalition" gave the market men another defense, for they argued that the people at large should ignore "the crusade," since it "was a plot by this small, aristocratic, and pleasure-seeking group" to destroy the livelihoods of commercial fishermen and monopolize the fish supply for themselves.[50] Of course, market hunters in this period were defending themselves against sportsmen in precisely the same language.

As a result of the uproar, the U. S. Fish Commission[51]—*the first federal agency created to deal with the conservation of a specific natural resource*—was established in 1871 and called in to settle the dispute. One well-known angler who had a part in bringing about federal intervention was Vermonter George Franklin Edmunds, who had been so instrumental in the appointment of his relative, George Perkins Marsh, to conduct his 1857 study of fish decline in the state in order to make recommendations for restoration. Then, Edmunds was Speaker of the Vermont legislature, but by 1871, he was a United States Senator and powerful enough to get his "intimate friend," the scientist Spencer Fullerton Baird, appointed to head the new federal agency.[52]

Even before the creation of the U.S. Fish Commission, Edmunds had used his influence to make a government vessel available to Baird for dredging off of Woods Hole, Massachusetts to collect specimens. While Baird and another scientist, Professor Henry E. Webster of Union College in New York, explored the sea life from the bottom of Vineyard Sound, the vacationing Edmunds joined them in the summer of 1870.[53] Like most elite, educated sportsmen of the nineteenth century, Edmunds seems to have been as fascinated with how the natural world "works" as he was with catching fish.

As discussed in Chapter One, one of the main reasons Marsh had recommended against state action in his 1857 *Report*, other than giving financial aid to private fish culturists, was because of the question of legal jurisdiction over the Connecticut River that runs through Connecticut, Massachusetts, and New Hampshire, in addition to Vermont. At least in terms of coastal waters, this issue seemed to be resolved with the creation of the U.S. Fish Commission, as the agency noted in its 1873 *Report on the Condition of the Sea Fisheries of the*

South Coast of New England in 1871 and 1872: "The alleged diminution of the fisheries was in the tidal and navigable waters of the United States, . . . over which the Federal Government exercises jurisdiction in other matters, [and thus] it was maintained by many that the state governments had no control, and that any enactments on the subject must be made by Congress; especially as, if left to the States, it would be impossible to secure that harmony and concurrence of action necessary for a successful result."[54]

With the publication of the Fish Commission's *Report,* detailed documentation finally existed for the incredible destruction of coastal and freshwater fishes (a section on the Great Lakes was also included) by commercial fishermen using nets, traps, and weirs. Other factors like pollution and bluefish predation were discussed, but Baird concluded that the impact of the fixed nets and similar devices were the most important reasons for the apparent decline of fish stocks. Predicting the virtual disappearance of some inshore species, he went so far as to threaten federal intervention if the states failed to pass proper legislation against the use of these contrivances by commercial fishermen.[55]

Baird was certainly ahead of his time in understanding that migratory wildlife species should be under the authority of the federal government, even though nonmigratory species must remain under the control of the individual state in which they are found. Not until the Federal Migratory Bird Treaty Act was passed in 1918 was this principle firmly established.

Although the Fish Commission's *Report* failed to produce any action against the market fishermen, hostilities between them and their hook-and-line opponents ceased with a return to abundance of the same species Baird claimed were passing out of existence—the Commissioner had simply failed to comprehend the importance of cycles in fish populations.[56] While the hated devices did take a fearful toll, the tremendous surpluses produced by some wildlife, especially fishes, allow large harvests without any permanent damage to the stocks. Apparently, when the clamor to stop the commercial fishermen began, several New England species were at a low point in their cycles, and with the return of the fish to abundance, the controversy died away.

Despite nature's resolution of this specific issue, general interest in the preservation and propagation of fish grew apace. By the mid-1870s, it was already approaching "mania"[57] dimensions. Soon, every part of the nation was clamoring for its fair share of the millions of food and game fish being produced by the hatcheries. Congressmen were continually besieged by their constituents to get the United States Fish Commission to supply them with adequate quantities of fish, including, unfortunately, the ecologically destructive carp, while the leading private fish culturists, like Seth Green and Fred Mather, added their substantial efforts to provide their fellow sportsmen with game fish.[58] It seemed that there was hardly a lake, river, or bay that missed being stocked with native or foreign species. As an indication of the movement's strength, the following is a partial list of the quantities of freshwater and saltwater species produced by the New York State Fish Commission from 1870 to 1881: 53,609,000 American shad; 10,990,000 "salmon trout" [lake trout]; 2,438,000 whitefish; 5,375,000 brook trout; 1,288,700 "California trout" [rainbow trout]; and 900,000 "frost fish" [Atlantic tomcod].[59]

As we have seen, sportsmen spearheaded the efforts in fish culture at the state level. Every one of the leading private culturists was a self-proclaimed "angler" as well as "scientist," and those who have left any substantial record of their lives indicate that boyhood fishing experiences initiated their fascination with fishes. In addition, it should be noted that sportsmen like Robert Barnwell Roosevelt and George Franklin Edmunds had played a key role in getting the federal government involved in fish culture.

Roosevelt served only one term as a United States Congressman, but he took that opportunity to introduce a bill for the establishment of a federal hatchery on the Pacific coast to produce salmon, and another on the Atlantic coast to produce American shad and other species; he also included an appropriation of $10,000 in the proposal to be spent under the direction of Baird. According to historian Dean C. Allard, Jr., Roosevelt's bill "can be seen as the genesis for the [U.S.] Fish Commission's participation in the fish cultural movement."[60]

Because the proposed legislation was stuck in the House Appropriations Committee, Roosevelt made an impassioned plea for the creation of a federal fish-culture program from the floor of the House on May 13, 1872. This " 'national matter'," he stressed, required a " 'unity of action' " that only the federal government could provide, since virtually all of the rivers that Atlantic salmon and American shad ran up were shared by more than one state.[61] Through federal control, Roosevelt eliminated the problem George Perkins Marsh had wrestled with in 1857 regarding the difficulty of Vermont acting alone to try and restore salmon and shad to the Connecticut River, a stream that ran through several state jurisdictions.

Roosevelt addressed another issue that Marsh had brought up in his 1857 *Report*. Like Marsh, Congressman Roosevelt hoped that artificial propagation would increase fish populations so much that hard-to-enforce restrictive laws would not be necessary after the fish were well established.[62] As an elite sportsman, he knew that every game law and effort at wildlife conservation had traditionally been viewed by a suspicious American public as an effort to restore Old World aristocratic privilege and dominance. So, "despite his personal interest in sport fishing," and his upper-class background (like Marsh), Roosevelt "stressed the humanitarian aspect of fish culture" and argued that "shad and salmon . . . could provide an abundance of cheap and nourishing food for the common man." Thus, he "used the same idealistic rhetoric that Marsh had employed fifteen years earlier"[63] and which gentlemen sportsmen would continue to use in the following years in order to gain public approval of their conservation programs.

This is not to say—as already noted—that Robert Roosevelt and those who came after him, like his nephew, Theodore, and his chief administrator, Gifford Pinchot, did not believe their own rhetoric. Their impulse to be conservationists may have begun with a concern mainly for the game species of animals, birds, or fishes they habitually pursued, but the code of the sportsman quickly widened that perspective to reach well beyond simple self-interest. In his address before the House, Congressman Roosevelt spoke of the need to replenish the nation's depleted fish stocks, but he could have been talking about any other natural resource just as easily. If the United States failed to act immediately to adopt a federal fish-culture program, he predicted that "each class [will take] all it can, blind to the future, which presses closer and closer on the heels of such want of foresight . . . [and] looks only to immediate gratification, and accepts the proverb 'after me a famine'."[64]

Although Roosevelt's draft of a law to get fish hatcheries established on the Atlantic and Pacific coasts under the direction of Baird and the U.S. Fish Commission was cut out of the annual Sundry Civil Appropriations bill of the House, Baird was determined to get it passed, in one form or another. Expanding Roosevelt's earlier proposal to include fish-stocking in the Mississippi Valley, the Gulf states, and the Great Lakes, he widened the political appeal of the proposed legislation to include most sections of the United States; he also added $5000 to the appropriation, for a total of $15,000.[65]

Still, the bill might never have become law if it had not been for the personal intervention of George Franklin Edmunds, who answered his friend's call for help. Because of Senator Edmunds' influence, Baird's revision of Roosevelt's original plan for federal involvement in fish culture was added to the Senate's Sundry Civil Appropriations bill. Reflecting the growing interest in fish culture, an Oregon Senator attached an amendment a few days later that required the federal government to introduce American shad from Atlantic waters to the Pacific coast. With renewed enthusiasm for the program in the House as well, that body accepted an amendment to their appropriations bill that was almost identical to Roosevelt's original proposal. At last, the consolidated Sundry Civil Appropriations Act became law on June 10, 1872, and Baird had his appropriations for the U.S. Fish Commission.[66]

The federal government now had a responsibility for fish propagation, for replenishing depleted waters and stocking new species that seemed to hold promise either as food or game, or both. One of the most spectacular successes was the introduction of American shad to the Pacific coast. Even before the passage of the federal fish-culture legislation, Seth Green, working under contract with the California Fish Commission, had made an effort to establish the species in the Sacramento River in 1871. Now, Baird supplemented Green's attempt with additional shipments in 1873, 1876, and 1877. Apparently, by the latter year, American shad had become established, and it would soon extend its range.[67] Though mainly considered a food fish at first, to be caught by commercial fishermen in nets, anglers later developed techniques for catching it on rod and reel, with artificial lures, and the American shad became a leading game fish on both coasts.

Another species that migrates from the sea into freshwater rivers to spawn would be the second great triumph in the federal fish-culture effort. Striped bass were originally found on the Atlantic and Gulf coasts, but in 1879 and again in 1882, the U.S. Fish Commission and California state culturists transported 435 young striped bass from New Jersey to San Francisco Bay. From these small beginnings, "this choice sport and food fish" quickly adapted to its new home and began to spread along the coast, furnishing, as does the shad, an extremely popular fishery.[68]

Other species that the U.S. Fish Commission successfully transplanted in the 1870s and 1880s were the native landlocked form of the Atlantic salmon into a wider area of New England, the California rainbow trout into the East, particularly the southern Allegheny region, and the German brown trout into the eastern waters of the United States.[69] Unfortunately, the Commission was also successful in transplanting the carp.

As already noted, the fish was first successfully introduced into the Hudson River in the 1830s, but Baird, who "seems to have been solely responsible for initiating the [Fish Commission's] carp program,"[70] saw to it that this form of what I call "living pollution" would be established in virtually every part of the country. With few exceptions, sportsmen rejected the fish, finding it unsuitable game in every respect, including taste. But Baird was determined to prove that the federal government could fulfill the dream of providing cheap food for the masses. Because it was held in high esteem in Asia and Europe, because it was incredibly hardy and grew rapidly, and because it could be transported long distances with no special care, the carp seemed like the perfect fish for farmers to raise. He "especially stressed its value for the hard-pressed southern farmer," and in 1877 went so far as to predict that a carp pond could produce "more meat per acre than cattle raising."[71]

Regrettably, many nonsportsmen across the country agreed with his favorable appraisal, and "so enthusiastic did Americans become over the carp that it spread to farm ponds in every part of the country."[72] By the early 1880s, Baird was sending fish to 298 out of 301 Congressional districts. In 1885, in addition to those he sent to the states to supplement their programs, Baird supplied about 350,000 carp to 6,200 private applicants. "Without doubt," one historian concludes, "the carp project was the most widespread and popular of any that the [Fish] Commission undertook."[73]

The carp, of course, never "caught on" in the way that Baird hoped, but the damage done to the ecology of aquatic systems by this alien species would continue to the present day. It is probably not an exaggeration to say that the establishment of the carp in North America was one of the greatest ecological calamities to strike the continent, analogous in some ways to the transplanting of English sparrows and European starlings.

While Baird and his agency succeeded in introducing a number of species to new habitats, they were less adept at restoring native ones to depleted waters. Though they enjoyed some initial success with the American shad, neither it nor the anadromous Atlantic salmon were able to return to former abundance because of netters, dams, and pollution.[74]

Despite their lack of interest in carp culture, sportsmen found enough in the Fish Commission's programs to continue their support of Baird's agency. The federal government's success in transplanting striped bass, rainbow and brown trout, and the landlocked form of the Atlantic salmon all proved very popular with anglers. As we have seen, they had laid the foundations for the fish-culture movement even before the guns fell silent at Appomatox. And while Baird was couching his efforts "in warm humanitarian terms as an attempt to give the common man a cheap supply of food"—an approach supported by patrician anglers—he never lost sight of the fact that a large part of his agency's "public appeal . . . was the promise that fish culture had for the large fraternity of sport fishermen, many of whom were men of at least local prominence and power."[75]

With the establishment of the sportsmen's journals in the 1870s, fish culture had been given a tremendous boost. *Forest and Stream,* for example, was the official organ of the American Fish Culturists' Association.[76] Thaddeus Norris, Seth Green, and Fred Mather ran fishing-fish culture columns in the sporting papers, and virtually all the important "scientists" involved with the subject, including the leading government culturist, Spencer Fullerton Baird, used the outdoor periodicals as their forum.[77] In addition, all the major papers furthered the movement by constant references to its achievements and potentialities.

Why the "fish culture idea" took hold with such success is not difficult to ascertain. For sportsmen, it meant a restoration of angling opportunities; for farmers and ranchers, it meant a profitable sideline, for, as we have seen, the U.S. Fish Commission repeatedly claimed that carp could be raised more cheaply than cattle and other stock with equal or better economic returns; for commercial fishermen, like shad netters, it meant never-ending profits despite systematic exploitation of the resource; and for the nation as a whole, it meant cheap food for the masses.

By the end of the century, it was clear to many that fish culture was not quite the bonanza it was first thought to be. Sportsmen found that the introduction of black bass and "German" brown trout often resulted in a drastic reduction of native brook trout; farmers and ranchers found that their promised profits never materialized; commercial fishermen found that fish propagation did not eliminate their responsibility for the resource, because each ecosystem only supports so many fish, regardless of how often it is stocked; and the nation as a whole found carp an indifferent food and rejected it as anything but a last resort.

Still, the early history of the U.S. Fish Commission, which later merged into the U.S. Fish and Wildlife Service, is important for a number of reasons. It was the first federal agency created to deal with the conservation of a specific natural resource, and "its work certainly represented the federal government's most important movement for the conservation of natural resources during this period."[78] Sport fishermen were central to its establishment and continued support, and its popular programs are another example of why wildlife, not forests, was the first resource to engender substantial public interest in favor of conservation. Finally, the fact that its efforts began in earnest right after the agency was created in 1871 shows that the original American conservation movement began in the 1870s, and not at the end of the century as claimed by Samuel Hays and those historians who have followed his lead.

To a greater degree than Baird and his fellow fish culturists, "pisciculturists" in the twentieth century stressed that the best way to produce more fish was to provide a healthy habitat, for fish always increase to the limit of their food supply, available cover, suitable breeding locations, etc. But in heavily fished streams with a small capacity for natural production, hatchery-bred fish introduced on a "put-and-take" basis do provide recreation for countless anglers, and the successful planting of Pacific-coast salmon in the Great Lakes in the second half of the twentieth century—which created a multi-million dollar sport fishery—proves that fish culture is still an important component of wildlife conservation.

In addition to their public services in stocking the nation's waters and protecting them from dams, pollution, and nets, sportsmen also made an important contribution in the private sector by establishing numerous game preserves. Virtually all of the sportsmen's clubs controlled, by leasing or direct ownership, large acreage that was kept in natural condition, thereby maintaining the ecosystems of those areas. Because each association enforced its own rules, in addition to state laws, game stocks were preserved; where game already had been reduced before the creation of the club, artificial propagation often filled the void. Nongame species also benefited by having their habitats guarded against "improvements." In many areas the only substantial acreage remaining in an undeveloped state was the land controlled by sportsmen's clubs.

Game preserves (in fact if not in name) date back to early Colonial days, and these "deer parks," as they were called, were considered by many in Virginia and Maryland to be an essential part of any country estate.[79] One of the more noteworthy deer parks of a later period was owned by Judge John D. Caton, a sportsman-naturalist who wrote frequently for both *American Naturalist* and the sporting press. About 1858, near Ottawa, Illinois, he set aside a sanctuary that eventually encompassed 200 acres and stocked it with white-tailed deer, elk, and other species. From studies made on these herbivores, Caton wrote his important work, *The Antelope and Deer of America* (1877).[80]

With the increase of sportsmen's self-consciousness in the 1870s, impetus was given to the game-preserve idea. Undoubtedly, the same British example that played such an important part in the development of American "sportsmanship" also was a factor in the creation of preserves, for the latter had long been used by English sportsmen as an instrument of conservation.

Another, more important, factor in the establishment of preserves was outdoormen's desire to perpetuate game and habitat in spite of the utter indifference of a nation seemingly obsessed with economic development. Instead of waiting for the indolent state and federal governments to assume their responsibility for natural resources, sportsmen decided to take the initiative themselves. Two of the earlier, better-known preserves were Blooming Grove Park and the Bisby Club.

According to T. S. Palmer, the leading authority on the subject, "the first game preserve belonging to an incorporated association was that established by the Blooming Grove Park Association in 1871, for the purpose 'of preserving, importing, breeding, and propagating game animals, birds, and fish, and of furnishing facilities to the members for hunting, shooting, and fishing on its grounds.' One of the important features was a deer park [of 1,000 acres]."[81] Located in Pike County, in eastern Pennsylvania, the Blooming Grove property consisted of 12,000 acres "in one of the wildest and most picturesque portions of the State."[82]

The founders of Blooming Grove were Fayette S. Giles, a wealthy jeweler; Genio C. Scott, author of *Fishing in American Waters* (1869); and Charles Hallock, future editor of *Forest and Stream*. Their idea of establishing "a grand park or inclosure . . . where game might be bred and protected" was based on an old European precedent, their specific models being "the grand forests of Fontainebleau and the Grand Duchy of Baden." (Giles had been a resident of France for six years and had "engaged actively in field sports, both in the forests of Fontainebleau and in Germany. . . .")[83]

In addition to the preservation and management of game animals, fish-culture and forestry programs were also initiated. The latter endeavor is particularly noteworthy, since *it was probably the first attempt to establish systematic forestry in the United States.*

As Hallock pointed out in 1873, "the cultivation of forests . . . and the selling of timber and surplus game of all kinds [will] . . . compensate in some degree for the frightful waste which is annually devastating our forests and exterminating our game."[84] It should be noted here that Gifford Pinchot is universally credited with initiating "the first systematic forest management" in the United States.[85] Though his work was far more extensive than that done at Blooming Grove, it did not begin until 1892, twenty years later.

Only one historian, Theodore W. Cart, seems to have perceived the importance of Blooming Grove Park in the history of conservation:

> The concept and execution of the Blooming Grove plan provided
> the first large-scale demonstration of integrated natural resource
> planning for primarily recreational purposes in America,
> something that would not be approached in the public sector for
> twenty years. . . . Yellowstone Park, created in the next year
> [1872], had no effective game protection until 1894 and had no
> plan to cultivate its timber. . . . Blooming Grove had no public
> counterparts until the national forest system provided for multiple
> use of timber and game resources. . . .[86]

The success of Blooming Grove encouraged sportsmen in other areas to emulate its example. One of these was the Bisby Club, established in New York's Adirondack Mountains. Believing "that the state would never take any action which would result in creating a grand park out of this vast wilderness" and feeling "an interest in preserving the forest from the incursions of civilization," a group of prominent sportsmen in 1877 leased a large tract of land in "the Northern Wilderness . . . to convert it into a park or preserve . . . where they might fish and hunt without molestation by the general public."[87] Its president was Richard U. Sherman, one of the state's fish commissioners, and other well-known sportsmen who became regular or honorary members were Thomas R. Proctor, banker; Seth Green, fish culturist; Horatio Seymour, former governor; and Verplanck Colvin, surveyor.[88]

By the spring of 1882, the club held lease to 9,000 acres of Herkimer County that embraced nine separate lakes, as well as some smaller waters. A spacious clubhouse had been built, and the waters stocked with game fish and planted with wild rice to attract waterfowl.[89]

In the early 1890s the Bisby Club merged with the much larger Adirondack League Club, which controlled 179,000 acres, and ceased to exist. The newer association "was organized in 1890 by a number of gentlemen of sporting proclivities, for the purpose of establishing a game preserve in a chosen quarter of the Adirondack wilderness and to put into practice the system of rational forestry prevailing on the continent of Europe, which reconciles the preservation and continual reproduction of forest areas with a continual and increasing income."[90] One of the prominent trustees of the club, and its "forestry adviser,"[91] was none other than Bernhard E. Fernow, Chief of the Division of Forestry of the United States Department of Agriculture. Describing the new association, guidebook-writer S. R. Stoddard stated that Fernow "is in . . . active management of its forest policy. A contract for the removal of the spruce above 12 inches in diameter at a stumpage price, which already guarantees the Club an income from this source of $30,000 a year, is in operation. . . ."[92]

Stoddard was probably writing in 1893, during the same period Pinchot was establishing his forestry program on George W. Vanderbilt's huge estate in western North Carolina. Even though it was planned in 1890, the Adirondack project was probably not put into operation until after Pinchot began his work in early 1892.[93] Nevertheless, it deserves mention, because it was one of the three earliest attempts to manage timber systematically and because it took place—like the Blooming Grove effort twenty years before—on a preserve established by sportsmen.

While these preserves allowed wealthy sportsmen to maintain their "world" despite the ravages of progress, hunters and anglers were not content merely to retreat into their sanctuaries and forget their responsibilities to the nation. Instead, they chose to establish a system of laws regulating virtually every facet of gunning and angling. And it should be emphasized that, contrary to popular belief, sportsmen urged these restrictions upon themselves, for no individual, group, or government agency forced them to limit their "bags," hunting and fishing seasons, or any other aspect of sport. If sportsmen failed to regulate themselves, no one else would, for they lived in a country characterized, first, by a Judeo-Christian tradition that separated man from nature and sanctified his dominion over it;[94] second, by a *laissez-*

faire economic order that encouraged irresponsible use of resources; third, by weak institutions, including the federal government, that seemed unwilling or unable to protect wildlife and habitat; and fourth, by a heritage of opposition to any restraint on "freedom," particularly that vestige of European tyranny, the game law.

American laws pertaining to wildlife appeared as early as the seventeenth century, but most of these statutes were not for the purpose of protecting wildlife but for killing it.[95] By paying Americans to destroy wolves, squirrels, crows, and other fauna, the bounty system was supposed to save livestock and crops. In reality, this unfortunate inheritance from England only wasted money and wildlife without resulting in any substantial benefits for the farmer. Even though it has been demonstrated time and again that bounties are worse than worthless as a wildlife-management technique, they have persisted even into recent years.

Sportsmen, too, originally supported the bounty system, but for them it was only one of many approaches to game conservation. For nonsportsmen, however, bounties represented the typical American orientation toward wildlife. Unless an animal or bird served some utilitarian purpose—usually economic in character—the usual question was: "What good is it?"

Farmers and ranchers usually made poor nature lovers, seeing wildlife primarily as competitors or sources of profit.[96] Sportsmen, on the other hand, regarded most animals and birds with nonutilitarian motives.[97] Not depending *directly* on nature for a livelihood, sportsmen were the only large group of Americans who came to woods and fields for mainly recreational and aesthetic reasons. It is no wonder, then, that they would take the initiative in preserving nonsporting species as well as those traditionally pursued as game.

From Colonial days, sportsmen had monopolized legislative efforts in regard to wildlife, and by the 1870s these "game laws"—as all wildlife regulations were called—had proliferated into a tangled mass of confusing and often contradictory statutes. For this reason, Charles Hallock, and later George Bird Grinnell, used *Forest and Stream* to demand "uniform laws for contiguous States which lie in the same isothermal belts."[98] Though ahead of its time, this idea would become the basis for determining the opening and closing dates of hunting and fishing seasons. Clearly, the editors of the leading outdoor journal of the time understood that the states had to cooperate with each other in the establishment of game laws if anything of permanent value was to be achieved.

Before efficient game laws could be passed, the public had to accept the necessity for legislation and be motivated to abide in it once enacted. Accordingly, at least once a year, the Forest and Stream Publishing Company printed a booklet containing the nation's game laws with a section explaining the purpose of the regulations. The pamphlet was distributed without charge.

In the effort to obtain respect for statutes protecting wildlife, one major obstacle the sporting journals had to overcome was the status resentment of nonsportsmen. Repeatedly, they received letters like the one printed in *Forest and Stream* on November 15, 1880. Ranting against the " 'aristocratic trespassers' " who were invading the farms of East Rockaway, Long Island (New York), with no other claim to hunt and destroy property than that they belonged to the " 'wealthier classes'," a farmer condemned these " 'encroachments . . . upon the liberties of the people.' "[99] Other letters were sent to *Forest and Stream* protesting that sportsmen exploited farmers and that game laws were only for the benefit of the rich, who had the time and money to pursue the game protected by the legislation.[100]

To counter these charges, Grinnell formulated his theory of democratic game protection. In an editorial in March, 1881, he denied the charge "that *Forest and Stream* was 'aristocratic' or that it favored measures which would make the enjoyment of legitimate sport by the poor man more difficult."[101] He argued, in fact, that it was the person of small income who most benefited by the enactment and enforcement of strict game laws. For "the rich man can travel to distant fields where game is plenty, and can have his shooting whether the laws are enforced or not. With the poor man it is not so; he has to take his day or half day in the field when he can get it, and has neither the time nor the money to travel far in search of game. It is, therefore, the man of modest means who is or should be interested in game preservation even more than he whose fortune is ample."[102] However, Grinnell noted, "no question of class or fortune should enter. . . ."[103] In a later editorial, " 'We, the People,' " he stressed that "laws prohibiting the destruction of game in its breeding season and of fish on their spawning grounds are not for the advantage of any narrow class or clique. They are for the good of us, the people." Sounding just like the Roosevelt administration twenty years later, Grinnell added that *Forest and Stream* takes the "broad tenable ground" of "the greatest good to the greatest number."[104]

Whereas Hallock had emphasized the need for additional game laws of a uniform kind, Grinnell put his stress on law enforcement. Shortly after becoming editor in 1880, he observed that game protectors for years had claimed that more legislation was the solution to wildlife depletion. The fact was, he asserted, most states had plenty of legislation, and some too much. What was really needed was not more statutes, but adequate enforcement of those already on the books.[105]

To accomplish this, he advocated the creation of a county game constable (now warden) system to be financed by a small fee from each hunter. After all, he reasoned, "those who dance must pay the fiddler."[106] Particularly important was that the office of the constable be nonpolitical and filled through appointments by the states rather than local citizen groups. He wanted the officers to be free from local pressure, so that their work could be performed efficiently and without interruption.[107]

This notion that the traditionally free and unstructured activity of hunting must now be financially supported by the sportsmen themselves and regulated by the states was a new idea. In the years ahead, however, it would become the cornerstone of game management. What was perhaps most significant about Grinnell's proposal was the insistence on the necessity of continuity—on a continual *process* of administration. This concept would become the basis of conservation itself.

Probably the most ambitious task *Forest and Stream* set for itself in the area of game legislation was its attempt to revolutionize the public's attitude toward lawbreakers. The paper had to struggle against massive indifference. Even those offenses that were generally condemned— like shooting deer at night after they were stunned by the glare of an artificial light—were not reported because of fear of retaliation by the relatives or friends of the poacher. Invariably, the informer would be visited by that ubiquitous fiend, the barn burner. *Forest and Stream* reported that "this deterrent fear of burning barns is not confined to any particular locality. We hear the same story from the West, from the Adirondacks, [and] from persons dwelling within five miles of New York City. . . ."[108]

Despite public opposition, the sporting journals never wavered in their efforts to pass good game laws and change American attitudes toward them. One of the more important goals the periodicals set for themselves was to end hunting of waterfowl and shore birds during the spring breeding season. Beginning in the late 1870s, *Forest and Stream* and *American Field* (the later name of *Field and Stream*) ran editorial after editorial attacking the traditional practice of spring shooting and censuring individual sportsmen who were slow to adopt the new creed; even President Cleveland was not immune from such public criticism.[109] As shown by the opinions of correspondents, sportsmen increasingly came to accept this latest piece of self-denial, even though it was not until the twentieth century that the practice was completely stopped (see the photograph of President Benjamin Harrison duck hunting in March, 1891, in the "Picture Album" of this book).

Market men, of course, had little regard for the campaign against spring shooting or any other "cause" that might reduce their profits. Sportsmen naturally felt frustrated to find their conservation efforts continually thwarted by the activities of commercial hunters and fishermen. They gradually came to realize that the biggest threat to game was its commercial, *systematic* exploitation, for even when habitat remained more or less intact, species like the elk and Eskimo curlew could be overharvested to such a degree as to imperil their very existence. Allowing them to be killed for market was the same as placing a bounty on their heads. Where the sportsman might shoot a dozen ducks or a pair of bison, market gunners often killed a hundred ducks and a score of bison. While the surpluses many wildlife species produce allow a certain amount of utilization without permanently endangering breeding stocks, market men rapidly exhausted surpluses—the "interest"—and began cutting into "capital" as well. Possessing no code of the sportsman to regulate the amount of wildlife killed or the methods used, market men saw no motive in killing other than the economic one.

All wildlife, no matter how elusive under ordinary circumstances, is highly vulnerable when unsporting methods are employed. Wild turkeys, for example, were easily baited with corn and captured in log traps, and deer were driven to water with dogs, forced to swim, and then clubbed to death from the bow of a canoe. Less wary species like passenger pigeons and bison were killed by the *millions*. With their nets, "pigeoners" usually caught hundreds of birds at one time. Descending on breeding grounds that might cover forty-five square miles, commercial pigeon hunters slaughtered so many that they filled freight cars with their stiff bodies. Once numbering in the hundreds of millions—some say billions—this magnificent species was already scarce in most areas by the 1880s, and the last of its kind died in the Cincinnati Zoo on September 1, 1914.[110]

The dramatic decline of wildlife species like the passenger pigeon and buffalo piqued the conscience of Americans and shattered their previous faith in the inexhaustibility of resources as did no other issue, including forest destruction. Though it had been declining for years, the bison still numbered in the millions as late as 1870. Yet, this symbol of Western expansion was utterly wiped out in thirteen years. With the close of 1883, the "thundering herds" were reduced to a pitiful remnant seemingly destined for extinction.

The passenger pigeon and bison were merely the most famous examples of the devastation wrought by a capitalistic democracy that treated wildlife resources as mere articles of commerce, available to everyone for the taking. Less well known today, but just as alarming to conservationists of the late nineteenth century, was the destruction of nongame birds for mindless fashion. Already disturbed by the systematic exploitation of wildlife, particularly the buffalo and the wild pigeon, environmentally conscious people discovered a new menace in the "taste" of American women.

Beginning in the late 1870s, the style of wearing hats stuffed with feathers, and even the birds themselves, became a craze. Countless American women, many of whom undoubtedly considered themselves animal lovers, saw no inconsistency in creating a demand that resulted in the slaughter of hundreds of thousands of birds. Even after the formation of the Audubon societies, it was not unusual for some female members to arrive at meetings wearing hats festooned with bird parts![111]

Because the plumage of egrets was most valuable in the breeding season, and because many bird species are concentrated at that time, nesting sites were invaded, the adult birds killed, and the young left to starve, bake in the sun, or be eaten by predators. Colony after colony was wiped out, and before many years passed, it began to look as if several species were headed for extinction. Yet with the price of some plumes higher than an equal weight in gold,[112] there was no stopping the slaughter. Like the "mountain man," hide hunter, "pigeoner," and commercial meat gunner, the man who shot for the millinery trade was no more responsible for the destruction than the society that spawned him. They were equally culpable, a fact often overlooked by environmental historians.

Despite the oft-repeated statement that sportsmen have only been interested in wildlife because they wanted a never-ending supply of targets, it was the sportsman-naturalist who led the movement to preserve *non*game species as well as those ordinarily pursued for sport. Because the commercialization of any species was against the code of the sportsman, it was only natural that his periodicals would be full of editorial attacks on the slaughter of bison, passenger pigeons, and nongame species like warblers, terns, and egrets. Sportsmen's efforts in behalf of nongame birds went back at least to the 1850s, as shown by game laws they passed in Massachusetts and Pennsylvania during that decade. And it was Frank Forester himself who "drafted New York State's first game law to include protection for insectivorous birds less than two months before he took his life in 1858."[113]

The real importance of sportsmen in ending the market hunting of song, sea, and wading birds has been obscured by the failure of historians to see that most of those they have labeled as "ornithologists," "scientists," or "nature lovers," could just as easily be categorized as "sportsmen." An example of this problem is the otherwise excellent doctoral dissertation by Theodore W. Cart that studies the events leading to the passage in 1900 of the Lacey Act, which ended the market hunting and interstate shipment of wildlife or wildlife products taken in violation of state law. Separating those who agitated in behalf of this legislation into "sportsmen," "scientific naturalists," "humanitarians," and "nature-lovers," Cart neglects to mention that many, if not most, of those in the "scientific naturalist" and "nature-lover" categories were also sportsmen; indeed, many were "killers" of birds and mammals, as well as fish. Nor does he make clear that John F. Lacey himself was an avid hunter and fisherman who appealed to the code of the sportsman in the Congressional speech advocating his bill. Lacey declared: " 'I have always been a lover of the birds, and I have always been a hunter as well, for today there is no friend that the birds have like the true sportsman—the man who enjoys *legitimate* [emphasis added] sport. He protects them out of season; he kills them in moderation in season.' " In addition, he attacked the " 'game hog' " and said that the Lacey Act was " 'directed against the pot hunter.' "[114] Even with his arbitrary categorization, Cart concludes that sportsmen were the most influential of his four groups in passing this landmark legislation.[115]

Although it may be difficult for some to accept, the great majority of the "ornithologists" who crusaded against bird destruction for millinery were sportsmen before and after they attained "scientist" status. Virtually all of those who founded the Nuttall Ornithological Club in Cambridge, Massachusetts in 1873 were self-avowed bird hunters, as were those who created the American Ornithologists' Union in 1883. In fact, the second association grew out of the Nuttall Club, though it was modeled on the British Ornithologists' Union.[116] One scholar goes so far as to claim that the "results" of the first meeting of the American Ornithologists' Union "were the wellspring from which flowed a large part of the modern conservation movement."[117] Charles

F. Batchelder, a member of the Nuttall Ornithological Club and its historian, later stated: "It should not be forgotten that in those days a hunting dog was very apt to be found a member of the household of any active ornithologist, for there seldom was much of a dividing line between ornithologists and sportsmen. Few were the ornithologists who, in season, did not turn keenly to the pursuit of game birds, and it was only the dullest-witted sportsmen whose eyes and guns were not directed instinctively toward any strange bird that appeared on the horizon."[118]

From John James Audubon to Frank Chapman, leading bird students made that critical first contact with the natural world through the vehicle of the gun. And most never lost their love for the hunt. The writings of Audubon, William Brewster, Elliott Coues, Robert Ridgway, Edward H. Forbush, Daniel G. Elliot, Charles Cory, Chapman, and others contain numerous references to recreational hunting as well as "scientific collecting." And Brewster and Coues were just two of the ornithologists who wrote extensively for sportsmen's journals.

Because the ornithologist's chief tool was the shotgun, he often used the same techniques and experienced the same feelings as the sportsman. A good example is Frank M. Chapman's description of his "capture" in 1890 of the now extinct, or nearly extinct, ivory-billed woodpecker on a collecting expedition down Florida's Suwannee River: "It was my good fortune to encounter the one ivory-billed woodpecker seen on the voyage. I knew its voice the moment its loud *yap-yap* fell on my ears. Then followed memorable moments as I stalked it through the cypress trees, until, *unbelievable glory* [emphasis added], it was actually in my hands."[119]

It is literally impossible much of the time to make a clear distinction between the ornithologist and the sportsman. A better term would be "sportsman-naturalist," because ornithologists' works are replete with hunting instructions and reminiscences; ornithologists often hunted for pleasure; the ornithologist's joy in "collecting" a rare specimen resembled in every way the pleasure experienced by the sportsman who bagged an unusual species of game bird for the first time; sportsmen themselves commonly kept "natural history cabinets" and collected for museums, George Bird Grinnell and Theodore Roosevelt being two well-known examples; and the level of the "scientific" papers in the best-known sporting books and periodicals often equaled that of journals like *The American Naturalist* and *The Auk* for the simple reason that they were written by the same men.

If this last point is hard to reconcile with today's clear distinction between hunting and fishing magazines, and scientific journals, all one has to do is look at statements made by "scientists" in the period. In 1873, the Assistant Curator (and future Curator) of the Smithsonian Institution, George Brown Goode, called *Forest and Stream* a "medium of communication between field-naturalists," and in 1879, Elliott Coues, "probably the best-known and most widely published American ornithologist of the late nineteenth century," observed that much of the "ornithological matter" in *Forest and Stream* and *The Field* (the later name of *Field and Stream*) is "precisely of the character of the shorter notes in the *Nuttall Bulletin* or . . . [the] *Zoölogist.*" Another ornithologist, Frank M. Chapman, recalled in later years that he first appeared in print in an 1883 issue of *Forest and Stream,* which "was [then] . . . not only the leading journal for sportsmen, but its high standing made it a recognized means of communication between naturalists." Obviously, the observation Goode had made in 1873 was still true a decade later.[120]

After compiling his monumental *American Game Mammals and Birds: A Catalogue of Books, 1582-1925,* published in 1930, the Harvard ornithologist and well-known sportsman, John C. Phillips, concluded that it had sometimes been difficult to separate sporting and scientific journals. And the next year, when his "Naturalists, Nature Lovers, and Sportsmen" appeared in *The Auk,* the journal of the American Ornithologists' Union, he commented that "years ago almost the whole field of conservation, sport, and ornithology could be followed in the pages of one or two journals."[121]

It was this "sportsman-naturalist" group that spearheaded the crusade to end destruction of song, sea, and wading birds for fashion. The American Ornithologists' Union and League of American Sportsmen played major roles in formulating and passing the Lacey Act of 1900, which was the "beginning of the end" for the "feather trade."[122]

In the earliest years, however, the most influential element in the movement was the Audubon Society, founded by sportsman-naturalist George Bird Grinnell in 1886. While there had been one or two prior organizations named after the great bird painter, these had been established by sportsmen for the perpetuation and propagation of game species. Grinnell's association, on the other hand, was solely for the preservation of nongame species, a category of wildlife generally considered less important up to that time. Once again, sportsmen-naturalists took the initiative in filling the void left by public indifference. Personal involvement with the natural world on a nonutilitarian basis and adoption of the aesthetic component in the code of the sportsman caused many sportsmen to be almost as concerned with the destruction of nongame birds as with those traditionally pursued for sport. As already noted, their early interest in species they had no intention of hunting is shown by Frank Forester's drafting, in 1858, of the first game law in New York State to include protection for insectivorous birds.

Grinnell announced the formation of his new society in *Forest and Stream* on February 11, 1886. Entitled "The Audubon Society," this front-page editorial is an important document in the history of conservation and deserves to be quoted in full:

> Very slowly the public are awakening to see that the fashion of wearing the feathers and skins of birds is abominable. There is, we think, no doubt that when the facts about this fashion are known, it will be frowned down and will cease to exist. Legislation of itself can do little against this barbarous practice, but if public sentiment can be aroused against it, it will die a speedy death.
>
> The *Forest and Stream* has been hammering away at this subject for some years, and the result of its blows is seen in the gradual change which has taken place in public sentiment since it began its work. The time has passed for showing that the fashion is an outrageous one, and that it results very disastrously to the largest and most important class of our population—the farmers. These are injured in two ways; by the destruction of the birds, whose food consists chiefly of insects injurious to the growing crops, and of that scarcely less important group the Rapaces,[123] which prey upon the small rodents which devour the crop after it has matured.
>
> *The reform in America, as elsewhere, must be inaugurated by women* [emphasis added], and if the subject is properly called to their notice, their tender hearts will be quick to respond. In England this matter has been taken up and a widespread interest in it developed. If the women of America will take hold in the same earnest way, they can accomplish an incalculable amount of good.
>
> While individual effort may accomplish much, it will work but slowly, and the spread of the movement will be but gradual. Something more than this is needed. Men, women and children all over our land should take the matter in hand, and urge its importance upon those with whom they are brought in contact. A general effort of this kind will not fail to awaken public interest,

and information given to a right-thinking public will set the ball of reform in motion. Our beautiful birds give to many people a great deal of pleasure and add much to the delights of the country. These birds are slaughtered in vast numbers for gain. If the demand for their skins can be caused to fall off, it will no longer repay the bird butchers [commercial hunters] to ply their trade, and the birds will be saved.

Statistics are as yet wanting to show the proportions to which this traffic has grown in North America, but we know that it reaches well into the hundreds of thousands. Some figures published in *Forest and Stream* of Aug. 4, 1884, showed that in a three months' trip a single taxidermist collected bird skins to the number of 11,018, which, including specimens too badly mutilated for preservation, and skins spoiled in the making, would perhaps represent a destruction of 15,000 birds. This same person states that he handles annually about 30,000 bird skins, almost all of which are used for millinery purposes. A single middleman, who collected the spoils of the shooters in one small district, brought to the taxidermists in four months about 70,000 birds.

The birds of the fields, the birds of the woods, the birds of the marshes, and those of the sea, all suffer alike. It is needless to repeat the oft-told story of destruction. How can we best go to work to combat this great and growing evil; what means can we best employ to awaken at once popular feeling against it?

We desire to enlist in this work every one who is interested in our birds, and we urge all such to take hold and assist us.

In the first half of this century there lived a man who did more to teach Americans about birds of their own land than any other who ever lived. His beautiful and spirited paintings and his charming and tender accounts of the habits of his favorites have made him immortal, and have inspired his countrymen with an ardent love for the birds. The land which produced the painter-naturalist, John James Audubon, will not willingly see the beautiful forms he loved so well exterminated.

We propose the formation of an association for the protection of wild birds and their eggs, which shall be called the Audubon Society. Its membership is to be free to every one who is willing to lend a helping hand in forwarding the objects for which it is formed. These objects shall be to prevent, so far as possible, (1) the killing of any wild birds not used for food, (2) the destruction of nests or eggs of any wild bird, and (3) the wearing of feathers as ornaments or trimming for dress.

To bring this matter properly before the public at large, we shall employ every means in our power to diffuse information on the subject over the whole country. Those who are willing to aid us in our labors are urged to establish local societies for work in their own neighborhood. To such branch societies we will send without charge circulars and printed information for distribution among their neighbors. A little effort in this direction will do much good. As soon as the association shall have a membership and shall be in position to organize and shall have attained an existence, we will hand the books and any funds which it may have, over to its members, who will thereafter take charge of it.

The work to be done by the Audubon Society is auxiliary to that undertaken by the Committee of the American Ornithologists' Union;[124] and will further the efforts of the A.O.U. committee, doing detail duties to which they cannot attend. Those who desire to join the Audubon Society, established on the basis and for the purpose above set forth, should send their names at once to the *Forest and Stream*, 40 Park Row, New York.[125]

The Audubon Society proved to be an instant success. Well-known Americans, like minister Henry Ward Beecher and nature-writer John Burroughs, immediately joined the organization and endorsed it in the pages of *Forest and Stream*.[126] In turn, they attracted a large number of followers—so many, in fact, that by the fall of 1888 the society had nearly 50,000 members.[127]

Paradoxically, the very success of the Audubon Society caused its demise. So many joined the new organization that Grinnell found all his time being consumed by its functions. Because membership was free, no money was coming in to offset the costs. Only by discontinuing it in 1889 could he maintain *Forest and Stream* at the high level he demanded.[128]

Despite the dissolution of Grinnell's organization, its efforts were hardly in vain. The movement he had set in motion continued to grow, and in 1896, sportsman-naturalist William Brewster organized the Massachusetts Audubon Society, the first permanent state association to model itself after Grinnell's original society; "as President of the Massachusetts State Sportsmen's Association, [Brewster] had [already] been actively working for wildlife preservation. . . ."[129] Many other state groups came into existence, and after they joined together in 1905 to form the National Association of Audubon Societies, Grinnell became a director of the new body.[130] It had been founded mainly through the efforts of William Dutcher, "a recreational hunter," who had brought together the thirty-six state Audubon societies, and who has been called "the principal creator of the modern Audubon movement."[131] The later National Audubon Society, organized in 1940, remains independent of some of the earliest state societies, despite the public's tendency to lump them all together as "The Audubon Society."

It would be interesting to know what percentage of the membership in the Audubon societies, which now numbers in the hundreds of thousands, would find it ironic, and maybe even disconcerting, to discover that many of the Audubon movement's founders were hunters of birds—just like their societies' namesake. Of course, it is only ironic and disconcerting if one does not understand how the code of the sportsman nurtured fascination and *love* for all wildlife, not just those that were pursued as game.

Before leaving the subject of the first Audubon societies, it should be pointed out that even though sportsmen were disproportionately influential in their creation, women quickly rallied to the cause, just as Grinnell had predicted in his 1886 *Forest and Stream* editorial. After women learned how extensive the millinery trade was and how the commercial slaughter was causing whole groups of birds, like egrets, herons, and terns, to disappear, they joined the early societies in droves, quickly making up a large part of the membership. Furthermore, they played a role in founding some of the first groups, including both the Massachusetts and Connecticut (1898) bodies.[132]

The slaughter of birds to adorn ladies' hats was merely one more example of the havoc wrought by a capitalistic democracy that gave everyone the "right" to exploit commercially animate and inanimate natural resources without the slightest regard for the needs of future generations. By the 1890s, some sportsmen had decided it was time America as a whole accept a major component of their code by putting an end to the commercialization of game. Though long in the making,[133] *Forest and Stream*'s announcement of this principle on February 3, 1894 was—in terms of its blanket, national coverage— the most revolutionary declaration up to that time on the subject of wildlife conservation.

Written, evidently, by George Bird Grinnell and his managing editor, Charles B. Reynolds,[134] the front-page editorial called "A Plank" is a watershed in the history of conservation. Here, in its entirety, is what it said:

> This is 1894. We have just been celebrating the four-hundredth anniversary of the coming to this continent of men equipped with firearms. For four centuries, from the time of Christopher Columbus to that of Charles Delmonico [presumably a reference to a member of the famous family of *restaurateurs*], we have been killing and marketing game, destroying it as rapidly and as thoroughly as we knew how, and making no provision toward replacing the supply. The result of such a course is that for

the most part the game has been blotted out from wide areas, and today, after four hundred years of wanton wastefulness, we are just beginning to ask one another how we may preserve the little that remains, for ourselves and our children.

With all the discussion of the subject in the columns of the *Forest and Stream* from 1873 to 1894, there has been and is a general consensus of opinion that the markets are answerable for a larger proportion of game destruction than any other agency or all other agencies combined. The practical annihilation of one species of large game [the bison] from the continent, and the sweeping off of other species from vast regions formerly populated by them, have not been brought about by the settlement of the country, but by unrelenting pursuit for commercial purposes. The work of the sportsman, who hunts for the sake of hunting, has had an effect so trivial, that in comparison with that of the market hunter, it need not be taken into consideration. The game paucity of today is due to the skin hunter, the meat killer, [and] the market shooter.

From the beginning wild game has played an important part in the development of the country. It has supplied subsistence when there was no other food for the pioneer and the settler. Buffalo and elk and deer and grouse and quail and wild goose and wild duck have sustained the men who first cut into the edge of the unbroken forests of the continent, who blazed the trails westward, and pushed their way, directed as mariners at sea by note of sun and stars, across the billowing prairies. Many a halt would have been made by these advancing hosts, had they been compelled to depend upon sutler trains, instead of foraging on the abundant game resources of the country as they took possession of it. For generations, then, it was right and proper, and wise and profitable that game should be killed for food; that every edible creature clothed in feathers or in fur should be regarded as so much meat to be spitted or potted or panned.

But times have changed. Conditions are not what they were. Game still affords food for the dweller in the wilderness, for those who live on the outskirts; and for people in such situations venison is a cheaper commodity than beef. But for the vast and overwhelming multitude of the people of the continent, game is no longer in any sense an essential factor of the food supply. It has become a luxury; it is so regarded, and it is sold at prices which make it such. With the exception, perhaps, of rabbits or hares, the supply of wild game as marketed is not such as to reduce the cost of living to persons of moderate means. The day of wild game as an economic factor in the food supply of the country has gone by. In these four hundred years we have so reduced the game and so improved and developed the other resources of the country that we can now supply food with the plow and reaper and the cattle ranges cheaper than it can be furnished with the rifle and the shotgun. In short, as a civilized people we are no longer in any degree dependent for our sustenance upon the resources and the methods of primitive man. No plea of necessity, of economy, of value as food, demands the marketing of game. If every market stall were to be swept of its game today, there would be no appreciable effect upon the food supply of the country.

Well, then, why not recognize this, and direct our efforts, in line with such a recognition, toward the utter abolition of the sale of game? Why should we not adopt as a plank in the sportsman's platform a declaration to this end—*That the sale of game should be forbidden at all seasons?* To share and express the sentiment is one thing, to put it into execution is quite another. Perhaps the time is not ripe for such stringent measures. Yet this very rule of no game traffic holds in certain county laws in this State [New York]; and one of these days it will hold in every state, East and West, North and South. It may not be brought about in a day, but the present moment is none too soon to adopt the plank as a working principle and to work for it.

That which stands in the way of the present prohibition of the sale of game in the larger cities is the magnitude of the commercial interests involved. The traffic is one of large proportions, much capital is invested, and the business not one which would readily be sacrificed. No one of these considerations, however, can withstand a campaign of education and the creation of a public sentiment which will surely follow when that education shall have taught the community the true place of wild game in the economy of the civilization of the present.[135]

Because *Forest and Stream*'s "plank" struck at the American economic system itself, many thought it an impossible dream. Yet, the paper continued to demand its acceptance, and environmentally aware men and women began rallying to its standard. With the passage of the Federal Migratory Bird Treaty Act in 1918—which was achieved largely through the efforts of sportsmen[136]—a custom as old as the country soon ceased to exist. No other single principle, before or since, has had as beneficial an effect on the continent's wildlife.

4

The Early Fight for the Forests

*If we have the most perfect code of game and fish laws which it is
possible to devise, and have them ever so thoroughly enforced, what
will they avail if there is no cover for game nor water for fish? . . .
The crop [from a well-managed woodlands] is one which is slow in
coming to . . . harvest, but it is a sure one, and is every year
becoming a more paying one. Furthermore, it breaks the fierceness of
the winds and keeps the springs from drying up, and is a comfort to
the eye. . . . Under its protecting arms live and breed the grouse, the
quail and the hare, and in its shadowed rills swim the trout. If we
would have these, we must keep the woods a-growing. No woods, no
game; no woods, no water; and no water, no fish.*

GEORGE BIRD GRINNELL'S EDITORIAL,
"Spare the Trees," in *Forest and Stream*, April 13, 1882

While their first concern was wildlife, sportsmen quickly
perceived that the effort in behalf of mammals, birds, and
fishes was a solution to only half the problem. It would do
little good to preserve wildlife if its habitat continued to shrink, for
eventually both would be gone. That part of the environment most
immediately threatened was the forest.

Without power saws, bulldozers, or any other modern machinery,
nineteenth-century Americans proved amazingly adept at timber
destruction. Whole forests of live oak, white pine, redwood, and other
species were cut down and burned over, and by the latter part of the
century almost every wooded section of the country had experienced
a logging boom. While these lumbering operations provided a boost
to the local economy, the prosperity rarely lasted, and when the loggers
moved out, they left in their wake a denuded landscape.

Paradoxically, a certain amount of deforestation improved wildlife
habitat. Ruffed grouse, wild turkeys, and white-tailed deer are among
the many species that profit by selective cutting that opens up clearings
in deep woods. In fact, the abundance of these species in wilderness
inhabited "only" by Indians proves that human beings had already
made their mark on the land long before Europeans arrived. With the

use of stone implements and fire, Native Americans had altered the ecology of vast regions, and enhanced the habitats of many kinds of animals, birds, and fishes. When the white invaders began pushing west from the Atlantic, they duplicated, and extended, the Indian's earlier alterations of the land, harming some species but benefiting others.

While in its initial stages lumbering may have helped some wildlife, widespread systematic logging operations, combined with the huge conflagrations that frequently followed them, ultimately did far more harm than good to the ecosystems involved. Soil damage and erosion, elimination of watersheds and wildlife cover, and siltation and flooding were only some of the adverse effects produced by the cut-and-run mentality of a nation that often looked upon trees as little more than overgrown weeds, and bragged about how many farms its citizens had worn out in their lifetimes. To many Americans of the nineteenth century, uncut woodlands were an offense to their "Manifest Destiny," for this was a society whose self-image was defined in terms of physical change and material success. Consequently, some of its leading folk heroes were "skinners" of natural resources—real men like Buffalo Bill Cody or mythological ones like the giant lumberjacks who figured in humorous tall tales until, after the turn of the century, they were synthesized into the single mighty character of Paul Bunyan.

Sportsmen, however, manifested a different orientation. Possessing an Old World code, they saw forests not as a challenge to the American mission of progress, but as one of the essential settings for that important activity called sport. Free from the prejudices of the frontiersman, farmer, and logger, sportsmen viewed trees as something more than a hiding place for Indians, an obstacle to plowing, or a source of financial gain. Woodlands were both the home of their quarry and the aesthetic backdrop for that avocation that many considered more rewarding—in a noneconomic sense—than their vocation. Regrettably, few historians have understood that an individual's recreation often tells us more about the person than the work he or she does.

The importance placed on woodlands by those who were, or had been, hunters or fishermen is revealed in their efforts to draw attention to forest destruction. Once again, this group led the way with protests that began long before the Civil War. In one way or another, the following called for timber preservation in the antebellum period: DeWitt Clinton, John James Audubon, William Elliott, Frank Forester, Elisha Lewis, Charles Lanman, and Samuel H. Hammond.[1]

After the Civil War, organized efforts in behalf of forest preservation and propagation increased, though not at the same rate as those in regard to wildlife. There was no national "timber movement" comparable to the crusade for fish culture, sportsmen's clubs, wildlife preserves, and better game laws. Nor were there any national periodicals devoted wholly, or in part, to forest conservation like those dealing with wildlife. One significant indication of the earlier public interest in wildlife is the fact that the states and the federal government established fish commissions before forest commissions.

The interest in woodlands did grow in the post-bellum period, however, with much of the activity centered in the federal government. The Timber Culture Act of 1873 represented one approach, though it can hardly be called a conservation measure. Based on the dubious notion that the planting of trees on the Great Plains would reduce the aridity of the region, the purpose of this legislation was to expand settlement by increasing rainfall.[2] The supposed climatic benefits obtained from tree planting also played a part in the 1872 suggestion of Nebraskan J. Sterling Morton to dedicate April 10th of every year as "Arbor Day."[3] Like the Timber Culture Act, Arbor Day was little more than a gesture that had only a vague relationship to forest conservation.

Fortunately, the Timber Culture Act was not the only federal activity relating to forests in the 1870s. More worthwhile was the 1876 Congressional appropriation of $2,000 to the Commissioner of Agriculture for the employment of an agent to investigate the rate of consumption of forests and the best methods for renewal.[4] Franklin B. Hough received the assignment on August 30, 1876, and according to one scholar, "thus began the first action by the federal government toward a forest policy."[5] Hough had become aware of forest destruction as superintendent of the 1870 United States census, and it was he who alerted the American Association for the Advancement of Science, who in turn submitted the petition to Congress that resulted in the 1876 appropriation and Hough's appointment.

After he received his assignment, Hough traveled widely in the United States and Europe studying forests and forestry. As a result of these investigations, he published a number of official reports that helped lead to the establishment in 1881 of the Division of Forestry of the United States Department of Agriculture.[6] Yet, apart from the work of Bernhard Fernow, who became its Chief in 1886, this understaffed and underfinanced bureau accomplished little until the end of the century. Despite the bureau's lack of early achievements—

in contrast to the tremendous environmental efforts of sportsmen, and the establishment of an active United States Fish Commission ten years before the Division of Forestry—the *Concise Dictionary of American Biography* states matter-of-factly that Hough's "activities paved the way for the successful conservation movement of later years."[7] Thus, we have yet another example of the omnipresent, but erroneous, twin assumptions that no conservation movement existed until the turn of the twentieth century and that concern for the forests initiated that movement.

Although the national government was establishing a poor record in regard to forest conservation, a few federal officeholders did attempt to arouse the public on this issue. Carl Schurz, who was something of a hunter in his youth,[8] was one of these men. In his position as Secretary of the Interior during the years 1877 to 1881, he advocated the adoption of a wide-ranging program of forest conservation, including the creation of forest reserves, a federal forest service, and a national forestry commission. Like the other German-born pioneers of American forestry, Bernhard E. Fernow and Carl A. Schenck, Schurz hoped to introduce into the United States what was essentially an Old World, patrician concept of state responsibility for resource stewardship. In a country that made a fetish of freedom, it was inevitable that Schurz's ideas would be attacked as aristocratic and un-American.[9]

Other federal officeholders who expressed a concern for the forests were Presidents Arthur, Cleveland, and Harrison; the last two men set aside forest reserves totaling millions of acres. All three were eminent sportsmen (see the pictures of them in the "Photo Album" of this book). Arthur was reputedly one of the finest fly-casters and salmon anglers America has ever produced; Cleveland loved freshwater fishing and bird hunting equally, and his classic *Fishing and Shooting Sketches* (1906) reveals much about a man who believed that the sporting life bestowed physical, mental, and spiritual benefits upon its followers; and Harrison had a penchant for duck hunting that knew no bounds. As leading members of the "fraternity" possessing the British-derived code of the sportsman, all three of these Presidents shared to a degree Carl Schurz's Old World perspective on natural resources. Undoubtedly, the responsibility for the *total* natural environment inherent in the sportsman's code played a part in their official statements, and actions, in behalf of forest protection.

While a number of federal officeholders cited the need for timber preservation in the 1880s, easily the most important pioneer in this area was Bernhard E. Fernow, who became Chief of the Division of Forestry of the Department of Agriculture in 1886. Despite Gifford Pinchot's efforts to bury his predecessor by ignoring him, Fernow's achievements as head of the Division were substantial, and they were obtained despite a woeful lack of financial support. He helped to keep the subject of forestry alive, and according to historian Sherry H. Olson, his approach was, in many ways, superior to his successor's; Fernow, for example, stressed the need for research in wood technology, while Pinchot's primary concern was for increasing timber production.[10]

In sum, Bernhard Fernow has been underrated by those who have accepted Gifford Pinchot's later claim that little of note occurred in conservation before he arrived on the scene. Fernow was the preeminent leader of the incipient forestry movement of the 1880s, and his conception of the state, which has been described by one environmental historian "as the highest expression of the social organism and the promotion of academics and professionals in governmental service," would later be adopted by the Roosevelt-Pinchot conservation team. As that scholar observes, Fernow's belief in federal responsibility for resource husbandry was one of the vehicles by which "the conservation movement merged with the evolving doctrine of the welfare state."[11] It is important to note that Fernow, Roosevelt, and Pinchot were all distinctly upper class in background, for despite the use of democratic rhetoric and the need to make frequent political compromises, the conservation program of the Roosevelt administration would manifest a patrician, *noblesse oblige* conception of the need, and the right, to manage the people's natural resources for their own good, whether or not they desired such stewardship.[12] In looking back on his early conservation efforts, Fernow wrote in 1907 that he had had "the disadvantage of being a foreigner who had to learn the limitations of democratic government."[13]

Besides his similar vision of the state's purpose, Fernow had something else in common with Roosevelt and Pinchot, for he, too, was very much a sportsman. In his native Germany professional foresters often pursued hunting, fishing, and forestry simultaneously, and Fernow was no exception. He later recalled: " 'I have in years gone by carried my gun and cast my line occasionally, and taken pleasure in it. Indeed, my profession as a forester in my native country where I studied and practiced it includes both, in the theoretical teaching and in the practice, the art of sportsmanship hunting and . . . conservative fishing, and I can assure you, there is a high standard of sportsmanlike behavior kept up by the foresters. . . .' "[14]

Like another German-born forester, Carl A. Schenck, Fernow would bring his penchant for sport with him to the United States.[15] Both men found out that forestry and hunting were also compatible in America. As we have seen, Fernow first practiced forestry in the United States on the game preserve of well-to-do sportsmen. Schenck's experience was somewhat similar. On Gifford Pinchot's recommendation, he was appointed in 1895 as forester of George W. Vanderbilt's 120,000-acre Biltmore estate in North Carolina, but on arriving in America to consult with Pinchot, Schenck found that avid sportsman more interested in talking about hunting and fishing than forestry.[16] Later, hunting excursions on the estate helped cement their friendship.[17]

Like Great Britain, Germany had a long sporting tradition, at least among the aristocracy. The responsibility for the natural environment inherent in the British sportsman's code—which had already influenced American sportsmen like Gifford Pinchot—had its counterpart in the German tradition. It helps to explain the origins of the commitment to conservation that Fernow and Schenck brought with them to the United States and helped to establish here.

Thus far, we have concentrated mainly on the genesis of the federal government's work in forest preservation and management, but the greatest amount of activity in this area during the earliest years was performed by private citizens. One of these individuals was William Henry Brewer, professor of agriculture at Yale's Sheffield Scientific School from 1864 to 1903. In former years he had assisted Josiah Dwight Whitney in his geological survey of California and combined deer hunting with geology on a number of occasions.[18] One reason Brewer is considered to be an outstanding pioneer of forest conservation is because in 1873 he began offering at Yale what were probably the first lectures on forestry ever given at an American university. In addition, he was on the committee of the American Association for the Advancement of Science that petitioned Congress in 1874 to recognize the importance of forest preservation and cultivation. As noted previously, Franklin B. Hough was appointed in 1876 to investigate that subject.

Of all the private groups interested in timber preservation in the 1870s, none was more active than sport hunters and fishermen. It has already been shown that even before the Civil War began, a number of sportsmen had attacked forest destruction. In the post-bellum period these scattered protests became an organized agitation, not as widely popular as the crusade for wildlife, but powerful nonetheless.

As in the case of wildlife depletion, the appearance in the early 1870s of the first national sporting periodicals, *American Sportsman, Forest and Stream,* and *Field and Stream,* helped focus sportsmen's anger over woodland eradication and unite them against it.[19] While Brewer was offering his lectures at Yale, these journals were giving their own lectures, and to a far greater audience. When *American Angler* appeared in the next decade, another voice for forest preservation was added to the sporting press. Like the other journals, *American Angler* endeavored to keep its readers informed of the most up-to-date information on "natural history," and that included the disastrous effects of unregulated logging and pulp-mill production on rivers and their inhabitants. In addition to the attacks on water pollution already cited (Chapter Three), the newspaper also explained in detail how uncontrolled lumbering ruined fishing waters by causing such habitat changes as bank erosion and higher water temperatures.[20] Like the other periodicals, *American Angler* illustrated a remarkable understanding of ecological principles.

Of the four major papers, *American Sportsman* and *Forest and Stream* proved to be most concerned with forest preservation. Founded in 1871, the first journal repeatedly lamented the extent and ramifications of woodland destruction, and as a solution to the problem, it suggested that European forestry techniques be adapted to American timberlands.[21]

When *Forest and Stream* was founded in 1873, it quickly proved that it was even more dedicated to forest conservation than its predecessor. Editor Charles Hallock stated every week in *Forest and Stream*'s subtitle that his paper was "Devoted to . . . Preservation of Forests," and he lived up to that claim by frequently calling attention to the depletion of timberlands and the need for their protection. The very first issue of the paper (August 14, 1873) stated: "For the preservation of our rapidly diminishing forests we shall continually do battle. Our great interests are in jeopardy . . . from the depletion of our timberlands by fire and axe."[22]

Hallock's interest in this issue may have been spawned, in part at least, by George Bird Grinnell. Although Grinnell did not join the paper's staff until 1876, when he became natural history editor, he was associated closely with it from the beginning as a writer, financial supporter, and scientific adviser. Since his graduation from Yale in 1870, he had also kept in touch with scientific developments through his close association with Othniel C. Marsh, a sportsman and paleontologist who was then one of the university's most prominent faculty members.

Grinnell assisted Marsh on his 1870 fossil-collecting expedition to the Far West, entered Yale's Sheffield Scientific School in early 1874, and received a Ph.D. under Marsh in 1880.[23] Undoubtedly, Grinnell knew of William Brewer's forestry lectures at Sheffield, then a tiny institution, and it seems probable that he would have advised Hallock of their significance.

As we have seen, Grinnell first concentrated on defining "sportsmanship" and preserving wildlife after becoming *Forest and Stream*'s editor and owner in 1880. It did not take long, however, for him to understand that more was also needed on the subject of forest conservation. In April, 1882, therefore, he began his editorial drive to transform the nation's orientation toward its woodlands. Years earlier, Hallock had pointed the way by drawing attention to how rapidly the timberlands were being depleted and by suggesting Europe's system of managed forests as an alternative to the wasteful methods of American lumbering. But Grinnell went far beyond his predecessor in publicizing the European science of forestry.

In "Spare the Trees," the opening editorial of his campaign in behalf of the forests, he manifested awareness of the interrelationship of all natural resources. "If we have the most perfect code of game and fish laws which it is possible to devise," he wrote, "and have them ever so thoroughly enforced, what will they avail if there is no cover for game nor water for fish?"[24] Employing the ideology of the business-farm community, he called for Americans to use their "proverbial thriftiness and forecast" to achieve "the proper and sensible management of woodlands." The forests must be seen as a "crop . . . which is slow in coming to the harvest, but it is a sure one, and is every year becoming a more paying one."[25] In addition, "it breaks the fierceness of the winds, and keeps the springs from drying up, and is a comfort to the eye. . . . Under its protecting arms live and breed the grouse, the quail and the hare, and in its shadowed rills swim the trout. . . ." Although the lesson was a simple one, it had not yet been learned by the American people: "No woods, no game; no woods, no water; and no water, no fish."[26]

In perceiving the subtle interconnection of all life, Grinnell foreshadowed the science of ecology. By his use of terms like "harvest," "crop," and "management," he articulated the gospel of the efficient administration of natural resources, an ideology taken from the scientific and business communities that presaged the thinking of the Progressive conservationists. As so often would be the case, Grinnell manifested a knack for advancing new ideas that, in time, would become the dominant ideology. Because of his belief in the environmental responsibilities inherent in the code of the sportsman and his incomparable training in paleontology, with its obvious lessons in the vulnerability of animal and plant species, it is not surprising that he was in the forefront of the American minority who was knowledgeable about the growing crisis in natural resource depletion. And that awareness was enhanced, poignantly, in the period 1870-83 by seeing, firsthand, the destruction of the "Great West," a land originally typified by huge bison herds and free-ranging Indians. All of these formative influences dovetailed when Grinnell became editor of the leading outdoor journal of the time. From that position, he received new information, as well as feedback, from all sources concerned with the natural world, putting him at the nucleus of the intellectual evolution of conservation.

Ever since the early days of *Forest and Stream,* the weekly's editors had been interested in the possible applicability to American conditions of European developments in sport, natural history, and science. Particularly significant in this regard was the Europeans' attitude toward their woodlands. In an 1883 editorial, "Forestry," Grinnell reported: "In parts of Europe forestry is a science, and officers are appointed by the governments to supervise the forests; and only judicious thinning of young trees and cutting of those which [have] attained their growth is allowed. . . ."[27]

He pointed out that the system was used not only on government lands, but on private holdings as well, "the theory being that the individual will pass away, but the forest must remain forever."[28] He contrasted the Continental emphasis on continuous resource management with the situation existing in America, where the sovereignty of private ownership allowed an individual to "buy a tract of land in the great water producing region of the State, and for his own pecuniary benefit render it forever sterile."[29] Grinnell suggested that laws regulating forest use, like those already existing in Europe, should be immediately passed in the United States. As in the case of game legislation, he believed that statutes protecting the forests would have democratic results and "work well for the people at large."[30]

In 1884 *Forest and Stream* stepped up its campaign to educate the American people in the principles and methods of forestry. Grinnell argued on pragmatic rather than aesthetic grounds that European practices be tried in the United States. Relying on figures supplied by the Canadian statistician James Little and the Harvard dendrologist Charles Sprague Sargent, Grinnell claimed that the "awfully wasteful modern methods of lumbering" cost the nation one billion dollars annually.[31] He noted that in the process of felling and transporting one mature tree, an average of fifty saplings were killed. In addition, dead brush was always left behind, resulting in a serious fire hazard.[32]

Unlike those who wanted forest tracts set aside that would remain completely undisturbed, Grinnell realized that this essentially negative approach was only a "holding action." Other possible approaches included substituting for wood when possible, using "economy in cutting and marketing," and protecting from fire and livestock grazing. He knew that all these suggestions had their place, "but after all, the great dependence must be upon reproduction. . . ." To have a healthy, productive forest, it had to be cared for by thinning mature and dead trees. To leave the timber untouched was "wasteful," an adjective used repeatedly in *Forest and Stream*.[33]

In March Grinnell used the recent floods of the Ohio and Mississippi Rivers as illustrations of "the terrible effects of our criminal waste of woodlands."[34] He asked for massive reforestation along the rivers' banks and the creation of state and federal forestry commissions.[35] Later that spring, he went further and demanded that the national government immediately appoint "A Competent Forestry Officer," a "trained professional" to lead in "the inauguration of a system of forest conservancy."[36] Because there were no American forestry schools, only foreigners had the requisite training. As one qualified for the job, Grinnell suggested Charles F. Amery, an alien residing in America who had over fourteen years of experience in the forest bureaus of Germany and elsewhere.

Grinnell noted that despite the increasing awareness of the "necessity of doing something for the maintenance of a permanent timber supply, action is paralyzed by the difficulty of deciding how best to set about it." Although the federal government had created a Division of Forestry several years before, the bureau remained tiny and inactive. Grinnell believed that "the appointment of such a man as Amery on the staff of the forestry department would be regarded as [proof] . . . that the Government had at length come to . . . face the problem squarely." The fact that Amery was an alien was an advantage in a sense, for it guaranteed an apolitical perspective.[37]

Although Grinnell's recommendations were not adopted, the editorial reveals that he now perceived that the natural resources of the nation must be administered on a continuous and efficient basis, and that the removal of all political considerations was a necessary prerequisite for achieving this goal. In time, this view would become the cornerstone of the Progressive conservationist faith.

In the five-part series, "Forests and Forestry" (1884-85), Grinnell consistently used almost the entire front page of his weekly to explain the fundamentals of the European science. He argued that forestry's concepts were applicable to every country. While American trees and soils were not exactly like those in Germany and France, the Continent's expert foresters were "capable of adapting general principles to changed conditions."[38] And "pending the theoretical and practical training of young Americans," these foreign professionals should staff the forestry bureau.[39] Under their direction, it could become an animated, functioning department.

If the administration of a "systematic conservancy" were established, it would not only protect water supplies but also produce a perpetual, annual supply of four-billion board feet of lumber. According to Professor Sargent, this was the "capacity" of the American forests.[40] In other words, if the government were to "husband" its "timber stock" intelligently, the woodlands of the nation would be perpetuated while, at the same time, producing wealth.

Although Grinnell's sophisticated understanding of forestry came mostly from European sources, some Americans also contributed. One, as we have seen, was Charles Sprague Sargent, whose statistical estimates Grinnell used. More important was George Perkins Marsh, whose *Man and Nature: or, Physical Geography as Modified by Human Action* (1864) influenced all subsequent thinking on natural resources. He was the first to provide detailed historical documentation for the argument that forests should be preserved because they were necessary for human prosperity, perhaps even for human survival.[41] This basic fact seemed so obvious to Marsh that he found it incredible that "man has . . . forgotten that the earth was given to him for usufruct alone, not for consumption, still less for profligate waste."[42]

Applying his ideas to the great wilderness north of New York City, the Adirondacks, Marsh argued that the water-holding properties of these woodlands made it imperative that they be retained in a wild state. The spongelike quality of the forest floor slowed and regulated the release of moisture, guaranteeing the continuous flow of water to the south.[43]

From the first numbers of *Forest and Stream*, Hallock had publicized Marsh's conclusions, including his thesis that the decline of Spain and other countries was in part caused by their thoughtless destruction of forests.[44] Hallock's desire to have the Adirondacks preserved probably grew out of the sportsman's code and the Romantic tradition, but as historian Roderick Nash has pointed out, he employed the watershed argument because it was the most likely to succeed.[45]

After Grinnell became *Forest and Stream*'s editor, he continued fighting for the Adirondacks on the basis of the Marsh-Hallock watershed defense. The area had to be set aside because it protected the sources of the Hudson River and other water supplies upon which New York City depended. If uncontrolled lumbering of the region continued, these supplies would wither away, and the future of the state would be imperiled. This is what Grinnell meant when, in "Save the Adirondacks," he declared: "The reasons why the forests should be preserved are not sentimental, but very practical."[46] From late 1883 on, he kept up a steady barrage of editorials on the subject, directed mainly at businessmen.

As with all later issues relating to natural resources, the dialogue on the future of the Adirondacks suffered from the abysmal ignorance of legislators. In March, 1884, a bill to preserve the region was being debated in the New York Assembly, and a number of members were in vehement opposition. One announced that the watershed argument was absurd, since the Hudson River was an arm of the sea and did not depend on drainage from the Adirondacks. Instead of trying to ensure the continued flow of water into the river, he thought that all its tributaries should be blocked off to eliminate the expense of dredging the channel![47]

Grinnell did not despair, however, for there were a few in the Assembly who took an intelligent position on the issue, and stuck to it. One of these was the young Theodore Roosevelt. Although the two men had already met, they still knew each other mainly by reputation: Roosevelt, the dynamic legislator, and Grinnell, the editor of the leading journal on hunting and natural history, two of Roosevelt's favorite subjects. Referring to the assemblyman who wanted to dam the Hudson's feeder streams, Grinnell wrote: "In agreeable contrast to the utterances above quoted are those of Mr. Roosevelt and a few other gentlemen, who in all matters pertaining to the public good, take liberal and advanced views. It is satisfying to see, now and then, in our legislative halls a man whom neither money, nor influence, nor politics can induce to turn from what he believes to be right, to what he knows to be wrong."[48] Never known for his self-effacement, Roosevelt undoubtedly appreciated this public tribute. More importantly, the reference reveals that his interest in the future of natural resources existed earlier than indicated by historians.

When Grinnell editorialized in behalf of the Adirondacks, he at first simply repeated the Marsh-Hallock watershed argument. Soon, however, he thought of using the wilderness as a testing ground for the theories of European forestry.[49] On January 17, 1884, he urged: "Protection and conservation, now, prompt, adequate—this is what the Adirondack forests demand, not restoration years hence, after the damage from unregulated lumbering shall have been wrought and ruin has followed."[50] This was the first time Grinnell used the expression "conservation," which, it should be remembered, did not become the catchword for dialogue on natural resources until more than twenty years later. Yet, the term's juxtaposition in the editorial, and his other concurrent writings on forestry, make it clear that he was already employing the word in its modern sense: as the wise *use* of resources so as to make them last indefinitely.[51]

In the above passage, the "protection" of the Adirondacks would be accomplished when they were set aside and the fire hazard controlled. This was the static aspect of Grinnell's plan for the region. "Conservation" was the dynamic part, the *process;* it would only be achieved when the woodlands were systematically managed on a continuous basis.

The watershed argument, although valid, did not go far enough. The problem was that most of its supporters, including New York City business groups, felt that if the Adirondack "preserve" were established, it should be kept in a wild state. After all, they reasoned, was it not the lumbering of the forests that threatened the watershed's usefulness? Grinnell, however, thought it impractical to attempt to keep an area the size of Connecticut in a permanently inviolate condition; in time, pressure to utilize it economically would become too great to resist. Why not, therefore, have the future of the Adirondacks shaped realistically from the beginning by illustrating that protection of the drainage area and utilization of its timber were not incompatible? Grinnell probably reasoned that since the watershed defense was favorably received by the state's businessmen, they would be doubly impressed when shown they could "have their cake and eat it too." Increasingly, this was the appeal he used to justify the creation of an Adirondack reserve.

Addressing himself to those who wanted to keep the territory undisturbed, and sounding just like Gifford Pinchot in later years,

Grinnell wrote: "It is now generally well understood that forests are not to be maintained in good order by excluding the axe, but that the great economic aim of forest administration is to raise the productive yield of the forests to the highest capacity of the soil."[52] Put another way, the woodland as a whole would be improved by harvesting dead and mature trees. Grinnell was so determined that the Adirondacks be used as a proving ground for forestry that he editorialized against setting aside a larger portion of the region than could be efficiently administered.[53]

With the New York Chamber of Commerce and other business organizations now demanding its passage,[54] on May 15, 1885, Governor David B. Hill signed a bill establishing a 715,000-acre Forest Preserve.[55] Having first been told that lumbering of the Adirondack drainage area endangered their economic future, the businessmen of the state found it difficult to readjust their thinking to Grinnell's later argument that the region's forests should be harvested. Instead, their continued support of the proposed reservation had been based on the understanding that it would be kept inviolate. This attitude prevailed, and the act creating the preserve stipulated that it would remain forever "as wild forest lands."[56]

Grinnell was pleased that the area would now be protected from wasteful lumbering, but because it had been put in a kind of quarantine, with no provision for forestry, he remained unsatisfied. In later years, Gifford Pinchot would express the same unhappiness over the status of the Adirondack forests, and for the same reason. One historian claims that in 1900, when Pinchot presented his idea for scientific forestry in the Adirondacks to Theodore Roosevelt, then Governor of New York, he "was most impressed"—suggesting that this was the first time he had heard such a proposal![57] In reality, Roosevelt had been reading all about how the Adirondack timberlands should be systematically managed in the country's leading outdoor periodical years before he had ever heard of Gifford Pinchot. As we will see later, Roosevelt would soon begin to hear the same ideas from George Bird Grinnell personally, when they began their close friendship in 1885; although he had briefly met Pinchot in 1894, Roosevelt did not become well acquainted with him until 1899.

Because of its continual attacks on logging, as distinct from scientific harvesting according to the principles of forestry, *Forest and Stream* shared much of the responsibility for instilling in the public a suspicion of all those who used an axe in the woodlands. Grinnell would have an uphill fight convincing New Yorkers that with forestry, the timber could be cut, the watershed protected, and the woods, as a whole, made healthier.

The distrust of the lumber companies, of course, was warranted. After interest in setting aside the Adirondacks had become widespread, the loggers in the region had worked at an ever-faster pace to fell its timber, "their objective being to get as much on the ground as possible before any law interfering with them shall be passed."[58] Having no understanding of forestry, their only "policy" was the making of short-term profit.

Even after the preserve had been established, the companies continued to lumber indiscriminately within its borders. In June, 1885, Grinnell attacked them by demanding: "Who are the forest skinners?" The answer, he said, was obvious: "They are capitalists who are taking away for a mess of pottage the birthright of the people." And "Who is responsible for the people's loss? First, the people themselves; and second, the men sent by the people to Albany to take care of the people's interest." In Grinnell's view, their indifference put both groups at fault.[59]

His application of the "skinner" image was apt, for the lumberman who stripped the forest cover from the land and the market gunner who flayed the hides from big game were from the same mold. Both were creations of rapid industrialization, and both regarded the natural world only as a source of quick profit. Incidentally, it should be noted that Theodore Roosevelt, many years later, would also use the "skinner" image, and in exactly the same way.[60]

It was characteristic of Grinnell to see the use—or misuse—of resources as part of a common pattern. If the ideology and organization of American business was so effective that the forests and big game of vast regions could be exploited into oblivion within a few years, then the only way to stop the depletion of natural resources was to adopt that same ideology and organization.

When, for example, he demanded that the nation adopt a systematic approach to its timberlands based on the principles of forestry, he sometimes employed the analogy of the corporation.[61] The federal government would act as the manager of the corporation, administering the forests for the benefit of its stockholders, the American people. Each year, it would be calculated how much of the woodland could be cut without infringing on the "capital." The resulting income would be a continuous source of revenue. As will be shown, his solution to the problem of diminishing game was similar. Only the "interest" of each animal population would be spent by hunters, leaving sufficient breeding "stock" to produce the next generation. Here again, perpetual revenue would be produced, directly, through taxes on licenses, guns, and ammunition, and indirectly, through increased incomes for local businessmen servicing visiting sportsmen.

As we have seen, Grinnell played a central role in alerting Americans to the need for stewardship of timberlands. But it should be stressed that while his editorial drive probably represents the earliest, extended campaign of any national newspaper in behalf of forest preservation *and* conservation, that effort was based on many earlier precedents. In regard to the specific issue of New York's Adirondack watershed, sportsmen had long been calling for the region's protection.

As early as 1822, the same year Daniel Webster introduced his bill in the Massachusetts House of Representatives to protect brook trout (Chapter One), New York sportsman, DeWitt Clinton, a leading political figure of his day, made a general recommendation for the preservation of Adirondack forests.[62] It should be emphasized that Clinton was not just a man who occasionally "went fishin'," but a well-known, "accomplished angler" in the "sporting fraternity." Daniel Webster acquired Clinton's fishing tackle, and a few years after his death, "presented" it to the Cincinnati Angling Club for their collection when Webster visited the city in June, 1833.[63]

What angling meant to Clinton is suggested by the fact that his son followed in his father's footsteps, and by 1833, was, in the words of the Club's secretary, " 'one of the best anglers in the country.' "[64] By "best," the Club's officer was probably describing more than just the younger Clinton's skill with a fly-rod; he was also referring to Clinton's adherence to the rules of the game—to the code of the sportsman. In the history of fishing, hunting, and conservation, we repeatedly see this bonding of older and younger relatives through the vehicle of sport, with the internalization of sporting values and conservation concepts by the younger person. Gifford Pinchot and Aldo Leopold are just two of the many well-documented examples.[65]

When DeWitt Clinton was Governor of New York, he was a leading supporter of the plan to build the Erie Canal. But does that mean that his interest in preserving the Adirondacks was simply because the region is the watershed for the Hudson River, the lower portion of the transportation route between the Atlantic Ocean and Lake Erie opened up by the completion of the Canal in 1825? That he was interested in the region for more than its economic potential is shown by his involvement in the debate over whether the "king of game fishes," the Atlantic salmon, had ever migrated up the Hudson River to spawn.

After careful study of the *Journal* of Henry Hudson's 1609 voyage, Clinton concluded in 1815 that the "salmons" the English navigator referred to were actually " 'our rock fish or streaked [striped] basse, which comes into the river . . . in great numbers.' " In Clinton's time, no salmon were ever seen in the Hudson, " 'except a few estrays [strays] who have missed their way into the Connecticut River,' " for " 'salmon delight in clear, cool, . . . limpid water, and the Hudson is, particularly at the period of their vernal [spring] migration, discoloured and muddy.' "[66]

This question over whether the Atlantic salmon was native to the Hudson was not simply an academic one. Anglers were already starting to express an interest in "fish culture," but before any proposals could be initiated to restore the salmon in a particular river, fishermen had to know if it had ever existed there in the first place! There can be little doubt that DeWitt Clinton developed his love for the wilderness of upstate New York while wading in the liquid sunshine of its lakes and streams and casting to the beautiful brook trout. It was when he was part of this " 'wild, romantic, and awful [awesome] scenery,' " to use his own words, that he experienced " 'a correspondent impression in the imagination' " that would " 'elevate all the faculties of the mind and . . . exalt all the feelings of the heart.' "[67] Historian Roderick Nash believes that Clinton's love for nature was the result of the Romantic movement that began in the late eighteenth century,[68] but the source of his sentiments goes farther back, to the patron saint of all fly-fishers, Izaak Walton. The subtitle of his 1653 classic, *The Compleat Angler,* is *The Contemplative Man's Recreation,* and the essential benefit of angling in Walton's mind was the peace it brought to its practitioner.

After Clinton's general recommendation for the preservation of the Adirondack forests, the first specific proposal, as discussed in Chapter One, was presented by another sportsman, Samuel H. Hammond. In 1857 he suggested that the nation "mark out a circle [in the Adirondacks] of a hundred miles in diameter, and throw around it the protecting aegis of the constitution." A prophet of the "wilderness idea," Hammond requested that this preserve be kept free of logging and settlement, "a forest forever," in which "the old woods should stand . . . always as God made them."[69]

Hammond was joined in 1857 by another sportsman, who wrote anonymously to *The Spirit of the Times* in May complaining about the declining populations of brook trout and white-tailed deer in the Adirondack Mountains. He called for the creation of "Vigilance Committees" to catch and prosecute all those breaking the game laws.

Most importantly, he also proposed that the region be set aside as a wilderness game preserve where wildlife habitat would be protected and maintained for the future.[70]

Two years after Hammond and his fellow member of the sporting fraternity made their recommendations,[71] a sportsmen's organization, the Northwoods [Izaak] Walton Club, requested legislation that would protect "our Northern Wilderness." If such a law were passed, the nation would possess a "vast and noble preserve" where game could thrive and where "no screeching locomotive [would] ever startle . . . Fauns and Water Sprites."[72]

To the members of this club, and to many other anglers and hunters as well, the Old World concept of the game preserve or park for noble sportsmen seemed like an idea worthy of emulation in the New World.[73] Across the Atlantic, huge tracts had been set aside for centuries to provide aristocratic disciples of the chase with a hunting ground untouched by civilization. Deliberately kept in a wild state to ensure game propagation and protected from poachers through the vigilance of gamekeepers, these preserves might have been an injustice to "the people," but they protected forests and wildlife that would have been quickly exhausted by a society possessing the freedoms of the United States.

As one scholar observes, "the use of forests to serve the function of recreation is as old as the Middle Ages. Indeed, the very word 'forest' meant an area reserved for the king's private pleasure," for "only in the modern age did the word come to signify any tract of land covered with trees and underbrush."[74] Actually, the idea goes back even farther than the Middle Ages. As anthropologist Carleton S. Coon points out, "the [ancient] Persians gave us the word *paradise,* which originally meant simply a hunting preserve."[75]

This is not to say that the Old World precedent was copied exactly. The fundamental differences—a better word might be antagonisms— between aristocracy and democracy forbade it. The closest representation was the private sportsmen's association possessing its own preserve or park. Made up of wealthy outdoorsmen, these organizations often maintained comfortable clubhouses and large protected tracts where their members could enjoy hunting and fishing without concern for "No Trespassing" signs, "improvements," and other hindrances to sport. Blooming Grove Park and the Bisby Club, already discussed, are merely two of the better-known examples of this kind of association.

But even in the case of this latter group, the sportsmen's organizations were more New World than Old World in character. Though often upper class in membership, the clubs reflected American political and economic customs. Officers were usually selected by majority rule, and while some associations required merely an initiation fee and yearly dues, others operated like joint-stock companies. For instance, *American Field* (the later name of *Field and Stream*) reported that the Fox Lake Club, an association established in 1879 near Chicago, "is a regular stock company, the members holding the shares, each being entitled to all the rights and privileges of the club. The initiation fee is $215; the year[ly] dues are $10."[76] Therefore, an aristocratic, precapitalistic precedent was altered to fit a democratic, capitalistic culture.

Another example of the desire to adapt the game-preserve idea to American conditions was the 1858 recommendation of Henry David Thoreau. Discussing Maine's northern wilderness in an article in *Atlantic Monthly,* he referred to the European tradition of setting aside hunting preserves for nobility and asked: "Why should not we . . . have our national preserves . . . in which the bear and panther, and some even of the hunter race [Indians], may still exist, and not be 'civilized off the face of the earth'—[and] our forests [saved] . . . not for idle sport or food, but for inspiration and our own true recreation?" In the same passage he asserts that the kings "were impelled by a true instinct" in setting aside these hunting areas.[77]

Obviously, Thoreau had a different object in mind from the members of the Bisby Club or Blooming Grove Park. Though an experienced and enthusiastic fisherman,[78] a hunter in his younger days,[79] and an admirer of the aesthetic aspects of hunting and fishing,[80] he remained ambivalent toward the sporting fraternity, and occasionally even expressed hostility toward it.[81] Still, it is suggestive—as discussed in Chapter One—that in *Walden* (1854) he made a direct comparison between the joyful "hunting and fishing grounds" of his boyhood contemporaries and "the preserves of an English nobleman."

Fortunately for the history of the Adirondacks, sportsmen did more than engage in Romantic fantasies of sanctuaries where the Indian and his game would remain forever in a primitive state of suspended animation. As in the case of other wild regions—like Florida's Everglades, Montana's northern Rockies, and Alaska's coast and Mount McKinley area[82]—sportsmen had been among the first to explore, map, and study the Adirondacks.[83] While not nearly as pristine as the other regions mentioned, New York's northern mountains still qualified as *bona-fide* wilderness, and sportsmen had been establishing preserves there since at least the 1850s.[84] By the 1870s, these sanctuaries dotted the wilderness, and the sportsmen who maintained them led the movement to create a huge public preserve occupying much or most of the Adirondacks. Only in that way could the borders of their own reserves be protected from the encroachments of loggers, sawmill operators, and others bent on exploiting the forests for short-term gain.

From the early 1870s on, sportsmen's newspapers called for the creation of a vast Adirondack reservation.[85] In other words, almost a decade of agitation preceded Grinnell's editorial campaign for forest conservation. While lacking the national appeal of the movement for wildlife, particularly fish culture, the efforts in behalf of the Adirondacks had been publicized enough to make the sporting fraternity receptive to the arguments presented by *Forest and Stream.*

As it turned out, however, most sportsmen accepted only half of Grinnell's proposal, rejecting his plan for scientific forestry. Historian Eugene J. O'Neill is correct in arguing that the drive to set aside an Adirondack forest preserve and the repeated rejections of recommendations for the introduction of forestry after the reservation had been established were based mainly on aesthetic and recreational considerations, rather than the desire for efficiency in the use of resources. Even the New York City civic and business groups that joined—but did not initiate—the crusade wanted the region forever barred to economic utilization. As O'Neill observes, Samuel Hays's widely accepted thesis on the origins of conservation proves erroneous when applied to this seminal issue in environmental history.[86]

Yet one may argue that Hays's thesis does apply, at least in part, if the aim of the 1885 law setting aside the reservation "was the preservation of wilderness, but for commercial ends."[87] Those holding this view can claim that the main reason for the victory of wilderness advocates was the utilitarian desire to protect New York City's economic life by maintaining the source of its water supply. It should be stressed, however, that sportsmen, and not downstate business interests, began the crusade, and they remained a key element in the campaign—even after the businessmen joined.

As in the case of other early conservation issues, concern for wildlife preceded concern for forests. Sportsmen wanted the preservation of their game and sporting grounds for aesthetic and recreational reasons, but they knew that the best way to accomplish their purpose was to couch it in utilitarian terms. Charles Hallock and George Bird Grinnell, for example, were *primarily* interested in protecting game and habitat for the enjoyment of future generations of sportsmen. Nevertheless, they admitted that in a society like the United States, another, more pragmatic argument must be used. As Hallock observed in "The Adirondack Park," an editorial appearing in September, 1873, "Our hope is that the whole subject [of an Adirondack reservation] will be placed before them [the members of the state legislature] in a practical way. We do not urge here the tourist or hunting question. As much as the *Forest and Stream* advocates the preservation of game, we would give it a secondary place, though the preservation of the woods is the life of the game." And elsewhere in the piece, Hallock argued that the only way to ensure the legislators' interest "is to have them look at the preservation of the Adirondacks as a question of self-interest."[88] In later editorials Hallock and Grinnell continued to fight for Adirondack preservation on the basis of practical, economic arguments, despite the fact that they were always most interested in wildlife conservation. It was a strategy based on an accurate appraisal of the utilitarian instincts of most of their countrymen, and sportsmen-conservationists from Hallock and Grinnell to Theodore Roosevelt and Gifford Pinchot would employ the same approach, regardless of their deeper motives.[89]

While most historians of conservation grant sportsmen a place in the crusade to save the Adirondacks, the latter group's true importance has been obscured not only by the tendency to take their public statements at face value, but also by scholars' failure to identify leaders of the drive as sportsmen. In his work on the early history of conservation in New York State, Marvin W. Kranz, for instance, cites name after name of those who pioneered Adirondack preservation without seeming to be aware that many of these individuals were sportsmen before they were conservationists. Included in this group are Verplanck Colvin, Charles E. Whitehead, Abram Hewitt, and Grover Cleveland. Even Bernhard E. Fernow, who helped draft the 1885 law establishing the Forest Preserve; James Husted, who steered the bill through the New York Assembly; and Governor David B. Hill, who supported and signed it, were all sportsmen.[90]

The creation of the 715,000-acre Adirondack preserve marks a high point in the early history of American environmental concern. As in the case of the game preservation-fish culture movement going on at the same time, sportsmen had initiated the effort to save New York's woodlands. Pragmatic arguments to the contrary, a desire to perpetuate wildlife and habitat for recreational and aesthetic enjoyment inspired both campaigns.

5

Development of the National Park Concept

*We have seen it [the West] when it was, except in isolated spots, an
uninhabited wilderness; have seen the Indian and the game retreat
before the white . . . tide of immigration. . . . There is one spot left, a
single rock about which this tide will break, and past which it will
sweep, leaving it undefiled by the unsightly traces of civilization.
Here in this Yellowstone Park the large game of the West may be
preserved from extermination; here . . . it may be seen by generations
yet unborn. It is for the Nation to say whether these splendid species
shall be so preserved, in this, their last refuge.*

GEORGE BIRD GRINNELL'S EDITORIAL,
"Their Last Refuge," in *Forest and Stream*, December 14, 1882

As we have seen, the responsibility for the total natural
environment inherent in the code of the sportsman aroused
hunters and fishermen to work in behalf of nongame and
forests as well as those animals, birds, and fishes traditionally pursued
for sport. It should not be surprising to learn, therefore, that they also
played a leading role in the creation—and protection—of national parks.
Even though these reservations sometimes lacked good fishing and
would eventually prohibit hunting entirely, no group was more
important in their early history than the American sportsman.

In fact, the first to suggest the national park idea—so far as we
know—was hunter George Catlin. Although best known as a student
and painter of Indians, he was also a self-proclaimed sportsman who
combined recreational hunting with his studies of the Western Indians.[1]
Preceding by a quarter of a century Thoreau's call for "national
preserves" (Chapter Four), Catlin proposed in 1832 that the federal
government establish "a *magnificent park*" to house the Indians,
buffalo, and wilderness—"a beautiful and thrilling specimen for
America to preserve and hold up to the view of her refined citizens
and the world, in future ages!"[2]

Like Thoreau's later recommendation, Catlin's idea was probably
based on the European precedent of large game parks where aristocratic

sportsmen preserved wildlife and habitat intact for their own personal enjoyment. And also like Thoreau, Catlin hoped to "freeze" the Native American and his game, particularly the bison, in a state of suspended animation.[3]

This fanciful goal suggests, however, that Catlin and Thoreau wished to alter the Old World precedent to fit New World circumstances. Like Thoreau, Catlin wanted "A *nation's Park*, containing man and beast, in all the wild[ness] and freshness of their nature's beauty!"[4] In other words, both men apparently envisaged a preserve for the whole country—for "the people"—instead of merely for the enjoyment of a privileged class. Aside from the impossibility of keeping Indians ignorant of the civilization outside, one can only wonder how Catlin and Thoreau thought a wilderness park could be for the whole nation and still remain in a pristine state.

That problem, of course, has never been solved. Today, many in the National Park Service seem to understand that unless visitors' freedoms are restricted, the preserves will be damaged irrevocably by overuse.[5] Yet, the debate continues between those who see a national park as untainted wilderness where individuals must find their own pleasures in their own way, and those who see it as a recreational area necessitating blanket automobile access, hotels, restaurants, and every other kind of convenience. Like the efforts in behalf of game laws and forestry, the attempt to adapt what was originally an aristocratic precedent—in this case the game preserve or park—to the requirements of a democratic society proved to be only partially successful.

Despite one or two earlier examples of federal action to set aside natural areas for public use,[6] the first real national park was Yellowstone, established in 1872. White men had been passing through the region, though not necessarily in the park proper, since at least the time of John Colter, a hunter for Lewis and Clark. A later visitor was that ubiquitous mountain man, Jim Bridger, who stumbled across the wondrous land of geysers, waterfalls, and hot springs in 1830. Although he told the outside world of his find, everyone knew that mountain men were notorious storytellers, and "Old Jim Bridger's lies" were long a source of amusement.[7] Not until forty years later did the real "discovery" of the region occur, "by which is meant its full and final disclosure to the world."[8] After the return of two expeditions made in 1869 and 1870, Bridger was no longer ridiculed.

The second of these explorations played a direct role in the creation of America's first national park. Led by Henry D. Washburn and

Gustavus C. Doane, a party of nineteen men traveled through the Yellowstone wilderness in August and September of 1870 and discovered for themselves the geysers, hot springs, and other marvels first described by Jim Bridger.

On September 19th the expedition camped where the Firehole and Gibbon Rivers join to form the Madison, and around the evening fire its members discussed the future of the Yellowstone. While most expressed an intention to file claims in the area to profit from future tourism, one of the party, Cornelius Hedges, had a different opinion. Rather than to have the "wonders" exploited for private gain, he proposed the creation of "a great National Park" to insure that future generations would enjoy these natural objects in their original form.[9] While Hedges's idea may not have been entirely new[10] and only envisaged the provision of small buffer zones around the geysers and along the rims of the canyons,[11] it is generally regarded as the beginning of the effort that resulted in the establishment of Yellowstone National Park.

Like so many other prophets of environmental concern, Hedges was a cultivated, extremely well-educated Easterner. In an age when only two percent of the American population received the advantages of a secondary-school education,[12] Hedges held a Bachelor's degree from Yale and a law degree from Harvard. Coming to Montana in the early 1860s, he became one of Helena's leading citizens.

Although historian Aubrey L. Haines asserts that Hedges "was not an outdoor type of person,"[13] an examination of the diary he kept on the expedition yields a very different interpretation. Hedges was, in fact, the most enthusiastic and accomplished angler of the party.[14] While the general influence of the Romantic movement undoubtedly had much to do with Hedges's proposal for "a great National Park," the code of the sportsman may also have played a part. A highly literate, even scholarly individual, Hedges had probably seen the writings of Frank Forester, Samuel Hammond, or other well-known authors who stressed the aesthetic aspects of fishing and hunting and reminded sportsmen of their responsibility for the natural world.

After returning to civilization, Hedges and another member of the expedition, Nathaniel P. Langford, publicized the national park idea and succeeded in inducing a small interest in the project. One of those to be stimulated was Ferdinand Vandiveer Hayden, director of the Geological and Geographical Survey of the Territories, who decided to lead an expedition through the Yellowstone in the summer of 1871.[15]

Among those he chose to accompany him were photographer William Henry Jackson and landscape artist Thomas Moran. These two gathered a pictorial record that would soon play an important role in the history of the region.

Like most expeditions to the Great West in those early years, Hayden's 1871 survey offered numerous opportunities for recreational as well as utilitarian hunting and fishing. Although many historians give the impression that these activities were pursued only to provide the camp with food, a close reading of the personal diaries and journals of expedition members proves otherwise. Often, simply the appearance of a big-game animal like an elk or grizzly bear caused the excited explorers to break formation and give chase. On the Hayden survey none were more enthusiastic in their sporting interests than William Henry Jackson, who shot a trophy grizzly,[16] and Thomas Moran, who repeatedly proved his expertise as a trout angler.[17]

On returning to the East, Hayden joined forces with Nathaniel P. Langford and Montana's Congressional delegate, William H. Clagett, in an effort to establish a reservation in the Yellowstone. One who came to their support was Jay Cooke, Philadelphia banker, Civil War financier, and angler. Cooke was a founding member of the Oquossoc Angling Association in northern Maine. Organized in 1869, the group prided itself on accepting only " 'gentlemen' " to join them in the " 'decorous frolic' " of brook-trout angling. Being concerned about " 'their reputations when abroad'," they apparently played the game of fly-fishing according to long-established rules of conduct.[18]

Jay Cooke had actually been interested in establishing a park in the Yellowstone months before the Hayden expedition visited the region. A financier of the Northern Pacific Railroad through Montana, Cooke hoped the creation of a park would result in a lucrative tourist business for the line.[19] In early 1871 he had helped to subsidize several lectures given by Langford in behalf of a Yellowstone preserve, and later he also defrayed the expenses incurred in pushing the park legislation through Congress.[20]

That body's consideration of the proposed bill began on December 18, 1871. The brief Congressional debate revealed a general lack of interest in the subject, though at least one Senator expressed a fear that the park would take potential farm land out of cultivation.[21] An important exception to the general indifference, or hostility, shown by Senators was George Franklin Edmunds of Vermont—"one of the earliest conservationists in Congress"[22]—who spoke in favor of the park bill. This was the same Edmunds who was a well-known angler and key figure in the early fish-culture movement at both state and federal levels. In order to accomplish their goal, park proponents found that they had to use a "practical" approach, and they claimed that the Yellowstone region's high altitude and cold climate would make farming impossible. Edmunds, for instance, employed that tactic.[23] As with some later national parks, the Yellowstone could be set aside only after it was successfully argued that the area was essentially useless for large-scale economic development.[24]

Using this strategy, plus the claim that the government would incur little expense for the preserve's maintenance, park advocates managed to slip their bill through Congress. They received invaluable aid from Jay Cooke, whose money helped finance the effort; Nathaniel P. Langford, whose published articles on the Yellowstone were copied and distributed to the legislators before they voted; and especially William Henry Jackson, whose magnificent photographs, given out at the same time as Langford's articles, backed up the claim that the Yellowstone's wonders were absolutely unique and must be set aside.[25] Soon, Thomas Moran's paintings would add another visual dimension to Americans' appreciation of the Yellowstone[26] (and other scenic areas as well) and play no small part in increasing public support for the creation of national parks.[27]

Finally, on March 1, 1872, President Ulysses S. Grant signed the bill establishing—at least on paper—"a park or pleasuring-ground."[28] As we shall soon see, it took many years of agitation by aesthetic conservationists to define just what had been created by the stroke of Grant's pen.

The deep involvement of sportsmen like Cornelius Hedges, Jay Cooke, William Henry Jackson, and Thomas Moran in the effort to establish and publicize a Yellowstone preserve was only the first of many such campaigns. Those who had avidly fished or hunted for recreation would also play a vital role in the founding of many later national parks, among them Yosemite (1890), Glacier (1910), Lassen Volcanic (1916), Denali (1917), Grand Canyon (1919), Great Smoky Mountains (1930), Isle Royale (1940), and Everglades (1947).[29]

But the treatment of all these preserves was based on precedents established in the handling of Yellowstone National Park, long the nation's only such reserve. After the latter's "creation" in 1872, over two decades would pass before the government and general public of the United States began to view a "national park" in the way we now take for granted: as an essentially inviolate wildlife and wilderness sanctuary.

Spearheaded by George Bird Grinnell's *Forest and Stream,* sportsmen initiated a movement that aimed, first, to define the meaning of Yellowstone Park for the American people and, second, to establish for it an effective administration. The 1872 act creating the reservation had for its object the protection of a natural "museum" of "wonders"— geysers, hot springs, and canyons.[30] The park was not intentionally preserved either as a wilderness or a game refuge.[31] The only concern of those few interested in the area was that the "curiosities" be made available to the public as soon as possible.[32] Instead of believing that the park should remain in a pristine state, most of these individuals assumed that it would soon be "improved" by a multitude of hotels, roads, and other conveniences.

During the rest of the 1870s and the very early 1880s, most of Congress, as well as the general public, virtually forgot about the park. Because there was no convenient access to its vicinity, the reserve's only visitors were hide hunters, sportsmen, and members of expeditions.

The statute creating the reservation provided that it "is hereby reserved and withdrawn from settlement, occupancy, or sale . . . and set apart as a public park or pleasuring-ground for the benefit and enjoyment of the people."[33] The Secretary of the Interior was authorized to draw up regulations to "provide for the preservation from injury or spoliation, of all timber, mineral deposits, natural curiosities, or wonders . . . and their retention in their natural condition."[34] This proclamation could be given a variety of interpretations. Clearly, however, the one held by the Secretary of the Interior would be crucial. The rules he promulgated would largely determine how Americans conceived of their first "national park." In the same way, the degree of enforcement of these decrees would indicate which infractions, if any, the government considered threats to the meaning of the park, and which it looked on as insignificant. In time, the failure to prosecute the latter would make what they prohibited accepted practices. Eventually, such practices would receive the sanction of tradition, making them almost unalterable.

Because of its inaccessibility, there was at first little danger to the park outside of the depredations of commercial hunters. But by 1881, the tracks of the Northern Pacific Railroad had approached the vicinity of the reservation. "Soon after," George Bird Grinnell recalled in his autobiography, "its [the railroad's] President, . . . [Henry] Villard, took out a special train carrying a number of guests—railroad men, capitalists, and scientific men—to show the public the country traversed by his road. Among those who then visited the Park were some men who saw its possibilities as a pleasure resort, and realized that the privileges offered to lessees through the Act establishing the Park would have a money value to those who might secure them."[35] Soon these men would begin their efforts to exploit the reserve, inspiring Grinnell to launch a campaign aimed at protecting the park by clarifying its status.

In large measure, Grinnell's crusade was the outgrowth of his experience in the West. Because the boundaries of Yellowstone Park were drawn with little real knowledge of the terrain, a number of expeditions were sent into the region to see exactly what Congress had, in fact, "preserved."[36] One of these was an 1875 reconnaissance led by engineer and sportsman[37] William Ludlow. As the expedition's official naturalist, Grinnell became thoroughly familiar with the park. The most obvious problem it faced was hide hunting, which he vehemently attacked in Ludlow's *Report,* published in 1876.[38]

Although all species of big game were being systematically slaughtered, he was most alarmed by the destruction of the buffalo, in this, their last stronghold. For seventy years, the dream of Western expansion had fed on buffalo meat, and the animal had become the symbol of the new land, the game Old World aristocrats and New World patricians—Grinnell[39] and Roosevelt[40] among them—had to shoot, as a kind of initiation rite into frontier Americanism.

Long before Grinnell first saw the animal on its native grounds in 1870, hunters George Catlin and John James Audubon had expressed the hope that this representative of the West would never die out.[41] Now, with the establishment of Yellowstone National Park, there appeared to be a possibility that the bison might be preserved, though the founders of the park had not conceived of it as a game refuge.

Perhaps the first to envisage the national park as a preserve for keeping the buffalo from extinction was Theodore B. Comstock, who made the recommendation in the journal *American Naturalist* in early 1874.[42] Three years later, Grinnell also suggested the game-preserve idea. In the very popular *Sportsman's Gazetteer and General Guide* (1877), he observed that "the rapid and appalling diminution in their [the buffalo's] numbers and range is owing entirely to their wanton and useless destruction by skin-hunters and pseudo-sportsmen." While governmental protection during the breeding season would be a help, "another and better method for saving the few remaining herds from utter annihilation may be suggested; namely, by forming a buffalo reservation." The ready solution, he pointed out, lay in Yellowstone Park, where "we have the necessary territory, and it is already stocked; but the skin-hunter, that ruthless destroyer of game, must be kept at a distance if we would hope to save this species."[43]

For several years, Grinnell wrote nothing more on the refuge concept. Perhaps he was waiting to see how the Secretary of the Interior and Congress would handle the park. In the meantime, he continued his attacks on the market gunner, that camp follower of industrialism's advance into the Western wilderness. In 1880 he observed: "There is nowhere in the world such systematic, business-like and relentless killing as on the buffalo plains."[44]

By early 1881, he had decided that the government did not intend to protect the park buffalo. In the March 17th issue of *Forest and Stream*, he reiterated the view that the survival of the bison, as a species, depended on those in this reservation and said that it was mandatory, therefore, that the federal government appoint at least six wardens to watch over the animals.[45]

The wardens were not appointed, and the reserve continued to be treated as a bonanza for hide hunters. Pseudo-sportsmen also took their toll. In 1882 *Forest and Stream* reported "The Very Latest," the incredible story of the "Yellowstone Valley Hunting Club." The group advertised that on payment of a fee, it would guarantee trophies for Eastern tourists. All guns, ammunition, and other requirements were supplied, and the game was even located ahead of time, so that the "pilgrim" could kill his prize without the slightest delay. Grinnell's weekly satirized the operation by suggesting the adoption of a kind of burglar-alarm system which could "intersect all the ravines, plateaus and hills in the Yellowstone Valley with wires, all converging to the club room, so that every time a brute stirred anywhere in the territory covered by the club, an alarm would be given, and the exact whereabouts of the game shown by an indicator in the club room." Another possibility was that "a large stock of game might . . . be corralled in substantial enclosures, where the timid tourist could pump away with his repeating rifle. . . . Or the animals might be roped and tied to a post and then slaughtered by proxy." What was fantastic to Grinnell was that the managers of the "club" failed to see that their project was self-defeating, for soon the game would be exterminated and they would be out of business.[46]

In response to Grinnell's editorial attack, the president of the club, H. S. Back, wrote to the editor of *Forest and Stream* on June 15, 1882. Not aware of Grinnell's Western experience, Back called him a "tenderfoot" and mocked his supposed ignorance of the Yellowstone region and its game. He finished by asserting that " 'Eastern hunters have no idea of the extent of this Territory or of the amount of game there is in the Northwest; and we give you the laugh when you talk of exterminating the game in this country.' "[47]

Despite the Westerner's assurance, in the next few years the buffalo would vanish, several subspecies of larger mammal forms would become extinct, and many others would dwindle to precariously low levels. What Back's letter exemplifies is the hostility and utter lack of communication between East and West, which would continue to plague the efforts of conservationists, mostly Easterners like Grinnell, to save the West from its own destructive inclinations.

Although Grinnell's conception of the national park as a wildlife preserve was articulated as early as 1877, it took several years for him to realize that if his idea was to become a reality, something more was required than sporadic protests. On December 14, 1882, he provided that "something more" by launching a crusade in *Forest and Stream* to define the status of Yellowstone National Park and protect it from commercialization. Only after a continuous campaign of a dozen years would his goal be achieved.

The first editorial, "Their Last Refuge," covered the whole front page and was both a plea for the buffalo and a detailed analysis of the deficiencies in the act creating the reserve. He pointed out that the statute put the destiny of the reservation completely in the hands of the Secretary of the Interior. This official had the power to grant leases to private persons and corporations for their purpose of building roads, hotels, and other facilities, and to decide what regulations should be devised for the park. With regard to wildlife, only their "wanton destruction" with "the purpose of merchandise or profit" was specified as one of the offenses the Secretary was to "provide against."[48]

Grinnell's editorial made it clear that the vagueness of the act subjected it to a number of interpretations and left huge loopholes for those who sought to use the reserve for their own profit.[49] An example was the section on wildlife, which seemed to suggest that individuals or corporations could kill all the game they wished, just so long as they were not too "wanton." The greatest deficiency, of course, was that the act provided no machinery for carrying out any regulations the Secretary of the Interior might promulgate. As Grinnell later recalled, the Secretary's rules "soon came to be regarded as a dead letter. Anyone was at liberty to cut down the forest, kill the game or carry away natural curiosities, and all these things were constantly done. . . ."[50]

He cogently summed up the problem in the 1882 editorial:

This "great and glorious government" has again stultified itself by enacting laws without supplying the means to enforce them. The Park is overrun by skin-hunters, who slaughter the game for the hides, and laugh defiance at the government. . . . The curse of politics has entered into the management of the reservation, and the little money appropriated for its maintenance is wasted by incompetent and ignorant officials. It is leased to private parties, who desire to make a peep show of its wonders.[51]

In this editorial Grinnell also expressed regret that the park's potential as a wildlife sanctuary was not yet realized. He asked that the recommendation he made in the *Report* of the 1875 Ludlow reconnaissance to end hide hunting be followed at last. He also repeated the proposal made by Ludlow in the same publication that the reservation be transferred to the War Department and guarded by troops,[52] for, as Grinnell emphasized, nothing could be expected from the Department of the Interior, "that sink of corruption." A final suggestion was that the park be extended to the east as far as Cedar Mountain, which would almost double its area while preserving crucial big-game habitat.

The editorial closed with an urgent plea for the retention of at least one place as it was before the coming of the white man. In his own time Grinnell had witnessed "the tide of immigration [into the West], once small, like a tiny mountain stream, move forward, at first slowly, and then, gathering volume and strength, advance with a constantly accelerated power. . . ." But "there is one spot left, a single rock about which this tide will break, and past which it will sweep, leaving it undefiled by the unsightly traces of civilization." Most importantly, "here in this Yellowstone Park the large game of the West may be preserved from extermination; here . . . it may be seen by generations yet unborn. It is for the Nation to say whether these splendid species shall be so preserved, in this, their last refuge."[53]

With the arrival of a new year, *Forest and Stream* stepped up its drive to have the park legislatively defined as a wildlife and wilderness preserve, all commercialism excluded, and a mechanism of enforcement established. In "The Park Grab," an editorial of January 4, 1883, Grinnell exposed the scheme of the so-called "Yellowstone Park

Improvement Company," the main group involved in exploiting the reserve for private gain. The corporation was endeavoring to obtain a lease of seven tracts in the park, all but one of which was to be 640 acres in size. For the tiny annual charge of $2.00 per acre, the company would be entitled to build hotels, stores, stage and telegraph lines, raise cattle, and have unlimited use of all water, timber, and arable land. Grinnell found it incredible that "the only National Park possessed by the American people" could be so flagrantly appropriated for the benefit of a few commercialists.[54]

There was some cause for optimism, however. Opposition to the "monopolists" had already been expressed by a few in Congress, notably Senator George G. Vest of Missouri. But because "it is whispered that his interest in the subject has on a sudden ceased," Grinnell urged the Senator to remove this doubt by reasserting his original position.[55] The editor's fear was unjustified, for Vest would prove to be the staunchest defender of the park in Congress. A member of the Woodmont Rod and Gun Club of western Maryland, whose official motto was "Protect and Enjoy,"[56] he was an enthusiastic sportsman and a believer, apparently, in the environmental obligation intrinsic to the code of the sportsman.

Despite the efforts of *Forest and Stream,* the "Improvement Company" succeeded in getting the requested lease from the Assistant Secretary of the Interior.[57] It covered Mammoth Hot Springs, Yellowstone Canyon and Falls, and all the larger geyser basins.[58] But the corporation was not to go unscathed. Grinnell's attack on January 4th was resumed the following week. In an editorial that occupied almost the whole front page, he revealed that in order to construct a 600-room hotel at Mammoth Hot Springs, the company had established a sawmill that was busily cutting up the reserve's trees. The park's wildlife was also in danger. In order to feed the large labor force that was to be in the area through the winter, "the company called for bids from contractors to furnish 20,000 pounds of wild meat. . . ."[59]

Still, there was a positive side to the situation. Senator Vest had renewed his opposition to the corporation and had even introduced a bill that incorporated many of the demands Grinnell had made in his editorials. The proposed legislation would extend the park east to Cedar Mountain and south to the 44th parallel, adding about 3,344 square miles to its size; detail troops within its borders if found necessary; provide heavy fines for traffic in game; and establish a force of ten wardens, accountable to a regularly paid superintendent of the park.[60]

The friends of the preserve appeared to be achieving results in other areas as well. The January 18th number of *Forest and Stream* printed a letter received from Secretary of the Interior Henry M. Teller addressed to the Superintendent of the Park. Dated the 15th, it prohibited "the killing, wounding or capturing at any time" of the reserve's wildlife and forbade, in addition, the cutting of timber without the Secretary's authorization. Grinnell thought these orders might not be too late, if only they could be enforced.[61]

Concerning the proscription on animal destruction, he argued that if put into effect, it would perpetually maintain good hunting in the region surrounding the preserve. Protected in their natural nursery, the big game would quickly increase. This reproductive spiral would be amplified by animals coming from the outside, which, in their search for safety, would concentrate within the reservation's borders. The wildlife inside the park would continually reproduce and spill over its edges to restock depleted adjacent territory.[62]

Here was another application of the concepts of business management to resource use. The reserve's wildlife would act as capital stock to produce interest for reinvestment in other areas. In the years ahead, Grinnell often repeated this theory. It added a "practical" touch to the battle over the park's future that would appeal to Western sportsmen. And it worked precisely as he predicted, making Theodore Roosevelt, among others, an enthusiastic endorser.[63]

The January 18th issue of *Forest and Stream* contained another seminal idea on the meaning of the nation's first national park. In "The People's Park" Grinnell emphasized that the reservation was owned by the American public as a whole rather than by the few commercial groups that were in the process of taking it over.[64] Since this idea is now the heart of the national park philosophy, it is difficult to envisage a time when public ownership was not a universally accepted truth.

Although the act setting aside the Yellowstone region had provided the basis for this view, by describing its product as "a public park or pleasuring-ground for the benefit and enjoyment of the people," this clause could just as well have sanctioned the creation of another Coney Island. Like the side shows of a carnival, the attractions of the Yellowstone were, for most, its "freaks and phenomena of Nature."[65]

Others looked to the example of Europe. In March, 1883, George G. Vest announced in the Senate that there was nothing new in Yellowstone Park, for "France has such a park, Germany has such a park, England has her royal parks, and why should not America have her republican park. . . ."[66]

Vest's statement illustrates the continuing influence of European ideas on the development of American environmental concern. As discussed earlier, the first national park proposals in American history were probably based on the precedent of the Continental and English game preserve or "park" set aside for aristocratic sportsmen. What is particularly interesting about the Senator's comment is that a number of the best-known city parks of Europe and England were originally the hunting preserves of nobility—London's Hyde and St. James Parks, for example.[67] It would appear that the evolution of the park concept on both sides of the Atlantic—whether in the form of a well-ordered, formal park like those in London and later in American cities like New York and Chicago or the wilderness parks created by the United States—can be traced back to a concern for wildlife first exhibited by European sportsmen.[68]

In view of this complex, somewhat shadowy history, it is no wonder that the "true" meaning of the American national park took many years to develop. The people of the United States had to be taught that they were the owners of the Yellowstone, and that their preserve was not to be an amusement park or a well-ordered, formal park. Instead, it was to be a great wildlife and wilderness sanctuary. Again, the basis for this interpretation was contained in the act establishing the reserve; the stipulation that the Secretary of the Interior "shall provide against the wanton destruction of the fish and game" would, in time, be construed as a prohibition against all killing of wildlife, and the phrase "their retention in their natural condition," as applied to "all timber, mineral deposits, natural curiosities, or wonders," would later justify the total exclusion of all but the most necessary of human works. The battle over the future of Yellowstone National Park was, in a sense, a battle over the language of the act that created it. The strict constructionists, led by Grinnell, eventually won out. This was fortunate, not only for this one reserve but for the future of the entire park system in America and, indeed, the world.[69]

When Grinnell began his editorial crusade, he had a somewhat naive understanding of the difficulties and setbacks he would have to overcome before achieving success. At the end of January, 1883, *Forest and Stream* headlined "The Park Saved." The weekly printed a letter from Secretary of the Interior Teller to Senator Vest stating that he would not grant the lease of the Improvement Company until Congress had taken action on the Senator's bill or until the session closed. With premature enthusiasm, Grinnell exclaimed, "This ends the fight. The grabbers are defeated. The people's rights are to be protected. The Yellowstone Park is not to become a second and greater Niagara [i.e., a commercialized tourist attraction]."[70]

Vest's bill, however, was not passed. Actually, the fight was just beginning, and Grinnell would have to battle over a decade longer to have the reserve adequately governed. But the struggle *Forest and Stream* had initiated was now joined by other periodicals, among them *American Field* (the later name of *Field and Stream*), *Harper's Weekly*, and the *New York Times* and *Herald*.[71]

In February Grinnell expressed the hope that Vest's bill would pass in the future and asked that it be amended to include the scenic Tetons to the south.[72] This proposal, introduced by the paper, would not become a reality until the establishment of the Grand Teton National Park nearly a half-century later.

The next month, Grinnell kept the issue alive by quoting in detail the lively Senate debate on the amendment to the Sundry Civil Service Bill submitted by Vest. The proposal was for a $2,000 annual salary for the Superintendent of the Park and $900 each for ten assistants, to be appointed by the Secretary of the Interior. They, as well as the Superintendent, were to reside permanently in the reserve, and their job would be "to protect the game, timber, and objects of interest therein." The Secretary of War, at the request of the Secretary of the Interior, would be authorized to detail troops in the park. Public access would be improved by new roads and bridges. Finally, a limitation would be placed on the power of the Secretary of the Interior to grant leases; they could not cover a larger area than ten acres, nor be near any geysers or "other objects of curiosity or interest."[73]

The view of much of the West was probably typified by Senator John J. Ingalls of Kansas, who condemned the amendment as a waste of money. The park, he asserted, was already becoming a burden on the federal government. He thought it should be surveyed and sold as other public lands were sold. Declaring "I do not understand myself what the necessity is for the Government entering into . . . show business in the Yellowstone National Park," he advised handing the reserve over "to private enterprise, which is the surest guarantee for proper protection for such objects of care as the great national curiosities in that region."

Sounding very much like earlier sportsmen, Vest defended his amendment by proclaiming: " 'Mr. President, the great curse of this age and of the American people is its materialistic tendencies. Money,

money, l'argent, l'argent, is the cry everywhere, until our people are held up already to the world as noted for nothing except the acquisition of money at the expense of all esthetic taste and of all love of nature and its great mysteries and wonders.' "[74] The Senate responded to this attack on the materialism of the times and approved Vest's amendment. Future events would prove, however, that the park was still a long way from having an adequate administration.

In late March, 1883, *Forest and Stream* reported that the Secretary of the Interior had asked the Secretary of War for a detail of troops for the park: "Things are, therefore, marching along in very satisfactory shape."[75] But the troops did not arrive, and the dismal situation remained unchanged.[76] In November the weekly's editor argued that the unenforced and unenforceable laws of the Wyoming and Montana territories against big-game destruction should be shored up by "a Federal law, backed by the power and resources of the Federal Government."[77] The state of the reservation continued to deteriorate, and by the end of 1883, *Forest and Stream* was informing its readers that the Superintendent of the park was either dishonest or incompetent, or both, and his assistants were not the experienced Westerners required but corrupt Easterners who were augmenting their income by selling the geyserite and game they were supposed to be protecting![78]

The beginning of a new year brought the news that the meager steps already taken to provide a government for the park could not be carried out. The Secretary of the Interior announced that because most of the reservation was in an unorganized county of Wyoming Territory, his regulations were null and void. Without a judge to try cases, vandals and market gunners could only be censured—they could not be prosecuted or even expelled from the park.[79] The Improvement Company had taken advantage of the situation—increasing the pasturing stock, killing the game with abandon, and even threatening to remove the helpless Superintendent if he failed to cooperate.[80]

Forest and Stream bitterly complained that "an effort has been made to care for the Park, and this effort has proved wholly abortive. The Government is now the laughing stock of the Improvement Company and the skin-hunters and trespassers."[81] Now, as never before, the paper's editor was convinced that only the Army could fill the void until a permanent administration was established.

Though disappointed, Grinnell had by no means given up. In the months ahead, he reemphasized the idea that the American people owned the reserve and were, as a result, responsible for it—"its geysers, its forests, its game, must be preserved for its owners."[82] He went so far as to claim that "public opinion" demanded a government for the park,[83] which was hardly the case. At this early date, the public had not the slightest concern for the area. Nevertheless, Grinnell was on the right track. The sanctity of private property was at the heart of the American value system. When the people eventually learned that they owned the Yellowstone country, they became anxious to save it. The warning to the nation that its property was rapidly being used up by commercialists and "monopolists" would prove one of his most effective appeals.

In March, 1884, a bill passed the Senate which, if it had become law, would have incorporated most of the provisions *Forest and Stream* had been advocating. These included extension of the park on the east and south, authorization for the use of troops to capture and expel lawbreakers, inclusion of the reserve within the judicial jurisdiction of Gallatin County, Montana, and the provision of fines for the destruction of game.[84]

As it happened time and again, the bill passed the Senate only to be killed in the House by amendments for "improvements." The lobbyists of the Improvement Company were working diligently to get sections of the park removed for commercial development. Their assault on the reservation had been joined by mining interests in Cooke City. Located just outside the northeastern corner of the park, the town wanted a rail connection with Gardiner, Montana, the terminus of the Northern Pacific. Spokesmen for the Cinnabar and Clark's Fork Railroad Company had succeeded in having riders added to Vest's bill which would have granted a right of way across the reserve.

Grinnell was particularly alarmed by this new menace.[85] He knew that if the railroad were built, a precedent would be set leading to the construction of others. Soon, the stillness of the wilderness would be broken by the whistle of locomotives and the clatter of the cars as they passed over the tracks. In addition, sparks from passing trains would be a perpetual fire hazard.

Partly as a response to the railroad threat, Grinnell now added another dimension to his rationale for wanting the park protected. If the Yellowstone region were seen as a vital watershed, the fire danger presented by sparks flying from passing locomotives would make it mandatory that railways be excluded from the reservation. In the simultaneous battle he was carrying on for the Adirondacks, the watershed argument was proving very effective. Why not apply it to the Yellowstone? Here, too, it would prove a powerful defense, so much so that it would become for many the primary justification for having the region protected.

One of these was Arnold Hague. From a distinguished New England family and a professionally trained geologist, he had been with Clarence King on his 1870 Survey of the Fortieth Parallel and in 1883 had taken charge of the Geological Survey work in Yellowstone Park. Grinnell's contributions to the *Report* of the Ludlow reconnaissance and his newspaper crusade for the reserve brought him to Hague's attention. The two became acquainted, and Hague asked Grinnell to accompany him on his 1884 summer survey of the park. This was the first of several such trips they made together,[86] the result of which was a friendship that would last their lifetimes.

While camped in the wilderness, the two had long talks about their hopes for the park,[87] and they found that they were in basic agreement. Undoubtedly, Grinnell spoke of the success the watershed rationale was having in gathering support for the Adirondacks, and Hague probably affirmed the validity of its application to the Yellowstone region. After their return to the East, they increasingly talked of the reserve in terms of its importance as a drainage area.

Grinnell led the way with a letter to the *New York Times*, published on January 29, 1885. He argued that the reservation's forests must remain inviolate, because they were situated on the watersheds of both the Missouri and Snake Rivers, and correctly predicted that the continued flow of these rivers would become important to the West as their potential for irrigation was realized. Hague followed Grinnell's example in a letter to a member of the Senate's Committee on Territories, published in *Forest and Stream* and in an article in *The Nation*.[88]

It is important to note that the watershed defense did not become Grinnell's sole argument for preserving the Yellowstone in an undisturbed condition; it was only added to the game-refuge idea and is one more illustration of the fact that conservation began with a concern for wildlife. An editorial appearing in *Forest and Stream* the same day the *Times* letter was printed combined these reasons in arguing for the park's protection.[89]

What is significant about Grinnell's position on the Yellowstone is how much it differed from his interpretation of the purpose of the Adirondacks. Although the campaigns for these areas were going on at the same time, the editor of *Forest and Stream* differentiated—from the start—between the state forest, which he hoped would be systematically utilized according to the principles of scientific forestry, and the national park, which, though serving a similar purpose as a watershed, must remain an unaltered wilderness. Grinnell was not a pure "preservationist," to use a term favored by some historians, who supposedly wished to leave all timberlands in a completely undisturbed condition, whether they were state forests, national forests, or national parks. Nor was he a purely utilitarian kind of "conservationist," an individual who supposedly cared little for aesthetic considerations and thought that any natural area was being wasted if it was not being utilized for timber, irrigation, grazing, or some other "practical" purpose. Grinnell's genius was his intellectual versatility, his ability continually to evoke working solutions for new problems, while remaining independent of those who sought to employ the same one-dimensional approach for every situation.

The one element common to all his approaches was the belief that *all* natural areas, and everything in them, benefited from continuous, nonpolitical, systematic management. This concept, which would later become the cornerstone of Progressive conservation ideology, was manifested both in his efforts to obtain a "government" for Yellowstone Park and in his attempts to have the Adirondacks scientifically utilized according to the principles of forestry. Just because the first reservation was to remain outside the commercial sphere did not eliminate its need for continual fire control, wildlife protection, trail maintenance, etc. The same would be true for the national wildlife refuges and "wilderness areas" created in the twentieth century, despite the common belief that no management of these reserves is necessary.

As we saw earlier, some historians have used the later antagonism between John Muir and Gifford Pinchot as their model, leading them to categorize every environmental activist as either a "preservationist" (like Muir) or a "conservationist" (like Pinchot). While this dichotomy may apply in some cases, a true conservationist like Grinnell knew that natural resources—"assets" might be a better word—must be conserved under a variety of administrative schemes. He would fight just as hard for the scientific utilization of national forests as for the preservation of natural conditions in national parks. Thus, he championed the forestry work of Gifford Pinchot, but joined John Muir in attacking the Hetch Hetchy dam project in Yosemite Park. And like another sportsman, Theodore Roosevelt, Grinnell would continue to love the chase, while at the same time campaigning for the establishment of wildlife sanctuaries. Neither man felt any inconsistency in his position, because there was none. They knew that one had to be *both* an "aesthetic conservationist" and a "utilitarian conservationist," depending on the issue involved. The "wise use of natural resources," a phrase the Roosevelt administration later popularized, meant that every unit in the conservation program—from national forests to national wildlife refuges—benefited from continuous, systematic management. And "management," of course, could mean no public use at all, if the area in question was one of special ecological concern.

Nowhere was this need for administrative continuity based on firmly established principles more obvious than in the early mismanagement of Yellowstone National Park. Because Grinnell conceived of the reserve as a kind of nonprofit corporation run for the benefit of the public, the man obviously most responsible for its efficient administration was its manager, the Superintendent. *Forest and Stream*'s editor remained ever vigilant to see that this official was performing well, but in the early years of the park, Grinnell was often disappointed. During the spring of 1885, he became so disenchanted with Robert Carpenter, the man then occupying the post, that he led a campaign to oust him.[90] The latter was like so many of the political appointees whose inefficiency and dishonesty plagued the reserve for years. One historian of the national parks has labeled him "a devotee of private enterprise, who tried to wreck the park."[91] Grinnell exposed how he was spending much of his time in Washington, D.C., lobbying for the Improvement Company. Even more incredible, it was learned that he had filed claim on 1,400 acres of park land with the intention of mining for coal.[92] In late May the Superintendent was finally removed. With justice, Grinnell claimed that "Carpenter's removal is the direct result of the ventilation of his acts by . . . *Forest and Stream*."[93]

During the fight to have Carpenter ejected, Grinnell had expressed the hope that after his ouster, the park would be put under a commission. It would consist of five men, to include the governors of Wyoming and Montana; the chief engineer in charge of road-building; a scientist, perhaps from the Geological Survey—he was probably thinking of Hague—and lastly, an intelligent, interested individual outside the agencies regularly concerned with the preserve.[94] A prime candidate for this last position was, of course, Grinnell himself. In the years ahead, commissions would become the dominant administrative forms for managing all natural resources.

By the summer of 1885, the guardians of the national park had still achieved almost nothing in the way of concrete results. Much of the problem lay in the fact that their struggle was taking place in an intellectual milieu shaped by the Romantic tradition. While the responsibility for the total environment inherent in the code of the sportsman had probably been part of the thinking of some of Yellowstone's founders, the park was created mainly to protect its "mysteries" and "wonders." One historian goes so far as to argue that the park's establishment was the culmination of the Romantic movement in America.[95] In a sense, those who had set the region aside might be compared to nineteenth-century reformers like the Greenbackers and Henry George's "single-taxers." For the supporters of these crusades, reform entailed a single panacea that, once accomplished, obviated the need for further action.[96] There was little or no realization of the need for continuity in handling problems. Those who had created the nation's first national park seemed to share this outlook. Laws had been enacted that proclaimed the curiosities of the Yellowstone officially preserved; nothing more was needed.

One who knew better was the editor and owner of America's most-respected sportsmen's periodical, George Bird Grinnell. In an editorial in behalf of the reserve, he had exposed the sham by declaring: "This 'great and glorious government' has again stultified itself by enacting laws without supplying the means to enforce them."[97] In one of the earliest muckraking campaigns in American history, he sought to supply the missing means by exposing the inaction of the government and the greed of the would-be "monopolist." Where there was only a vacuum, Grinnell hoped to establish a *process*, an ongoing administration. Although he would have to struggle almost a decade longer to achieve this goal, his cause was becoming more popular.

One who found the message appealing was the young sportsman-naturalist, Theodore Roosevelt. Although he had already shown an interest in the future of the environment by supporting the creation of an Adirondack forest preserve, it was not until Roosevelt became involved in the battle over Yellowstone National Park that he initiated his career as an active conservationist. Grinnell was the man most responsible for bringing about this involvement, the genesis of which was a book review in *Forest and Stream*.

6

The Boone and Crockett Club

(1) To promote manly sport with the rifle. (2) To promote travel and exploration in the wild and unknown, or but partially known, portions of the country. (3) To work for the preservation of the large game of this country, and, so far as possible, to further legislation for that purpose, and to assist in enforcing the existing laws. (4) To promote inquiry into, and to record observations on, the habits and natural history of the various wild animals. (5) To bring about among the members the interchange of opinions and ideas on hunting, travel, and exploration; on the various kinds of hunting rifles; on the haunts of game animals, etc.

The "purposes and objects" of the
Boone and Crockett Club, founded in 1887,
AS FORMULATED BY THEODORE ROOSEVELT,
GEORGE BIRD GRINNELL, AND ARCHIBALD ROGERS

When the twenty volumes of *The Works of Theodore Roosevelt* (New York,1926) were being compiled by Scribner's, Roosevelt's widow asked that George Bird Grinnell write the Introduction to the first volume,[1] which included *Hunting Trips of a Ranchman* (1885) and *Ranch Life and the Hunting-Trail* (1888). The basis for her request is explained by Grinnell: "It was the writing of a review of 'Hunting Trips of a Ranchman' that brought me into intimate contact with Theodore Roosevelt. I had known him casually as a young man carrying on at Albany a fight for good politics, which commanded wide sympathy, and as interested in the cattle business in Dakota, in which, at the same time, I also was interested in another Territory [Wyoming]; but I had seen little of him until the appearance of this first book of his on hunting and Western life."[2]

The review appeared on July 2, 1885, in "New Publications," one of *Forest and Stream*'s regular sections. It began encouragingly: "Luxurious books upon the better class of field sports are certainly more highly appreciated now than they used to be. . . . Its author is Mr. Theodore Roosevelt, who is best known as an earnest and energetic politician of the best type," and "the excellent work which he has accomplished at Albany shows him to be—if nothing more—a person of exceptionally well-balanced mind, and calm deliberate judgement, and these qualities cannot fail to make their impression in any pursuit to which their possessor may choose to turn his attention."[3]

Continuing, Grinnell took a new tack: "Mr. Roosevelt is not well known as a sportsman, and his experience of the Western country is quite limited, but this very fact in one way lends an added charm to his book. He has not become accustomed to all the various sights and sounds of the plains and . . . mountains, and for him all the differences which exist between the East and the West are still sharply defined." Conversely, "the old-timer who attempts to write of life in the Far West is almost sure to grow prosy. He takes too much for granted, and regards as commonplace a great many features of that life which are, in fact, extremely interesting to those before whom they are brought for the first time. Mr. Roosevelt's accounts of life on a ranch are delightful from their freshness." Despite the favorable elements in Grinnell's comments, it is unlikely that the proud Roosevelt was pleased with the notion that his volume was charming because of its naiveté.

As the review went on, the criticism became more specific: "Where Mr. Roosevelt details his own adventures he is accurate, and tells his story in a simple, pleasant fashion, which at once brings us into sympathy with him. We are sorry to see that a number of hunting myths are given as fact, but it was after all scarcely to be expected that with the author's limited experience he could sift the wheat from the chaff and distinguish the true from the false." In regard to the work's illustrations, Grinnell pronounced most of them "admirable." Nevertheless, he thought a few were very bad, and one, a sketch of a cow elk, he characterized as a "hydrocephalous dwarf."

Grinnell later justified the patronizing tone of his critique by reminding the reader that at the time it was written, "there were not many active writers who had seen so much of the West as I, and who in travelling through it had also given the same careful attention to the ways of the wild creatures."[4] His claim was valid. Whereas Roosevelt's experience was then limited to a two- or three-year period in what is now western North Dakota and eastern Montana, Grinnell's involvement with the Far West began fifteen years earlier, extended over much of its wilderness, and included close association with some of the region's most competent hunters and observers of nature, men like "Lonesome Charley" Reynolds and the North brothers, Frank and Luther.[5] His greater experience is best shown by the fact that he had passed through the valley of the Little Missouri with General George Armstrong Custer's 1874 expedition a decade before the young Roosevelt would begin a ranch there;[6] the same landmarks Grinnell had gazed at, and even helped to name, would be seen years later by an exuberant Roosevelt, who first came to the region to shoot a trophy buffalo.[7]

While Grinnell's criticism of *Hunting Trips* may have been justified, Roosevelt was piqued by the review. He called at the *Forest and Stream* office soon after it appeared to ask for an explanation. Grinnell remembered that "we talked freely about the book, and took up at length some of its statements." The editor must have made a strong case, for Roosevelt "at once saw my point of view."[8]

"After we had discussed the book and the habits of the animals he [Roosevelt] had described," Grinnell recalled,

> we passed on to the broader subject of hunting in the West, which was still to some extent unexplored and unhunted, and to the habits of the animals as modified by their surroundings. I told him something about game destruction in Montana for the hides, which, so far as small game was concerned, had begun in the West only a few years before that, though the slaughter of the buffalo for their skins had been going on much longer and by this time . . . , the last of the big herds had disappeared.

Because of their deep mutual interests,

> Roosevelt called often at my office to discuss the broad country . . . we both loved, and we came to know each other extremely well. Though chiefly interested in big game and its hunting, and telling interestingly of events that had occurred on his hunting trips, Roosevelt enjoyed hearing of the birds, the small mammals, the Indians, and the incidents of travel of early expeditions on which I had gone. He was always fond of natural history, having begun, as so many boys have done, with birds; but as he saw more and more of outdoor life his interest in the subject broadened and later it became a passion with him.[9]

Grinnell's involvement with the natural world had proceeded along the same lines. In passing, it should also be noted that their fascination with the "Wild West" seems to have been sparked in youth by reading the same Romantic novels of Thomas Mayne Reid.[10]

The two had something else in common: "We were both familiar with life on a cow ranch. . . ." After working in western Nebraska on a ranch belonging to William F. ("Buffalo Bill") Cody and the North brothers, Grinnell had decided to buy a spread of his own. In 1883 he purchased land in one of his old hunting grounds, the Shirley Basin of southeastern Wyoming Territory.[11] Like Roosevelt, who bought land in Dakota Territory the same year, he had been lured into ranching by the cattle boom of the early 1880s. Both would suffer large losses when, during the winter of 1886-87, blizzards lashed the ranges of the northern Great Plains and wiped out cattle by the tens of thousands. With the coming of spring, many ranchers found that they were ruined. Only their wealth kept Grinnell and Roosevelt from being included.

As the two talked about their experiences in the West, Grinnell returned often to the subject of hide hunting and showed Roosevelt the published protest he made in the *Report* of the 1875 Ludlow expedition against the commercialization of big game.[12] This document, plus his verbal descriptions of the killing, "much impressed Roosevelt, and gave him his first direct and detailed information about this slaughter of elk, deer, antelope, and mountain sheep. No doubt it had some influence in making him the ardent game protector that he later became, just as my own experiences had started me along the same road [earlier]."[13] In Grinnell's usual self-effacing way he suggested that he may have had some part in shaping the viewpoint of the future President; in fact, as this study will show, he was one of the two individuals who most influenced Roosevelt's conservation philosophy; the other, of course, was Gifford Pinchot.

Grinnell's gentlemanly desire to remain in the shadows, giving others the credit for actions he had initiated, is one major reason why his true importance in the conservation movement has so long been obscured. Unlike Roosevelt and Pinchot, he made no effort to publish an autobiography, and he gave the bulk of his invaluable papers, other than those that dealt with ethnography and Western travels, to a personal friend rather than a public archive. As he wrote a friend in 1897, "Of course, I would rather keep in the background in this matter so far as the public is concerned. . . ."[14]

During those first conversations between Roosevelt and Grinnell, the latter recalled that "we talked of these things [the commercialization of wildlife] at length, and in a vague way foresaw the dangers that already threatened big game in many parts of the West as soon as a point should be reached where their products could be turned into dollars." They perceived that the key factor was "available transportation, for as soon as the skins could be brought to a market, the animals that yielded them would be killed. Destruction had already taken place near the railroads, but though we felt that in time it would follow everywhere, we did not comprehend its imminence and the impending completeness of the extermination." And he added: "Neither had we any comprehension of the attempts that would at once be made to turn into money all our natural things, whether big game, birds, or forests."[15] This statement is typical of Grinnell's self-effacement, for his editorials in *Forest and Stream* prove that he was not as naive as he later suggested.

Grinnell recalled too that "those who were concerned to protect native life were still uncertainly trying to find out what they could most effectively do, how they could do it, and what dangers it was necessary to fight first. We regretted the unnecessary destruction of game animals, but we did not know all it meant, nor had we the vision to look forward and imagine what it portended. So, though we discussed in a general way the preservation of game, it must be confessed—in the light of later events—that we were talking of things about which we knew very little."[16]

Even though Grinnell and Roosevelt may have underestimated the rapidity with which the wildlife of the country would be decimated, they agreed that the game should be preserved "chiefly with the idea that . . . there might still be good hunting which should last for generations."[17] Both men soon decided that some sort of organized effort in this direction should be started. Although hundreds of sportsmen's associations with a similar goal were already in existence, too many of them were concerned only with local wildlife conservation or spent more time talking about protecting game than in actually working for it. As he stated in an 1884 *Forest and Stream* editorial, Grinnell wanted "a live [national] association of men bound together by their interest in game and fish, to take active charge of all matters pertaining to the enactment and carrying out of the laws on the subject. There is abundant material for such a body. Why can it not be organized?"[18]

The establishment of the Boone and Crockett Club, named after two of America's most famous hunters, was the result of this thinking. After Grinnell became intimately associated with Roosevelt, he emphasized the need for an effective sportsmen's society, to do for the larger mammals what the Audubon Society—founded by Grinnell in 1886—was doing for birds. Roosevelt agreed.[19]

Undoubtedly, another influence on both men was the long history of conservation work performed by the New York Association for the Protection of Game, the name the New York Sportsmen's Club, founded in 1844, had assumed in 1874. The organization could, during the 1870s and early 80s, take credit for "much of the legislation . . .

aimed at conserving wildlife in the Empire State. . . ."[20] Robert Barnwell Roosevelt, the uncle of Theodore, was the group's president from 1877 until his death in 1906.[21]

Documentation for the connection between the New York Association for the Protection of Game and the later Boone and Crockett Club is the fact that the longtime counsel for the New York Association, Charles E. Whitehead, later became a member of the Boone and Crockett. It had been Whitehead who had successfully prosecuted the 1875 *Phelps vs. Racey* case against a game dealer in New York City for selling quail out of season. In upholding the verdict, the state appeals court made "a landmark decision supporting state authority to limit the sale of game."[22]

But by the late 1880s, the New York Association for the Protection of Game "was in deep trouble" according to the historian of the Boone Crockett Club, James Trefethen. Its members were being caught up in the "trapshooting craze" sweeping the country, and spending an ever decreasing amount of time on conservation matters.[23]

It was, in other words, an opportune time for a new organization, one that would have a national scope, as well as the self-discipline to stay focused on what was important. With all of these influences, plus his own deep commitment to the code of the sportsman, Theodore Roosevelt invited a number of his sportsmen friends to a dinner party in Manhattan in December, 1887, at which he suggested the formation of a national conservation association.[24] The recommendation was accepted by those present, who included, in addition to Roosevelt and Grinnell, Roosevelt's brother Elliott and his cousin, J. West Roosevelt, Archibald Rogers, E. P. Rogers, J. Coleman Drayton, Thomas Paton, Colonel James E. Jones, John J. Pierrepont, and Rutherford Stuyvesant.[25] All were prominent, wellborn New Yorkers.

A little later, Roosevelt, Grinnell, and Archibald Rogers "formulated the purposes and objects of the organization."[26] There were five in number: (1) "To promote manly sport with the rifle." (2) "To promote travel and exploration in the wild and unknown, or but partially known, portions of the country." (3) "To work for the preservation of the large game of this country, and, so far as possible, to further legislation for that purpose, and to assist in enforcing the existing laws." (4) "To promote inquiry into, and to record observations on, the habits and natural history of the various wild animals." (5) "To bring about among the members the interchange of opinions and ideas on hunting, travel, and exploration; on the various kinds of hunting rifles; on the haunts of game animals, etc."[27]

Regular membership was limited to one hundred men, all of whom had to "have killed with the rifle in fair chase, by still-hunting or otherwise, at least one individual of three of the various kinds of American large game." In its constitution the club declared against "killing bear, wolf or cougar in traps"; "killing game from a boat while it is swimming in the water"; "fire-hunting" (also called "jacklighting," or simply "jacking," which was shooting, at night, animals stunned by the light of a torch or artificial light); and "crusting" (killing animals immobilized in deep snow). From long before the Civil War, American sportsmen had been campaigning against these methods, labeling them as violations of gentlemanly behavior.[28] The emphasis the club's constitution placed on "fair chase" meant that the reform potential in what I have called the code of the sportsman was at last going to be fully realized.

It was probably Grinnell who first pointed out that some provision should be made for those who were not big-game hunters, but who had worked for wildlife preservation. Examples were his two friends, geologist Arnold Hague and Supreme Court lawyer William Hallett Phillips. Though not a hunter, Hague applauded the "healthy manly sport" of hunting and relished eating the game others had killed! It was not hunting, but fishing, that Phillips loved, and he was an enthusiastic member of the "sportsmen's fraternity."[29] Their service for Yellowstone Park entitled them to membership, even though neither man had killed any big game.[30] After some consideration, it was decided that nonhunters could be elected to associate or honorary membership.[31] This rule and article (3) of the constitution were indications that the society was to be more than a dining club of select outdoorsmen.

Another such indication was the fact that when the suggestion was made for organizing the association, those present at the dinner "agreed that such a club could do some good." As soon as the society was formed, Grinnell made every effort to publicize it, hoping thereby to spur the members to action. In the announcement of the club in *Forest and Stream* on February 16, 1888, he wrote: "It would seem that an organization of this description, composed of men of intelligence and education, might wield a great influence for good in matters relating to game protection." And the weekly promised that "the public will be kept advised."[32]

In time its members would include many of the most famous and respected men in America, individuals like Henry L. Stimson, Henry Cabot Lodge, Elihu Root, Owen Wister, Wade Hampton, Gifford

Pinchot, and many others. As a result, the organization's influence would prove far in excess of any ordinary association of similar size. In fact, the Boone and Crockett Club—and not the Sierra Club—was the first private organization to deal effectively with conservation issues of national scope.

Virtually all of the early regular members were from a somewhat similar social background. They had attended college, often at Ivy League schools; they possessed venerable family names; they were financially well-off, if not wealthy; and all were from the East, particularly the New York area. They were part of what some historians have called the American patrician class.[33] The exclusive Union, Metropolitan, University, Cosmos, and Century Clubs were their usual social haunts. Until 1909, when the Boone and Crockett acquired its own center, most of the society's meetings were held in either the University Club in Manhattan or the Metropolitan Club in Washington, D.C.[34]

As is usually the case, the work of the organization was accomplished by only a small number of members, the rest being content merely to attend the annual dinner. Of these active members, Grinnell was the most influential. He formulated almost every idea the club came to stand for; he brought up most of the issues it became involved in; he did a great part of the work on the Boone and Crockett book series on hunting and conservation; and he effectively used *Forest and Stream* as the "natural mouthpiece of the club."[35] In 1896 George S. Anderson, then Superintendent of Yellowstone National Park and a regular member of the Boone and Crockett, expressed the belief that without Grinnell, the club could not continue to exist.[36] And in a letter to Grinnell a year later, Roosevelt acknowledged him as one of the two or three "leaders of our organization."[37] A subsequent director of the society, the noted explorer and naturalist of Alaska, Charles Sheldon, went so far as to declare: "The Boone and Crockett Club . . . has been *George Bird Grinnell* [emphasis in original] from its founding. All its books, its work, its soundness, have been due to his unflagging work and interest and knowledge."[38] Because the statement was substantially correct, its significance lies in the fact that some of the most important figures in the first conservation movement—including its two future leaders, Roosevelt and Pinchot—were members of the club. As former Secretary of the Interior, Stewart L. Udall, has pointed out, "the Boone and Crockett wildlife creed . . . became national policy when Theodore Roosevelt became President."[39] Forests and water could be included in that "creed," for in time the club took as its basic approach Grinnell's idea that all "natural resources"—including national parks—benefited from efficient administration.

This concept, taken from the ideology of the scientific and business worlds, was reinforced by the code of the sportsman, with its emphasis on the use, without waste, of all game killed. As shown by its constitution, one of the club's essential *raisons d'être* was to achieve the wider acceptance of this code. After a year of existence, Grinnell claimed in *Forest and Stream* that the Boone and Crockett had already obtained notable success in this endeavor among "the best classes of society." He observed that with the exception of market gunners, the greatest destroyers of Western wildlife in the past had been upper-class pseudosportsmen. He affirmed, however, that in the last year the members of the club had ceaselessly expressed "their views about the folly and the wrong of wanton butchery, and their opinions on sport are therefore spread among that very class which in the past has given most offense in this respect." As a result, "those who used to boast of their slaughter are now ashamed of it, and it is becoming a recognized fact that a man who wastefully destroys big game, whether for the market, or only for heads, has nothing of the true sportsman about him."[40]

The importance the club's leaders placed on the etiquette of sport is illustrated by their stance in regard to Adirondack deer "hounding" (the use of dogs to drive deer into water where they are shot or clubbed to death). As usual, Grinnell had led the way with an editorial in *Forest and Stream* published three years before the club was founded. In the issue of November 6, 1884, he asked rhetorically: "What is Adirondack deer hounding? . . . Is hounding a legitimate way to kill deer in the Adirondacks? . . . Ought it to be abolished? Can it be abolished? Will it be abolished?"[41] This was the beginning of a seven-month campaign to end the practice, which he described as "destructive, unsportsmanlike and brutal."[42] *Forest and Stream* printed petitions against hounding and sent them all over the state.[43] After being returned with thousands of signatures, they were forwarded to the Assembly in Albany.[44]

Tangible results were achieved when, in late winter, 1885, a bill was introduced in the Assembly to prohibit the custom. *Forest and Stream* agitated for its passage,[45] and by May this had been accomplished—twice in fact[46]—but Governor David B. Hill hesitated to add his signature.[47] Adirondack hotel owners and guides, as well as wealthy visiting "sportsmen," were against the legislation. Nevertheless, the anti-hounders had their way, and the bill became law the next month.[48]

Although the statute quickly resulted in a greatly reduced slaughter of deer,[49] the more effective it became in eliminating hounding, the greater the agitation by hotel keepers, guides, and pseudosportsmen to have it repealed. By early 1886, this effort had become a groundswell.[50] Though *Forest and Stream* circulated petitions to retain the law,[51] the opposition was too great, and in May, 1886, the New York Assembly repealed the prohibition.[52]

Although hounding again became one of northern New York's favorite fall pastimes in the following years, *Forest and Stream* had succeeded in making this form of recreation suspect among many of the state's sportsmen. One who needed no further encouragement to be anti-hounding was the Boone and Crockett Club's president, Theodore Roosevelt. Then on the Civil Service Commission in Washington, D.C., he wrote Grinnell on January 13, 1894: "Don't you think the executive committee plus Madison Grant[53] . . . might try this year to put a complete stop to hounding in the Adirondacks? Appear before the Legislature, I mean. I wish to see the Club do something."[54] Later in the same month, he again urged Grinnell to "meet Madison Grant and have a talk over whether the Club could not take some action . . . about hounding deer in the Adirondacks."[55]

This was the beginning of a Boone and Crockett effort that continued sporadically for several years. Finally, in May, 1897, New York's governor signed a bill prohibiting, for five years, both hounding and jacklighting. Several members of the club—including Grinnell, who testified at the hearings—were responsible for the introduction of the legislation and its passage. Nevertheless, the lion's share of the credit belonged to Madison Grant, who carried on a series of face-to-face negotiations with various senators and assemblymen.[56]

When the five years expired, New York's deer hunters had decided that the use of dogs and lights was unsportsmanlike, and the prohibition became permanent. Other Eastern states quickly followed New York's example by forbidding these practices.

The club's interest in the preservation of big game naturally inclined it toward Yellowstone National Park. By the time that book review brought Grinnell and Roosevelt together, *Forest and Stream* and Senator Vest had already spent several years in crusading for the reserve. They had been joined in this effort by Samuel S. Cox. A graduate of Brown and an eminent member of the lower house of Congress, this New Yorker was the most faithful defender of the park in the House until his death in 1889.[57] Cox was also a dedicated angler—he once made what he called a "pilgrimage" to the tomb of Izaak Walton—

and he worked diligently to preserve fishing opportunities in the Potomac.[58] Though historian Roderick Nash asserts that Cox's advocacy of the reserve was "in the tradition of the Transcendentalists and Frederick Law Olmsted [the landscape architect],"[59] it is more likely that his commitment was based on the code of the sportsman, a tradition far older than American Transcendentalism or even European Romanticism.

Another adherent to the code of the sportsman was Theodore Roosevelt.[60] Describing his early relationship with Roosevelt, Grinnell later recalled that "the original attempt by a certain group of men to secure for their own profit control of all the important attractions of the park had been defeated before I knew him well, but as soon as he understood about the conditions in Yellowstone Park, he gave time and thought to considering its protection."[61] It would not be long before he joined Grinnell, Vest, Phillips, and Hague in actively working to establish a "government" for the park.

Between the time Grinnell and Roosevelt got together and the beginning of Roosevelt's active participation in the crusade, *Forest and Stream* continued to supply the public with a barrage of information on the park, including the state of the Vest bills in Congress, the dangers to the preserve, exposés of ineptitude and corruption in its handling, and definitions of the reservation's meaning for the American people.[62] Besides his newspaper efforts, Grinnell also acted as a lobbyist for the Vest bills, despite the fact that his patrician contempt for political maneuvering made the work disgusting to him. In early 1887 he wrote the well-known plainsman, Luther North, that "lobbying is the meanest work I ever did. I would rather break broncos for a living than talk to Congressmen about a bill. It makes me feel like a detested pickpocket to do it." And the worst part was that after enduring "this shame," the bill he had worked for failed to pass.[63] It was Grinnell's deep sense of public service that kept him from giving up. With the commitment of the true muckraker, he told a friend: "We failed at Washington as I supposed we would, but I feel that, after all, truth is mighty and will prevail, and it is a newspaper's duty to kick with as much regularity and vigor as possible."[64]

Forest and Stream continued to "kick." Its newest tactic was the publishing of a seven-part model petition containing Grinnell's justifications for protecting the park, which he asked all sportsmen's clubs to copy, endorse, and send to Congress.[65] Later, *Forest and Stream* began issuing its own petitions, which it distributed across the country. Each week the names of the signatories were printed in the weekly.[66]

The first public record of Roosevelt's participation in the crusade for Yellowstone is found in the *Forest and Stream* issue of April 3, 1890. The paper reported that he, Phillips, Hague, Captain F. A. Boutelle, the Superintendent of the reservation, and a few other "friends of the park" had been present at a recent meeting of the House's Public Lands Committee.[67] Under consideration was the latest Vest bill. Although Hague and others spoke, Roosevelt remained silent; evidently, he was still only an interested observer.

Soon, however, he was actively involved. By late April, Grinnell was able to write Hart Lyman of the *New York Tribune* that Roosevelt could now be counted among the reserve's most enthusiastic defenders. Like Phillips, Hague, and the others of its guardians, Grinnell believed that Roosevelt had no other "motive in this matter, except the proper preservation of the Park."[68]

But exactly what that "preservation" entailed soon became a source of potential disunity among the group. The issue was over whether a railroad should be allowed in the park. Captain Boutelle thought that such an "addition" would reduce Western opposition to the reserve, while doing it no material harm. To obtain a better idea of its needs, Roosevelt visited the reservation in late 1890. When he returned, it appeared to Grinnell "that Boutelle had converted him to a belief that a [rail]road would be beneficial to the Park."[69] Grinnell was particularly upset about this development, both because of his friendship with Roosevelt and because it would remove one of the preserve's most influential allies.[70]

Despite these considerations, Grinnell's commitment to his principles was then, as always, more important than friendship. He asked Hague and Archibald Rogers, another member of the Boone and Crockett interested in the park,[71] to try and "win Roosevelt back to his allegiance on this matter." But if they could not, "of course, we must throw him overboard."[72] Luckily, such a drastic move proved unnecessary, as one or both of these men did manage to bring him back to his original position. On December 24, 1890, Grinnell wrote Rogers: "I am glad to hear that Roosevelt is going to stand back on the question of railways in the Park and not to work against us."[73]

With the arrival of 1891, the leaders of the Boone and Crockett galvanized themselves for a new effort in behalf of Yellowstone. The club's annual dinner was going to be held on January 14th at the Metropolitan Club in Washington, D.C., and Roosevelt wanted to use the occasion to emphasize to government officials the need for action. At the time, Grinnell was so busy with *Forest and Stream* matters that he thought he would be unable to attend. He changed his mind only after receiving an urgent plea from Roosevelt.[74] The dinner was kept informal,[75] even though Roosevelt had invited a gallery of notables. As president of the Boone and Crockett, he presided over the table. On his left sat Secretary of War Redfield Proctor,[76] and on his right, Speaker of the House Thomas B. Reed. Grinnell sat opposite Roosevelt, with Secretary of the Interior John W. Noble on one side and Samuel Pierpont Langley, physicist and Secretary of the Smithsonian Institution, on the other. A number of Congressmen, including Henry Cabot Lodge, Arnold Hague, William Hallett Phillips, and a few others, also attended.[77]

At a business meeting beforehand, Grinnell and Roosevelt drew up a series of resolutions which were read at the dinner: "*Resolved*, That the Boone and Crockett Club, speaking for itself and hundreds of [sportsmen's] clubs and associations throughout the country, urges the immediate passage by the House of Representatives of the Senate bill for the protection and maintenance of the Yellowstone National Park. *Resolved*, That this club declares itself emphatically opposed to the granting of a right of way to the Montana Mineral Railroad or to any other railroad through the Yellowstone National Park."[78]

After Roosevelt and Phillips made short speeches on the requirements of the reservation, one of the Congressmen asked a number of questions that were answered by Hague and Roosevelt.[79] "We then got to the subject of . . . large game," Grinnell reported to Archibald Rogers, "and Langley, in response to a request from Roosevelt, said that he believed from what he had heard, that the large game of the Continent would be practically exterminated except in such preserves as the Yellowstone Park, within the life of the present generation of men." The Secretary had probably obtained this viewpoint from Grinnell. The two had been in communication on wildlife matters for some time, and Langley had already incorporated at least one of Grinnell's suggestions. This was his idea for having the National Zoological Park, which the Smithsonian controlled, acquire the Yellowstone reserve's surplus bears and other unwanted predators, rather than destroying them as was done formerly.[80]

After the Secretary had made his comment, "Roosevelt . . . asked me to say something of the way in which game had disappeared in my time," Grinnell continued in his letter to Rogers, "and I told them a few 'lies' about buffalo, elk, and other large game in the old days." Clearly, Grinnell's long and varied experience in the presettlement West had entitled him to Roosevelt's esteem.[81] When he finished his description of "the old days," a general conversation followed until about eleven o'clock when the group broke up.[82]

Grinnell felt that the dinner had been a success, because "we excited a real interest," and he was now "more hopeful than . . . for two or three years."[83] Despite his optimism, the railroad lobby proved successful in keeping the House from considering the Senate bill before the end of the session.[84]

The future was not all black, however, as the issue was gaining a wider currency in the nation's periodicals. For some time, Grinnell had successfully used his position as the editor of *Forest and Stream* to foster unity of the press by encouraging fellow newspapermen to join his banner.[85] In view of the growing demand by the press that the park be protected, Robert Underwood Johnson of *Century Magazine* asked Grinnell to head a "Defense Association" that he hoped to found for the purpose of fighting for Yellowstone and the recently created Yosemite Park. Because Grinnell was the leader in the Yellowstone movement, Johnson thought he was the logical man for the job. But Grinnell declined, confidently asserting that the Boone and Crockett Club would be able to achieve, at least for Yellowstone, the necessary legislation. He told Johnson that though the society appeared superficially to be only "a dining club of about 30 big game hunters," the "good social standing and more or less position and influence" of its members meant that the association had great potential.[86] Events would prove him right.

It should be noted here that this is the same "R.U." Johnson who had to goad John Muir into writing articles for *Century* in behalf of expanding an already existing state reserve into Yosemite National Park. Johnson's effort began in 1889, though Muir did not publish the requested articles until late 1890.[87] As we have seen, George Bird Grinnell needed no such prodding to launch his campaign to protect Yellowstone National Park, which included enlarging it, and defining how all national parks should be treated in the future. And his editorial barrage against the inactivity of the federal government began in 1882, with some preliminary "shots" even earlier. Yet, historian Stephen Fox published a book in 1981 entitled *John Muir and His Legacy: The American Conservation Movement,* obviously implying that the entire conservation crusade derived from this one man, who was, in reality, a relative latecomer to conservation—and a reluctant one at that! But because Fox cannot ignore Grinnell, he labels *Forest and Stream*'s editor "the ubiquitous early leader of eastern conservation,"[88] seeming to suggest that there were two conservation movements, one in the East and one in the West. Of course, there were not, as demonstrated by the fact that both Grinnell and Johnson were editors of New York periodicals fighting for Western lands.

Johnson's offer to Grinnell to direct an association for defending national parks did have one result, however; it encouraged the leaders of the club to think about expanding their organization. On May 7, 1891, Grinnell wrote to Hague that "I am rather disposed to think with you that it is quite within the purview of the Boone and Crockett Club to care for these Parks, but in order to do that it will be necessary, as you say, to enlarge the scope of the club and to get in a great number of new members." The distribution of influence in the association is revealed by Grinnell's admonition that Hague consider the other side of the question: "You and I can now control the action of the Boone and Crockett in these matters, as you say, but if that club were ten or one hundred times as large, could we still do so?"[89]

By 1892, the park situation had changed little. The *Forest and Stream* office continued to act as a kind of clearinghouse for information received from Phillips, Roosevelt, and Hague in Washington, and from various Western informants, including the superintendents and Elwood ("Billy") Hofer, an experienced hunter and the reserve's principal guide and outfitter.[90] These intelligence reports were digested and incorporated into both editorials and pamphlets; the latter were distributed to the leading newspapers and every member of Congress.[91]

Forest and Stream's activity was matched by the park's Washington guardians. Roosevelt, Phillips, and Hague participated in hearings on the park held by the Public Lands Committee of the House early in 1892, and defended the reservation against the railroad lobby.[92] Later in the year, they sent Grinnell the endorsements he had requested[93] for his editorials. When *Forest and Stream* published "A Standing Menace" on December 8th, which attacked the railroad interests, the paper followed it the next week with supporting letters from Phillips, Roosevelt, and George S. Anderson, a sportsman and the reserve's latest superintendent.[94]

By now, the railroad threat had taken a new form. Because those who were pushing for the right of way had been effectively blocked on the grounds that a line through the park would be an infringement on its "integrity," they reasoned that the perfect solution to the dilemma was to have the area in question cut off from the rest of the preserve and returned to the public domain. Legislation known as the "segregation bill" was introduced into Congress to accomplish that end. If passed, it would have removed 622 square miles from the northeastern portion of the park. This was the "Standing Menace" alluded to in Grinnell's editorial. Roosevelt's letter on the subject, dated December 5, 1892, is noteworthy:

> I have just read the article "A Standing Menace," printed in the *Forest and Stream*, in reference to the attempts made to destroy the National Park in the interests of Cooke City.[95] I heartily agree with this article. It is of the utmost importance that the Park shall be kept in its present form as a great forestry preserve and a National pleasure ground, the like of which is not to be found on any other continent than ours; and all public-spirited Americans should join with *Forest and Stream* in the effort to prevent the greed of a little group of speculators, careless of everything save their own selfish interests, from doing the damage they threaten to the whole people of the United States, by wrecking the Yellowstone National Park. So far from having this Park cut down, it should be extended, and legislation adopted which would enable the military authorities who now have charge of it to administer it solely in the interests of the whole public, and to punish in the most vigorous way people who trespass upon it. The Yellowstone Park is a great park for the people, and the representatives of the people should see that it is molested in no way.[96]

Obviously, Roosevelt had resolved his earlier indecision on the issue of railroads in the park. He now firmly believed that they represented a grave threat to the reservation, even in the form of "segregation." This is all the more significant, since he held this opinion in the face of "backsliding" by one of his Washington co-workers. Arnold Hague now favored segregation. He was weary of the seemingly endless crusade and wanted to finish his survey work, which was being held up by the controversy over the park's future. It is also possible that political pressure had been exerted on him through the Geological Survey to drop his opposition to the railroad interests.[97] This defection pained Grinnell. As he told Phillips, "I felt badly that he [Hague] should disagree with the rest of us. I must say that I am sick of this whole Park business, but it is one of the cases where you cannot very well stop fighting."[98]

Despite the desertion in his camp, Grinnell found the American public coming around to his position. The pamphlets *Forest and Stream* was continually printing and distributing were proving especially effective. The many thousands who saw the paper each week were met with the following appeal: "Every reader who appreciates the gravity of the situation, who would see the Park preserved, for his children and his children's children . . . is invited to assist in the Park defense movement by putting these circulars where they will best create public sentiment." And, he added, "the reprints will be sent in any desired numbers, post paid, to any address."[99] So many readers responded that the company most involved in trying to "develop" Yellowstone was receiving such a volume of adverse mail that its publicity agent visited the *Forest and Stream* office to demand that its side also be printed.[100]

Even when the segregation bill passed the Senate in February, 1893, Grinnell successfully used his paper to keep it from passing the House. P. J. Barr, a paid lobbyist for the railroad interests, had sent a telegram to leading Democrats in Montana asking them to apply pressure on Charles F. Crisp, Speaker of the House, to have the legislation forced through. A copy of the telegram fell into Grinnell's hands, and he printed it in *Forest and Stream,* accompanied by a sarcastic editorial entitled "Will Speaker Crisp Be Deceived?" The Speaker may not have been deceived, but he was certainly embarrassed, and the hopes of the railroad lobby were crushed for that session of Congress.[101]

Although the reserve's guardians were making some progress in their efforts to involve the public in the future of Yellowstone, they would not obtain final victory until they received the unwilling aid of a poacher. It all began when Superintendent Anderson assigned his chief scout, Felix Burgess, to watch the Pelican Creek area of the national park. In October, 1893, a buffalo herd had been sighted there, and Anderson knew that if the notorious poacher, Edgar Howell, were in the park, he would concentrate his activities in that vicinity. At the time, buffalo heads and robes were bringing large sums from taxidermists who hoped to stock up before the species became extinct.

A few months later the Superintendent's hunch paid off. It was a cold March day, and the snow was so deep that Burgess and his companion, a trooper named Troike, were using skis to make their reconnaissance. While scouting Astringent Creek in Pelican Valley, they happened on a man's trail. Following it, they found a cache of half a dozen fresh buffalo heads hanging in a tree and, farther on, a tepee. While the two were examining the lodge, six shots sounded close by. Moving to the top of a wooded slope, they looked down on a human figure busily skinning a fallen buffalo, while several others lay in the snow near him. Burgess recognized Edgar Howell. The situation was delicate, since Burgess and Troike had only a single .38-caliber revolver between them, while Howell, a man known for his savage temper, had a repeating rifle. Still, there was one chance. Because Howell needed both hands free to flay his kill, he had leaned his rifle against one carcass while working on another. Taking this opportunity, the scout drove his ski poles into the snow and raced down the slope. Howell was so intent on his work that by the time he looked up, it was too late. Burgess was standing only a few feet away, his gun pointed in the poacher's direction.[102]

What made this incident more than an isolated encounter in the wilderness was the presence in the park of a *Forest and Stream* reporter, Emerson Hough.[103] In addition to being a dedicated sportsman,[104] he achieved fame for his many historical romances, including *The Story of the Cowboy* (1897), *The Passing of the Frontier* (1918), and *The Covered Wagon* (1922). In later years, Hough demanded full credit for supposedly seizing on Howell's arrest as an opportunity for publicizing the needs of the park. In reality, he was at first "unwilling to take the responsibility of sending a telegram to *Forest and Stream*" and finally did so only after being argued into it by Anderson and Hofer.[105]

The story first appeared on March 24, 1894. In "A Premium on Crime" the weekly protested: "The occurrence calls public attention again and most forcibly to the criminal negligence of which Congress has been guilty for all these years in failing to provide any form of government for the Park, or to establish any process of law by which crimes against the public committed within its borders can be punished."[106] Succeeding issues continued to hammer away in the same vein.[107] In "Save the Park Buffalo" *Forest and Stream* asked "that every reader who is interested in the Park or in natural history, or in things pertaining to America, should write to his Senator and Representative in Congress asking them to take an active interest in the protection of the Park." Another editorial dramatically underscored its point with three photographs of slain buffalo in the snow.[108]

The call was answered by the American people.[109] Eight years earlier, a railroad spokesman's rhetorical question—"Is it true that the . . . demands of commerce [meaning a right of way through the park] . . . are to yield to . . . a few sportsmen bent only on the protection of a few buffalo"[110]—went almost unchallenged. Now, these "few sportsmen" were joined by a significant percentage of the articulate public. After other papers followed *Forest and Stream*'s lead, the Howell capture "created an interest throughout the country. . . ."[111] Carefully prepared by the continuous teachings of Grinnell's weekly, the nation was at last beginning to realize that it owned Yellowstone National Park and its wildlife. The poaching incident revealed the speed with which its property was being eaten up by a greedy few. The resulting sense of loss was intensified by the sentimental attachment felt for the buffalo, the symbol of the virgin West, now that the animal and the life it represented seemed doomed. *Forest and Stream* had perpetuated the idea that the survival of the species depended on those in the park. As a consequence, what alarmed the public about the Howell case was that even though the poacher had destroyed only a few buffalo, he had killed "enough to show that, with a little more time, he would have exterminated the herd altogether."[112]

Only a week after *Forest and Stream* first reported the incident, Congressman John F. Lacey of Iowa, a member of the Boone and Crockett Club, introduced a bill in the House similar to the ones Vest had presented in the Senate so many times before. But now the legislation found little opposition. In early May it emerged from committee, passed both Houses, and was signed by President Cleveland on the 7th.[113]

The "Act to Protect the Birds and Animals in Yellowstone National Park" was the victory that Grinnell, and later the Boone and Crockett Club, had fought for so long. It incorporated the park within the United States judicial district of Wyoming, making the laws of that state applicable except where federal law took precedence. Killing animals, except to protect human life or property, was forbidden. All traffic in wildlife, alive or dead, removal of mineral deposits, and destruction of timber were also prohibited.

The emphasis in the act was on enforcement. A commissioner appointed by the United States Circuit Court would reside in the park to judge cases. He would be backed up by a force of United States marshals who could arrest, without process, anyone caught violating a regulation. Possession of dead wildlife was to be considered *prima-facie* evidence of guilt. The penalty for this or other infractions was a fine of up to $1,000 or a jail sentence of up to two years, or both. To house the lawbreakers, a jail would be constructed in the preserve.[114]

Despite the satisfaction the passage of this legislation brought the guardians of the park, they knew the law was not perfect. All believed, for example, that the clause allowing the killing of animals that endangered life or property would be misused in the future. Still, the act was as close to ideal as could be had. Although "the . . . bill is not perfect," Grinnell wrote Roosevelt, "with a good man at the head of the Interior Department, and a good superintendent, it will prove effective."[115] To ensure the proper enforcement of the regulations, Roosevelt and Phillips immediately took "steps to see that good men are appointed for deputy marshals."[116]

Historians agree that Grinnell and *Forest and Stream* deserve most of the credit for passage of the Lacey bill.[117] But as we have seen, the publicity given the Howell case entailed an attack on the "criminal negligence" of Congress. In a manifestation of an attitude that would later produce the famous assault on the "muckrakers," Roosevelt complained that Grinnell's blanket condemnation of the national assembly had been uncalled for. Because Roosevelt was a latecomer to the Yellowstone crusade, Grinnell may have been irritated by this somewhat presumptuous judgment of his tactics. Nevertheless, he politely answered: "I am glad to have your suggestions and entirely agree with you that as a rule it does not do much good to blackguard Congress as a whole. This has been done in a very moderate way in *Forest and Stream,* and for a particular purpose, which purpose seems to have been accomplished in just the way we wished to have it." Although he felt that William Hallett Phillips "has of late years done more than anyone else for the Park," Grinnell fed Roosevelt's substantial ego by declaring: "You personally have done a great deal and ought to be 'blown off' for your help." As was customary, he took no credit for himself.[118]

In founding a policy and administration for the nation's first national park, Grinnell and his co-workers had established precedents that would be followed in the handling of all later parks. As one historian has observed, "the provisions of the Lacey Act . . . formed the basis for the present law and policy under which the National Park Service has administered the natural treasures of the United States since 1916,"[119] the year that agency came into existence.

In *A Brief History of the Boone and Crockett Club* (1910), Grinnell explains that "the attempt to exploit the Yellowstone National Park for private gain in a way led up to the United States forest reserve system as it stands to-day,"[120] because "as a natural sequence to the work that they [the club's leaders] had been doing" in regard to Yellowstone Park "came the impulse to attempt to preserve western forests generally."[121] Since their original concern had been the park, it might seem odd that concrete results on the forestry question were obtained three years before the passage of the Lacey bill. The reason for this was simply that the battle over the park took place in a public arena against determined Western opposition, while the results in forestry were achieved by circumventing the popular forum. Nevertheless, the interrelationship of the two issues is shown by the fact that the first forest reserve President Harrison chose to set aside in 1891 was the Yellowstone National Park Timberland Reserve adjacent to the national preserve. "In essence," says one observer, "the Yellowstone became the birthplace for both the national parks and national forests."[122] He might have added that the systems for managing both were created largely by members of the Boone and Crockett Club.

As in the case of Yellowstone National Park, Grinnell led the club on the forestry issue. The editorial effort he began in 1882 to transform the nation's orientation toward its woodlands continued unabated throughout the decade.[123] The central thrust of these sophisticated but simply stated expositions was that "the Federal government must husband its resources and place them under systematic management,"[124] the purpose of which was utilization without waste. Grinnell emphasized, in fact, that not to use resources was in itself wasteful: "The proposal to lock up the forests and prevent all further utilization of their products is one that cannot be entertained."[125] The latter statement was made in 1888 and matches exactly the policy that would be established in future years by two other Boone and Crockett members, Gifford Pinchot and Theodore Roosevelt.

In the late 1880s *Forest and Stream* repeatedly asserted that the concepts and techniques of scientific forestry could only be effectively adapted to American conditions "by entrusting the administration of the forests to a skilled executive." Until forestry schools could be established in the United States capable of producing such a man, Grinnell requested "the importation of a competent staff of European officers."[126] Given the situation then existing, with the forests being wastefully cut down and burned over and the government unwilling or unable to reverse the destruction, he urged that the timberlands be "absolutely closed and the laws against trespass rigidly enforced."[127] But it is plain that he thought this drastic move should only be a stopgap, to save the woods until a plan for their administration could be drawn up and put into effect.

In "Popular Forestry Instruction," *Forest and Stream*'s editorial for December 6, 1888, Grinnell included a brief history of the weekly's crusade for the introduction of forestry in the United States.[128] He claimed, and probably with justice, that it had been the paper's seven-year campaign that had stimulated so much interest in the subject throughout New York State that the Assembly was finally forced into action. "They drafted a bill admirable in every detail, and displayed a praiseworthy zeal in incorporating every good suggestion in it; they appointed a Forest Commission, whose duty it would be to undertake the economic and scientific administration of the State forests, restock denuded areas, bring the whole under a high system of conservancy, establish chairs of forestry in our universities and colleges, and above all, to diffuse among the people at large a mass of popular literature, designed to enlighten them as to the economic importance of properly conserved forests." Now, he complained, the public thought that no further action was necessary when, in reality, nothing substantial had been accomplished. The reason, he affirmed, was that the men filling the newly created offices had no professional training or expertise.[129]

With an attitude approaching resignation, Grinnell wrote: "And so there is nothing for us [to do] but to recur to the subject from time to time, and keep alive the public interest in the problem, the attempted solution of which will probably constitute the severest test of the capacity of a republican government to deal with great economic questions, which the Government of the United States has ever been exposed to."[130] How right he was became increasingly obvious as the democratic West tried to block every federal effort to bring about land stewardship—an effort initiated mainly by the Eastern elite.

While Grinnell was acting in his usual capacity as the instigator of public opinion, William Hallett Phillips was busy in his customary role as a behind-the-scenes negotiator. He was "a resident of Washington [D.C.], a Supreme Court lawyer with a large acquaintance there." Because of this position, and the fact that he was a member of "one of the oldest and best-known Washington families," he was "tuned in" to all the latest legislative and political developments.[131]

Like others in the Boone and Crockett Club, Phillips had arrived at his interest in forestry via his involvement in the crusade over the Yellowstone. "In 1887 Phillips . . . had succeeded in interesting Mr. [Lucius Q.C.] Lamar, Secretary of the Interior, and a number of Congressmen, in the forests, and gradually all these persons began to work together. At the close of the first Cleveland Administration, while no legislation had been secured looking toward forest protection, a number of men in Washington had come to feel an interest in the subject."[132]

In 1889 President Benjamin Harrison appointed John W. Noble of Missouri Secretary of the Interior. As in the case of his predecessors, Noble received the "treatment" from the directors of the Boone and Crockett as soon as he entered office. This consisted of personal visits from Phillips, Hague, and Roosevelt, and invitations to the club's dinners. But one all-important difference was that Noble, unlike his forerunners, was highly receptive to the organization's expression of concern for the forests.

Why this should be true is not entirely clear. Although Noble was later an associate member of the Boone and Crockett Club, it is not known whether he ever hunted for recreation or accepted the environmental obligation inherent in the code of the sportsman. But it is known that he admired hunters and hunting, as he revealed in an obituary of his old chief, Benjamin Harrison. In that memoir Noble argued that it was Harrison's well-known love for sport hunting (see the "Photo Album" of the present work) that helped explain his success as a lawyer and a man.[133] This claim was, of course, one of the basic themes in the sporting tradition.

Regardless of whether Noble was a sportsman himself, he seemed to enjoy the attentions of the prestigious Boone and Crockett Club, and he was in close touch with at least two of its members, Phillips and Grinnell, by 1889. In fact, the latter believed that it was Phillips, who was already a good friend of the Secretary of the Interior, who was most responsible for involving Noble in the effort to preserve Western forests.[134] On March 9, 1893, Grinnell published "Secretary Noble's Monument" in *Forest and Stream,* in which he wrote: "It will be remembered that *beginning* [emphasis added] with the Yellowstone National Park, which was brought to the notice of Mr. Noble early in his administration, he has given much attention to the question of our parks and timber reservation[s]"; this statement undoubtedly refers mainly to the efforts of William Hallett Phillips.[135]

Grinnell's relationship with Noble began in the spring of 1889. In addition to his conservation work, Grinnell was also a dedicated champion of Native Americans.[136] After trying for months to oust an Indian agent who was exploiting the Blackfeet of northwestern Montana, he suddenly achieved success when the new Secretary of the Interior interceded personally in the affair after being alerted by Phillips.[137] From that time to the end of Noble's term in office, the Secretary and *Forest and Stream*'s editor were in frequent communication on both conservation and Indian matters.

Parenthetically, it should be noted that Noble played a key role in placing federal control over the region around Yosemite Valley, which had been set aside as a state park in 1864. President Benjamin Harrison, who had been an "aesthetic conservationist" for years—as shown by his proposal for a Grand Canyon national park as early as 1882— enthusiastically signed a bill to preserve the area around Yosemite Valley on October 1, 1890. Noble helped to determine the future of Yosemite by deciding, on his own, to change the name of the reservation from "reserved forest land" to *national park.*[138] The earlier efforts of the

Boone and Crockett Club in behalf of Yellowstone National Park and Western woodlands, and the personal friendship between W. H. Phillips and Noble, undoubtedly helped make the Secretary of the Interior receptive to the arguments of John Muir and R. U. Johnson for Yosemite preservation.

Following the position long held by *Forest and Stream,* Noble came to agree that in order to save the timberlands, they would have to be withdrawn from the public domain.[139] The means for accomplishing this end were provided on March 3, 1891, when "An Act to Repeal Timber Culture Laws and for other Purposes . . ." was signed by President Harrison. Pushed through at the close of the Fifty-First Congress, the legislation was an effort to revise the land laws of the United States. Those who worked hardest among the members of Congress to have the bill approved were Bernhard Fernow, Chief of the Division of Forestry, and to a lesser degree, Hague and Phillips.[140]

The granting of power to the President to set aside woodlands was the last of the bill's twenty-four sections, being "inserted in [the] Conference Committee in the last hour of Congress," Fernow recalled later, "by the insistence of Mr. Noble, that he would not allow the bill to be signed by the President unless the clause was added."[141] Soon after the passage of the bill, Hague "saw Secretary Noble and [suggested] . . . the setting aside of the Yellowstone Park Forest Reserve adjoining the Park."[142] His aim, as Grinnell explained at the time, was "protection for the territory south and east of the Park, which it has so long been hoped might be added to the reservation."[143] Noble liked Hague's idea, but before acting, he wanted to be sure there were no legal pitfalls. To resolve this question, Hague returned the next day with William Hallett Phillips, Noble's friend and adviser, and all three discussed the legal question. After dismissing all doubts, Noble carried the project to the President, who promised to give the order. The dimensions of the proposed tract were discussed in several conferences between Noble and Hague and, finally, on March 30, 1891, President Harrison issued the proclamation setting aside the first forest reserve. Calling the tract the Yellowstone National Park Timberland Reserve, Harrison defined its boundaries in exactly the same language Hague had used in his proposal to Noble.[144]

Though this land would be administered differently from the national park, it eventually obtained real protection when the Forest Service eliminated wasteful logging and uncontrolled fire, the two factors that had previously threatened its existence. At the same time, crucial wildlife habitat was preserved and hide hunting eliminated. In one sense, therefore, Harrison's proclamation was the culmination of the effort Grinnell had begun in 1882 to have Yellowstone Park extended on the east and south, an effort which Phillips and Hague had later taken up.

The Yellowstone reserve contained 1,239,040 acres, all in Wyoming, and was the inauguration of the national forest system, which presently totals about 191 million acres. Shortly after its establishment, Roosevelt, representing the Boone and Crockett Club, endorsed the action and commended Harrison and Noble.[145] The Secretary's reply of April 16, 1891, is one of the most significant documents in the early history of American conservation, because Noble told Roosevelt why he proceeded as he did. After thanking Roosevelt for the club's generous endorsement, Noble stated: "*Your associates, Mr. Phillips and Mr. Hague, brought the business to my attention* [emphasis added]. Having been familiar with the subject, I had no hesitation in immediately advising the President favorably as to the proclamation, and I am glad to see that he has promptly appreciated the situation and acted as he did."[146] The fact that Noble mentions Phillips first reveals just how important he was in convincing Noble to take this all-important step.

In crediting Noble with inserting the key lines in the 1891 act, most historians have followed John Ise, who published *The United States Forest Policy* (1920). Although he admitted that the history of this issue was vague, Ise nevertheless accepted Bernhard E. Fernow's later claim that he and Edward A. Bowers of the American Forestry Association "had educated Noble up to the point" of demanding the insertion of the forest-reserve clause.[147] While Fernow and Bowers deserve credit for exerting some influence, Phillips, who was a personal friend of Noble's, was more important—as shown by the Secretary's letter. But unlike Fernow, Phillips left no readily accessible documentation of his role. Like some other patrician pioneers of conservation, "he . . . labored long and earnestly for the public good [but] . . . preferred that his efforts should not be known, and that others should receive the credit for what he did." This quotation comes from George Bird Grinnell's unsigned obituary of Phillips, who drowned near Washington, D. C., on May 9, 1897, but Grinnell could have been describing his own penchant for anonymity just as easily.[148]

Besides the letter of thanks coming from Roosevelt and the Boone and Crockett Club, Grinnell also expressed his gratitude to Noble and Harrison in *Forest and Stream,* and urged the public to accept the reserve and the policy it represented.[149] Some years later, Noble would gratefully acknowledge the aid Grinnell and "his very popular and influential paper" had given him, before and after the forest reserve system was initiated.[150]

From this discussion, it would appear that Yellowstone National Park was a focal point of the early dialogue on "natural resources"—to use that term in its broadest sense. After "conservation" gained currency, some of its supporters employed the word only in reference to resource "use"; those areas emphasizing the aesthetic were ordinarily excluded. As we have seen, when Grinnell was working out his ideas for the future of the Adirondacks, he may have shared this outlook. Soon, however, he came to regard the handling of all natural resources, including national parks, as being part of "conservation," since they all benefited from *continuous,* efficient management. This sense of the need for process was inherited by the directors of the Boone and Crockett Club, who, under Grinnell's leadership, became involved in the future of the national park. Their approach was his approach, the basis of which was the demand for a "government" for the reserve. By this, they meant an administration that would have the power and assured continuity to enforce effectively a series of regulations. This emphasis on the need for continuous, efficient enforcement is clearly evident in the 1894 act, and the application of its provisions to the national park was the first time a specific, publicly owned natural resource had received such systematic treatment.

The second reason the battle over the Yellowstone was a focal point of early conservation was because it was one of the first times a resource-related issue gained national popular support that included nonsportsmen as well as hunters and fishermen. Only the fish-culture movement (Chapter Three) attained a similar popularity, but it lacked the emotionalism attending the crusade to preserve Yellowstone. The uproar caused by the Howell poaching incident shows that by 1894 there existed something approaching a mass concern for the park. While other issues like forestry and irrigation remained without public understanding or backing, a significant segment of "the people" clamored for the protection of "their" national park. Their involvement in the drive was based on sentimentality—the desire to see the buffalo saved—rather than on a deep scientific or aesthetic appreciation. Yet it was the beginning of an ever-greater willingness to acknowledge the crisis in natural resources and accept the need for concerted national action.

In later years, as we saw in Chapter Three, both Roosevelt and Pinchot maintained that forestry was the first issue to gain and keep mass support for conservation. Roosevelt is attributed with saying: "The conservation movement was a direct outgrowth of the forest movement. . . . Without the basis of public sentiment which had been built up for the protection of the forests, and without the example of public foresight in the protection of this, one of the great natural resources, the conservation movement would have been impossible."[151] But these words came from the conservation chapters of Roosevelt's *Autobiography*, which historian Samuel Hays is probably correct in assuming were written by Gifford Pinchot and James R. Garfield, Roosevelt's last Secretary of the Interior.[152] Because of their central positions in the Progressive conservation crusade, historians have uncritically accepted the Roosevelt-Pinchot viewpoint.[153]

It is likely, however, that the two were reflecting their own, later concentration on forestry as the focus of conservation, rather than their memory of how the movement actually began. An example of Roosevelt's selective "memory" is the fact that in his autobiographical sketch for *Who's Who,* he neglected to mention that he had unsuccessfully run for the Presidency in 1912![154] As to Pinchot's concern for what occurred in conservation before he arrived on the national scene, we have the following comments from the beginning of his published memoirs: "This is not a formal history, decorated and delayed by references to authorities. As to nearly every statement it contains, you will have to take it or leave it on my say-so. About many parts of the story of forestry in America from 1885 to 1910, I am the only living witness," and "that is another reason why you must take my word or leave it."[155]

Long before the public had a comprehension of the principles and practices of scientific forestry, or even an awareness that the timber stocks were supposedly[156] in danger of being exhausted, it knew that many kinds of mammals, birds, and fishes were rapidly disappearing. The public's attention was drawn first to wildlife because the disastrous consequences of unregulated industrial growth were most obvious in terms of this resource. As the most accessible, it was depleted first; and as the most conspicuous, its loss was noticed first. An individual might not understand nor care about forestry statistics, but he or she felt regret at viewing an empty prairie that had been darkened only a few years before by thousands of buffalo. The completeness with which the supposedly countless bison was wiped out provided the earliest, and the most dramatic, challenge to the nineteenth-century myth of the inexhaustibility of resources.[157]

One person who eventually perceived the incompatibility between myth and reality was Theodore Roosevelt. Although he had expressed an interest in 1884 in the movement to set aside an Adirondack Preserve, his orientation toward the outdoors was still as a sportsman-naturalist who had not yet fully accepted the environmental obligation intrinsic to the code of the sportsman. Except for two ornithological studies published in the 1870s and one history work in the early 1880s, his first books dealt with hunting in the West. While they reveal that Roosevelt possessed the code of the sportsman, these volumes do not manifest the same commitment to the perpetuation of natural resources so much a part of the later Boone and Crockett Club book series created and edited by him and Grinnell. Under the latter's tutelage, Roosevelt's love for big-game hunting soon developed into a concern for the future of big game, as he became increasingly aware of the speed with which it was disappearing. The belief that Yellowstone National Park was its last refuge was the origin of his involvement in the crusade for that preserve, which, in turn, was the beginning of his active career as a conservationist. It was only somewhat later that he became concerned, first, for the forests of the Yellowstone, and still later, for the Western forests generally.

The third reason for calling the campaign for the Yellowstone a focal point of early conservation was that it brought together for the first time several of the most important leaders of the national conservation movement. These included Arnold Hague, who would become Gifford Pinchot's assistant and co-worker in the forestry field, Roosevelt, and Pinchot himself. Although Pinchot was not actually involved in the Yellowstone fight, it was the extension of the Boone and Crockett Club's interest in Yellowstone's forests to Western forests as a whole that made them want Pinchot for a member when they heard of his professional ability; he joined the organization in 1897.

The fourth and last reason why the crusade for Yellowstone represents a focal point of early conservation has already been given: Yellowstone was not only the birthplace of the national parks and the policy for administering them—it was also the cradle of the forest reserves. These were the building blocks of the national forest system, the single most important element in the Roosevelt-Pinchot conservation program.

By the middle 1890s, a conservation movement that had started to take shape two decades earlier was now well-developed, and its full flowering was just around the corner. Of those who had set the course for the future, none had been more important than George Bird Grinnell. For all those twenty years, he had been at the center of the evolution of conservation and was intimately involved in legitimizing the place of the sportsman in American society and consolidating that group's increasing dissatisfaction with disappearing game and habitat; in bringing about better enforcement of game statutes by changing the public's attitude toward lawbreakers; in fighting off the assaults on the nation's first and, for a long time, only national park; in achieving a clear-cut definition of the meaning of the park and establishing a policy for its administration, and for all the parks to follow; in co-founding and directing the Boone and Crockett Club, the first conservation organization in the United States to deal effectively with issues of national scope; in arousing an interest, first in New York State and later throughout the country, in the future of the nation's forests; and in planting in the public mind an incipient awareness of the fact that in order for "natural resources" to be used and enjoyed by human beings, while lasting indefinitely, they must be administered on a continuous, scientific, apolitical basis.[158]

Grinnell's impact had been great, but it would be greater still when a friend, whose conservation philosophy he had done much to form, became Governor of New York and then President of the United States. The friend, of course, was Theodore Roosevelt.

7

Establishment of a
National Conservation Policy

*George Bird Grinnell . . . and Gifford Pinchot were the two strongest
influences in shaping the conservation philosophy of Theodore
Roosevelt, which is largely the basis of the modern conservation
program in America.*

LETTER OF JAMES B. TREFETHEN,
historian of the Boone and Crockett Club,
to the author, October 23, 1967

When Roosevelt assumed the governorship of New York in
early 1899, he discovered that all ideas for improving the
handling of the state's natural resources had to be channeled
through an already existing administrative body: the New York State
Fisheries, Game, and Forest Commission. Although the agency was
established some years before, it had accomplished little, as its members
were customarily appointed solely on the basis of political influence.
Grinnell had been editorializing since 1888 to have the administration
of New York's resources separated from politics; efficient management
of the state's natural assets would be obtained, he asserted, only if
they were put into the hands of impartial experts.[1]

With the ascendancy of his friend to New York's highest political
office, Grinnell's wish for a reconstituted commission might now be
granted. As he observed in May, "the state of New York is fortunate at
present in having a Governor who is not only deeply interested in all
matters of game, fish and forest preservation, but [who] also has so
clear an acquaintance with these subjects that he can always be
depended upon to act on them for the public good." And, he added,
even when Roosevelt's own great knowledge proved insufficient, he
knew exactly which "expert advisers" to call on for aid.[2] Of these,
Grinnell would continue to be the most important.

One of the manifestations of the commission's ineptitude was its
total failure to enforce game laws. Inadequate law enforcement was a
problem Grinnell had been publicizing for almost two decades, and

175

one which Roosevelt had taken up when he joined the crusade for the Yellowstone. In a letter addressed to the commission, dated November 28th and printed in *Forest and Stream,* the Governor attacked the utter inefficiency of the state's game wardens and requested the commissioners to provide him with a full report on the wardens' capabilities, distribution, and numbers.[3]

In referring to the needs of New York's northern mountain region, Roosevelt foreshadowed his later emphasis on forestry as the focus of his national conservation program. He asked that the commissioners concentrate their efforts on the Adirondacks, "both from the standpoint of forestry and from the less important but still very important standpoint of game and fish protection."[4] Here, in capsule form, was the Roosevelt plan for the state's—and later the nation's—natural assets. Although wildlife and other resources would be a significant part of the plan, its major emphasis would be the woodlands.

It was probably for this reason that the Governor's first proposal for improving the efficiency of the commission was to eliminate four of its members, making it a single-headed agency.[5] The source of this idea was Gifford Pinchot, who had visited Roosevelt soon after he took office, and offered his suggestions for reforming the administration of New York's natural resources.[6] As in later years as Chief Forester and President Roosevelt's lieutenant, Pinchot revealed a lack of interest—at least as far as *public policy* was concerned[7]—in any resource except the forests. In proposing an agency headed by a single commissioner, he expected that the official's time would be spent wholly in adapting the principles and practices of scientific forestry to the state's timberlands. Then, as later, Pinchot seemed to assume that if the forests were properly managed, all other resources would be adequately protected in the process.

Grinnell could not agree. One man might be sufficiently versed in forestry to administer the woodlands properly, but it was highly unlikely that he would be equally knowledgeable about the other major resource categories. To ensure that the whole field was covered, the editor of *Forest and Stream* advocated splitting up the commission into sections and putting a commissioner at the head of each. The number of commissioners would then be reduced from five to three, and their departments would be forestry; game and fish protection; and fish culture and oyster farming. As in his earlier editorials on this subject, he emphasized that the only way to establish efficiency in the agency's functioning was to staff it with apolitical professionals.[8]

Grinnell's continuing influence on Roosevelt is shown by the fact that when the Governor announced his reconsidered plan for the makeup of the commission, he had discarded Pinchot's suggestion for a single commissioner and adopted Grinnell's proposal for a three-headed agency, differentiated into separate departments.[9] Evidently, Roosevelt had concluded that even though Pinchot's plan was simpler and had the advantage of stressing forestry, it inadequately provided for the administration of the other major resources.[10]

In the end, neither plan was adopted. Because the commission was a source of patronage, the state's politicians were unalterably opposed to any change in its basic character. Under the circumstances, Roosevelt's last hope for improving the agency lay in his right to nominate new members for the commission when the old one expired by limitation on April 25, 1900. If qualified men could be appointed, the fact that their terms would be five years long meant that much future good might be accomplished. Particularly important, of course, was the president of the commission. A competent individual in this position could affect for the better the whole tenor of the agency.

When Roosevelt announced his nominations, it was immediately apparent that he had picked such a man. The Governor's choice was W. Austin Wadsworth, sportsman and president of the Boone and Crockett Club. In his editorial of March 10th Grinnell applauded the Wadsworth nomination, but in regard to Roosevelt's other selections, he proved that once again his commitment to principle was more important than friendship. He expressed the hope that Wadsworth would be able to control the other members, for he was the only one "who appears not to have been selected without regard to politics." In brief biographical sketches Grinnell condemned in turn each of the other four nominations.[11]

Soon after the editorial appeared, Roosevelt wrote Grinnell in dismay: "Today I found . . . your paper . . . being actively circulated by the men who are here [in Albany] in the interest of the lumber . . . and cold storage [shippers of game] lobby to defeat my nominees for the Forest, Fish and Game Commission, the argument being that as the men interested in forest, fish and game preservation cared so little for the new nominees, and as every political and financial interest was enlisted against them, there was no possible object in making the change." Ironically, those who desired the perpetuation of unregulated lumbering and game traffic had discovered an unexpected ally in one who had long been their worst enemy.

As the Governor's letter went on, it was obvious that he was more hurt than angry. Feeling that Grinnell had unfairly censured his nominees, he proceeded to give a detailed, self-justifying explanation of how and why each of them was selected. Roosevelt told Grinnell that he had no idea of the obstacles the Governor had to overcome when there was "no effective popular feeling one way or the other about the forest or the preservation of fish and game," and when the lobbyists of the lumber and cold-storage interests and "every politician in the state" were working to have the old commission retained. In an implied slap at Grinnell's "armchair politics," Roosevelt asserted: "I chose the men the way I did because my business was to improve the Commission—not to issue a manifesto about them."[12]

In essence, Roosevelt's defense was valid. Although Grinnell was not a stranger to political maneuvering, he was still somewhat naive about the difficulties a politician had to face, and surmount, before a reform measure could be implemented. While Roosevelt was in full agreement as to the value of Grinnell's goal, the Governor knew, as an experienced political tactician, that compromise was the key to success.

Roosevelt's letter points out another, more important, difference between the two men. When it came to reform, Roosevelt prided himself on being a "doer," a man of action. Grinnell, on the other hand, was a creator and amalgamator of ideas, who, as the historian of the Boone and Crockett Club has observed, "was a pusher rather than a leader, working behind the scenes and quietly steering the energies of more active public officials into constructive channels."[13] Despite their occasional disagreements, this is precisely the relationship he had with Roosevelt.

Evidently, the Governor had adequately vindicated himself, for Grinnell told him on March 17th that his additional information on the nominees put them in a different light. "A pretty strong point in their favor," Grinnell concluded, was "the fact that the wood pulp . . . and cold storage men are trying to prevent . . . their confirmation. . . ."[14]

Despite the opposition, the New York Senate confirmed the nominees on March 20th. Four days later, Grinnell backed up his new view of the men by cautiously endorsing the Senate's action in *Forest and Stream*. He commented that because of Roosevelt's genuine interest in the work the commission was to undertake, it was inconceivable that he would have picked unqualified men. But, he added, "the work of the new commission will be watched with great interest."[15]

As if to obtain a more positive endorsement of his action, the Governor asked Grinnell to attend the preliminary meeting of the new commission at which Roosevelt was to give a talk outlining his expectations of the officials. The fact that Grinnell was still foremost among those whose opinions on natural resources Roosevelt trusted is shown by the Governor's question: "Can you suggest any first class men interested in forestry and fish and game whom it would be a good thing to have come here at the same time?"[16] Grinnell did attend, and he brought along a few of the "first class men" Roosevelt had asked for.[17] Afterwards, Grinnell told the Governor he was pleased with the speech to the commissioners and thought that it would achieve the desired result.[18]

Under President Wadsworth's leadership, the agency did accomplish much good. At the beginning of the administration of Governor Benjamin B. Odell, Roosevelt's successor, a sportsman's periodical, *The Gun,* stated that "in checking pollution of streams alone, its service has been of inestimable value. . . ."[19] Pollution had been a target of the commission ever since Governor Roosevelt's annual message of January, 1900. Besides sounding very much like Grinnell in emphasizing that what was needed in the field of natural resources was not more laws but better enforcement of existing statutes, the Governor also spoke out against pollution. Repeating arguments that had been appearing in sporting literature since before the Civil War, Roosevelt put particular stress on the contamination caused by pulp mills and its ruinous effects on fishing.[20]

Because the editor of *Forest and Stream* had been unsure at first of how conscientious the new conservation commission would prove, it may seem strange that its course was laid out largely according to ideas that he himself had formulated. This is not really surprising, however, when it is remembered that the agency's director was also president of the Boone and Crockett Club and very much under Grinnell's intellectual sway. Most of the recommendations made by the commission had been expressed earlier in *Forest and Stream* or at the meetings of the Boone and Crockett Club, and they had originated, invariably, in Grinnell's fertile mind. Examples were the proposed amendment to the state constitution that would permit the practice of "conservative forestry" in the Adirondack Preserve, the setting aside of state game refuges, and the abolition of spring waterfowl shooting.[21]

Roosevelt's tenure in the office of governor came to an end in late 1900. His major conservation accomplishments were the expansion of public concern for the state's natural resources and the vitalization of the agency responsible for administering them. The two-year term was really too short, however, to do more than begin the work required. When Roosevelt received, and accepted, the Vice-Presidential nomination in June, 1900, Grinnell was disappointed that he had not "held out" for the Presidency, believing that the lesser post might prove to be a dead end for his friend's political career.[22] Ironically, an assassin's bullet gave him the opportunity for implementing conservation that Grinnell thought was lost. When Theodore Roosevelt took the Presidential oath of office at 3:00 p.m. on September 14, 1901, a new era in the history of the American land began.

The conservation achievements of his administration were vast. The most important were the addition of 148 million acres to the forest reserves,[23] called "national forests" after 1907; the creation of a professional Forest Service that would efficiently manage the tracts according to the principles and practices of scientific forestry; the establishment of five national parks and eighteen national monuments; and the founding of an extensive system of wildlife refuges containing fifty-one units.[24]

Although Roosevelt's conservation program has been thoroughly examined by historians—who now consider it his most enduring accomplishment—they have overlooked the fact that the fundamentals of that program were foreshadowed in a series of books he coedited years before. These were the three Boone and Crockett Club volumes on hunting and conservation that he and Grinnell compiled during the 1890s: *American Big-Game Hunting* (1893), *Hunting in Many Lands* (1895), and *Trail and Camp-Fire* (1897). In one or more of these works can be found the demands that the federal government expand the national parks and forest reserves, establish a means for systematically administering them, and create a series of game refuges. As we have seen, all these proposals had been expressed earlier in *Forest and Stream*.

It was during the late 1880s that Roosevelt began acquiring the ideas he would later establish as national policy, and the fact that he repeatedly chose Grinnell to be his coeditor pinpoints the special advisory relationship the latter had to the future President. About 1891, the two men had first begun to talk of the desirability of publishing a book made up of contributions by club members on hunting and natural history, plus editorial material furnished by themselves. They seemed to feel that such a volume would help to consolidate the members and their ideas, and increase the prestige of the club by making its reform efforts better known. The first book was such a success that they decided to initiate a series, and their literary partnership continued until Roosevelt became President.

Whenever there was a problem in interpretation, Roosevelt customarily acceded to Grinnell's greater experience and knowledge. When, for example, he wrote him about a paper submitted by a club member for the 1897 volume, Roosevelt told Grinnell: "Of course, whatever you wish to do . . . , I will gladly agree to."[25] Later, in discussing another matter pertaining to the same book, he replied to Grinnell: "All right—I am sure your judgment is correct. Early in July I will be able to send you my two articles."[26]

As the book neared completion, Grinnell—who, as usual, seemed to be doing most of the work—informed Roosevelt that he still had not received all the papers requested of the club members. Roosevelt replied: "I am sorry you should be so short of copy. . . . If there is any real difficulty about copy, I should suggest that you and I write a composite article (unless, which I believe, you could do it alone) on the past and present distribution of the big game animals of temperate North America, with a short description of each." As a bit of encouragement, he added: "Our first two volumes are really very good. I was looking over them the other day; and we must try to make this [one] up to the [same] level." If they were successful in this, he told Grinnell, and "the fellows don't come forward better in the future than in the past, we will simply stop publishing volumes until they do."[27]

When *Trail and Camp-Fire* appeared later that year, Roosevelt's expectations were fulfilled. In a letter to Grinnell, he judged it "the best volume we have put out yet." He was especially pleased with Grinnell's title choice, which he called "a particularly good one."[28] The critics seemed to share Roosevelt's enthusiasm, for in a list of 4,332 volumes published during 1897-98, the New York State Librarian ranked it as one of the best fifty.[29]

From their close association as the leaders of the Boone and Crockett Club, Roosevelt received a thorough exposure to Grinnell's ideas for handling the nation's natural resources. There is little question that he was the original source of many of the concepts Roosevelt later established as national policy. During the formative 1885-97 period, Roosevelt absorbed not only Grinnell's ideas, but also his point of view. In reviewing the evolution of Grinnell's thought on natural resources, three main themes can be delineated.

The first was a product of his involvement with the more sophisticated, academic approach to Western exploration initiated by the Yale University dinosaur-hunting expedition of 1870 (Chapter Four). At the same time that Grinnell's field work in paleontology and zoology under Professor Othniel C. Marsh had made him aware of the changes the earth and its life forms had undergone, he had witnessed, first-hand, what I have called, in a book on his early life, *The Passing of the Great West*—the destruction in the period 1870-83 of both the remaining bison herds and the free-ranging Indian cultures that depended on them. His scientific studies leading to the Ph.D. and his Western experiences, particularly the shock of discovering commercial hide hunters operating inside Yellowstone National Park on the 1875 Ludlow expedition, taught Grinnell that the land was vulnerable. This insight helped lead to a concern about how natural resources were being abused, a major source of his commitment to reform.

The second theme in Grinnell's conservation thought was his application of the business community's ideology to the handling of natural resources, especially the idea that they could be "managed" like a firm. Whether forests or wildlife, if only the "interest" was used and sufficient "capital" left behind to produce the next generation, renewable resources could be utilized indefinitely without fear of shortages.

The third and most important theme in Grinnell's thinking is what I have termed the "code of the sportsman," the Old World, aristocratic ethic that had been taking hold in America since at least the time of William Elliott and Henry William Herbert. After Grinnell absorbed the code himself, he disseminated it through the pages of his *Forest and Stream,* the leading outdoor newspaper of the last quarter of the nineteenth century. It became part of the value system of countless hunters and anglers across the nation, including the members of the Boone and Crockett Club.

The assumption that there was only one correct way for a "gentleman"—or a would-be gentleman—to pursue game, and that all other methods were crude, or even immoral, was the most fundamental component of the code. But there were other key ingredients as well. One was the requirement of noncommercial use, without waste, of all game killed. Another part of the code that would achieve ever-greater importance as time went on was the demand that sportsmen take responsibility for the perpetuation of their sport, which meant that they must work for the conservation of the game and the habitat on which it depended. Finally, they would extend this concern even to nongame, as Grinnell did with the creation of the Audubon Society, and Roosevelt did, when, as President, he established fifty-one national wildlife refuges.

In passing, it should be emphasized that the claim of one historian that the purpose of these refuges was the "perpetuation [of hunting] by protecting the reproductive cycles of key game species"[30] is simply mistaken. In fact, the first sanctuaries were set aside mainly to protect birds from *commercial* hunters, who were shooting nongame species for the millinery trade. These were the same hated market hunters who Grinnell had established the Audubon Society to stop. The original refuge, Pelican Island in Florida, was created in 1903, and while it may have had some pelicans nesting on it, the main breeding species there were egrets, ibises, and roseate spoonbills. None of these, of course, had ever been considered game birds by sportsmen.

Despite the claims of virtually every academic historian since Samuel Hays published his *Conservation and the Gospel of Efficiency* in 1959, wildlife, and not forests, was the first natural resource to attract enough support to produce a public policy for its preservation and management in perpetuity. As a Boone and Crockett Club publication put it in 1915:

> The fact must be emphasized that the history of conservation will show that a generation or more before that [concept] was made a principle to be applied to our other natural resources, the sportsmen of this country had established and applied it to the preservation of our game.[31]

It can be seen that the three themes in Grinnell's thinking had certain elements in common. All, for example, tended toward an emphasis on the need to eliminate waste and produce efficiency. This was even true of the code of the sportsman, with its taboo against the wanton destruction or waste of game. The primary common factor, however, was a belief in the *perpetual* responsibility of the nation for its natural resources, including national parks and nongame wildlife, and a confidence that these assets could be enjoyed forever if only administered on a continuous, apolitical, systematic basis.

This is the "point of view," mentioned above, that Grinnell passed on to Roosevelt. When the latter became President, he too made the efficient administration of resources the cornerstone of the Progressive conservation creed. Both men, and Pinchot as well, shared a patrician's sense of *noblesse oblige* about their innate right, and ability, to set policies for protecting "the people's" natural assets from those who would use them up for short-term financial gain. As we saw in Chapter One, this ideology, which to those who disagreed with it probably seemed like paternalism, had long been a part of the thinking of elite sportsmen. By always stressing the utilitarian and democratic aspects of their program, Roosevelt and Pinchot were able to obtain at least the minimal political support required for success. As those who have worked in the environmental field know, the charge of "elitism" against those who try to protect the natural world is still heard today, particularly in the West.

In examining the development of Grinnell's thinking on conservation, one is struck by its versatility. Beginning with Samuel Hays, academic historians have tended to pigeonhole the environmental leadership in American history into "conservationists," those who want to use and "manage" the natural world for human benefit and who implicitly possess an inferior ecological and aesthetic understanding, and "preservationists," those who want to keep the natural world as it is and who implicitly possess a superior ecological and aesthetic understanding. Like so many other sportsmen activists, Grinnell bridged these two categories, which are more theoretical than real.

In fact, all aspects of human interaction with the natural world benefit from continuous, apolitical, systematic "management." This is just as true of national parks and wilderness areas as it is of national forests and wildlife refuges. Among the issues that have to be addressed on an on-going basis are infrastructure maintenance, fire control, elimination of alien flora and fauna, and regulating human-wildlife interplay; this last activity can include everything from park rangers keeping campers and grizzly bears apart, to federal wardens checking anglers' catches in waterfowl refuges.

It is time to discard the old preservation-versus-conservation dichotomy and realize that, in the end, it is all "conservation." When Grinnell editorialized against hunting in Yellowstone National Park, in order to turn the reservation into an inviolate wilderness and wildlife sanctuary, he was an "aesthetic conservationist"; the same was true when he conceived, and led, the later effort to establish Glacier National Park in northwestern Montana. But when he called for the adoption of systematic forestry in the United States, based on the European model, he was a "utilitarian conservationist"; the same could be said, of course, for his efforts to perpetuate waterfowl populations and duck hunting—which he loved to the end of his life—by campaigning to establish bag limits and set seasons.

By the time Roosevelt reached the Presidency, he, too, understood that if one is concerned about the entire natural world and humankind's relationship with it, one has to be both a utilitarian and aesthetic conservationist. Thus, he not only proclaimed national forests that would be selectively "harvested" according to the principles of scientific forestry, but also national wildlife refuges and national monuments, some of which, like the Grand Canyon in Arizona and Mount Olympus in Washington, would become the cores of great national parks.

There can be little doubt that his urgency in protecting these "monuments," which seemed to exceed his executive authority under the Antiquities Act of 1906,[32] was at least partly the result of his experience in the early fight to save Yellowstone National Park from despoliation. After he had joined Grinnell's campaign for the Park, which was the beginning of his active career as a conservationist, Roosevelt found that years more of effort would be necessary before legislative success came in 1894. As President, he found it so much more "efficient" to use his executive authority to set aside areas he wanted preserved.

In addition to ignoring Grinnell's influence on Roosevelt's thinking in the period before 1900, historians have also exaggerated the role of Gifford Pinchot. Because Roosevelt appointed him as his chief administrator, historians have focused on the forester. The literature on him is extensive and includes several biographies.[33] Scholars appear to assume that before Pinchot made his appearance, Roosevelt had little real interest in conservation reform. Even those who point to his record as New York's governor emphasize that it was at the beginning of Roosevelt's tenure in that office that Pinchot became his adviser. This portrait of the forester's indispensability is partly the result of Pinchot's own brush strokes, for in his autobiography he spares no efforts to prove that *he* was the conservation movement.[34]

The fact is that Pinchot originated few ideas. His great contribution to conservation lay in his talents as a manager, one who implemented concepts already familiar to Roosevelt. In essence, he was the "trained professional" Grinnell had first called for in 1884, who would lead the nation in the "inauguration of a system of forest conservancy."[35]

After leaving the Presidency, Roosevelt stated that the men most responsible for the success of the original conservation movement were Pinchot and James R. Garfield, his Secretary of the Interior: "I saw them work while I was President, and I can speak with the fullest knowledge of what they did. They took the policy of conservation when it was still nebulous and they applied it and made it work. They actually did the job that I and the others talked about."[36] Here, as elsewhere, Roosevelt pays tribute to the public officials who administered his conservation program, but at no time does he acknowledge those who influenced him *before* he came to the Presidency.

There is, in fact, much evidence to indicate that Grinnell played a crucial role in bringing Pinchot and Roosevelt together. In his autobiography the forester states that it was through C. Grant LaFarge, son of the famous artist and Secretary of the Boone and Crockett Club, that he met Roosevelt in 1897, although they did not begin to work together until early 1899. Actually, Pinchot had met Roosevelt on May 21, 1894, but the encounter seems to have been forgotten by the forester. While LaFarge may have actually arranged the 1897 meeting, Grinnell, and probably Arnold Hague, induced it. Since 1894, Grinnell had been publicizing Pinchot's forestry work, emphasizing that he was one of the first to apply to American conditions the theoretical principles of the European science. By 1896, he and Pinchot were well acquainted, and the latter thought enough of Grinnell, as an expert in his own right, to ask him to be one of the contributors to a special issue on the forest reserves that Pinchot was compiling for *The Forester,* a publication of the American Forestry Association.[37]

In attempting to explain the origins of national conservation, historians have neglected the intellectual antecedents of Roosevelt's policy. This study has found that Grinnell, the originator and synthesizer of ideas, *prepared* Roosevelt for Pinchot, who executed those ideas. From the first consultation with the Governor in 1899, Pinchot was impressed with Roosevelt's grasp of forestry and his enthusiasm for suggestions on how the timberlands could be utilized and perpetuated simultaneously.[38] Behind that receptivity were almost fifteen years of tutelage by George Bird Grinnell.

Probably the best demonstration of Roosevelt's deep respect and admiration for Grinnell was his effort to save *Forest and Stream.* Two years after Roosevelt left the Presidency, in April 1911, Grinnell parted with the weekly after an association of thirty-five years. When he left, the quality of the periodical, particularly the natural history section, rapidly declined. Roosevelt was so alarmed by this development that he arranged a luncheon at Oyster Bay to which he invited Grinnell, together with *Forest and Stream*'s new editor and several of the nation's leading naturalists, to talk over what might be done to rectify the situation. It was decided to establish a "Governing Board" picked by Roosevelt to advise the journal's new owners. But the editor put the names of famous naturalists like Grinnell, C. Hart Merriam, George Shiras, 3d., Carl E. Akeley, Edmund Heller, and Wilfred H. Osgood in the periodical's masthead simply as a gimmick for selling newspapers; the "governing" board was never allowed to govern. With much sadness, Grinnell and Roosevelt watched *Forest and Stream*'s standing continue to deteriorate; it went from a weekly to a monthly in 1915, and finally ceased publication in August, 1930, after first selling its subscription lists to the present *Field & Stream*.[39]

Historians may be oblivious to Grinnell's place in the development of the original conservation movement, but Roosevelt's contemporaries were not. After he died, a group of his friends formed the Roosevelt Memorial Association and in 1923 created the Roosevelt Medal for Distinguished Service. When, in the spring of 1925, the presentations were made in the outdoor-conservation field, it was no accident that Grinnell and Pinchot were given medals at the same time and coupled as "pioneers"—the word President Coolidge used in the White House ceremony. Because there was only one award in each category, Pinchot appropriately received the medal for conservation, while Grinnell's prize was in the "promotion of outdoor life."[40] The important point is that in the minds of the Association's members, many of whom were Roosevelt's old friends and fellow naturalists, Grinnell, Pinchot, and the late President were inextricably linked.[41]

Only one scholar has perceived this relationship. James B. Trefethen, historian of the Boone and Crockett Club, delineated it in a letter to the author: "George Bird Grinnell . . . and Gifford Pinchot were the two strongest influences in shaping the conservation philosophy of Theodore Roosevelt, which is largely the basis of the modern conservation program in America."[42]

It is indeed ironic that the individuals who established that program were sportsmen, for if they lived today, they would find themselves being increasingly accused of insensitivity to nature and its wild things. But if an affinity for hunting and fishing—which often entails the taking of life—is a manifestation of insensitivity, then how does one explain the fact that American sportsmen were, by far, the single most important group in the making of conservation?

Epilogue

Aldo Leopold and the Continuing Tradition of the Sportsman-Conservationist Ideal

To My Father, Carl Leopold, Pioneer in Sportsmanship.

DEDICATION PAGE OF ALDO LEOPOLD'S
Game Management (1933)

cologist, conservationist, and philosopher Aldo Leopold was
born in Burlington, Iowa, on January 11, 1887, the same year
the Boone and Crockett Club began half a continent away.
Though of different generations, Leopold and the founders of the
Boone and Crockett shared a common tradition, the foundations of
which had been laid down across the Atlantic even before the United
States came into being. Leopold, Roosevelt, and Grinnell grew up in
a sportsman's world, where they not only had abundant opportunities
to hunt and fish, but where they learned to accept responsibility for
the game and its habitat.

On July 16, 1933, Leopold became Professor of Game Management
at the University of Wisconsin, a post he would hold until his death.
Though the title description of his position had been "narrowed down
to game management" from the broader, original "chair[man] of
conservation,"[1] it was clear that preserving wildlife for the future would
be the focus of Leopold's research and teaching.

Elated conservationists from around the United States wrote
congratulatory letters, including the mercurial and hyperbolic William
Temple Hornaday, who had predicted the imminent extinction of
numerous species. He called the appointment " 'a helpful gesture in
the struggle to save American game *and sport* [emphasis added] from
finally going over the precipice, A.D. 1940.' "[2]

During his years at the University, Leopold would become
increasingly well-known among wildlife biologists, forest managers,
and wilderness advocates. His book, *Game Management*, published
shortly before he accepted his professorship, would become the
definitive work in the field. Terms like game "harvesting" and the

"carrying capacity" of the habitat, when applied to issues like deer overpopulation, are in such wide use today that we forget that it was Leopold who popularized them, and established the discipline of wildlife management.

It would not be for his 1933 *Game Management*, however, that Leopold would become celebrated around the world, but for another work, *A Sand County Almanac*, first published in 1949, a year after his death. The book sold only moderately well until 1966, when Oxford University Press published a paperback edition that rode the tidal wave of rising environmental concern sweeping across the nation. Rachel Carson had awakened the country to the dangers of pesticides in *Silent Spring*, which appeared in 1962, and Congress had passed the Wilderness Act two years later. As Curt Meine, the biographer of Leopold, tells us, "Sales of *A Sand County Almanac* skyrocketed as a new generation of readers, eager to learn about and understand their natural surroundings, seized upon Leopold's words." He "became the 'priest' and 'prophet' of the environmental movement" and "*A Sand County Almanac* . . . the movement's 'bible' or . . . 'scripture'."[3] A founder of the radical environmental organization, Earth First!, went so far as to call Leopold's book " 'not only the most important conservation book ever written, [but] . . . the most important book ever written' "![4]

Academic historians have been equally laudatory. Beginning with Roderick Nash's well-known *Wilderness and the American Mind*, first published in 1967, and coming down to the present in works by William Cronon, Donald Worster, and Hal Rothman, among many others, Leopold's reputation as a "visionary" continues to grow.[5] According to these scholars, every element of the *proper* relationship between human beings and the natural world can be found in *A Sand County Almanac*.

The book was the culmination of a lifetime of thinking about our species' place in nature. "Providing the core for modern conservation ethics,"[6] it is probably best known for Leopold's advocacy of "the land ethic." People "abuse land," he wrote, "because we regard it as a commodity belonging to us. When one sees land as a community to which we belong, we may begin to use it with love and respect." Simply put, "A thing is right when it tends to preserve the integrity, stability, and beauty of the biotic community. It is wrong when it tends otherwise."[7]

If we take the ethic literally, as Leopold intended, a sport hunter who assumes, however unwittingly, the role of the exterminated wolf and cougar and "preys" on a white-tailed deer, removing it from an ecosystem where deer have exceeded the carrying capacity of their habitat, is following the land ethic. But an animal-rights advocate, however well-intentioned, who succeeds in getting deer hunting banned in the same ecosystem, even though both the habitat and the deer herd itself are degraded in the process, is acting against the land ethic. Rather than being incompatible with this code of conduct toward the natural world, the sportsman-conservationist tradition was, in fact, the cornerstone of Leopold's ethical edifice. Documentation for this conclusion comes from the writings of Leopold himself, from the memories of his eldest daughter, Nina Leopold Bradley, and from a book entitled *Aldo Leopold: The Professor* (1987), written by Robert A. McCabe, who received his Master of Science and Doctor of Philosophy degrees under Leopold and who would later occupy the same position, now entitled "Professor of Wildlife Ecology," at the University of Wisconsin.

McCabe became a close friend of Leopold and his hunting and fishing partner. According to him, Leopold "learned the ethics of the chase and the value of wildlife from his father, who was a sportsman/hunter when game was plentiful in the Midwest, prior to the turn of the [twentieth] century."[8] Despite game abundance, Leopold "and his brothers were schooled in hunting behavior, restraint, moderation, and subtlety, a reverence for the species hunted."[9] In the many years since Leopold's death, McCabe grew weary of trying "to explain the respect and reverence that a hunter feels toward his quarry"; it was, he said, "like trying to describe the color blue to a person born blind." Despite the frustration that Leopold and McCabe experienced in trying to communicate with those who had not grown up in the traditions of the rod and the gun, McCabe believed that "in the years that I knew A. L. (and before), he tried with a skill possessed by no other to articulate the compatibility of a hunter's love for the object of the hunt." Leopold "taught, as he learned from his father, that without reverent rapport with game animals, the person behind the weapon is reduced [merely] to a shooter who resists any management effort that interferes with his own [innate] desire to exploit."[10]

The recollections of Leopold's eldest daughter, Nina Leopold Bradley, corroborate McCabe's characterizations of his mentor's thinking. In a 1995 paper, "How Hunting Affected Aldo Leopold's

Thinking and His Commitment to a Land Ethic," she concluded: "To him [Leopold], hunting was an expression of love for the natural world; you might even say it initiated a kind of bonding with the land." And like McCabe, Nina understood the importance of her grandfather, Carl's, teachings. "Imbued" by his father "since childhood with the lessons of fair play, Aldo saw the rules of sportsmanship as the only reasonable behavior for a young outdoorsman and hunter." Without understanding how "Carl's love for the outdoors and for the hunt were a guiding force for himself and for his whole family," one cannot comprehend, Nina affirms, how his son's "enjoyment of the hunt led to his later pioneering efforts in wilderness protection and toward an ethical approach to land use. . . ."[11]

Growing up in the late 1800s in Burlington, Iowa, in a house overlooking the Mississippi River, Aldo was reminded continually by his father of how much damage the market hunters were doing to the nation's waterfowl population, a quarter of which came down the Mississippi Flyway. "By the time his [Carl's] boys began to hunt, they had a well-developed personal code of sportsmanship."[12] As one of Burlington's most prominent sportsmen, Carl endorsed the sporting press's attacks on spring waterfowl hunting and the sale of game.

Proof that his son had internalized his father's "conservation conscience" comes from a letter of March 21, 1904, when he was just seventeen. From New Jersey's elite Lawrenceville Preparatory School, where Leopold studied before going to Yale, he wrote his father: "I am very sorry that the ducks are being slaughtered as usual, but of course could expect nothing else. When my turn comes to have something to say and do against it and other related matters, I am sure that nothing in my power will be lacking to the good cause."[13]

About thirty years later, Leopold would still be acknowledging the huge ethical debt he owed his father, who died in 1914. As I first pointed out in 1975, the fact that Leopold dedicated *Game Management* (1933) to his father, "Pioneer in Sportsmanship," meaning, of course, the code of the sportsman, tells us much about the genesis of his land ethic. According to Nina, her father never stopped developing "his ideas on the ethics of sportsmanship," which "anticipated Leopold's later philosophical development, and addressed an issue long debated among conservationists: the seeming inconsistency in being both a hunter and a protector of game." For him, "the title 'sportsman' was the highest honor to which a hunter could aspire," because "sportsmanship was a personal matter . . . of human conscience" that went well beyond written laws. What had been "consistent in Aldo Leopold's philosophy from childhood to maturity," she believes, was—to use her father's own words—" 'a respect for living things.' " In the final analysis, she knew that "to Aldo Leopold, hunting was not an abomination nor an inconsistency," but "a way for active participation in the drama of life, to be conducted in an ecologically balanced and civil manner."[14]

In September, 1992, I interviewed Leopold's hunting and fishing partner, Robert McCabe, and asked him if he agreed with my caption for the Leopold photograph in the "Picture Album" of this book: Is it correct to claim that Leopold's "land ethic represents the highest development of the environmental responsibility inherent in the code of the sportsman"? His answer was that this characterization accurately reflects the central role played by fishing and hunting, particularly the latter, in the evolution of Leopold's thinking about the natural world and humankind's place in it. Nina supported this conclusion on June 20, 1995, during my visit to "The Shack" property made famous in *A Sand County Almanac*.

As noted earlier, this interpretation of the development of Leopold's world view can be documented in his own writings. When we read *A Sand County Almanac* we can ignore, or even condemn, his fishing and hunting accounts, or we can try and understand how these experiences shaped his thinking. Three examples from the book should suffice.

One day, after driving "two hundred miles of hot, dusty road" to fish for trout, Leopold found only low, warm, poorly oxygenated water, and no fish. While the average angler might have given up, Leopold remembered that "high up near the headwaters we had once seen a fork, narrow, deep, and fed by cold springs that gurgled out under its close-hemmed walls of alder." The essence, and chief appeal, of fishing and hunting for many is "to solve the problem" at hand, which in this case was finding the trout. Therefore, Leopold asked the question: "What would a self-respecting trout do in such weather? Just what we did: go up."[15] His analysis proved correct; he found the fish just where he "knew" they would be, and "shortly," he could hear the satisfying sound of a trout "kicking in the bed of wet alder leaves at the bottom of the creel."[16]

Another example from *A Sand County Almanac* of this appeal of "solving the problem" in fishing and hunting by "bonding with the land"—to use his daughter's words—is found in his account of how, as a boy, he "formulated" his "first ornithological hypothesis" while hunting rabbits. On the way to his "favorite rabbit patch," he recalled, "I noticed that the lake, then covered with ice and snow, had developed a small 'airhole' at a point where a windmill discharged warm water from the shore." Although he knew that most ducks had already migrated southward, he hypothesized that "if there were a duck left in the region, he (or she) would inevitably, sooner or later, drop in at this airhole." Suppressing his "appetite for rabbits," he "sat down in the cold smartweeds on the frozen mud, and waited."[17]

With the poetic language that makes *A Sand County Almanac* such a beautiful piece of nature writing, Leopold described how "I waited all afternoon, growing colder with each passing crow, and with each rheumatic groan of the laboring windmill. Finally, at sunset, a lone black duck [*Anas rubripes*] came out of the west, and without even a preliminary circling of the airhole, set his wings and pitched downward."[18]

He could not remember taking the shot, "only my unspeakable delight when my first duck hit the snowy ice with a thud and lay there, belly up, red legs kicking."[19] The boy had bagged one of the wariest of all duck species, the black duck, but he had done much more: he had solved the problem and was now well on his way to becoming a hunter and naturalist.

Another hunting story from his boyhood found in *A Sand County Almanac* is particularly good in demonstrating the relationship between Leopold's code of the sportsman, inherited from his father, and the development of his land ethic. When his father gave the boy his first shotgun, Leopold remembered, "he said I might hunt partridges [ruffed grouse] with it, but that I might not shoot them from trees. I was old enough, he said, to learn wing-shooting."[20]

The ruffed grouse is perhaps the most difficult target in shotgunning because of the thick cover in which they are found and their ability to maneuver in and around trees with amazing speed and agility. For the young Leopold, "to forego a sure shot in the tree in favor of a hopeless one at the fleeing bird was my *first exercise in ethical codes* [emphasis added]. Compared with a treed partridge, the devil and his seven kingdoms was a mild temptation."[21]

At last, at the end of his "second season of featherless partridge-hunting," the boy made the "swinging shot of the sort the partridge hunter dreams about, and the bird tumbled dead in a shower of feathers and golden leaves." Even though a half century had passed, Leopold believed he "could draw a map today of each clump of red bunchberry and each blue aster that adorned the mossy spot where he lay, my first partridge on the wing. I suspect my present affection for bunchberries and asters dates from that moment."[22]

The young Leopold had proven that he could master his temptations and play the game of hunting according to a long-established set of rules, a code of the sportsman followed by Theodore Roosevelt, George Bird Grinnell, Henry William Herbert, and William Elliott before him. Because a grouse flushing out of a tree is one of the most difficult shots to make, and because he missed many times before finally downing the bird in the bunchberries and asters, Leopold learned to value the species in a way he never would have done if he had simply "potshot" them while sitting.

When *A Sand County Almanac* appeared, these hunting accounts "bothered some readers . . . but the balance and fullness of . . . that book . . . made it . . . possible to overlook."[23] But to be embarrassed by Leopold's hunting, or to feel the need to make excuses for it, does him, and history, a disservice. Historians, in particular, have been guilty of this compulsion to remove the stain of "blood sports" from their hero's portrait by claiming that Leopold grew out of these youthful exuberances as both he and his conservation ethic matured. Roderick Nash makes exactly that point at the beginning of his chapter on "Aldo Leopold: Prophet" in *Wilderness and the American Mind*.[24] Stephen Fox, in *John Muir and His Legacy: The American Conservation Movement* (1981), goes even farther. Analyzing what he calls "the familiar syndrome of the repentant hunter," Fox lists seven individuals, among them Leopold, who supposedly gave up hunting because of guilt.[25] In Fox's self-fulfilling prophecy, Leopold developed a "mature conservationism," and because "as an archer Leopold killed little game," he at least "met the repenters halfway by giving up his rifle in favor of bow and arrow."[26]

Like so many similar treatments of hunting, Fox's interpretation tells us more about his own sentiments than it does about the historical figure he is discussing. When I asked McCabe in September, 1992, if Leopold had given up gun hunting for bow hunting, he snapped, "Nonsense!"[27] Ironically, it was bow hunting, not gun hunting, that Leopold "terminated . . . about 1937."[28] So eager was he to continue his "wing shooting," despite worsening health, that he hunted ruffed grouse and pheasants with McCabe in 1947, the last autumn of his life.[29] Avoiding the thickest "covers" so that he would not have to "fight brush," and carrying a canvas folding chair—shown in the Leopold photograph in the "Picture Album" of this book—for frequent stops, he was able to have one last October doing what he loved more than anything else in the outdoors.

There is no doubt that anti-hunting, and even anti-fishing, sentiment has grown dramatically since the paperback edition of *A Sand County Almanac* appeared in 1966, but that fact is—or should be—irrelevant for the study of history. In perceiving how the land ethic evolved out of the code of the sportsman and the continuing tradition of the sportsman-conservationist ideal, we acquire not only a deeper understanding of Aldo Leopold, but of the whole history of American conservation.

A Picture Album of Sport and Conservation

1. "Frank Forester" (Henry William Herbert),
English-born crusader for an American code of the
sportsman. (Courtesy of the New York Public
Library.)

2. John James Audubon as he looked *circa* 1841; a portrait painted by his sons, John Woodhouse and Victor Gifford Audubon. Like Louis Agassiz Fuertes, Lynn Bogue Hunt, and many later wildlife artists, the great ornithological artist loved to hunt the birds he painted. (Courtesy of the American Museum of Natural History.)

4. An illustration from [Thomas] Mayne Reid's *Boy Hunters* (1852). His Romantic tales of the frontier endeared him to multitudes of youthful readers. Among those who believed that Reid's books sparked their first interest in the "Wild West" were George Bird Grinnell and Theodore Roosevelt.

3 (opposite, below). George Catlin, the first American—so far as we know—to suggest the national park idea. While painting and studying the Western Indians, he hunted buffalo for sport. From an 1849 oil painting by William Fisk. (Courtesy of the National Portrait Gallery, Smithsonian Institution.)

5. Like many sportsmen's clubs, the Currituck Club on Currituck Sound, North Carolina, preserved wildlife habitat that might otherwise have been lost to human encroachment. Hunting was regulated by club rules, which preceded state laws. The Currituck Club was one of the earliest such associations, founded in 1857 by a group of Yankees. Its "grounds" included 3,100 acres of marsh. This is a photograph of the "new" clubhouse, built in 1879 about 75 yards from the original one. It had 21 rooms, one for each member. Until a series of heart attacks eliminated all outdoor activity, George Bird Grinnell hunted at the nearby Narrows Island Club, often with his fellow ornithologist, Daniel G. Elliot. From Eugene V. Connett, ed., *Duck Shooting Along the Atlantic Tidewater* (1947). (Courtesy of William Morrow and Company.)

6 (opposite, top). An 1867 Currier and Ives lithograph entitled *Home From the Woods. The Successful Sportsmen.* (Courtesy of the Library of Congress.)

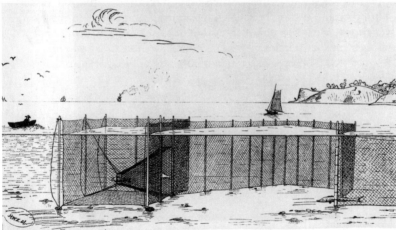

7. A "heart-pound" net in Lake Michigan. Variations of the pound net, used on both coastal and inland waters, were despised by sport and commercial hook-and-line fishermen. Opposition to these contrivances on the part of New England's coastal inhabitants was the major factor in the organization in 1871 of the U.S. Fish Commission, the first federal agency to deal with conservation of a specific natural resource. In the illustration the "leader" is the net fence extending out from the shore to guide fish into the middle section, or "heart." Fish mill around the heart until they pass through the "tunnel" into the "pot," also called the "bowl" or "crib." From the U.S. Fish Commission's *Report on the Condition of the Sea Fisheries of the South Coast of New England in 1871 and 1872* (1873).

8. One of the basic themes of the sporting tradition is that the disciples of hunting and fishing benefit physically and mentally from these avocations. Meant to poke fun at the more enthusiastic proponents of this idea, this illustration from *Harper's New Monthly Magazine* (August, 1870) shows a city man before and after a trip to the Adirondacks.

9. "Seth Green Taking Spawn from a Salmon Trout [lake trout]. The Proper Position." Green, a dedicated angler, was the preeminent nongovernmental fish culturist of his day. From Robert Barnwell Roosevelt and Seth Green, *Fish Hatching, and Fish Catching* (1879).

10. An interior view of the New York State hatching house at Caledonia, as it looked in 1875. Several years later, two of the nation's leading fish culturists reported that "in it have been hatched in one season two million and a half of whitefish, two million salmon trout [lake trout], and one million and a half of brook trout together with several hundred thousand [Atlantic] salmon, these figures . . . being taken by . . . actual count." The 1870s witnessed the rise of the "fish culture movement," a crusade spearheaded by sportsmen-naturalists. Despite what virtually all historians claim, wide-scale conservation efforts in regard to wildlife preceded those in behalf of forests. From Robert Barnwell Roosevelt and Seth Green, *Fish Hatching, and Fish Catching* (1879).

11. George Perkins Marsh, whose book *Man and Nature* (1864) has been called the "fountainhead of the conservation movement." An enthusiastic angler in his youth, he was a proponent of fish culture as early as 1857, when he wrote a sportsmen-inspired report for the Vermont legislature on the decrease of game and food fishes in the state. Believing in the beneficial "effects on the character of the sportsman" of both hunting and fishing and understanding that anglers led the efforts for fish conservation, Marsh argued that sport fishing should be "promoted . . . by public and even legislative patronage."

12. "Lonesome Charley" Reynolds, expert hunter and "generally ranked as the greatest of the Western scouts" (*Concise Dictionary of American Biography*). Close association with such authentic frontiersmen was a mark of pride for Easterners like George Bird Grinnell and Theodore Roosevelt.

13. Robert Barnwell Roosevelt, political reformer, advocate of the code of the sportsman, well-known hunting and fishing author, member of the New York Association for the Protection of Game, and prime mover in the effort to establish a federal fish-culture program. He undoubtedly played a part in formulating the outdoor interests, and concerns, of his nephew, Theodore Roosevelt. From Charles Hallock, *An Angler's Reminiscences* (1913).

14. Thaddeus Norris. Like every other pioneer in the science of fish culture, he was first an angler. From Fred Mather, *My Angling Friends* (1901).

15. "Englishmen in Colorado: Fishing for Breakfast," an illustration from the *London Graphic*, August 17, 1872. Well-born foreign sportsmen were attracted to America, and some of them contributed to the early conservation movement. (Courtesy of the Western History Department, Denver Public Library.)

16. With a "jacklight" in the bow to stun the birds, boatmen quietly row down on ducks massed on the water and will fire when the greatest number can be killed. The caption accompanying this illustration— "The Nefarious Pot-Hunter"—indicated what sportsmen thought of such activities. From *Scribner's Monthly*, November, 1877.

17. Carp—pride and joy of government fish culturists, led by Spencer Fullerton Baird. The carp was introduced throughout the United States, disrupting ecosystems wherever established, a classic example of the tragic consequences often attending the introduction of alien organisms. Photograph by Donald W. Pfitzer. (Courtesy of the Bureau of Sport Fisheries and Wildlife.)

18. Because every true sportsman was expected to have an interest in natural history, glass cabinets containing mounted specimens of animals and birds bagged on outings were very much in vogue. Taxidermy flourished, and the practice of this art encouraged more systematic studies. Entitled "Room in a Taxidermist's Shop," the illustration is from *Century Magazine,* December, 1882.

19. This ad is typical of those that appeared frequently in sportsmen's newspapers and books in the last quarter of the nineteenth century, and is an example of the interrelationship between sport and natural history. From Charles Hallock's *Camp Life in Florida: A Handbook for Sportsmen and Settlers* (1876).

20. Charles Hallock, founder of *Forest and Stream,* as he looked in 1896. From Fred Mather, *My Angling Friends* (1901).

21. The front page of the first issue of *Forest and Stream*, August 14, 1873.

22. "Summer Life at North Mountain House." Located "in the centre of an unbroken primeval forest of 25,000 acres" in northeastern Pennsylvania, this resort had "fishing for those who like it, and hunting in the woods. . .." From John B. Bachelder, *Popular Resorts, and How to Reach Them* (1874).

23. James Henry Moser's well-known painting of *The Still Hunt* (1888). A market hunter, using a Sharps rifle, has already killed more than a dozen buffalo. (Courtesy of the National Park Service Collection, Yellowstone National Park.)

24. Skinning a buffalo on the northern Great Plains in the last years of the commercial buffalo slaughter. (Courtesy of Huffman Pictures, Miles City, Montana.)

25. Because of the growing demands of tanneries and fertilizer plants, the commercial destruction of the buffalo became a year-round industry. This woodcut, *circa* 1874, shows the curing of hides and bones in the West. Raw hides were pegged out to dry before being pressed (to the right) and baled for shipment to the East. In the background are heaps of buffalo bones that will also be sent East to be ground into fertilizer. (Courtesy of the Bettman Archive.)

26. Guns and shooting were an integral part of the lives of most males in late nineteenth-century rural America. Entitled *The Turkey Shoot*, this 1879 oil painting by John W. Ehninger shows a match taking place near Saratoga, New York. Using a percussion arm, a contestant is firing from a rack. The man on the left has proven his marksmanship by winning a turkey. While most males, of all classes, probably had at least some experience with hunting, only a small percentage of them would become the gentlemen sportsmen who launched the conservation movement.

28. "Martha," the last passenger pigeon. She died in the Cincinnati Zoo on September 1, 1914, when she was 26 years old. Her species, once perhaps the most abundant avian form ever to have lived on the planet, became extinct mainly because of forest destruction and systematic killing by *commercial* hunters. (Courtesy of the Zoological Society of Cincinnati.)

27 (opposite, below). Unlike sportsmen—who usually did not depend directly on the natural world for a livelihood—farmers of the nineteenth century usually manifested little appreciation of nature, at least when it came to any living thing that seemed to be a "competitor." Here, Iowa farmers are shooting passenger pigeons over their newly sown grain field. From *Leslie's Illustrated Newspaper,* September 21, 1867.

29. Commercial pigeon netters at work. When the passenger pigeons in the dead trees all drop to the ground, a trigger mechanism will be released by the men in the blind and a net will be thrown over the whole flock. To attract passing flocks, the "pigeoners" often baited the area with buckwheat or some other food, then tethered live decoy pigeons on small platforms called "stools" (hence the term "stool pigeon"). When these were raised and lowered, the captive birds fluttered as if alighting and thus lured flying pigeons. From *Leslie's Illustrated Newspaper*, September 21, 1867.

30. Angler Cornelius Hedges, whose idea for "a great National Park" in the Yellowstone region may have been the beginning of the effort that eventually led to the establishment of America's first such reserve. The illustration shows him as he looked when he graduated from Yale in 1853. (Courtesy of the Montana Historical Society.)

31. The Lower Falls of the Yellowstone, taken by hunter and pioneer photographer William Henry Jackson. His photographs played a major part in the passage of the bill creating Yellowstone National Park. (Courtesy of the Library of the State Historical Society of Colorado.)

32. The Fulton Meat Market in Durango, Colorado, in the 1880s. The mounted elk indicated that game was for sale. Elk carcasses hang on the right. Commercialization of wildlife threatened many species, and sportsmen were the only significant group that opposed the market gunner. (Courtesy of the Western History Department, Denver Public Library.)

33. In the 1840s surf fishing with rod and reel began to replace the traditional hand line, and by the post-bellum period, it was a popular sport for gentlemen anglers in the Northeast. Entitled *Playing a [Striped] Bass in the Surf,* the illustration is from Genio C. Scott, *Fishing in American Waters* (1875); first published in 1869.

34. The chase inspired many of the nineteenth century's leading artists, among them Albert Bierstadt, Frederic Remington, and Winslow Homer. All three of these men were sportsmen, as was Arthur B. Frost, who "by 1900 . . . was probably the country's most popular illustrator" (*Concise Dictionary of American Biography*). This lithograph is entitled *Quail—A Dead Stand*. From Frost, *Shooting Pictures* (1895-96).

35. An Arthur B. Frost lithograph entitled *Rail Shooting*. In the stern a "pusher" propels his clinker-built double-ender with a 12-foot pole, while the gunner in the bow fires at a sora rail. Once a popular sport along tidal rivers in the East, rail shooting (for several species) has vanished in many areas, a casualty of industrial pollution and development. From Frost, *Shooting Pictures* (1895-96).

36. Expert hunter Galen Clark, who, in the words of
historian Shirley Sargent, "did more than anyone else
to preserve and protect the Yosemite Grant [1864],
now Yosemite National Park." Although the wide
publicity given to John Muir's much later efforts have
overshadowed Clark's importance, he deserves the
title of "father of Yosemite Park." Photograph by
George Fiske, showing Clark in Yosemite Valley.
(Courtesy of the California State Library.)

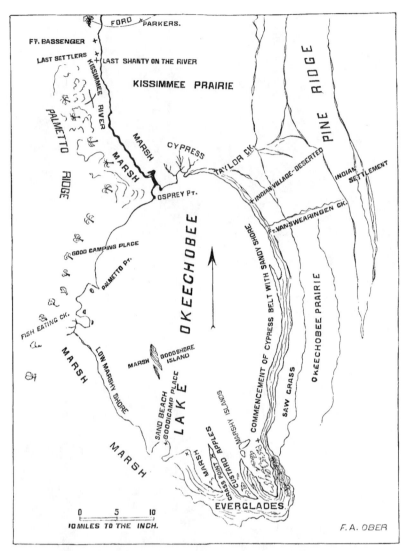

37. One of the little-known facts of sporting history is that outdoorsmen played an important role in "opening up" wild regions by sponsoring scientific expeditions. Less was known about the interior of southern Florida in the early 1870s than almost any part of the "Wild West." This is one of the first good maps published of Lake Okeechobee, compiled on an 1873 expedition sponsored by *Forest and Stream*. From *Forest and Stream*, April 16, 1874.

38. Commercial elk and deer hunters and their kill (which also includes a bighorn sheep and mountain lion) in Colorado in 1885. Men like these were despised by sportsmen. (Courtesy of the Western History Department, Denver Public Library.)

39. George Bird Grinnell, crusading editor of *Forest and Stream* from 1880 to 1911 (natural history editor from 1876 to 1880). Pioneer in the preservation and management of wildlife, forests, and scenic areas; influential adviser to Theodore Roosevelt; and the author of the effort that resulted in the creation of Glacier National Park, he played a leading role in the early development of the conservation movement, both in its utilitarian and aesthetic forms. When he died in 1938, the *New York Times* noted that Grinnell had often been referred to as "the father of American conservation."

40. Using "a dozen flat painted strawboard decoys" in wheat stubble, two goose hunters follow their sport on the "prairie shooting grounds" of Minnesota. By Charles A. Zimmerman, the sketch is from the *Chicago Field* (later name of *Field and Stream*), October 12, 1878. Through an increasing use of illustrations, the sporting press educated hunters on what was considered "fair" as a method for pursuing their prey.

41. Before 1885—when commercial fishermen and "progress" began to move in—catches of eight or nine brook trout averaging over four pounds were common along the south shore of Lake Superior on Michigan's Upper Peninsula. The photograph shows a sportswoman landing a four-pounder in 1886. Recent research shows that more women engaged in hunting and fishing, especially in the West, than previously thought. Photograph by George Shiras, 3d. From his *Hunting Wild Life With Camera and Flashlight* (1936), I; first published in 1935. (Courtesy of the National Geographic Society.)

42. Weathered stumps are the sole evidence that a forest once covered this barren area on Mt. Rose near Virginia City, Nevada. The timber went to the Comstock Lode in the 1870s for mining purposes. Photograph taken on July 3, 1938, by R. C. Wilson. (Courtesy of the U.S. Forest Service.)

43. The Hudson River above Lake Sanford in New York's Adirondacks. The region was the scene of the first large-scale campaign to save American forests, and the movement was spearheaded by sportsmen. An 1888 photograph taken by S. R. Stoddard. (Courtesy of the Adirondack Museum, Blue Mountain Lake, New York.)

44 (overleaf, top). Gifford Pinchot fishing near his home in Milford, Pennsylvania. Because of political opposition to the Roosevelt administration's forest-conservation programs, Pinchot couched every public statement in utilitarian terms. Away from the public arena, he was, however, a very different man. In his writings on angling, which have been ignored by historians, Pinchot reveals that from an early age, he was a deeply sensitive "nature lover." It was, in fact, a boyhood fishing trip to the Adirondacks that sparked his interest in becoming a forester. Probably the best demonstration of his spiritual relationship with fishing was the act of his son and angling partner, who made sure his father had his favorite fly-rod with him in the coffin when he was placed in the ground. Entitled "In the Spring the Angler's Fancy Lightly Turns to Thoughts of Trout," the photograph is from Pinchot, *Just Fishing Talk* (1936).

45. Looking out at the Great Smoky Mountains from a terrace of the
Biltmore mansion near Asheville, North Carolina. Once part of George
Vanderbilt's 120,000-acre Biltmore estate and now part of the Pisgah
National Forest, this area was the home of Gifford Pinchot's early
efforts at systematic forestry in the United States. The first such
endeavor—despite the fact that historians have always given that honor
to Pinchot—seems to have taken place on the lands of the Blooming
Grove Park Association, a sportsmen's club in eastern Pennsylvania.
Photograph by Daniel O. Todd, July, 1961. (Courtesy of the U.S.
Forest Service.)

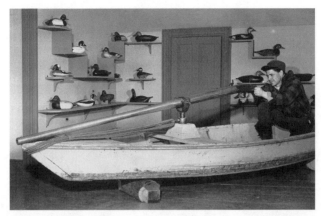

46. A swivel "big gun" mounted (incorrectly) on a skiff, used by market hunters to fire huge quantities of shot into waterfowl massed on the water. Scores of ducks and geese might be killed or crippled at one blast. (Courtesy of the Shelburne Museum, Shelburne, Vermont.)

47. Angler, fish merchant, ichthyologist, and New York State Fish Commissioner, Eugene G. Blackford (in top hat in center), did much to popularize the study of fishes. In New York City's famous Fulton Market for several days every spring—beginning on opening day of trout season—he exhibited a large collection of live and dead specimens of numerous species. Because he specialized in the rare and exotic, both the sporting and scientific communities awaited Blackford's openings with keen anticipation. The illustration is from the *Chicago Field,* April 12, 1879.

48. August prairie-chicken shooting in the West. From *Scribner's Monthly*, August 1877.

49. Several members of a sportsmen's club smoking and talking in front of the evening fire after a day of fishing. Entitled *Telling Fish Stories,* the illustration appeared in *Scribner's Monthly,* February 1877.

50. Fly-casting contest of the second Anglers' Tournament of the
National Rod and Reel Association in 1883, at Harlem Mere, Central
Park, New York City. In the lower right-hand corner a judge is
weighing the contestants' fly-rods. From Herbert Manchester, *Four
Centuries of Sport in America, 1490-1890* (1968); first published in
1931. (Courtesy of Benjamin Blom, Inc.)

51. John Burroughs, probably the best-known nature writer of the late
nineteenth century, engaging in what he called his "favorite pastime."
He is holding large cutthroat trout he has just caught in the
Yellowstone River during a trip with Theodore Roosevelt in the spring
of 1903; the man in the background is unidentified. From George Bird
Grinnell, ed., *American Big Game in Its Haunts* (1904).

52. "Founders of the American Ornithologists' Union, 1883."
Virtually all of these men began their studies by hunting birds. Indeed,
many of them remained avid sportsmen after they achieved "scientist"
status. In the top row, beginning at the left, are Nathan C. Brown, E.
A. Mearns, Thomas McIlwraith, J. B. Holder, Daniel G. Elliot, Charles
Aldrich, J. M. Wheaton, A. K. Fisher; second row: R. W. Shufeldt (in
uniform), Robert Ridgway, H. W. Henshaw, Spencer Fullerton Baird,
George N. Lawrence (wearing glasses), Elliott Coues, Charles F.
Batchelder; third row: C. B. Cory (in profile), C. Hart Merriam, J. A.
Allen, Montague Chamberlain (below Allen), William Brewster, D. W.
Prentiss (wearing glasses); and fourth row: H. A. Purdie, Charles E.
Bendire, Eugene P. Bicknell, H. B. Bailey. From Frank M. Chapman,
Autobiography of a Bird-Lover (1935); first published in 1933.
(Courtesy of Hawthorn Books.)

53. C. Hart Merriam, hunter, member of
the League of American Sportsmen, and
founder (in 1885) of the Division of
Economic Ornithology and Mammalogy in
the U.S. Department of Agriculture, out of
which evolved the U.S. Fish and Wildlife
Service. (Courtesy of the Library of the
Museum of Comparative Zoology, Harvard
University.)

54. A proponent of forest conservation, Chester A. Arthur is shown "fighting" a salmon on the Cascapédia River of Quebec's Gaspé Peninsula. Copied from a photograph by Carl Beckstead. From Charles Eliot Goodspeed, *Angling in America* (1939). (Courtesy of George T. Goodspeed and the Houghton Mifflin Company.)

55. An early advocate of woodland conservation in New York State, Grover Cleveland set aside millions of acres in forest reserves during his second term as President, and signed the 1894 "Act to Protect the Birds and Animals in Yellowstone National Park." His *Fishing and Shooting Sketches* (1906) reveal his deep commitment to the code of the sportsman. He is shown fishing for bass in Duncan Lake, Ossipee, New Hampshire. Photographed by John H. Finley. From Charles Eliot Goodspeed, *Angling in America* (1939). (Courtesy of George T. Goodspeed and the Houghton Mifflin Company.)

57. Editor of *American Angler,* William C. Harris, who crusaded for fish conservation, fish culture, and pollution abatement. From Charles Hallock, *An Angler's Reminiscences* (1913).

56. Bernhard E. Fernow, German-born sportsman and leading pioneer in forestry. He personifies the tremendous debt Americans owe to Old World conservationists and their ideas. As the "forestry adviser" of the Adirondack League Club, a sportsmen's association, in upstate New York in the 1890s, he continually worked for the integration of wildlife and forest conservation, as was the case in Europe. He later recalled: "I have in years gone by carried my gun and cast my line occasionally, and taken pleasure in it. Indeed, my profession as a forester in my native country where I studied and practiced it includes both, in the theoretical teaching and in the practice, the art of sportsmanship hunting and . . . conservative fishing, and I can assure you, there is a high standard of sportsmanlike behavior kept up by the foresters. . .." (Courtesy of the Library of Congress.)

VOLUME 7, No. 19.   MAY 9, 1885.

THE AMERICAN

THE TARPUM—TARPON—SILVER KING—(*Megalops thrissoides*).
For description, modes of capture, etc., see THE AMERICAN ANGLER of Dec 8th and 15th, 1883, and April 18th and 25th, 1885.

ANGLER

NEW YORK
WILLIAM C HARRIS
EDITOR

58. Because they had to know their quarry in order to hunt or fish successfully, nineteenth-century sportsmen added much to the knowledge of wildlife habits. For example, almost nothing was known about the life histories of grayling and tarpon before anglers began to seek them out. In the 1880s the latter species became the new "glamour fish," and anglers flocked to Florida to see if they could conquer the "silver king." Almost unheard-of a few years before, the fish was so well known by the spring of 1885 that it rated a front-page illustration in *American Angler*, the leading periodical on sport fishing.

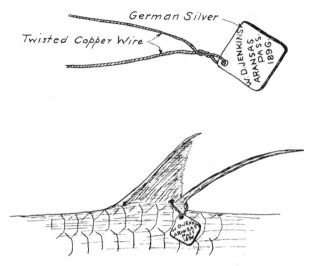

59. Many believe that the technique of marking or "tagging" fish to trace their migration patterns is a relatively recent development, but Izaak Walton mentions it in his *Compleat Angler*, first published in 1653! In America, the practice goes back to the nineteenth century. The picture shows a tag devised by angler W. D. Jenkins of Texas. Made of "German silver," it was attached to the dorsal fin of a tarpon by means of a twisted copper wire. From *American Angler*, October-November, 1896.

60. William Hallett Phillips, a Supreme Court lawyer and ardent angler who wielded a powerful, behind-the-scenes influence in the efforts to preserve Yellowstone National Park and set aside forest reserves. (Courtesy of the Haynes Foundation, Bozeman, Montana.)

61. Attempting to look like the frontiersmen he admired, a buckskin-clad Theodore Roosevelt poses with his rifle in a studio in 1884. He later said that he would never have become President if it had not been for his Western ranching experience, which began with a desire to shoot a trophy buffalo. Roosevelt's "conservation philosophy . . . is largely the basis of the modern conservation program in America," and in terms of concrete conservation achievements, like the amount of land brought under federal protection, his Presidency was the most important in the history of the United States. From Hermann Hagedorn, *Roosevelt in the Bad Lands* (1921). (Courtesy of the Houghton Mifflin Company.)

62. The White House dining room during Theodore Roosevelt's Presidency, showing the trophy heads of elk, bison, bear, and moose (partially visible). From Roosevelt's *Outdoor Pastimes of an American Hunter* (1905). (Courtesy of the Theodore Roosevelt Collection, Harvard College Library.)

64. Sleeping black-duck decoy, carved by Obediah Verity of Long
Island, *circa* 1880. Some believe that the wooden decoy, created to lure
game birds, was the highest expression of American folk art. That it
reached its greatest development here cannot be denied, but it was not
unique to North America. Apparently without realizing the importance
of his discovery, a Swedish author, Gunnar Brusewitz, in his book
Hunting (translated into English and published in New York in 1969),
shows that painted wooden decoys were in wide use in Scandinavia by
the first quarter of the nineteenth century. (Courtesy of the Shelburne
Museum, Shelburne, Vermont.)

63 (opposite, below). The first wildlife sanctuaries in America were
established by gentlemen sportsmen who adapted an Old World
precedent to New World conditions. The photograph shows the
entrance gate to the Adirondack game, fish, and forest preserve of
banker John Pierpont Morgan in upstate New York. 1899 photograph
by S. R. Stoddard. (Courtesy of the Adirondack Museum, Blue
Mountain Lake, New York.)

65. President Benjamin Harrison (on right) in his blind on the property of the Bengies Ducking Club near Baltimore. On his left is William Joyce Sewell, powerful Republican politician from New Jersey. From the crouching position of the guide on the right and the concentration of the retriever, it appears that ducks are at that moment coming to the decoys, which are barely discernible in the distance in the original photograph. This picture was taken in March, 1891, the same month Harrison proclaimed the first forest reserve. He would follow it with millions of additional acres in what would become known as the national forests, including the Grand Canyon Forest Reserve (he had proposed it as a national park as early as 1882), "the first act to protect the region from private encroachment." In addition, he set aside what can be considered the first national wildlife refuge and first federal "wilderness area," the Afognak Reserve in Alaska in 1892, as well as the "Casa Grande [Pre-Columbian] Ruins Reservation" in Arizona, also in 1892; the latter proclamation anticipated the Antiquities Act of 1906. (Courtesy of Indiana Historical Society Library.)

66. President Harrison after the hunt. With his double-barreled shotgun and bag of ducks, which includes both his and Sewell's, he stands on the steps of the Bengies Ducking Club. (Courtesy of the Indiana Historical Society Library.)

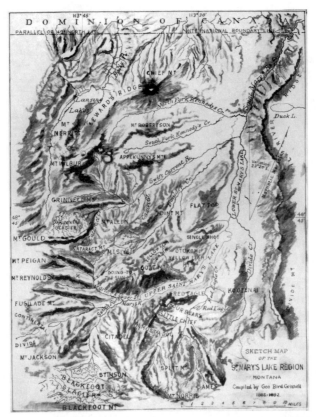

67. By the mid-1880s, there were few regions of the United States
outside of Alaska that had not been explored thoroughly. One
exception was the St. Mary's Lake country in the northwestern corner
of Montana. This is a "sketch map" of the region compiled by George
Bird Grinnell between 1885 and 1892. By the latter year, he had
already begun his campaign to have this magnificent area preserved as a
national park. Largely through his efforts, Glacier National Park
became a reality in 1910. (Courtesy of the National Park Service.)

68 (opposite, top). The Woodmont Rod and Gun Club, established in
western Maryland in 1880. As in the case of other sportsmen's
associations, Woodmont's members accepted the responsibility for the
total environment implicit in the code of the sportsman. The Club's
official motto was "Protect and Enjoy," and one of its prominent
members was Senator George Graham Vest, staunchest Congressional
defender of the threatened Yellowstone National Park. From *American
Angler,* October 21, 1882.

69. The published works of ornithologists like William Brewster, Elliott Coues, Daniel G. Elliot, and Frank M. Chapman reveal that a prerequisite for knowing birds was to have a knowledge of how to hunt them. Like so many other naturalists of the nineteenth century, the Curator of Chicago's Field Museum, Charles B. Cory, began his "faunal studies" with a gun and never lost his love for the chase. Entitled *Brant Shooting: "Get Ready,"* the illustration shows two hunters in a pit blind using both wooden and live decoys. From Cory, *How to Know the Ducks, Geese, and Swans of North America* (1897).

70. New York City's American Museum of Natural History in 1889. As in the case of the National Museum in Washington, D.C., and the Field Museum in Chicago, sportsmen-naturalists like George Bird Grinnell, Charles B. Cory, and William Temple Hornaday played an important role in building up this institution's early collections of mammals and birds. (Courtesy of the American Museum of Natural History.)

71. "*Ovis stonei*," once believed to be a new form of mountain sheep, on exhibit in the American Museum of Natural History. It was discovered and "collected" by an expedition sent out under the auspices of George Oliver Shields' *Recreation*, a popular sportsmen's magazine founded in 1894. "Stone's Sheep" is now generally regarded as simply a blackish color phase of the Dall's, or white, sheep (*Ovis dalli*). From *Recreation*, June, 1897.

72. A watercolor by Edmund H. Osthaus, about 1904, called *Just Look at Them!* Gazing out of a window of their clubhouse at flights of waterfowl, the hunters and their dog—perhaps an American water spaniel—are eager to be off. (Courtesy of the Eleutherian Mills Historical Library, Greenville, Delaware.)

73. For sportsmen-naturalists like Theodore Roosevelt—who had
hunted wilderness bears uncorrupted by people—"the effect of
protection upon bear life in the Yellowstone [Park] has been one of the
phenomena of natural history." By the 1890s, incidents between bears
and ignorant tourists were common, but the feeding of "tame" bears at
the park dumps continued for many years into the twentieth century.
From George Bird Grinnell, ed., *American Big Game in Its Haunts*
(1904).

74 (opposite, below). While variations of the term "game hog" had been in use for some time (e.g., "trout hog," "grouse hog," etc.), sportsman George Oliver Shields gave it a far wider circulation when he established the magazine *Recreation* in 1894. Subscribers sent in information regarding those who had violated a basic component of the code of the sportsman by killing game in excess, and Shields "roasted" them in *Recreation,* using names, addresses, photographs, and humorous commentary to embarrass these pseudo-sportsmen. Another technique was the satirical cartoon, as shown here. Entitled *A Distinguished Member of the Herd,* it appeared in the April, 1898, issue.

75. James T. Rothrock, pioneer in forestry at the state level and a dedicated sportsman. (Courtesy of the University of Pennsylvania Archives.)

76 (overleaf, top). "The Hunter's Cabin" at the World's Columbian Exposition, held at Chicago from May to November, 1893. Symbolizing the central role of the wilderness hunter in the making of American history, the cabin "is the headquarters of the Boone and Crockett Club, an organization of prominent sportsmen throughout the United States, whose object is to preserve the large game of the country, especially that of the Yellowstone or National Park. The structure is built of rough logs, and within, over the rude fireplace, is the skull of a grizzly bear." Standing out front is Elwood Hofer, hunter, guide, and packer, who was brought from Yellowstone Park by the Boone and Crockett Club to act as the exhibit's interpreter. Photograph and quoted passage from Hubert Howe Bancroft, *The Book of the Fair* . . . (1894). (Courtesy of Crown Publishers.)

77. Madison Grant. A founder of
the New York Zoological Society
(which established the "Bronx
Zoo"), the Save-the-Redwoods
League, and other organizations,
he was one of the Boone and
Crockett Club's most active
members. This leading
representative of the New York
patrician class typifies the all-
important role of upper-class
individuals in the making of
conservation. (Courtesy of the
American Museum of Natural
History.)

78. After George Bird Grinnell, *Forest and Stream*'s editor, launched his crusade to define the meaning of Yellowstone National Park and establish for it an effective administration, he succeeded in interesting other editors in the issue. This cartoon from *Harper's Weekly* (January 20, 1883) shows what will happen if the "Yellowstone Park Improvement Company" is allowed to exploit the reserve for private gain—a visitor is set upon by profiteers at the Park entrance. Note that the tourist brings a cased gun with him, for hunting was an accepted activity in the Park for many years. Not until 1894, when sportsmen obtained passage of the "Act to Protect the Birds and Animals in Yellowstone National Park," was hunting entirely stopped.

79. An avid sportsman and a Republican Congressman who represented Iowa almost continuously from 1889 to 1907, John F. Lacey was responsible for drafting much of the key legislation of early conservation, including the 1894 act to protect Yellowstone National Park, which established the definition of a "national park"; the "Lacey Act" of 1900, which stopped market hunting and interstate shipment of wildlife or wildlife products in violation of state law; and the original transfer act for forest reserves, which set the stage for the establishment of the U.S. Forest Service. As he suggested in his Congressional speech favoring passage of the Lacey Act, which was printed in *Recreation* (July, 1900), the genesis of his commitment was the responsibility for the *total* environment inherent in the code of the sportsman. He stated: "'I have always been a lover of the birds, and I have always been a hunter as well, for today there is no friend that the birds [and by implication all wildlife] have like the true sportsman—the man who enjoys *legitimate* [emphasis added] sport'." (Courtesy of the Iowa State Department of History and Archives, Des Moines.)

80. During his active career, some of the posts held by angler-ichthyologist George Brown Goode were United States Fish Commissioner, Assistant Secretary of the Smithsonian Institution, and chief administrator of the National Museum. (Courtesy of the Smithsonian Institution.)

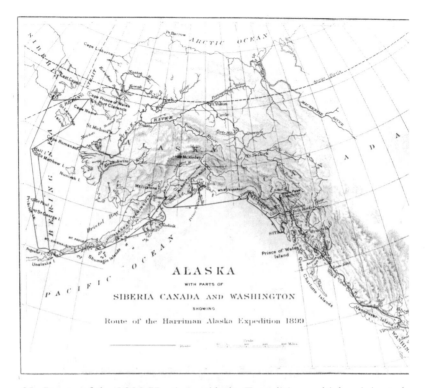

81. Route of the 1899 Harriman Alaska Expedition, which originated in the desire of railroad executive Edward H. Harriman to shoot a trophy Alaskan brown bear. Using a luxurious steam yacht provided by him, a group of the country's leading naturalists—including C. Hart Merriam, George Bird Grinnell, John Burroughs, and John Muir— explored and studied the wild coasts of Canada, Alaska, and Siberia, journeying as far north as the Bering Strait. Despite the fact that Muir accepted Harriman's hospitality, he condemned him for shooting the bear he had come for. From Harriman Alaska Expedition, *Alaska* (1901), I.

82. The Catalina Tuna Club at Avalon on Santa Catalina Island, California. Founded in the 1890s by angler-ichthyologist Charles Frederick Holder, the organization was confined to "gentleman anglers" and pioneered in the study and conservation of marine game fishes. From Holder's *Game Fishes of the World* (1913).

83 (opposite, top). While his greatest contribution to conservation was the realization that the federal government—not the states—had jurisdiction over migratory birds, sportsman George Shiras, 3d., also contributed through the medium of photography. He increased the public's appreciation of wildlife by pioneering a number of photographic techniques, one of which was the use of the pot-hunter's "jacklight" to obtain stunning pictures of animals on their nocturnal rounds. Taken in the 1890s on his hunting grounds in Michigan's Upper Peninsula, this picture is entitled *A Midnight Reflection* and is one of a series that won the highest awards at the World Exposition in Paris in 1900 and the Louisiana Purchase Exposition in St. Louis in 1904. From George Shiras, 3d., *Hunting Wild Life with Camera and Flashlight* (1936), I; first published in 1935. (Courtesy of the National Geographic Society.)

84 (opposite, below). The dividing line between scientific "collecting" and recreational "hunting" was often indistinct or nonexistent. This is a National Museum exhibit of lions "bagged" ("collected") by sportsman-naturalist Theodore Roosevelt on the Smithsonian-Roosevelt African Expedition of 1909. (Courtesy of the Smithsonian Institution.)

85. Hunting for science—"collecting"—could be as exciting as hunting for sport, especially when the quarry was elusive and very rare. Here is the future president of the Massachusetts Audubon Society, William Brewster, on a houseboat on Florida's Suwannee River in 1890 holding the now extinct, or nearly extinct, ivory-billed woodpecker, shot by Frank M. Chapman, who is probably the man holding the main collecting tool, a double-barreled shotgun, in his hands. As he recalled in his *Autobiography:* "It was my good fortune to encounter the one ivory-billed woodpecker seen on the voyage. I knew its voice the moment its loud *yap-yap* fell on my ears. Then followed memorable moments as I stalked it through the cypress trees, until, *unbelievable glory* [emphasis added], it was actually in my hands." Among his many later accomplishments, Chapman would found the magazine *Bird-Lore,* now *Audubon,* and create the Christmas Bird Census held every year across the United States. (Courtesy of the Library of the Museum of Comparative Zoology, Harvard University.)

86. In the nineteenth century well-meaning sportsmen as well as some anti-hunter, self-proclaimed "animal lovers" believed that the killing of "vermin" like cougars and wolves was beneficial because it resulted in greater numbers of "good" animals like deer and elk. Tragically, they were right. By the early part of the twentieth century, herbivores were so numerous in some places that they were destroying their habitats and beginning to starve. In the photograph a deer stands on its hind legs, reaching for forage. Having already destroyed the ground cover and lower branches, the deer has to stretch for the upper branches. When they are consumed, the animal will starve, and the quality of the whole herd may be impaired. In such a situation only human beings—assuming their natural role as predators—can restore the balance and save both the deer and its habitat. Photograph by Charles McDonald. (Courtesy of the U.S. Forest Service.)

87. *Trouting*, from Henry
Van Dyke's *Little Rivers*
(1895). Van Dyke was a
popular writer who was
revered for conveying the
beauty, even the spirituality,
of sport fishing. Like most
influential outdoor writers
of his time, he was as
interested in the pursuit of
his quarry—and in the
aesthetics of his
surroundings—as he was in
catching fish.

88. A commercial gunner of Elliott Island, Maryland, holding a
shotgun with which he killed—so he claimed—35,000 ducks in the
early part of the twentieth century. Shooting for sport had a relatively
small impact on waterfowl populations compared to the havoc wrecked
by market hunters. From Harry M. Walsh, *The Outlaw Gunner* (1971).
(Courtesy of Tidewater Publishers, Cambridge, Maryland.)

89. Sportsmen-naturalists perpetuated the code of the sportsman by inculcating it in the youth of America. From left to right, the photograph shows Ernest Thompson Seton, Lord Baden-Powell, and Daniel Carter Beard, the founders of the Boy Scout movement. All three were sportsmen. (Courtesy of the Boy Scouts of America, New York, N.Y.)

90 (overleaf, top). Because of a penchant for self-flattery, William Temple Hornaday has been accepted by literal-minded historians as one of the greatest wildlife conservationists. As the first Director of the New York Zoological Park and a crusader for the bison, Hornaday deserves a place in the history of conservation—but not the one he chose for himself. Far more important conservationists like George Bird Grinnell and Charles Sheldon believed that Hornaday actually did more harm than good by splitting the ranks of conservationists through his bitter attacks on anyone who did not agree precisely with "Mr. Hornaday," as he often called himself. In recent years anti-hunting historians have quoted him for his assaults on hunters, failing to understand that he was against those hunters who, in his opinion, abused the sport, but he certainly was not against all hunting. Hornaday believed that only he and a small minority of hunters who agreed with his often erroneous notions of wildlife management were the true adherents of the code of the sportsman. This photograph, taken by naturalist John M. Phillips, shows a middle-aged Hornaday clutching the hide of a mountain goat he has just shot in British Columbia, and the caption he chose for the picture was "'The Moment of Triumph'—Caught Unawares [by the Camera]." From Hornaday, *Camp-Fires in the Canadian Rockies . . .* (1916); first published in 1906.

91. The New York Zoological Park ("Bronx Zoo"), one of the world's great zoos and a pioneer in the creation of natural "habitats" for its collections, was established by the Boone and Crockett Club in the 1890s to preserve wildlife from extinction, particularly big-game animals. As an institution closely linked with hunters, it included among its exhibits a museum containing the trophy heads of various big-game animals collected by sportsmen-naturalists. The photograph shows this "Heads and Horns Museum Building," which opened in 1922. (Courtesy of the New York Zoological Society.)

92. Aldo Leopold, "father of the American land ethic," weighing and measuring a woodcock after a hunt in the fall of 1946; note the shotguns on top of the car's fender. His land ethic represents the highest development of the environmental responsibility inherent in the code of the sportsman. The photograph was taken by his hunting partner, Robert A. McCabe, who generously shared his thoughts with me on what hunting meant to Leopold. (Courtesy of the University of Wisconsin Archives.)

Notes

Introduction

1. In a review of Robert McHenry, ed., *A Documentary History of Conservation in America* (New York, 1972), Richard A. Bartlett states: "For anyone involved with the conservation movement, or, to use a more modern word, ecology, it will provide sources for countless arguments and speeches"; *History: Reviews of New Books,* I (November-December, 1972), 32.
2. Herbert C. Hanson, *Dictionary of Ecology* (New York, 1962), 121. Of course, "ecology" is not only the study of those interrelationships, but it is the interrelationships themselves.
3. In his autobiography, *Breaking New Ground* (New York, 1947), Pinchot says he discovered this concept while horseback riding one evening in Rock Creek Park near Washington, D.C. See 322-26.
4. I am using this term to mean the history of the writing of history.
5. The best example of this thesis is J. Leonard Bates, "Fulfilling American Democracy: The Conservation Movement, 1907 to 1921," *Mississippi Valley Historical Review,* XLIV (June, 1957), 29-57.
6. See Peter G. Filene, "An Obituary for 'The Progressive Movement,'" *American Quarterly,* XXII (Spring, 1970), 20-34. Also see Richard L. McCormick, "The Discovery that Business Corrupts Politics: A Reappraisal of the Origins of Progressivism," *American Historical Review,* 48 (April, 1981), 247-74, and Daniel T. Rogers, "In Search of Progressivism," *Reviews in American History,* 10 (December, 1982), 113-32.
7. Except for *Forest and Stream,* the names of these newspapers changed frequently. These changes are traced in my "Annotated Bibliography." The *Field and Stream* discussed in this study is not the magazine of the same name in existence today.
8. This phrase was suggested to me by Stewart L. Udall's term: "Myth of Superabundance." See his *The Quiet Crisis* (New York, 1967), 66. Udall's book was first published in 1963.
9. John W. Noble to George Bird Grinnell, March 15, 1910, Grinnell File. (The latter is the name I have given to a mass of uncatalogued, miscellaneous material pertaining to pioneer conservationist George Bird Grinnell I found stored in the library of the Birdcraft Museum of the Connecticut Audubon Society, and now at Yale University.)

Chapter 1
Precursors of Conservation:
American Sportsmen Before the Civil War

1. John Quincy Adams, *Life in a New England Town: 1787, 1788. Diary of John Quincy Adams, While a Student in the Office of Theophilus Parsons at Newburyport* (Boston, 1903), 23.

2. William B. Greeley, *Forests and Men* (Garden City, New York, 1951), 54; William R. Adams, "Florida Live Oak Farm of John Quincy Adams," *Florida Historical Quarterly*, LI (1972), 129-42.
3. As examples of book-length works that deal to some degree with sportsmen and conservation, see James B. Trefethen, *An American Crusade for Wildlife* (New York, 1975); Thomas L. Altherr, "'The Best of All Breathing': Hunting as a Mode of Environmental Perception in American Literature and Thought from James Fenimore Cooper to Norman Mailer" (Ph.D. dissertation, Ohio State University, 1976); Thomas A. Lund, *American Wildlife Law* (Berkeley, California, 1980); George B. Ward, III, "Bloodbrothers in the Wilderness: The Sport Hunter and the Buckskin Hunter in the Preservation of the American Wilderness Experience" (Ph.D. dissertation, University of Texas, 1980); James A. Tober, *Who Owns the Wildlife? The Political Economy of Conservation in Nineteenth-Century America* (Westport, Connecticut, 1981); Donald W. Klinko, "Antebellum American Sporting Magazines and the Development of a Sportsmen's Ethic" (Ph.D. dissertation, Washington State University, 1986); Dunlap, *Saving America's Wildlife*, already cited; Stuart A. Marks, *Southern Hunting in Black and White: Nature, History, and Ritual in a Carolina Community* (Princeton, New Jersey, 1991); Lisa Mighetto, *Wild Animals and American Environmental Ethics* (Tucson, Arizona, 1991); Wiley C. Prewitt, Jr., "'The Best of All Breathing': Hunting and Environmental Change in Mississippi, 1900-1980" (M.A. thesis, University of Mississippi, 1991); Jon G. Donlon, "Hunting for Leisure: The Social Components and Historic Foundations of American Sport Hunting" (Ph.D. dissertation, University of Illinois, 1995); Sarah E. Broadbent, "Sportsmen and the Evolution of the Conservation Idea in Yellowstone: 1882-1894" (M.A. thesis, Montana State University, 1997); Karl H. Jacoby, "The Recreation of Nature: A Social and Environmental History of American Conservation, 1872-1919" (Ph.D. dissertation, Yale University, 1997); Louis S. Warren, *The Hunter's Game: Poachers and Conservationists in Twentieth-Century America* (New Haven, Connecticut, 1997); and Nicolas W. Proctor, "Bathed in Blood: Hunting in the Antebellum South" (Ph.D. dissertation, Emory University, 1998). Of these, only Klinko and Proctor concentrate on sportsmen before the Civil War.
4. John C. Phillips (comp.), *American Game Mammals and Birds: A Catalogue of Books, 1582 to 1925.* (Boston, 1930), 355.
5. *Ibid.*
6. Anonymous ("A Gentleman"), *The Sportsman's Companion; or, An Essay on Shooting* (Harrisburg, Pennsylvania, 1948), 30. Reprint of first (1783) edition, edited by Jan Thornton.
7. *Ibid.*, 6.
8. *Ibid.*, "Editor's Notes," 118-19.
9. Where there is the possibility of confusion, scientific names have been provided.
10. Actually, Massachusetts had a closed season for white-tailed deer as early as 1694; T. S. Palmer (comp.), *Chronology and Index of the More Important Events in American Game Protection, 1776-1911.* U.S. Department of Agriculture, Biological Survey Bulletin No. 41 (Washington, D.C., 1912), 14.

11. Anonymous, *The Sportsman's Companion*, 62, 64, and 67.
12. Phillips, *American Game Mammals and Birds*, 211.
13. *Ibid.*
14. "A Gentleman of Philadelphia County" ["Dr." Jesse Y. Kester], *The American Shooter's Manual* (Philadelphia, 1827), ix-x. Throughout, I have silently "modernized" the idiosyncratic punctuation found in these works.
15. Kester, *The American Shooter's Manual*, 13-15.
16. *Ibid.*, 144-45, and 149.
17. *Ibid.*, 154-55.
18. *Ibid.*, 168-69.
19. J. Kenneth Callahan (comp.), *A Dictionary of Sporting Pen Names* (Peterborough, New Hampshire, 1995), 127.
20. "One Who is Considered Nobody" [John Davis], *Essays on Various Subjects, Written for the Amusement of Everybody* (New York, 1835), 7. I am indebted to Thomas L. Altherr for bringing this work to my attention.
21. Davis, *Essays*, 9-10.
22. To be killed "cleanly" in the air, a bird usually has to be "centered" in the pattern, with several pellets hitting it.
23. Davis, *Essays*, 10.
24. Anonymous, *The Sportsman's Companion*, "Editor's Notes," 119.
25. Davis, *Essays*, 12.
26. *Ibid.*, 13.
27. John James Audubon and Alexander Wilson are two of the best-known examples. For Audubon's hunting, see his *Delineations of American Scenery and Character* (New York, 1970); this is a reprint of a book first published in 1926 that contains an Introduction by his biographer, Francis Hobart Herrick. For Alexander Wilson, see his *Wilson's American Ornithology* (Boston, 1840); his term "met with"—for encountering a bird he wanted—was a synonym for "shot," as on p. 614 he stated that he "met with" or "shot" the gadwall duck in various locations.
28. J. P. Giraud, Jr., *The Birds of Long Island* (New York, 1844), iii-iv.
29. *Ibid.*, vi-viii.
30. *Ibid.*, 305, 189, and 194.
31. *Ibid.*, 207-08.
32. Rails are still hunted in this fashion, and some sportsmen continue to find them too easy to shoot. After a trip to the Georgia coast, former president Jimmy Carter recalled that "I soon reached the legal limit without missing a shot, and . . . remember the facile experience with distaste. I've never wanted to shoot another rail." Carter, *An Outdoor Journal: Adventures and Reflections* (New York, 1988), 14.
33. Giraud, *Birds of Long Island*, 256-57.
34. *Ibid.*, 267-68.
35. *Ibid.*, 294.
36. *Ibid.*, 295.
37. *Ibid.*
38. Charles Eliot Goodspeed, *Angling in America: Its Early History and Literature* (Boston, 1939), 30.
39. *Ibid.*, 73-74.
40. Quoted in *ibid.*, 133.
41. *Ibid.*

42. Paul Schullery, *Royal Coachman: The Lore and Legends of Fly-Fishing* (New York, 1999), 65-66. I am indebted to Schullery for bringing this material pertaining to Gibson to my attention.
43. *Ibid.*, 66; Schullery notes that "there were earlier articles, but they were less personal and specific and may have been mostly plagiarized from British publications."
44. Quoted in *ibid.*
45. *Ibid.*, 67.
46. *Ibid.*
47. *Ibid.*, 75.
48. *Ibid.*
49. Goodspeed, *Angling in America*, 108.
50. *Ibid.*, 108-113.
51. *Ibid.*, 113.
52. Jerome V. C. Smith, *Natural History of the Fishes of Massachusetts, Embracing a Practical Essay on Angling* (New York, 1970), 344-46; this is a reprint of a work first published in 1833.
53. Goodspeed, *Angling in America*, 159.
54. John J. Brown, *The American Angler's Guide; or, Complete Fisher's Manual For the United States: Containing the Opinions and Practices of Experienced Anglers of Both Hemispheres . . .* (New York, 1857), 231-32. The enlarged edition of Brown's work, containing the section quoted here, first appeared in 1849.
55. *Ibid.*, 232.
56. *Ibid.*
57. *Ibid.*, 233.
58. *Ibid.*, 233-34.
59. *Ibid.*, 264-65.
60. *Ibid.*, 265.
61. *Ibid.*
62. Peter Matthiessen, *Wildlife in America* (New York, 1987), 186; first published in 1959. A. J. McClane, ed., *McClane's Field Guide to Freshwater Fishes of North America* (New York, 1978), 56.
63. *Ibid.*
64. Brown, *American Angler's Guide*, 266.
65. Henry William Herbert, *Frank Forester's Fish and Fishing of the United States, and British Provinces of North America* (London, 1849), 84-89, 256, and 293-96.
66. *Ibid.*, 86.
67. Dean C. Allard, Jr., "Spencer Fullerton Baird and the U.S. Fish Commission: A Study in the History of American Science" (Ph.D. dissertation, George Washington University, 1967), 113-14.
68. Lewis Mumford, *The Brown Decades: A Study of the Arts in America, 1865-1895* (New York, 1931), 78.
69. David Lowenthal, *George Perkins Marsh: Versatile Vermonter* (New York, 1958), 3, 17-18, and 185.
70. *Ibid.*, 139-40.
71. Allard, "Spencer Fullerton Baird," 114.
72. Goodspeed, *Angling in America*, 274; Allard, "Spencer Fullerton Baird," 65 and 112.

73. George Perkins Marsh, *Report, Made Under Authority of the Legislature of Vermont, on the Artificial Propagation of Fish* (Burlington, Vermont, 1857), 8-9.
74. *Ibid.*, 12-13.
75. *Ibid.*, 13-14.
76. *Ibid.*, 14-15.
77. *Ibid.*, 15.
78. *Ibid.*, 10.
79. *Ibid.*
80. *Ibid.*
81. *Ibid.*, 11.
82. *Ibid.*, 20-21.
83. *Ibid.*, 11-12.
84. *Ibid.*, 17.
85. *Ibid.*
86. *Ibid.*, 16-17.
87. Lowenthal, *George Perkins Marsh*, 186.
88. Allard, "Spencer Fullerton Baird," 114.
89. Lowenthal, *George Perkins Marsh*, 253.
90. George Perkins Marsh, *Man and Nature; or, Physical Geography as Modified by Human Action* (New York, 1864), 280-84.
91. Lowenthal, *George Perkins Marsh*, 186.
92. William Elliott, *Carolina Sports By Land and Water* (New York, 1967), 166. This is a reprint of the first (1846) edition, published in Charleston, South Carolina.
93. *Ibid.*, 166.
94. *Ibid.*, 166-67.
95. *Ibid.*, 167.
96. *Ibid.*
97. *Ibid.*
98. *Ibid.*
99. *Ibid.*, 168.
100. *Ibid.*
101. *Ibid.*, 168-69.
102. *Ibid.*, 172.
103. William Southworth Hunt, *Frank Forester [Henry William Herbert], A Tragedy in Exile* (Newark, New Jersey, 1933), vii, 1, 21-27, 54, and 57-58.
104. *Ibid.*, 57; the series began in *The American Turf Register and Sporting Magazine* in the May/June, 1839 issue, and a month earlier in *The Corsair*. For a reprint of the first installment of the series, see Larry K. Menna, ed., *The Origins of Modern Sports, 1820-1840; Vol. 2 of Sports in North America, A Documentary History* (Gulf Breeze, Florida, 1995), 60-68.
105. Klinko, "Antebellum American Sporting Magazines," iv-v. As Klinko points out, "confusion . . . exists in distinguishing magazines from newspapers at this early date," because "their physical aspects were usually very similar. . . ." Essentially, "a newspaper existed primarily to report the current news, while a magazine was intended to instruct or entertain its audience" (p. 9). For another examination of early sporting journalism, see Jack W. Berryman, "The Tenuous Attempts of Americans to 'Catch-Up with John Bull': Specialty Magazines and Sporting Journalism, 1800-1835,"

Canadian Journal of History of Sport and Physical Education, X (May, 1979), 33-61.

106. Menna, *The Origins of Modern Sports,* Vol. 2, 305; also see 306-08.

107. Quoted in Klinko, "Antebellum American Sporting Magazines," 79.

108. *Ibid.*

109. *Ibid.,* 111.

110. *Ibid.,* 111-12.

111. *Ibid.,* 180.

112. *Ibid.*

113. *Ibid.,* 181-82.

114. *Ibid.,* 182.

115. *Ibid.,* 182-83.

116. *Ibid.,* 42, 90, 92, and 98.

117. For some idea of the range and quantity of his works, see William Mitchell Van Winkle (comp.), *Henry William Herbert [Frank Forester]: A Bibliography of His Writings, 1832-1858* (Portland, Maine, 1936).

118. Although published in the United States in October, 1848, the American edition was post-dated to 1849, and that is the year on the title page; *ibid.,* 25.

119. Henry William Herbert, *Frank Forester's Field Sports of the United States and British Provinces of North America,* 2 vols. (New York, 1849), I, v.

120. An archaic term, usually spelled "venery."

121. Herbert, *Field Sports,* I, 11-12.

122. *Ibid.,* 14.

123. *Ibid.,* 17. For another view of rural people, at least in one area of the United States, see Richard W. Judd, *Common Lands, Common People: The Origins of Conservation in Northern New England* (Cambridge, Massachusetts, 1997). Judd argues that country people in the region of his study were not opposed to conservation, but actually initiated it. Jacoby, in "The Recreation of Nature," also studies rural inhabitants' attitudes toward conservation.

124. Herbert, *Field Sports,* I, 17-18.

125. *Ibid.,* 18. For a study of these types of land uses, see Gordon G. Whitney, *From Coastal Wilderness to Fruited Plain: A History of Environmental Change in Temperate North America, 1500 to the Present* (New York, 1994).

126. Herbert, *Field Sports,* I, 18.

127. Matthiessen, *Wildlife in America,* 69.

128. Two analyses of how this development in law took place are Lund, *American Wildlife Law,* and Tober, *Who Owns the Wildlife?*

129. Herbert, *Field Sports,* I, 18-19.

130. *Ibid.,* 19-20.

131. Thoreau, *Walden, or Life in the Woods* (New York, 1942), 143; first published in 1854. The author does not know what Thoreau meant by the "Humane Society." Perhaps it was a local group, for the first "national" association with this orientation seems to have been the Society for the Prevention of Cruelty to Animals (SPCA), established in New York by Henry Bergh in 1866. By "animals," Bergh meant chiefly the domestic kinds, not wildlife; he was, for instance, "interested especially in horses" (Mighetto, *Wild Animals,* 46).

For an interesting article comparing the world views of Transcendentalist Henry David Thoreau and sportsman William Elliott, see Charles R. Anderson, "Thoreau Takes a Pot Shot at *Carolina Sports*," *Georgia Review*, XXII (Fall, 1968), 289-99. For his conflicting feelings toward hunting, see Thomas L. Altherr, "'Chaplain to the Hunters': Thoreau's Ambivalence Toward Hunting," *American Literature*, LVI (October, 1984), 345-61; and Thomas L. Altherr and John F. Reiger, "Academic Historians and Hunting: A Call for More and Better Scholarship," *Environmental History Review*, XIX (Fall, 1995), 48-50.

132. Tober, *Who Owns the Wildlife?*, 49.

133. Herbert, *Field Sports*, 1, 267.

134. George Bird Grinnell, "American Game Protection, A Sketch," in Grinnell and Charles Sheldon, eds., *Hunting and Conservation: The Book of the Boone and Crockett Club* (New Haven, 1925), 221-24.

135. Lewis was a Philadelphia physician, who studied at Princeton and graduated from the medical school of the University of Pennsylvania; Krider was also from Philadelphia, a gun maker and owner of a well-known "sportsmen's depot," established in 1826, which supplied hunters and anglers all over the country; and Samuel Hammond was a prominent journalist from Albany.

136. Samuel H. Hammond, *Wild Northern Scenes; or, Sporting Adventures with the Rifle and the Rod* (New York, 1857), 82-84. An earlier, less-ambitious version of Hammond's proposal for a preserve can be found in his *Hills, Lakes, and Forest Streams; or, A Tramp in the Chateaugay Woods* (New York, 1854), 168. For the development of fly-fishing as a sport among gentleman anglers, see Paul Schullery, *American Fly-Fishing: A History* (New York, 1987).

137. Klinko, "Antebellum American Sporting Magazines," 180.

138. *Ibid.*, 187-94.

139. *Ibid.*, 196.

140. Quoted in *ibid.*, 199.

141. *Ibid.*, 200-02.

142. *Ibid.*, 202-08.

143. *Ibid.*, 209-12.

Chapter 2
Makers of Conservation:
American Sportsmen After the Civil War

1. As we have seen, articles on hunting and fishing had appeared earlier in "sporting" periodicals like *American Turf Register and Sporting Magazine*, and *The Spirit of the Times*, but these journals were not devoted primarily to hunting and fishing. The one subject they carried most seems to have been horse racing.

2. *Forest and Stream*, July 2, 1885, XXIV, 451. For a different interpretation of this period, see Klinko, "Antebellum Sporting Magazines," 42.

3. Interestingly, under the various definitions of the word "nature," the *American Heritage Dictionary of the English Language* states that "against nature" means something "profoundly wrong or unnatural: '*the taking [of] fish in spawning-time may be said to be against nature*' (Walton)."

4. Francis J. Grund, *The Americans in Their Moral, Social, and Political Relations* (London, 1837), II, 263-64. Grund immigrated to Boston from his native Austria about 1827.

5. The life expectancy of Americans is now 76.5 years; see *The World Almanac and Book of Facts, 1999* (Mahwah, New Jersey, 1998), 875.

6. *Sports Afield*, II (January 17, 1889), 5; Dwight W. Huntington, *Our Big Game: A Book for Sportsmen and Nature Lovers* (New York, 1904), 29.

7. In almost all cases, the editorials appearing in the sporting periodicals were unsigned, but I am assuming that they were written by the editor. That assumption will be followed throughout this work. In this instance, the paper was theoretically conducted by the "Parker Brothers"—as noted in the masthead—but Wilbur seems to have been responsible for the editorial matter. The Parker family is best remembered today for the making of fine shotguns.

8. Volume II, 24.

9. *Ibid.*

10. *Ibid.*

11. December, 1872, II, 40; October 11, 1873, III, 26; November 22, 1873, III, 120; November 29, 1873, III, 139; April 18, 1874, IV, 40.

12. George Bird Grinnell to Charles Sheldon, March 6, 1922, Letter Book, 206. Grinnell's Letter Books were found by me in the library of the Birdcraft Museum of the Connecticut Audubon Society. Arranged chronologically, most volumes have approximately 1,000 pages of copied letters. Thirty-eight books in all, they extend, with few gaps, from August 2, 1886, to October 17, 1929. In 1984 they were transferred to Yale.

13. *Forest and Stream*, September 11, 1873, I, 73; *ibid.*, April 29, 1875, IV, 186; "Fishculture" was a regular column of the weekly; *Forest and Stream*, March 18, 1875, IV, 88; Grinnell to C. A. Hazen, September 20, 1916, Letter Book, 402.

14. I am indebted to George M. Fredrickson for suggesting this possibility.

15. "A New Gospel of Aesthetics," *Forest and Stream*, August 24, 1876, VII, 40.

16. *Ibid.*

17. *Ibid.*, August 14, 1873, I, 8.

18. *Ibid.*

19. Grinnell to Charles Sheldon, March 4, 1925, Grinnell File. "Memoirs," 86-87. A typewritten autobiography written between November 26, 1915, and December 4, 1915, and covering Grinnell's life up to about 1883, the "Memoirs" (other copies of this manuscript have surfaced, like the one in the Glacier National Park Archives, but with the title of "Memories") abruptly end in the middle of a sentence on page 97. The manuscript is in the Grinnell File, but when citing this source, I will simply refer to it as the "Memoirs."

20. His early life (1849-83) is dealt with in John F. Reiger, editor and commentator, *The Passing of the Great West: Selected Papers of George Bird Grinnell* (Norman, Oklahoma, 1985); first published in 1972. Grinnell is best known today for his writings on the American Indian.

21. "A Ten Years' Review," *Forest and Stream*, January 1, 1880, XIII, 950.

22. "A Much Abused Title," *ibid.*, August 10, 1882, XIX, 21-22.

23. "Pot-Hunters," *ibid.*, April 20, 1882, XVIII, 223; "The Order of Trout Hogs," *ibid.*, June 16, 1881, XVI, 379.

24. *Ibid.*, February 12, 1880, XIV, 31.
25. *Ibid.*
26. *Ibid.*
27. See his *Age of Reform: From Bryan to F.D.R.* (New York, 1955), 135-66.
28. This term comes from a novel of the same name written by Mark Twain and Charles Dudley Warner and published in 1873. Their book castigates the vulgarity of the time, and its title has been used by historians to characterize the years from about 1877 to about 1896.
29. *The Inner Civil War: Northern Intellectuals and the Crisis of the Union* (New York, 1968), 221.
30. Grinnell to Frank G. Page, September 15, 1926, Letter Book, 421-22; *Forest and Stream,* December 24, 1891, XXXVII, 445; "Memoirs," 44.
31. Reiger, *The Passing of the Great West,* 57-58 and 78-80.
32. *The Inner Civil War,* 266.
33. Of these businesses, the Bosworth Machine Company of Milford, Connecticut, was the largest. It made sewing machines for heavy industrial uses.
34. Leopold, *A Sand County Almanac* (1966 edition), 213. For the claim that hunting involves one intimately with his or her quarry and the natural world, also see Ortega y Gasset's *Meditations on Hunting;* the idea is scattered throughout. For merely one example of the same belief in the period under discussion, see "Science and Field Sports," *American Field* (later name of *Field and Stream*), August 7, 1886, XXVI, 121.
35. Robert Henry Welker, *Birds and Men: American Birds in Science, Art, Literature, and Conservation, 1800-1900* (New York, 1966), 119; first published in 1955. For Muir, see Stephen Fox, *John Muir and His Legacy: The American Conservation Movement* (Boston, 1981), 81-82. Muir claimed to accept evolution as fact, but gutted Darwin's thesis by rejecting natural selection—because it interfered with the "divine plan."
36. Of course, some Romantics probably thought these areas appealing because they were "mysterious," but they rarely actually entered them—unlike the hunter.
37. Under the leadership of Jay N. ("Ding") Darling and other sportsmen-conservationists, the Migratory Bird Hunting Stamp Act was passed in 1934. It obligates waterfowl hunters to purchase a stamp before they can shoot, and the money brought in is used to preserve waterfowl habitat. This device and the actions of private sportsmen's groups such as Ducks Unlimited have reserved huge areas in the United States and Canada that would otherwise have been lost to agricultural and industrial development.
38. Roosevelt, *Superior Fishing; or, the Striped Bass, Trout, and Black Bass of the Northern States . . .* (New York, 1865), 184-85.
39. Because of its almost universal use, I sometimes employ the term "buffalo," even though "bison" is the only technically correct name for the wild cattle of North America. A later member of the Boone and Crockett Club, Parkman "ran" buffalo on this trip for pleasure, not simple necessity: "My chase was more protracted, but at length I ran close to the bull and killed him with my pistols." See page 360.
40. Parkman, *The Oregon Trail: Sketches of Prairie and Rocky-Mountain Life* (Boston, 1872), ix-x.
41. Issue of February 20, 1875, V, 328.

42. For an appraisal of Murray's impact, see the 1970 edition of his famous book, edited by William K. Verner and with an Introduction of over sixty pages by Warder H. Cadbury; published in Syracuse, New York, by Syracuse University Press.

43. *Rod and Gun and American Sportsman* (same paper but with a new title), October 7, 1876, IX, 5.

44. Actually, this is the last of several titles; *Field and Stream* changed its name to *The Field, Chicago Field,* and finally *American Field.*

45. "Long Island As It Was—The Lesson It Teaches," *American Field,* July 1, 1882, XVIII, 8. Paragraphing eliminated.

46. For a history of what was perhaps the first club, the Schuylkill Fishing Company, founded in 1732, see *Rod and Gun* (formerly *American Sportsman*), December 4, 1875, VII, 150; Robert Adams, Jr., "The Oldest Club in America," *Century Magazine,* XXVI (August, 1883), 544-50; and Goodspeed, "The Schuylkill Fishing Company," *Angling in America,* 29-54.

47. Exceptions to this statement were the duck-hunting clubs, already common by the antebellum period in some waterfowl regions.

48. Burnham, "The Old Era—and the New," *Bulletin of the American Game Protective [and Propagation] Association,* XIV (January, 1925), 13.

49. This group was originally called the American Fish Culturists' Association; since 1884 it has been known as the American Fisheries Society.

50. Pages 61-68. I have left out a number of clubs formed by Americans in Canada. Hallock's book was published in New York.

51. Hallock does not specifically state this, but it was a common practice of the day to name clubs after famous outdoorsmen and their leading periodicals.

52. *American Club List and Sportsman's Glossary,* 33-37 and 43. I have also left out four fox-hunting clubs in Canada.

53. There are many sources of documentation for the fact that most wildlife legislation originated with sportsmen and that their efforts go back to the beginning of American history. By the 1870s, they had forced the passage of a huge number of laws in every part of the country—the main problem was enforcement. For merely a sample of the literature pertaining to this subject, see Palmer, *Chronology and Index of the More Important Events in American Game Protection;* Ralph M. Van Brocklin, "The Movement for the Conservation of Natural Resources in the United States Before 1901" (Ph.D. dissertation, University of Michigan, 1952); John Henry Reeves, Jr., "The History and Development of Wildlife Conservation in Virginia: A Critical Review" (Ph.D. dissertation, Virginia Polytechnic Institute, 1960); Eugene T. Petersen, "The History of Wild Life Conservation in Michigan, 1859-1921" (Ph.D. dissertation, University of Michigan, 1953); and Marvin W. Kranz, "Pioneering in Conservation: A History of the Conservation Movement in New York State, 1865-1903" (Ph.D. dissertation, Syracuse University, 1961). Kranz, for example, states that "most of the laws restricting shooting appeared to be, and in fact were, designed by wealthy sportsmen" (p. 102). As an illustration of how strong this movement had become by the 1870s, *Forest and Stream* reported in 1874 that 30,000 petitioners were backing up an effort by some Ohio legislators to pass new game laws; see the issue of April 16, 1874, II, 153.

54. Volume III, 53.

55. *American Sportsman,* December 20, 1873, III, 188. As in most cases of this kind, the correspondent included the names of the elected officers.
56. This, of course, is untrue.
57. *American Sportsman,* June 13, 1874, IV, 168. Paragraphing has been eliminated.
58. *Ibid.,* August 29, 1874, IV, 344.
59. The great majority of these individuals have publications written by them, or pertaining to them, in my "Annotated Bibliography" that document their hunting or fishing. There are some, however, whose experience in these activities cannot be readily ascertained by consulting the titles in that compilation: Ainsworth was a wealthy angler who pioneered in fish culture (Thaddeus Norris dedicated his early work on that subject to Ainsworth and cites him as an angler); Anderson was a hunter (George Bird Grinnell to Anderson, September 7, 1892, Letter Book, 371); Arthur, Clinton, Harrison, and Webster were anglers (see Goodspeed, *Angling in America*); Baird's youthful angling and hunting are mentioned in Dall's biography, while his later angling interests are cited in George Reiger, *Profiles in Saltwater Angling;* Bierstadt and Grant were regular members of the Boone and Crockett Club and both hunters; the fact that Cox, Vest, and Moran were sportsmen will be documented later in this study; Dutcher was a hunter (see John B. Burnham's article, "Conservation's Debt to Sportsmen"); Edmunds was an angler (see Dean C. Allard, Jr., "Spencer Fullerton Baird and the U.S. Fish Commission. . ."); Harris, Parker, and Rowe were editors of leading sporting periodicals and well-known sportsmen; Ludlow was a hunter (see photograph of grizzly bear he helped to "bag" on Custer's 1874 Black Hills expedition in Reiger, *The Passing of the Great West*); and Merriam was a hunter and a member of the League of American Sportsmen. All the works mentioned above are in my "Annotated Bibliography."
60. Mighetto, *Wild Animals,* 32.
61. David Popenoe, *Sociology* (Englewood Cliffs, New Jersey, 1980), 294-99; first published in 1971.
62. Glenda Riley, *Women and Nature: Saving the "Wild" West* (Lincoln, Nebraska, 1999), xiii.
63. *Ibid.,* photograph #23, following page 96.
64. Tom Fegley, "Women Drawn to Hunting," *Chillicothe Gazette,* January 16, 2000, page 6B.
65. Mary Zeiss Stange, *Woman the Hunter* (Boston, 1997).
66. Fegley, "Women Drawn to Hunting"; some of the television programs mentioned in the Preface of the present work cite the growing numbers of sportswomen in sport-related conservation organizations.

Chapter 3
Conservation Begins with Wildlife

1. Their statement of this position can be found in their memoirs. See Roosevelt, *Theodore Roosevelt: An Autobiography* (New York, 1913); and Pinchot, *Breaking New Ground,* already cited.
2. Nicholas Roosevelt, *Conservation: Now or Never* (New York, 1970), 9. For the idea that Roosevelt continually stressed the utilitarian objectives of his

conservation program because of political necessity rather than from a lack of aesthetic appreciation, see Pinchot to Alden Sampson, November 15, 1901, Boone and Crockett Club File (this "File" is the designation I have given to the large mass of uncatalogued material pertaining to the Boone and Crockett Club and its members, formerly located at the Theodore Roosevelt Birthplace and now at the Boone and Crockett Club and the University of Montana, both in Missoula). Roosevelt to Roger S. Baldwin, October 13, 1903, in Elting E. Morison and John M. Blum, eds., *Letters of Theodore Roosevelt* (Cambridge, Massachusetts, 1951-54), III, 329-30; Grinnell, "Theodore Roosevelt," in Grinnell, ed., *American Big Game in Its Haunts* (New York, 1904), 15-16; and Roosevelt to Robert Underwood Johnson, January 17, 1905, in Morison and Blum, *Letters of Theodore Roosevelt*, IV, 1104-05.

3. Frank M. Chapman, *Autobiography of a Bird-Lover* (New York, 1935), 181; first published in 1933. Also see Willard B. Gatewood, "Theodore Roosevelt: Champion of 'Governmental Aesthetics'," *Georgia Review*, XXI (1967), 172-83.

4. Paul Russell Cutright, *Theodore Roosevelt: The Making of a Conservationist* (Urbana, Illinois, 1985), 223.

5. John Ise, *Our National Park Policy: A Critical History* (Baltimore, 1961), 109.

6. *Ibid.*, 152. John F. Lacey, "Let Us Save the Birds: Speech of Hon. John F. Lacey in the House of Representatives," *Recreation*, XIII (July, 1900), 33.

7. Hal Rothman, *Preserving Different Pasts: The American National Monuments* (Urbana, Illinois, 1989), 69-70 and 234.

8. *Ibid.*, 70.

9. *Ibid.*, 68. Cutright, *Theodore Roosevelt*, 195.

10. *Ibid.*

11. One scholar who was an early "exception to the rule" was Lawrence Rakestraw. In his writings that touched on Pinchot, Rakestraw tried to set the record straight. See his book review of Frank Graham, Jr., *Man's Dominion: The Story of Conservation in America* (New York, 1971), in *Forest History*, XVI (April, 1972), 31-32; his article, "Conservation Historiography: An Assessment," particularly 278-81; and his book review of Henry Clepper's *Professional Forestry in the United States* (Baltimore, 1971), in the *Pacific Historical Review*, XLII (February, 1973), 118. In the latter piece Rakestraw cites Pinchot's "'Forest Reserve Order No. 19' which ordered classification and special protection for areas of 'popular, historic or scientific interest'. . . ."

12. Grinnell to J. B. Monroe, May 3, 1897, Letter Book, 395.

13. See Reiger, "Gifford Pinchot with Rod and Reel."

14. *Ibid.*, 28.

15. Marguerite Ives, "Gifford Pinchot," in *Seventeen Famous Outdoorsmen Known to Marguerite Ives* (Chicago, 1929), 57.

16. Nicholas Roosevelt, *Conservation*, 15.

17. Pinchot to Roosevelt, November 11, 1901, Boone and Crockett Club File. Dedicated national park defender George Bird Grinnell—who began his continuous editorial effort to preserve the Yellowstone years before John Muir initiated a similar drive in regard to Yosemite Valley—had the greatest admiration for the utilitarian Pinchot and worked closely with him on

matters pertaining to both wildlife and forest conservation; proof for this statement may be found in correspondence in Grinnell's Letter Books and in his editorials in *Forest and Stream*. See, for example, Grinnell to Pinchot, June 11, 1901, Letter Book, 712-13; Grinnell to Pinchot, September 30, 1901, *ibid.*, 895-96; Grinnell to Pinchot, October 5, 1901, *ibid.*, 918; Grinnell to Pinchot, December 4, 1901, *ibid.*, 959-60; Grinnell to Sampson, December 23, 1901, *ibid.*, 12; Grinnell to Pinchot, January 28, 1904, *ibid.*, 509; Grinnell to Rosewell B. Lawrence, June 4, 1906, *ibid.*, 415-16; Grinnell to Pinchot, June 3, 1907, *ibid.*, 953; Grinnell to John J. White, Jr., February 5, 1908, *ibid.*, 344; Grinnell to Madison Grant, March 6, 1908, *ibid.*, 392; Grinnell to Pinchot, March 25, 1908, *ibid.*, 444; "The Biltmore Forest," *Forest and Stream,* January 6, 1894, XLII, 1; "Yale School of Forestry," *ibid.*, March 24, 1900, LIV, 221; *ibid.*, January 30, 1904, LXII, 81; "Transfer of Forest Reserves," *ibid.*, February 11, 1905, LXIV, 109; "The Forest Service," *ibid.*, January 26, 1907, LXVIII, 127; and "Gifford Pinchot," *ibid.*, January 15, 1910, LXXIV, 87.

After Roosevelt left office, Grinnell and Pinchot would find themselves on opposite sides of the fence in the controversy over whether a portion of Yosemite National Park should be flooded to create a reservoir, but this was one issue and did not mean that they had split over their general approach to conservation. Pinchot's stand in favor of the reservoir has been treated frequently by historians; for Grinnell's position, see "The Hetch-Hetchy Project," *Forest and Stream,* February 6, 1909, LXXII, 207; "Hetch-Hetchy Valley," *ibid.*, March 5, 1910, LXXIV, 367; "Hetch Hetchy Next Year," *ibid.*, June 18, 1910, LXXIV, 967; Grinnell to H. L. Myers, September 23, 1913, Letter Book, 486-87; Grinnell to R. U. Johnson, September 25, 1913, *ibid.*, 515; and Grinnell to James A. O'Gorman, October 7, 1913, *ibid.*, 548.

This unity in regard to basic goals was shared by most of the leaders of the aesthetically oriented Boone and Crockett Club during Roosevelt's administration, as shown by papers in the Boone and Crockett Club File. See Pinchot to Roosevelt, November 11, 1901; George B. Cortelyou to Pinchot, November 30, 1901; Pinchot to Sampson, November 15, 1901; "Report of Committee on Game Refuges Submitted to Executive Committee at Players' Club, New York on January 7, 1902"; Pinchot to Sampson, January 13, 1902; Pinchot to Sampson, January 15, 1902; Pinchot to Sampson, March 6, 1902; Pinchot to Sampson, April 2, 1902; John F. Lacey to Grant, June 12, 1902; Pinchot to Grant, January 31, 1903; Sampson to Grant, October 28, 1903; and Grinnell to Grant, March 6, 1907.

18. Bernard E. Fernow, *A Brief History of Forestry in Europe, the United States and Other Countries* (Toronto, Canada, 1907), 413; VanBrocklin, "The Movement for the Conservation of Natural Resources," 32; Kranz, "Pioneering in Conservation," 138; and Andrew Denny Rodgers III, *Bernhard Eduard Fernow: A Story of North American Forestry* (New York, 1968), 51; first published in 1951.

19. Henry Clepper, "American Forestry Association," in Richard C. Davis, ed., *Encyclopedia of American Forest and Conservation History* (New York, 1983), I, 17.

20. Roosevelt, *Game Fish of the Northern States of America* . . . (New York, 1862), 52-53, 89, 95, and 230-35; Norris, *American Fish-Culture* . . .

(Philadelphia, 1868), 20-21 and 143-44; Scott, *Fishing in American Waters* (New York, 1875), 151-54, 365-66, 379, and 407-18; Scott's book was first published in 1869. For merely a sample of the large number of attacks on these evils found in the sporting periodicals, see "Fishways in Streams," *American Sportsman*, February, 1872, I, 7; "The Pollution of Rivers and Streams," *ibid.*, May 2, 1874, IV, 72; "Dirty Water," *ibid.*, December 5, 1874, V, 152; "The Pollution of Rivers," *Forest and Stream*, March 18, 1875, IV, 88; "Pollution of Streams," *The Rod and the Gun* (later name of *American Sportsman*), August 14, 1875, VI, 296; Seth Green, "Destruction of Fish by Paper Mills," *American Angler*, November 19, 1881, I, 28; "Destruction of Food Fishes" and "The Poisoned Schuylkill," both in *Forest and Stream*, July 13, 1882, XVIII, 463; "The Sawmill and the Trout," *American Angler*, September 23, 1882, II, 199; *American Field* (later name of *Field and Stream*), July 14, 1883, XX, 25; "The Pollution of the Schuylkill River, Pa.," *American Angler*, August 22, 1885, VIII, 118; "Polluting New York Harbor," *Forest and Stream*, June 10, 1886, XXVI, 387; *American Angler*, January 1, 1887, XI, 8; "Fertilizers Destructive to Fish Life," *ibid.*, January 8, 1887, XI, 30; "Fish Slaughter and Stream Pollution," *ibid.*, August 13, 1887, XII, 97; Seth Green, "Can Stream Pollution Be Stopped?" *ibid.*, August 13, 1887, XII, 107; and "River Pollution in Ohio," *Forest and Stream*, December 22, 1887, XXIX, 421.

21. Arnold Gingrich, *The Fishing in Print: A Guided Tour Through Five Centuries of Angling Literature* (New York, 1974), 28, 149, 151, and 155.

22. Thaddeus Norris, *The American Angler's Book: Embracing the Natural History of Sporting Fish, and the Art of Taking Them, With Instructions in Fly-Fishing, Fly-Making, and Rod-Making, and Directions for Fish-Breeding* . . . (Philadelphia, 1864), 459-60.

23. *Ibid.*, 60.

24. Kranz, "Pioneering in Conservation," 37 (Footnote #28) and 65-66.

25. *Ibid.*, 33-34.

26. Robert Barnwell Roosevelt, *Superior Fishing*, 14 and 20-21.

27. I have borrowed, and extended to fishing, this phrase from philosopher Paul Shepard. See his *The Tender Carnivore and the Sacred Game* (New York, 1973), which argues that modern humans' most cherished qualities and abilities are the result of our hunter-gatherer past.

28. Roosevelt, *Superior Fishing*, 184-86.

29. *Ibid.*, 188-90.

30. *Ibid.*, 186-87, and 193.

31. *Ibid.*

32. *Ibid.*, 193-94.

33. *Ibid.*, 191-92 and 195. The Hudson was probably never a salmon river.

34. *Ibid.*, 183-84.

35. Richard P. Harmond, "Robert Barnwell Roosevelt and the Early Conservation Movement," *Theodore Roosevelt Association Journal*, XIV (Summer, 1988), 4.

36. Kranz, "Pioneering in Conservation," 53.

37. Harmond, "Robert Barnwell Roosevelt," 5.

38. Charles F. Waterman, *Fishing in America* (New York, 1975), 84.

39. Harmond, "Robert Barnwell Roosevelt," 6.

40. *Ibid.*

41. *Ibid.*, 8.
42. John T. Cumber, "The Early Making of an Environmental Consciousness: Fish, Fisheries Commissions and the Connecticut River," *Environmental History Review,* XV (Winter, 1991), 79-80.
43. *Ibid.*, 83 and 90 (Note #44).
44. *Ibid.*, 91 (Note #61).
45. This was a term sportsman employed for those who used unsporting methods to catch fish mainly for food or commerce. Not only did these individuals supposedly have no sense of the "art" and "science" of angling, but they caught, and kept, too many fish, and often sold their catch as well, which, of course, was one of the most serious infractions of the code of the sportsman. Yet another example of the interconnection between hunting and fishing was the fact that the term "pot-hunter" was used interchangeably for those who broke the rules, whether in fishing or hunting. For example, in *Superior Fishing* Robert Roosevelt complained about what had happened in one of his favorite angling destinations in New York State: "The rapidity with which a section of country can be fished out by energetic *pot-hunters* [emphasis added] where the law places inadequate restraint, and often in spite of the law's restraint, has been remarkably evidenced in the history of Sullivan County" (185).
46. See United States Commission of Fish and Fisheries, *Report on the Condition of the Sea Fisheries of the South Coast of New England in 1871 and 1872* (Washington, D.C., 1873), IX and 197; hereinafter, this source will be referred to as the *U.S. Fish Commission Report.*
47. Allard, "Spencer Fullerton Baird," 71.
48. *Ibid.*, 73.
49. *Ibid.*, 72.
50. *Ibid.*
51. Though the agency's official designation was the "United States Commission of Fish and Fisheries," it was usually called by this shorter name. As the "Notes" will indicate, I have relied heavily on Dean C. Allard, Jr.'s excellent Ph.D. dissertation for much of my discussion of the U.S. Fish Commission.
52. Allard, "Spencer Fullerton Baird," 58, 65, and 84.
53. *Ibid.*, 65.
54. *U.S. Fish Commission Report,* X.
55. Allard, "Spencer Fullerton Baird," 93; *U.S. Fish Commission Report,* XXXIV-XXXVI.
56. Allard, "Spencer Fullerton Baird," 97-101 and 164-65.
57. Genio C. Scott, "Spring Birds and Fishes," *The Rod and the Gun* (later name of *American Sportsman*), April 17, 1875, VI, 34; Fred Mather, "Stall Fed vs. Wild Trout," *ibid.*, May 1, 1875, VI, 72.
58. Allard, "Spencer Fullerton Baird," 111-63, 284, 293-94, and 352; Theodore W. Cart, "The Struggle for Wildlife Protection in the United States, 1870-1900: Attitudes and Events Leading to the Lacey Act" (Ph.D. dissertation, University of North Carolina, 1971), 159.
59. Seth Green, "Fish Culture in New York," *American Field* (later name of *Field and Stream*), July 1, 1882, XVIII, 2. Because Green fails to say exactly when the "frost fish" were produced, I am assuming that it was during the same period as the other species cited.
60. Allard, "Spencer Fullerton Baird," 127.

61. From the *Congressional Globe,* cited in *ibid.,* 128.
62. *Ibid.*
63. *Ibid.*
64. From the *Congressional Globe,* cited in *ibid.*
65. *Ibid.,* 129-30.
66. *Ibid.,* 130.
67. *Ibid.,* 136.
68. *Ibid.,* 279-80.
69. *Ibid.,* 266 and 274-77.
70. *Ibid.,* 146.
71. *Ibid.,* 147 and 150.
72. *Ibid.,* 272.
73. *Ibid.*
74. *Ibid.,* 264-65.
75. *Ibid.,* 157.
76. *Forest and Stream,* February 19, 1874, II, 26.
77. For merely one example, see Baird's letter in *ibid.,* January 1, 1874, I, 330.
78. Allard, "Spencer Fullerton Baird," 293.
79. T. S. Palmer, *Private Game Preserves and Their Future in the United States* (Washington, D.C., 1910), 2-3.
80. *Ibid.,* 3. Also see *American Sportsman,* December 20, 1873, III, 187, for Caton's own description of the animals in his preserve.
81. Palmer, *Private Game Preserves,* 3 and 4. The purpose of the protected deer park was to provide a continual supply of game to the surrounding area, and wardens were employed to ensure that no poaching took place.
82. "Fall Sport at Blooming Grove Park," *American Sportsman,* November 8, 1873, III, 85. Though modified from earlier years, Blooming Grove still exists.
83. Charles Hallock, *The Fishing Tourist: [An] Angler's Guide and Reference Book* (New York, 1873), 225-26.
84. *Ibid.,* 227. The timber-management program was under the direction of "Grand Forester" F. W. Jones; see *American Sportsman,* December 27, 1873, III, 201.
85. Henry Clepper, "Gifford Pinchot" in Clepper, ed., *Leaders of American Conservation* (New York, 1971), 259; for a similar statement, see Harold T. Pinkett, *Gifford Pinchot: Private and Public Forester* (Urbana, Illinois, 1970), 22.
86. Cart, "The Struggle for Wildlife Protection," 92.
87. H. J. Cookingham, "The Bisby Club and the Adirondacks," *American Field* (later name of *Field and Stream*), March 10, 1883, XVIII, 172.
88. *Ibid.*
89. *Ibid.,* 173; "The Bisby Club," *ibid.,* April 22, 1882, XVII, 272. Also see "Wonderful Trout Growth at Bisby Park," *American Angler,* June 6, 1885, VII, 359, for a discussion of the results of planting hybrid brook-rainbow trout in the waters of Bisby Park.
90. S. R. Stoddard, *The Adirondacks* (Glen Falls, New York, 1893), 215-16; this is the 24th (1894) edition of his guide and has a copyright date of 1893.
91. *Ibid.,* 216.
92. *Ibid.*
93. Rodgers, *Bernhard Eduard Fernow,* 253.

94. Though flawed, the "classic" statement of this position is Lynn White, Jr., "The Historical Roots of Our Ecological Crisis," *Science*, CLV (March 10, 1967), 1203-07.
95. Matthiessen, *Wildlife in America*, 57.
96. For a different view, at least in northern New England, see Judd, *Common Lands, Common People*.
97. The exception was the predatory mammal or bird, which was regarded as "evil" because it killed "innocent" species. The common, but erroneous, belief, shared by sportsmen and nonsportsmen alike, was that the diminution of predators would result in an absolute, permanent increase in almost every other species. While temporary increases did occur, the long-run results were overpopulation, habitat destruction, and staggering losses to disease, crippling, etc.
98. "Uniform Game Laws," *Forest and Stream*, February 21, 1884, XXII, 61; also, see *ibid.*, February 19, 1874, II, 24; and *ibid.*, April 29, 1875, IV, 186, for Hallock's earlier statements of this position.
99. "A Proposition to Gentlemen Sportsmen," XV, 319.
100. *Ibid.*, March 24, 1881, XVI, 139.
101. "New Facts on Game Protection," *ibid.*
102. *Ibid.*
103. *Ibid.*, January 26, 1882, XVII, 503.
104. *Ibid.*
105. "Should the Gun be Taxed?" *ibid.*, January 22, 1880, XIII, 1010.
106. *Ibid.*
107. *Ibid.*
108. *Ibid.*, July 23, 1885, XXIV, 505.
109. "A Bad Example," *American Field*, April 10, 1886, XXV, 337.
110. With tragic irony, the Cincinnati Zoo also has the distinction of having been the home of the last Carolina parakeet; the latter died on February 21, 1918, in the same building that housed the last passenger pigeon.
111. Graham, *Man's Dominion*, 50.
112. One historian states that "by the turn of the century the prices paid for egret plumes had risen to $32 an ounce (four herons contributed an ounce), or twice the price of gold"; *ibid.*, 48.
113. Even a casual reading of the leading sportsmen's papers already cited in this study—with the exception of *American Angler*—will reveal that during the commercial buffalo slaughter of the 1870s and early 1880s, they frequently attacked the market hunters. For a sample of these papers' protests against the commercial pigeon hunters, see William B. Mershon (comp.), *The Passenger Pigeon* (New York, 1907), 77, 93, and 223-25. The latter citation refers to a *Forest and Stream* editorial of July 14, 1881, attacking the "sport" of using live passenger pigeons in trapshooting contests; it condemned the shooters directly and the commercial netters indirectly—for supplying the living targets. For merely an indication of the sporting press's attitudes concerning the destruction of nongame birds, see "Spare the Small Birds," *American Sportsman*, October 4, 1873, III, 9; "Game Laws and the Protection of Birds," *ibid.*, January 24, 1874, III, 260; *ibid.*, August 29, 1874, IV, 344; "Killing Insectivorous Birds," *The Rod and the Gun* (later name of *American Sportsman*), July 10, 1875, VI, 232; *The Field* (later name of *Field and Stream*), August 21, 1875, IV, 8; "Protect the Birds," *Chicago Field* (later name of *Field and Stream*), September 21,

1878, X, 81-82; *Forest and Stream,* April 22, 1880, XIV, 230; "Destruction of Song Birds," *ibid.,* March 23, 1882, XVIII, 143; "The Destruction of Small Birds," *ibid.,* March 30, 1882, XVIII, 163; "A Spring Plague," *ibid.,* April 27, 1882, XVIII, 244; "The Destruction of Insectivorous and Song Birds," *American Field* (later name of *Field and Stream*), January 5, 1884, XXI, 1; "The Sacrifice of Song Birds" and "The Destruction of Small Birds," both in *Forest and Stream,* August 7, 1884, XXIII, 21 and 24; "Birds, Bonnets and Butchers," *ibid.,* September 25, 1884, XXIII, 161; "Bird Destruction," *ibid.,* January 14, 1886, XXV, 482; "Fashion and the Birds," *American Field,* March 20, 1886, XXV, 265; "Save the Birds," *ibid.,* April 17, 1886, XXV, 361; "Unsportsmanlike Destruction," *ibid.,* May 29, 1886, XXV, 505; "Birds of Plumage," *ibid.,* June 12, 1886, XXV, 553; "The Audubon Society," *American Angler,* September 25, 1886, X, 201; and "The Audubon Society," *ibid.,* December 25, 1886, X, 410. For the source of the laws to protect songbirds in the 1850s, see Klinko, "Antebellum American Sporting Magazines," 206-07; and for the Herbert citation, see Cart, "The Struggle for Wildlife Protection," 87.

114. See Lacey, "Let Us Save the Birds," 33.

115. See Cart, "The Struggle for Wildlife Protection." He summarizes his arguments in "The Lacey Act: America's First Nationwide Wildlife Statute," *Forest History,* XVII (October, 1973), 4-13.

116. Matthiessen, *Wildlife in America,* 165. Graham, *Man's Dominion,* 29 and 32.

117. *Ibid.,* 32.

118. See his *Account of the Nuttall Ornithological Club, 1873 to 1919. Memoirs of the Nuttall Ornithological Club, No. VIII* (Cambridge, Massachusetts, 1937), 13-14.

119. Chapman, *Autobiography,* 93.

120. *Forest and Stream,* October 23, 1873, I, 174; Michael J. Brodhead, "Elliott Coues," in Keir B. Sterling, *et al.,* eds., *Biographical Dictionary of American and Canadian Naturalists and Environmentalists* (Westport, Connecticut, 1997), 174-75; Coues, "Sketch of North American Ornithology in 1879," *American Naturalist,* XIV (January, 1880), 21; and Chapman, *Autobiography,* 32. The following is a random selection of leading "naturalists" and "scientists," in all fields, whose contributions I have found in one or more of the "big four" sportsmen's periodicals: Spencer Fullerton Baird, William Brewster, Elliott Coues, Joel A. Allen, Albert K. Fisher, C. Hart Merriam, Frank M. Chapman, Robert Ridgway, Joseph T. Rothrock, Livingston Stone, Seth Green, Fred Mather, Thomas M. Brewer, George Brown Goode, David Starr Jordan, Othniel C. Marsh, John Burroughs, Theodore N. Gill, Joseph Bassett Holder, Charles Frederick Holder, Theodatus Garlick, Henry W. Henshaw, and Edward Drinker Cope.

121. Phillips, *American Game Mammals and Birds,* 9-10, and "Naturalists, Nature Lovers, and Sportsmen," *The Auk,* XLVIII (January, 1931), 40.

122. See Cart's dissertation and article, already cited, for a full discussion of the importance of the Lacey Act.

123. Perhaps this is a misprint—the original being a reference to the now abandoned order of "*Raptores,*" consisting of those species loosely called "birds of prey": hawks, eagles, owls, and vultures; the latter, of course, feed only on dead or dying animals and do not catch their own prey.

124. Grinnell was a prominent member of the Committee.

125. Volume XXVI, 41.
126. See *Forest and Stream*, February 25, 1886, XXVI, 83; and *ibid.*, March 4, 1886, XXVI, 104, for pledges of support.
127. T. Gilbert Pearson, *Fifty Years of Bird Protection in the United States* (New York, 1933), 201.
128. *Ibid.* Also see Grinnell to C. Hart Merriam, December 20, 1887, Letter Book, 238; Grinnell to Frank M. Chapman, November 10, 1898, *ibid.*, 949; and Grinnell to Minnie K. Anderson, March 13, 1900, *ibid.*, 792-93.
129. Pearson, *Fifty Years of Bird Protection*, 201. The Pennsylvania Audubon Society was organized in the fall of 1886, modeling itself after Grinnell's original society, "but it became dormant"; *ibid.*
130. Grinnell to William Dutcher, November 3, 1906, Letter Book, 666. Although a loose federation—the National Committee of Audubon Societies—was organized in 1901, it was not until 1905 that the National Association of Audubon Societies was incorporated.
131. Arthur A. Belonzi, "William Dutcher," in Sterling, *Biographical Dictionary,* 231 and 232.
132. Fox, *John Muir*, 342.
133. As early as February 12, 1859, the editors of *The Spirit of the Times* had published an editorial entitled "Preservation of Game" in which they had called for an end to the sale of game. But their statement had been directed mainly at the New York City market and was, therefore, rather limited in scope. See Klinko, "Antebellum American Sporting Magazines," 198.
134. Grinnell to Charles B. Reynolds, March 1, 1918, Letter Book, 418. In fact, Grinnell gives Reynolds credit for originating the proposition.
135. Volume XLII, 89.
136. See Trefethen, *An American Crusade for Wildlife,* especially Chapter 12.

Chapter 4
The Early Fight for the Forests

1. All of these individuals are discussed elsewhere in this study.
2. See David M. Emmons, "Theories of Increased Rainfall and the Timber Culture Act of 1873," *Forest History,* XV (October, 1971), 6-14.
3. *Ibid.*, 12; Henry Clepper, "Julius Sterling Morton," in Clepper, *Leaders of American Conservation,* 230.
4. The German-born pioneer of forestry, Bernhard E. Fernow, later commented that "it is to be noted as characteristic of much American legislation . . . that this . . . was secured only as a 'rider' to an appropriation for the distribution of seed"; Fernow, *A Brief History of Forestry*, 408.
5. Henry Clepper, "Franklin Benjamin Hough," in Clepper, *Leaders of American Conservation,* 173.
6. *Ibid.*
7. Page 456. The *Concise Dictionary of American Biography* (New York, 1964) is merely a one-volume abridgement of the multivolume, supposedly authoritative, *Dictionary of American Biography.*
8. Schurz, "Reminiscences of a Long Life," *McClure's Magazine*, XXVI (November, 1905), 6 and 4; and *ibid.*, XXVI (December, 1905), 170-71.
9. Udall, *The Quiet Crisis,* 99.
10. Olson, *The Depletion Myth: A History of Railroad Use of Timber* (Cambridge, Massachusetts, 1971), 40, 75, and 192.

11. Donald Worster, ed., *American Environmentalism: The Formative Period, 1860-1915* (New York, 1973), 73; editor speaking.
12. James Penick, Jr., is one of the few to understand this idea. In his review of Harold Pinkett's *Gifford Pinchot,* he states that forestry was an example of patrician reform that depended on the backing of upper-class conservationists; *Pacific Northwest Quarterly,* LXII (October, 1971), 141. For a good discussion of the *noblesse oblige* orientation of the Roosevelt conservation program, see G. Edward White, *The Eastern Establishment and the Western Experience: The West of Frederick Remington, Theodore Roosevelt, and Owen Wister* (New Haven, 1968), 171-83. Although he does not discuss conservation specifically, another scholar presents a wealth of insights regarding the patrician class, including Roosevelt, that can be applied directly to the latter's conservation program; see Michael D. Clark, "American Patricians as Social Critics, 1865-1914" (Ph.D. dissertation, University of North Carolina, 1965). The same is true of Walter E. Burdick, Jr., "Elite in Transition: From Alienation to Manipulation" (Ph.D. dissertation, Northern Illinois University, 1969).
13. Fernow, *A Brief History of Forestry,* 416.
14. Quoted in Rodgers, *Bernhard Eduard Fernow,* 28.
15. Fernow's membership in an Adirondack sportsmen's association has already been discussed. For Schenck's hunting, see his *The Biltmore Story: Recollections of the Beginnings of Forestry in the United States* (St. Paul, Minnesota, 1955), 36 and 60. Schenck's book is edited by Ovid A. Butler.
16. *Ibid.,* 20.
17. *Ibid.,* 36.
18. Scattered references to this fact can be found in Francis P. Farquhar, ed., *Up and Down California in 1860-1864: The Journal of William H. Brewer* (New Haven, 1930).
19. The interest shown in this subject by *American Sportsman, Forest and Stream,* and *American Angler* will be documented shortly. For *Field and Stream,* see, for example, "Game—Its Extinction: The Cause and the Remedy," *Chicago Field* (later name of *Field and Stream*), August 3, 1878, IX, 392; "Why the Prairies are Treeless," *ibid.,* January 29, 1881, XIV, 394; "Tree Planting," *American Field* (later name of *Field and Stream*), July 21, 1883, XX, 49; "A Public Park," *ibid.,* December 22, 1883, XX, 577; "State School of Forestry," *ibid.,* July 16, 1884, XXII, 49; and "Nurseries for Game," *ibid.,* October 24, 1885, XXIV, 385.
20. See, for example, *American Angler,* May 17, 1884, V, 310; *ibid.,* May 24, 1884, V, 328; *ibid.,* December 20, 1884, VI, 386; "Destruction of the Trout and Trout Streams of Central New York," *ibid.,* January 1, 1887, XI, 8-9; "How Shall We Preserve Our Water Supply?" *ibid.,* March 5, 1887, XI, 145-46.
21. See, for example, "Forest Legislation," *American Sportsman,* October 25, 1873, III, 56; "Foreign Sporting Notes," *ibid.,* March 7, 1874, III, 361; "Wood and Forest," *ibid.,* November 21, 1874, V, 120; *ibid.,* March 13, 1875, V, 377; "Our Trees," *ibid.,* March 20, 1875, V, 392; "Forest Preservation in Europe," *The Rod and the Gun* (later name of *American Sportsman*), July 10, 1875, VI, 231; A. S. Collins, "Decrease of Brook Trout in the United States," *ibid.,* August 7, 1875, VI, 280; "Waste Land and Forest Culture," *ibid.,* March 18, 1876, VII, 390; "Are We Drying Up?" *ibid.,* January 20, 1877, IX, 246.

22. For some other examples of Hallock's interest in the subject, see: "Woodman Spare that Tree," *Forest and Stream*, August 21, 1873, I, 26; "The Preservation of Our Forests," *ibid.*, September 4, 1873; I, 56; "The Adirondack Park," *ibid.*, September 11, 1873, I, 73; "What the Germans Say About Wood Cutting," *ibid.*, September 18, 1873, I, 89; *ibid.*, September 25, 1873, I, 101; "The Waste of Timber," *ibid.*, October 2, 1873, I, 121; "The State Park," *ibid.*, October 9, 1873, I, 136-37; *ibid.*, October 16, 1873, I, 149; *ibid.*, November 27, 1873, I, 244; "The Forests and Their Effects on Man," *ibid.*, December 25, 1873, I, 321; "Adirondack Park and the Preservation of Our Forests," *ibid.*, March 19, 1874, II, 88.

23. For a detailed discussion of his early career, see Reiger, *The Passing of the Great West.*

24. *Forest and Stream*, April 13, 1882, XVIII, 204.

25. *Ibid..*

26. *Ibid.*

27. *Forest and Stream*, July 19, 1883, XX, 481.

28. *Ibid.*

29. *Ibid.*

30. *Ibid.*

31. "Forest Wealth," *ibid.*, January 31, 1884, XXII, 2.

32. *Ibid.*

33. *Ibid.*

34. "Unheeded Lessons," *ibid.*, March 27, 1884, XXII, 161.

35. *Ibid.*

36. *Ibid.*, May 15, 1884, XXII, 301.

37. *Ibid.*

38. "Forests and Forestry V," *ibid.*, January 22, 1885, XXIII, 502.

39. *Ibid.*

40. "Forests and Forestry III," *ibid.*, January 8, 1885, XXIII, 461-62; *ibid.*, January 15, 1885, XXIII, 482.

41. Nash, *Wilderness and the American Mind*, 104-05.

42. Marsh, *Man and Nature*, 35, quoted in Nash, *Wilderness and the American Mind*, 104-05.

43. Marsh, *Man and Nature*, 234-36, cited in *ibid.*, 105.

44. *Forest and Stream*, September 4, 1873, I, 56.

45. "The Adirondack Park," *ibid.*, September 11, 1873, I, 73, cited in Nash, *Wilderness and the American Mind*, 118.

46. *Forest and Stream*, December 13, 1883, XXI, 381.

47. *Ibid.*, March 13, 1884, XXII, 121.

48. *Ibid.*, 121-22.

49. As early as 1873, Hallock had cited the possibility of using European methods of timber-cutting in the Adirondacks: see *ibid.*, October 9, 1873, I, 136-37. Yet he made no effort to follow up this idea, and his later editorials reverted to the watershed justification.

50. *Ibid.*, XXI, 489.

51. This, of course, applies only to wildlife, forests, ranges, and water. But even nonrenewable resources like minerals and oil can be administered according to what Roosevelt later called "wise use," so as to make them last as long as possible.

52. "The Adirondack Forests," *Forest and Stream*, January 29, 1885, XXIV, 2.

53. *Ibid.*
54. Nash, *Wilderness and the American Mind,* 119.
55. *New York Laws,* 1885, Chap. 238, p. 482, cited in *ibid.*
56. *Ibid.*
57. G. Wallace Chessman, *Governor Theodore Roosevelt: The Albany Apprenticeship, 1898-1900* (Cambridge, Massachusetts, 1965), 250.
58. *Forest and Stream,* April 17, 1884, XXII, 221.
59. "Who Are the Skinners?" *ibid.,* June 11, 1885, XXIV, 385.
60. For one example, see U.S. Congress, House, *Message from the President of the United States Transmitting a Message on Conservation and Water Management* (90th Cong., 2nd Sess., House, Doc. 273), I; in this message of March 8, 1968, President Johnson quotes Roosevelt.
61. *Forest and Stream,* January 15, 1885, XXIII, 482.
62. Gurth Whipple, *Fifty Years of Conservation in New York State, 1885-1935* (Syracuse, 1935), 16; Van Brocklin, "The Movement for the Conservation of Natural Resources," 12-13.
63. Goodspeed, *Angling in America,* 112.
64. Quoted in *ibid.*
65. For Pinchot, see Reiger, "Gifford Pinchot With Rod and Reel," and for Leopold, see the Epilogue of the present study.
66. Quoted in Goodspeed, *Angling in America,* 246-47.
67. Quoted in Nash, *Wilderness and the American Mind,* 70.
68. *Ibid.*
69. Hammond, *Wild Northern Scenes,* 83. Hammond was a dedicated believer in the code of the sportsman: see *ibid.,* x-xi, 23, 43, 48, 81-82, and 341. In an earlier work, as already noted in Chapter One, Hammond made a similar recommendation for an Adirondack preserve, but without specifying its size: Hammond, *Hills, Lakes, and Forest Streams* (1854), 168. As in the later volume, this work contains many examples of his commitment to the code of the sportsman.
70. Cited in Klinko, "Antebellum American Sporting Magazines," 197.
71. I am assuming, of course, that Hammond and the anonymous contributor to the *Spirit of the Times* were not one and the same!
72. Quoted in Harold C. Anderson, "The Unknown Genesis of the Wilderness Idea," *Living Wilderness,* V (1940), 15; cited by Nash, *Wilderness and the American Mind,* 117.
73. For merely two examples, see "Forest Wardens," *Rod and Gun and American Sportsman* (later name of *American Sportsman*), September 30, 1876, VIII, 424; and "An Adirondack Preserve," *Forest and Stream,* January 26, 1882, XVII, 511. For the importance of this idea, see Eugene J. O'Neill, "Parks and Forest Conservation in New York, 1850-1920" (Ed.D. dissertation, Columbia University, 1963), 4, 10, 51, 183-84, 187, and 201.
74. *Ibid.,* 4.
75. Coon, *The Story of Man: From the First Human to Primitive Culture and Beyond* (New York, 1962), 112; this is a revised edition of a work first published in 1954.
76. See issue of June 9, 1883, IX, 463.
77. Thoreau, *The Maine Woods* (New York, 1950), 321; this is Dudley C. Lunt's edition of a book first published in 1864. The article was incorporated into the later book, published after Thoreau's death.

78. See, for example, Thoreau, *The Concord and The Merrimack* (New York, 1954), 33-39; this is Dudley C. Lunt's edition of *A Week on the Concord and Merrimack Rivers*, published by Thoreau in 1849.
79. Thoreau, *The Maine Woods*, 65.
80. Thoreau, *A Week on the Concord and Merrimack Rivers*, 6, 8, 24-27, 48-49; and Thoreau, *Cape Cod* (New York, 1951), 178; this is Dudley C. Lunt's edition of a book first published in 1865.
81. For example: Thoreau, *The Maine Woods*, 24 and 86.
82. In the early 1870s *Forest and Stream* sent into the Lake Okeechobee-Everglades region two expeditions that uncovered much new information concerning its topography and fauna; in the 1880s George Bird Grinnell explored and mapped the still-wild country in what became—largely through his efforts—Glacier National Park; the famous Harriman Expedition of 1899, that studied the coast of Alaska, began with the desire of sportsman Edward H. Harriman to shoot an Alaskan brown bear; and sportsman-naturalist Charles Sheldon explored the Mount McKinley region in the early years of the twentieth century and spearheaded the effort to make it a national park.
83. This is a well-established fact of Adirondack history; for merely one indication of its truth, see Goodspeed, *Angling in America*, 187, for the 1856 statement of a Herkimer County historian.
84. *Ibid.*
85. Their interest in forest preservation has been documented in my earlier "Notes"; a number of the editorials cited, particularly those in *Forest and Stream*, refer to the need for establishing a wilderness park in the Adirondacks.
86. For O'Neill's conclusions, see his "Parks and Forest Conservation in New York"; Hays's thesis is discussed elsewhere in the present work.
87. Nash, *Wilderness and the American Mind*, 119; while he does not cite Hays, Nash's discussion of this issue comes to the same conclusion.
88. *Forest and Stream*, September 11, 1873, I, 73.
89. This idea is discussed elsewhere in the present study.
90. See Kranz, "Pioneering in Conservation," 43, 46-47, 50-51, 142, 150, 156-57, 161-62, 174, 178-79, 181-84, and 261-63. Colvin, Whitehead, Cleveland, and Fernow have already been identified as sportsmen. For Hewitt as a sportsman, see *American Angler*, June 19, 1886, IX, 391; for Husted, see *ibid.*, July 4, 1885, VIII, 8; and for Hill, see *ibid.*, August 15, 1885, VIII, 106.

Chapter 5
Development of the National Park Concept

1. Catlin, *North American Indians: Being Letters and Notes on their Manners, Customs, and Conditions, Written During Eight Years' Travel Amongst the Wildest Tribes of Indians in North America, 1832-1839* (Philadelphia, 1913), I, 27-29. On the latter page, in describing a chase after buffalo, he says: "I went not for 'meat,' but for a trophy; I wanted his head and horns." This two-volume work, originally published in London in 1841, was a collection of articles Catlin had written in the previous decade.
2. *Ibid.*, I, 294-95.

3. The context of their statements reveals that both Catlin and Thoreau were just as concerned about the future of large game as they were about the fate of the Indians.
4. Catlin, *North American Indians*, I, 295.
5. For example, visitors to Alaska's Denali National Park must use shuttle buses provided by the National Park Service, instead of taking their own cars anywhere they please. Special areas in other national parks have also been designated for restricted use.
6. Arkansas Hot Springs (1832) and Yosemite Valley (1864). For the fact that neither was really a national park, see Ise, *Our National Park Policy*, 13.
7. Hiram Martin Chittenden, *The Yellowstone National Park* (Cincinnati, 1905), 44-51. This book was first published in 1895.
8. *Ibid.*, 60.
9. Nathaniel P. Langford, *The Discovery of Yellowstone Park: Journal of the Washburn Expedition to the Yellowstone and Firehole Rivers in the Year 1870* (Lincoln, Nebraska, 1972), 117-118; this is a later edition—with a Foreword by historian Aubrey L. Haines—of a work first published in 1905.
10. *Ibid.*, xix-xx.
11. Nash, *Wilderness and the American Mind*, 110.
12. U.S. Bureau of the Census, *Historical Statistics of the United States: Colonial Times to 1957* (Washington, D.C., 1960), 207; this figure includes public and nonpublic schools and refers to the percentage of 17-year-old Americans who had graduated from secondary school in 1870. It might also be noted that 20 percent of the population ten years old and over were illiterate in 1870; *ibid.*, 214.
13. Langford, *The Discovery of Yellowstone Park*, xi.
14. Hedges, "Journal of Judge Cornelius Hedges," *Contributions to the Historical Society of Montana . . .*, V (1904), 370-94; scattered fishing descriptions throughout.
15. Nash, *Wilderness and the American Mind*, 110-11.
16. See William H. Jackson and Howard R. Driggs, *The Pioneer Photographer: Rocky Mountain Adventures with a Camera* (Yonkers-on-Hudson, New York, 1929), 300-02, for Jackson's own account of shooting the bear, including his pains to preserve its hide as a trophy.
17. *Ibid.*, 104-05 and 109; and Lewis W. Selmeier, "First Camera on the Yellowstone—A Century Ago . . ." *Montana, the Magazine of Western History*, XXII (Summer, 1972), 49.
18. Goodspeed, *Angling in America*, 207-08.
19. Nash, *Wilderness and the American Mind*, 111.
20. *Ibid.*
21. Ise, *Our National Park Policy*, 16.
22. *Ibid.*
23. Nash, *Wilderness and the American Mind*, 112. Ise, *Our National Park Policy*, 16.
24. For a discussion of this mentality, see Alfred Runte, *National Parks: The American Experience* (Lincoln, Nebraska, 1997); this is the third edition of a book first published in 1979. Also, see "Alaska: Preserving the Public Domain," *Sierra Club Bulletin*, LIX (February, 1974), 17, for the same attitude in regard to national wildlife refuges.
25. Nash, *Wilderness and the American Mind*, 111-12; and Selmeier, "First Camera on the Yellowstone," 52.

26. The first of these did not appear until shortly after the park bill was passed; *ibid.*

27. Clarence P. Hornung, "A Gallery of Western Art," in Jay Monaghan, ed., *The Book of the American West* (New York, 1963), 579.

28. Ise, *Our National Park Policy,* 17-18.

29. Galen Clark, a key figure in the early history of what became Yosemite National Park, was a hunter. See Shirley Sargent, "Galen Clark—Mr. Yosemite," in Yosemite Natural History Association, *Yosemite: Saga of a Century, 1864-1964* (Oakhurst, California, 1964), 19-20; and Introduction by W. W. Foote in Galen Clark, *Indians of the Yosemite Valley: Their History, Customs and Traditions* (Yosemite Valley, 1904), xiii-xv. For the crucial part played by two sportsmen, Theodore Roosevelt and E. H. Harriman, in getting Yosemite Valley taken out of state hands and added to Yosemite National Park in 1905-06, see Udall, *The Quiet Crisis,* 129-30.

The "fathers" of Glacier and Denali National Parks were George Bird Grinnell and Charles Sheldon, respectively; see Madison Grant, "The Beginnings of Glacier National Park" and "The Establishment of Mt. McKinley [Denali] National Park," in Grinnell and Sheldon, *Hunting and Conservation,* 438-70. Sheldon was a member of the Boone and Crockett Club and a well-known author on hunting and natural history. Lassen Volcanic and Grand Canyon National Parks were first set aside as national monuments by Theodore Roosevelt, and the legislation allowing him to take this action was passed mainly through the efforts of another sportsman, John F. Lacey; see Ise, *Our National Park Policy,* 151-52 and 156-57.

For the fact that the original proposals for a national park in the southern Appalachians came from sportsmen, see Charles D. Smith, "The Appalachian National Park Movement, 1885-1901," *North Carolina Historical Review,* XXXVII (January, 1960), 38, 41-42, and 65. Also, see James B. Trefethen, *Crusade for Wildlife: Highlights in Conservation Progress* (Harrisburg, Pennsylvania, 1961), 285, for the impact of Charles Sheldon. One of the main groups backing the effort that led to the creation of Isle Royale National Park was the Izaak Walton League, an organization of sport anglers; see Ise, *Our National Park Policy,* 333.

Among the very first to draw public attention to the need for preserving the Everglades were sportsmen A. W. Dimock, Frank M. Chapman, and William Dutcher. See Charleton W. Tebeau, *Man in the Everglades: 2000 Years of Human History in the Everglades National Park* (Miami, 1968), 168-69. This is the second, revised edition of a book originally published in 1964 under a different title. Chapman and Dutcher have already been identified as sportsmen, and Dimock wrote the angling classic: *The Book of the Tarpon* (New York, 1911). Also, see John C. Phillips, "Conservation of Our Mammals and Birds," in Grinnell and Sheldon, *Hunting and Conservation,* 64, for a call for Everglades preservation.

30. Nash, *Wilderness and the American Mind,* 108-13.

31. *Ibid.,* 112.

32. "The Yellowstone National Park," *Scribner's Monthly,* IV (May, 1872), 121, cited in Nash, 113.

33. Ise, *Our National Park Policy,* 18.

34. *Ibid.*

35. "Memoirs," 94.

36. Ise, *Our National Park Policy,* 21-22.

37. See the photograph of a grizzly bear he helped to "bag" on George Armstrong Custer's 1874 Black Hills expedition in Reiger, *The Passing of the Great West*.

38. William Ludlow, *Report of a Reconnaissance from Carroll, Montana Territory, on the Upper Missouri, to the Yellowstone National Park, and Return, Made in the Summer of 1875* (Washington, D.C., 1876), 61. Also, see Reiger, *The Passing of the Great West*, 117-19.

39. For Grinnell's buffalo hunting, see *ibid.*, 58-72; also, see Grinnell's "Last of the Buffalo," *Scribner's Magazine*, XII (September, 1892), 267-86, for his poetic tribute to the vanished multitudes. The weathered skulls of the bull and cow bison he describes picking up on the prairie, "to keep as mementoes of the past," are in the Birdcraft Museum of the Connecticut Audubon Society, Fairfield.

40. Roosevelt first went West to shoot a trophy buffalo; see Trefethen, *Crusade for Wildlife*, 2.

41. Catlin's desire to preserve the bison has already been discussed; for Audubon, see Francis Hobart Herrick, *Audubon the Naturalist: A History of His Life and Times* (New York, 1917), II, 255-56.

42. See Volume VIII (February, 1874), 65-79; on page 78 he implies that he is an angler.

43. Pages 34-35. For the fact that Grinnell wrote this section of the book while Hallock took the credit, see Reiger, *The Passing of the Great West*, 167.

44. *Forest and Stream*, February 19, 1880, XIV, 51.

45. "Where Some Game Goes To," *ibid.*, March 17, 1881, XVI, 119.

46. *Ibid.*, May 11, 1882, XVIII, 283.

47. "The President Speaks," *ibid.*, June 29, 1882, XVIII, 423.

48. *Ibid.*, XIX, 382.

49. *Ibid.*, 382-83.

50. "Memoirs," 95.

51. *Forest and Stream*, XIX, 382-83.

52. Ludlow stated his belief that if the government would only assume its obligation to the park, "the day will come . . . when this most interesting region, crowded with marvels and adorned with the most superb scenery, will be rendered accessible to all; then, thronged with visitors from all over the world, it will be what nature and Congress, for once working together in union, have declared it should be, a National Park"; Ludlow, *Report of a Reconaissance*, 37.

53. *Forest and Stream*, December 14, 1882, XIX, 383.

54. *Ibid.*, XIX, 441.

55. *Ibid.*

56. "The Woodmont Rod and Gun Club," *American Angler*, October 21, 1882, II, 259.

57. Ise, *Our National Park Policy*, 36.

58. *Ibid.*

59. "Memoirs," 94; "The Park Monopolists," *Forest and Stream*, January 11, 1883, XIX, 461-62.

60. *Ibid.*

61. *Ibid.*, XIX, 481.

62. *Ibid.*; "Game in the Yellowstone Park," *ibid.*, February 18, 1886, XXVI, 62.

63. Roosevelt, "Introduction," in Allen G. Wallihan, *Camera Shots at Big Game* (New York, 1901), 7; Roosevelt *et al., The Deer Family* (New York, 1902), 23; and "Forest Reserves as Game Refuges," *Forest and Stream,* February 8, 1902, LVIII, 101. In the last item Grinnell is quoting Roosevelt.

64. *Ibid.,* XIX, 481.

65. Edwin J. Stanley, *Rambles in Wonderland* (New York, 1880), 63, quoted in Nash, *Wilderness and the American Mind,* 113.

66. *Forest and Stream,* March 8, 1883, XX, 107.

67. Nathan Cole, *The Royal Parks and Gardens of London, Their History and Mode of Embellishment . . .* (London, 1877), 19-20. Also, see Michael Brander, *Hunting and Shooting: From Earliest Times to the Present Day* (New York, 1971), 74, for the fact that Regent's Park was originally "Mariebone Park," a royal hunting ground.

68. For examples of the importance of the Old World influence on the development of city parks in America and the idea that their origins can be traced back to the hunting preserves of royalty, see Grinnell to G. A. Parkson, March 2, 1921, Letter Book, 216; O'Neill, "Parks and Forest Conservation," 51 and 183-84; Jon A. Peterson, "The Origins of the Comprehensive City Planning Ideal in the United States, 1840-1911" (Ph.D. dissertation, Harvard University, 1967), 74-75, 77-78, and 102; and John B. Jackson, *American Space—The Centennial Years: 1865-1876* (New York, 1972), 217-18.

69. For the spread of the national park idea to other countries, see Ise, *Our National Park Policy,* 658-69; and Nash, *Wilderness and the American Mind,* 342-78.

70. *Forest and Stream,* January 25, 1883, XIX, 501.

71. "The Yellowstone National Park," *American Field* (later name of *Field and Stream*), January 13, 1883, XIX, 21-22; "Congress Proposes to Check the Yellowstone National Park Grab," *ibid.,* January 20, 1883, XIX, 41; *ibid.,* February 3, 1883, XIX, 83; "The Yellowstone Park," *ibid.,* March 3, 1883, XIX, 145; "The Syndicate Rules," *ibid.,* March 10, 1883, XIX, 165; "The Yellowstone Park," *Harper's Weekly,* January 20, 1883, XXVII, 46-47; "Grabbing a Great Park," *New York Times,* January 20, 1883, XXXII, 1; *ibid.,* 4; "Yellowstone Park Leases," *New York Herald,* January 21, 1883, 10.

72. "Park Protection," *Forest and Stream,* February 15, 1883, XX, 41.

73. "Mr. Vest's Victory," *ibid.,* March 8, 1883, XX, 101.

74. *Ibid.,* 107.

75. *Ibid.,* March 22, 1883, XX, 141.

76. Troops were not stationed in the park until August, 1886. One historian claims that the Army "saved" Yellowstone and later national parks by protecting them from vandals, poachers, forest fires, etc. But the question might well be asked: Who deserves more credit—the soldiers who followed orders or the civilians like Grinnell who got them into the parks in the first place? See H. Duane Hampton, *How the U.S. Cavalry Saved Our National Parks* (Bloomington, Indiana, 1971).

77. "Congress and the Large Game," *Forest and Stream,* November 15, 1883, XXI, 301.

78. "The Yellowstone Park," *ibid.,* December 20, 1883, XXI, 401-02.

79. "Yellowstone Park Matters," *ibid.,* January 17, 1884, XXI, 494.

80. *Ibid.,* 489.

81. *Ibid.*
82. "Yellowstone Park Bill," *ibid.*, February 7, 1884, XXII, 21.
83. *Ibid.*
84. *Ibid.*; "Yellowstone Park Matters," March 13, 1884, XXII, 121.
85. *Ibid.*
86. Grinnell to T. E. Hofer, May 15, 1917, Letter Book, 642; Grinnell to W. H. Phillips, November 7, 1889, *ibid.*, 453-54.
87. "Diary, Through Two-Ocean Pass, Aug. 1884" (item no. 301 of Grinnell Collection checklist), entry of August 29, 1884; George Bird Grinnell Collection of Journals, Field Notes and other Materials on the Plains Indians, 1870-1930; Southwest Museum Library, Los Angeles. Hereinafter, this source is cited as the Grinnell Collection.
88. Hague to Senator Charles F. Manderson, February 4, 1886, *Forest and Stream*, February 25, 1886, XXVI, 83; Hague, "The Yellowstone Park as a Forest Reservation," *The Nation*, XLVI (January 5, 1888), 9-10.
89. "The Care of the National Park," *Forest and Stream*, XXIV, 1.
90. "Remove the Superintendent," *ibid.*, April 9, 1885, XXIV, 201; "A Change Needed," *ibid.*, April 23, 1885, XXIV, 245; "The Park Needs a Superintendent," *ibid.*, May 14, 1885, XXIV, 305.
91. Ise, *Our National Park Policy*, 41.
92. *Forest and Stream*, April 9, 1885, XXIV, 201.
93. "A New Park Superintendent," *ibid.*, May 28, 1885, XXIV, 345.
94. "Needs of the Park," *ibid.*, May 7, 1885, XXIV, 287-88.
95. William H. Goetzmann, *Exploration and Empire: The Explorer and the Scientist in the Winning of the West* (New York, 1966), 330.
96. For an exposition of this thesis, see Robert H. Wiebe, *The Search for Order, 1877-1920* (New York, 1967), especially 62-75.
97. "Their Last Refuge," *Forest and Stream*, December 14, 1882, XIX, 382-83.

Chapter 6
The Boone and Crockett Club

1. Representative—signature is illegible—of the Roosevelt Memorial Association to Grinnell, January 23, 1923, Grinnell File.
2. Grinnell, "Introduction," *The Works of Theodore Roosevelt* (National Edition, New York, 1926), I, xiv.
3. *Forest and Stream*, XXIV, 451.
4. Grinnell, "Introduction," *The Works of Theodore Roosevelt* (National Edition), I, xiv.
5. Grinnell's friendship with these men is treated in Reiger, *The Passing of the Great West*. The Reynolds cited here is no relation to Charles B. Reynolds, who was on the staff of *Forest and Stream*.
6. Grinnell's experiences on Custer's 1874 Black Hills expedition are described in Reiger, *The Passing of the Great West*, 78-107.
7. Trefethen, *Crusade for Wildlife*, 2.
8. Grinnell, "Introduction," *The Works of Theodore Roosevelt* (National Edition), I, xv.
9. *Ibid.*, xv-xvi.
10. See Roosevelt, *Theodore Roosevelt: An Autobiography;* and Reiger, *The Passing of the Great West*.
11. "Memoirs," 96.

12. See earlier discussion, above.
13. Grinnell, "Introduction," *The Works of Theodore Roosevelt* (National Edition), I, xvi.
14. Grinnell to G. W. H. Stouch, November 26, 1897, Letter Book, 186. For other examples of this compulsion to remain anonymous, even when it meant bending the truth, see Madison Grant to Grinnell, May 26, 1910, Boone and Crockett Club File; Grinnell to Grant, May 26, 1910, Letter Book, 217; Grinnell to W. Austin Wadsworth, June 10, 1910, *ibid.*, 269; and John B. Burnham to Grinnell, June 7, 1920, Grinnell File.
15. Grinnell, "Introduction," *The Works of Theodore Roosevelt* (National Edition), xvi-xvii.
16. *Ibid.*, xvii.
17. *Ibid.*
18. *Forest and Stream*, May 15, 1884, XX, 301.
19. Grinnell to T. E. Hofer, January 15, 1919, Letter Book, 269.
20. Harmond, "Robert Barnwell Roosevelt," 4.
21. *Ibid.*
22. Tober, *Who Owns the Wildlife?*, 147, 169, and 216.
23. Trefethen, *Crusade for Wildlife*, 75. Trapshooting was competition shooting with shotguns at artificial targets and live pigeons, first the wild passenger pigeon and later the common barnyard variety (the rock dove of Europe). Not all sportsmen were caught up in the "craze," as Grinnell shows in a *Forest and Stream* editorial of July 14, 1881. He condemned the shooters for being cruel and unsporting, and the commercial netters for supplying the living targets. Cited in Mershon, *The Passenger Pigeon*, 223-25.
24. *Forest and Stream*, February 16, 1888, XXX, 61.
25. Grinnell to Arnold Hague, February 22, 1888, Letter Book, 297.
26. Grinnell to Cromwell Childe, March 24, 1899, *ibid.*, 215.
27. "The Boone and Crockett Club," *Forest and Stream*, March 8, 1888, XXX, 124.
28. For a typical *Forest and Stream* attack on jacklighting and "floating" (killing deer in the water), see "Jack Bluff and Bluster," *Forest and Stream*, August 20, 1885, XXV, 61.
29. Hague, "The Yellowstone Park as a Game Reservation," in Theodore Roosevelt and George Bird Grinnell, eds., *American Big-Game Hunting* (New York, 1901), 257; and Joseph P. Iddings, "Memorial of Arnold Hague," *Bulletin of the Geological Society of America*, XXIX (1918), 45; the first work originally appeared in 1893. Also, see Grinnell to W. H. Phillips, June 5, 1889, Letter Book, 354.
30. Grinnell to Arnold Hague, February 22, 1888, *ibid.*, 297.
31. Because of Grinnell's influence, Hague and Phillips in fact became regular members, but they seem to have been the only nonhunters to receive that honor. And despite the rule that nonsportsmen could become associate or honorary members, almost all of those who joined under those classifications were—or had been—hunters.
32. Grinnell to Arnold Hague, February 22, 1888, *ibid.*, 297. *Forest and Stream*, February 16, 1888, XXX, 61; and "The Boone and Crockett Club," *ibid.*, March 8, 1888, XXX, 124.
33. Edward N. Saveth, "The American Patrician Class: A Field for Research," *American Quarterly* (Summer, 1963), XV, Pt. 2, 235-52.

34. Trefethen, *Crusade for Wildlife,* 21.
35. Grinnell, ed., *A Brief History of the Boone and Crockett Club, With Officers, Constitution and List of Members for the Year 1910* (New York, 1910), 20. After talking with Grinnell's co-workers in the Boone and Crockett, a later member believed: "His [Grinnell's] sane judgment guided the [Boone and Crockett] Executive Committee" and "in facing every problem that confronted the Club throughout its entire life, the court of last resort always seemed to rest within the mind of this one man. No course of action was determined until his judgment had been sought and no conclusions reached until his opinion had been given"; John P. Holman, "A Tribute to George Bird Grinnell," in "Boone and Crockett Club Officers, By-Laws, Treasurer's Report and List of Members for the Years 1938-1939" (July, 1939), 29-30, Boone and Crockett Club File.
36. Anderson to Grinnell, January 29, 1896, *ibid.*
37. Roosevelt to Grinnell, November 30, 1897, Theodore Roosevelt Papers, Library of Congress, Series 2. Also, see Roosevelt to William Austin Wadsworth, February 4, 1898, in Morison and Blum, *The Letters of Theodore Roosevelt,* I, 768.
38. Sheldon to W. Redmond Cross, May 3, 1926, Boone and Crockett Club File.
39. Udall, *The Quiet Crisis,* 161.
40. *Forest and Stream,* January 17, 1889, XXXI, 513.
41. "Adirondack Deer Hounding," *ibid.,* XXIII, 281.
42. "Adirondack Deer Hounding," *ibid.,* January 15, 1885, XXIII, 481.
43. *Ibid.*
44. "The Deer Bill," *ibid.,* February 26, 1885, XXIV, 81.
45. "The Deer Hounding Bill," *ibid.,* February 19, 1885, XXIV, 62; "The Deer Bill," *ibid.,* February 26, 1885, XXIV, 81; "The Adirondack Deer Law," *ibid.,* March 5, 1885, XXIV, 101; and "Pass the Deer Hounding Bill," *ibid.,* March 26, 1885, XXIV, 161.
46. *Ibid.,* May 14, 1885, XXIV, 305.
47. *Ibid.*
48. "The Deer Hounding Law," *ibid.,* June 18, 1885, XXIV, 405.
49. "The Adirondack Deer Law," *ibid.,* December 31, 1885, XXV, 441.
50. "The Adirondack Deer," *ibid.,* January 21, 1886, XXV, 501.
51. *Ibid.,* January 28, 1886, XXVI, 7.
52. *Ibid.,* May 20, 1886, XXVI, 325.
53. A leading representative of the New York patrician class, Grant was also a lawyer and a hunter-naturalist. He is best known for his *The Passing of the Great Race* (1916), a racist work that played a part in bringing about the anti-immigration legislation of the 1920s. A founder of the New York Zoological Gardens ("Bronx Zoo"), the Save-the-Redwoods League and other organizations, he was one of the Boone and Crockett Club's most active members. After being proposed by Grinnell, he joined in 1893. Grant and Roosevelt soon became close friends and co-workers in conservation. The latter wrote Grinnell in early 1894: "I am inclined to think that Madison Grant is a genuine acquisition; he strikes me as a good fellow"; Roosevelt to Grinnell, January 13, 1894, Boone and Crockett Club File.
54. *Ibid.*
55. Roosevelt to Grinnell, January 30, 1894, *ibid.*

56. *Forest and Stream,* May 15, 1897, XLVIII, 381. Also, see William Cary Sanger, "The Adirondack Deer Law," in George Bird Grinnell and Theodore Roosevelt, eds., *Trail and Camp-Fire* (New York, 1897), 264-78.
57. Grinnell to T. E. Hofer, December 20, 1886, Letter Book, 51-52; *Forest and Stream,* January 12, 1888, XXVIII, 481; Grinnell to Archibald Rogers, August 8, 1888, Letter Book, 444; *Forest and Stream,* September 12, 1889, XXXIII, 141; Grinnell to William Hallett Phillips, November 7, 1889, Letter Book, 454; and Grinnell to William M. Springer, May 9, 1890, *ibid.,* 309.
58. "The Hon. S. S. Cox on Angling and Fish Protection," *American Angler,* June 21, 1884, V, 385-89.
59. Nash, *Wilderness and the American Mind,* 114.
60. For example, Roosevelt, *Hunting Trips of a Ranchman: Sketches of Sport on the Northern Cattle Plains* (Upper Saddle River, New Jersey, 1970), 149; this is a reprint (Literature House) of a work first published in 1885. Also, see Roosevelt, *Ranch Life and the Hunting-Trail* (New York, 1969), 134-35; this is a reprint (Winchester Press) of a work first published in 1888.
61. Grinnell, "Introduction," *The Works of Theodore Roosevelt* (National Edition), I, xxiii.
62. As a sample: "A Territorial Dogberry," September 3, 1885, XXV, 101; "Another Syndicate," November 12, 1885, XXV, 301; "A Report on the National Park," December 3, 1885, XXV, 361; "Game in the National Park," December 17, 1885, XXV, 401; "The Yellowstone National Park," December 24, 1885, XXV, 421; "Senator Vest's Park Bill," December 31, 1885, XXV, 441; "No Railroad in Yellowstone Park," February 18, 1886, XXVI, 62; "A Railroad to Cooke City," March 11, 1886, XXVI, 121-22; "Is There an African in the Woodpile?" March 25, 1886, XXVI, 161-62; "Railroad Routes to Cooke," April 8, 1886, XXVI, 201-02; "The Railroads and the Park," May 13, 1886, XXVI, 301; "How the Case Stands," May 20, 1886, XXVI, 325; "Waking Up at Last," June 3, 1886, XXVI, 365; "The National Park in 1887," September 15, 1887, XXIX, 141; "The National Park in 1887," September 22, 1887, XXIX, 161; "Park Matters in Congress," January 12, 1888, XXIX, 481; "In Behalf of the Park," March 8, 1888, XXX, 121; "The Park Bill in the House," April 5, 1888, XXX, 201; "Mr. Plumb's Ignorance," April 19, 1888, XXX, 241; "Important Measures," July 26, 1888, XXXI, 1; August 2, 1888, XXXI, 21; September 12, 1889, XXXIII, 141; December 5, 1889, XXXIII, 381; "The New Park Bill," January 30, 1890, XXXIV, 21; "Scheming for a Railroad," February 20, 1890, XXXIV, 81; February 27, 1890, XXXIV, 101; "The Yellowstone Park Bill," April 3, 1890, XXXIV, 205 and 207; "To the House of Representatives," April 24, 1890, XXXIV, 265; "A Natural Reservoir," May 1, 1890, XXXIV, 285; "Mr. Carey's Responsibility," May 15, 1890, XXXIV, 325; "Game in the Great West," July 3, 1890, XXXIV, 469; "What About the Park?" December 11, 1890, XXXV, 409; "The National Park Bill," March 12, 1891, XXXVI, 145; "Yellowstone Park Legislation," February 25, 1892, XXXVIII, 169; "The National Park Grab Bag," March 17, 1892, XXXVIII, 245; "Danger to the Park," May 19, 1892, XXXVIII, 469 and 474; "An Individual Appeal," December 15, 1892, XXXIX, 507; and "Patriotism in 1893," December 29, 1892, XXXIX, 551.
63. Grinnell to Luther H. North, February 17, 1887, Letter Book, 70.
64. Grinnell to George Gould, March 18, 1887, *ibid.,* 92.

65. "In Behalf of the Park," *Forest and Stream*, March 8, 1888, XXX, 121.
66. *Ibid.*, March 29, 1888, XXX, 186.
67. *Ibid.*
68. Grinnell to Lyman, April 23, 1890, Letter Book, 289.
69. Grinnell to Archibald Rogers, December 19, 1890, *ibid.*, 129.
70. *Ibid.*; Grinnell to Captain F. A. Boutelle, December 9, 1890, *ibid.*, 80-81.
71. Rogers was a regular member of the club and, of course, an avid hunter; see his "Big Game in the Rockies," in Roosevelt and Grinnell, *American Big-Game Hunting*, 90-128, an article originally appearing in *Scribner's Magazine*.
72. Grinnell to Arnold Hague, December 1, 1890, Letter Book, 64-65.
73. Grinnell to Archibald Rogers, December 24, 1890, *ibid.*, 133.
74. Grinnell to Arnold Hague, January 13, 1891, *ibid.*, 183.
75. Grinnell to Archibald Rogers, January 17, 1891, *ibid.*, 186-88.
76. Since the summer of 1886, the park had been under the control of the army; Grinnell, *A Brief History of the Boone and Crockett Club*, 16-17.
77. "Boone and Crockett Club Meeting," *Forest and Stream*, January 22, 1891, XXXVI, 3.
78. *Ibid.*; a third resolution endorsed "the efforts now being made to preserve the groves of big trees [giant sequoias] in California" and thanked "the Secretary of the Interior for his interest in this matter."
79. Grinnell to Archibald Rogers, January 17, 1891, Letter Book, 186-87.
80. "Cages in Place of Bullets," *Forest and Stream*, August 21, 1890, XXXV, 85; *ibid.*, January 8, 1891, XXXV, 489.
81. An important manifestation of the regard Roosevelt had for *Forest and Stream*'s editor is the fact that he very much wanted Grinnell to be his hunting partner, which for Roosevelt was the ultimate compliment. See Grinnell to James Willard Schultz, May 24, 1888, Letter Book, 361; and Grinnell to Archibald Rogers, August 8, 1888, *ibid.*, 444. Another example of Roosevelt's admiration for Grinnell is an 1894 letter of his to their mutual friend, Madison Grant. In it, he urges Grant to send Grinnell some photographs of Roosevelt, apparently showing the big-game animals the future President had just shot in the West; Roosevelt to Grant, October 10, 1894, in Morison and Blum, *The Letters of Theodore Roosevelt*, I, 401.
82. Grinnell to Archibald Rogers, January 17, 1891, Letter Book, 187.
83. *Ibid.*
84. "The National Park Bill," *Forest and Stream*, March 12, 1891, XXXVI, 145.
85. See earlier discussion, above; plus Grinnell to "Editor of Scribner's Magazine," April 28, 1887, Letter Book, 109; and Grinnell to Hart Lyman (*New York Tribune*), April 23, 1890, *ibid.*, 289. For later efforts, see Grinnell to W. H. Phillips, March 28, 1892, *ibid.*, 865, describing interview with editor of *Garden and Forest Magazine;* and Grinnell to Caspar W. Whitney (*Harper's Weekly*), October 11, 1894, *ibid.*, 241.
86. Grinnell to R. U. Johnson, May 6, 1891, *ibid.*, 407-08.
87. Fox, *John Muir*, 97-99, and 105.
88. *Ibid.*, 94.
89. Grinnell to Arnold Hague, May 7, 1891, Letter Book, 412-13.
90. Grinnell to W. H. Phillips, February 23, 1892, *ibid.*, 780; Grinnell to W. H. Phillips, March 28, 1892, *ibid.*, 865; Grinnell to Arnold Hague, May 14, 1892, *ibid.*, 102; Grinnell to George S. Anderson, December 13, 1892,

ibid., 639; Grinnell to W. H. Phillips, December 23, 1892, *ibid.*, 692; and Grinnell to T. G. Pearson, March 28, 1921, *ibid.*, 324.
91. Trefethen, *Crusade for Wildlife*, 35-36; Grinnell to George S. Anderson, November 28, 1892, Letter Book, 571; and *Forest and Stream*, December 15, 1892, XXXIX, 507. *The Louisville Commercial* (December 20, 1892), the *New York Sun* (December 20, 1892), and the *New York Times* (December 25, 1892) were three of the papers that backed up *Forest and Stream*'s stand in behalf of the park.
92. *Forest and Stream*, March 17, 1892, XXXVIII, 245.
93. Grinnell to George S. Anderson, November 28, 1892, Letter Book, 571; Grinnell states that he is also asking for letters from Phillips, Roosevelt, and Hague.
94. "A Standing Menace," *Forest and Stream*, December 8, 1892, XXXIX, 485; and "A Standing Menace," *ibid.*, December 15, 1892, XXXIX, 514; the letters were supposedly a spontaneous response to the editorial. (Anderson has already been identified as a sportsman—see Chapter Two.)
95. Mining interests and real-estate speculators in Cooke City, Montana, just outside the northeastern corner of the park, were the ones pushing for the railroad.
96. *Forest and Stream*, December 15, 1892, XXXIX, 514.
97. Grinnell to W. H. Phillips, December 15, 1892, Letter Book, 648; Grinnell to Charles Sheldon, January 30, 1920, *ibid.*, 134.
98. Grinnell to W. H. Phillips, December 15, 1892, *ibid.*, 648.
99. "An Individual Appeal," *Forest and Stream*, December 15, 1892, XXXIX, 507.
100. Grinnell to W. H. Phillips, March 1, 1892, Letter Book, 803.
101. *Forest and Stream*, February 23, 1893, XL, 155; Trefethen, *Crusade for Wildlife*, 36.
102. "The Account of Howell's Capture," *Forest and Stream*, May 5, 1894, XLII, 377-78.
103. See Hough, *Getting a Wrong Start: A Truthful Autobiography* (New York, 1915), 132-42, for a description of George Bird Grinnell and the inner workings of *Forest and Stream*.
104. *Ibid.*, 69 and 141.
105. Grinnell to Horace Albright, February 23, 1922, Letter Book, 169-70; Grinnell to T. E. Hofer, May 3, 1922, *ibid.*, 378.
106. *Forest and Stream*, XLII, 243.
107. "Dangers of Segregation," *ibid.*, March 31, 1894, XLII, 265; "Save the Park Buffalo," April 14, 1894, XLII, 309; and "The Account of Howell's Capture," May 5, 1894, XLII, 377-78.
108. *Ibid.*, 377.
109. Grinnell, *A Brief History of the Boone and Crockett Club*, 19; Theodore Roosevelt and George Bird Grinnell, eds., *Hunting in Many Lands* (New York, 1895), 9-10.
110. Nash, *Wilderness and the American Mind*, 114; Nash is quoting the *Congressional Record*.
111. Grinnell, *A Brief History of the Boone and Crockett Club*, 19.
112. Chittenden, *The Yellowstone National Park*, 119-20. In 1892 Grinnell estimated the number of bison in the park at 400, but by 1894, this figure

had been sharply reduced; a year later, the Superintendent thought there were only about 200 in the reserve; Mark Sullivan, "The Bison Still Lives," *Boston Evening Transcript*, October 10, 1900.

113. Trefethen, *Crusade for Wildlife*, 140.

114. "Protection for the Park," *Forest and Stream*, May 12, 1894, XLII, 327; and Ise, *Our National Park Policy*, 45-46.

115. Grinnell to Roosevelt, May 8, 1894, Letter Book, 57-58.

116. *Ibid.*; Grinnell is paraphrasing what Roosevelt had written him.

117. Chittenden, *The Yellowstone National Park*, 119-20; and Robert Shankland, *Steve Mather of the National Parks*, 45.

118. Grinnell to Roosevelt, May 8, 1894, Letter Book, 57-58.

119. Trefethen, *Crusade for Wildlife*, 42.

120. Page 21.

121. Page 23.

122. Ernest F. Swift, *The Public's Land: Our Heritage and Opportunity* (Washington, D.C., 1963), 7.

123. "Utilize the Streams," *Forest and Stream*, August 11, 1887, XXIX, 41; "Forests of the Rocky Mountains I," *ibid.*, October 25, 1888, XXXI, 261-62; "Forests of the Rocky Mountains II," *ibid.*, November 1, 1888, XXXI, 282-83; "Forests of the Rocky Mountains III," *ibid.*, November 8, 1888, XXXI, 301-02; "Popular Forestry Instruction," *ibid.*, December 6, 1888, XXXI, 381; "Practical Forest Restoration I," *ibid.*, February 28, 1889, XXXII, 105; "Practical Forest Restoration II," *ibid.*, March 14, 1889, XXXII, 149; "Practical Forest Restoration III," *ibid.*, March 21, 1889, XXXII, 169; and "Practical Forest Restoration IV," *ibid.*, March 28, 1889, XXXII, 189.

124. "Forests of the Rocky Mountains I," *ibid.*, October 25, 1888, XXXI, 261-62.

125. *Ibid.*

126. "Forests of the Rocky Mountains III," *ibid.*, November 8, 1888, XXXI, 301-02.

127. *Ibid.*, 302.

128. Volume XXXI, 381.

129. *Ibid.*

130. *Ibid.*

131. *Forest and Stream*, May 15, 1897, XLVIII, 381; and Grinnell to N. P. Langford, July 25, 1905, Letter Book, 742-43. Besides being Grinnell's close friend, he was also his lawyer; Grinnell to W. H. Phillips, September 3, 1888, *ibid.*, 476-77.

132. Grinnell, *A Brief History of the Boone and Crockett Club*, 23.

133. Noble, "General Benjamin Harrison," *The Independent*, LIII (March 21, 1901), 646.

134. For an example of Phillips' early dedication to the forests of Yellowstone, see *Forest and Stream*, February 11, 1886, XXVI, 41. For examples of the close working relationship between Phillips and Noble, see Grinnell to Phillips, May 25, 1889, Letter Book, 322; Grinnell to Noble, May 25, 1889, *ibid.*, 321 (letter crossed out and apparently never sent); Grinnell to Phillips, May 28, 1889, *ibid.*, 329; Grinnell to Phillips, June 5, 1889, *ibid.*, 354; Grinnell to Phillips, November 7, 1889, *ibid.*, 453-55; Grinnell to Phillips, December 4, 1889, *ibid.*, 16; and Grinnell to Phillips, April 24, 1891, *ibid.*, 383.

135. Vol. XL, 203.
136. From the late 1880s on, *Forest and Stream* and Grinnell's Letter Books are replete with examples of his efforts in behalf of Indians.
137. Grinnell to Phillips, May 25, 1889, Letter Book, 322; Grinnell to Noble, May 25, 1889, *ibid.*, 321 (letter crossed out and apparently never sent); Grinnell to Phillips, May 28, 1889, *ibid.*, 329; "Secretary Noble and the Indians," *Forest and Stream*, May 30, 1889, XXXII, 373; Grinnell to Phillips, June 5, 1889, Letter Book, 354; and Grinnell to Noble, June 19, 1889, *ibid.*, 380-81.

For some examples of Grinnell's efforts to get the Indian agent removed, see Grinnell to Commissioner of Indian Affairs, November 20, 1888, *ibid.*, 497-502; Grinnell to Commissioner of Indian Affairs, November 30, 1888, *ibid.*, 39-66; Grinnell to J. W. Schultz, December 4, 1888, *ibid.*, 7-9; Grinnell to L. H. North, December 13, 1888, *ibid.*, 34-35; Grinnell to Joseph Kipp, December 20, 1888, *ibid.*, 86-87; Grinnell to George Gould, December 26, 1888, *ibid.*, 96-97; Grinnell to H. H. Garr, January 3, 1889, *ibid.*, 180; Grinnell to Garr, January 7, 1889, *ibid.*, 128-29; Grinnell to William Russell, February 13, 1889, *ibid.*, 212; Grinnell to Gould, April 26, 1889, *ibid.*, 267-68; Grinnell to Garr, May 11, 1889, *ibid.*, 282; and Grinnell to J. B. Monroe, April 29, 1913, *ibid.*, 27-28.
138. Rothman, *Preserving Different Pasts*, 64; Ise, *Our National Park Policy*, 57; and Udall, *The Quiet Crisis*, 128.
139. Patrician angler George Edmunds, Senator from Vermont, who has been discussed above for his efforts in behalf of fish culture and Yellowstone National Park, had already obtained, on two different occasions, Senate approval of a bill to establish a forest reserve "at the headwaters of the Missouri River." In both cases, however, the House showed no interest in the bill. See John Ise, *The United States Forest Policy* (New York, 1972), 113-14. This is a reprint of a work originally published in 1920.
140. Arnold Hague to Grinnell, April 11, 1910, Grinnell File.
141. Bernard E. Fernow to Grinnell, April 12, 1910, *ibid.*
142. Arnold Hague to Grinnell, April 11, 1910, *ibid.*
143. *Forest and Stream*, April 9, 1891, XXXVI, 225.
144. Arnold Hague to Grinnell, April 11, 1910, Grinnell File.
145. A copy of this resolution, dated April 8, 1891, is in the Boone and Crockett Club File.
146. Noble to Roosevelt, April 16, 1891, Yellowstone Archives, Doc. No. 254, cited in Broadbent, "Sportsmen and the Evolution of the Conservation Idea in Yellowstone," 108.
147. Page 115.
148. "William Hallett Phillips," *Forest and Stream*, May 15, 1897, XLVIII, 381.
149. *Forest and Stream*, April 9, 1891, XXXVI, 225; *ibid.*, October 22, 1891, XXXVII, 265; and *ibid.*, December 3, 1891, XXXVII, 385.
150. Noble to Grinnell, March 11, 1910, Boone and Crockett Club File; and Noble to Grinnell, March 15, 1910, Grinnell File.
151. *Theodore Roosevelt: An Autobiography*, in *The Works of Theodore Roosevelt* (Memorial Edition, New York, 1923-26), XXII, 463.
152. Samuel P. Hays, *Conservation and the Gospel of Efficiency: The Progressive Conservation Movement, 1890-1920* (New York, 1969), 280-81; first

published in 1959. Also, see Pinchot's memoirs, *Breaking New Ground*, and his article, "How Conservation Began," *Agricultural History*, XI (October, 1937), 255-65.

153. Henry Clepper, "The Conservation Movement: Birth and Infancy," in Clepper, ed., *Origins of American Conservation* (New York, 1966), 9; Arthur B. Meyer, "Forests and Forestry," *ibid.*, 43; and Pinkett, *Gifford Pinchot*, 8. In its conclusions, the last work is an uncritical rehashing of *Breaking New Ground*, Pinchot's autobiography.

154. Jacques Barzun and Henry F. Graff, *The Modern Researcher* (New York, 1970), 84-85; this is a revised edition of a work originally published in 1957.

155. Pinchot, "On Writing History," in *Breaking New Ground*, xvii.

156. See Olson, *The Depletion Myth*, for the thesis that there was really no approaching "timber famine," despite the warnings of Roosevelt and others.

157. Harold T. Pinkett's assertion that "the ruthless exploitation of natural resources was first most obvious and alarming in the continuing devastation of the nation's forests" is simply inaccurate; Pinkett, *Gifford Pinchot*, 8.

158. I am speaking here, of course, not only of renewable categories of resources like wildlife and forests, but of specific places like national parks and refuges.

Chapter 7
Establishment of a National Conservation Policy

1. "The Smirch of Politics," *Forest and Stream*, August 30, 1888, XXXI, 101; *ibid.*, November 17, 1894, XLIII, 419; *ibid.*, December 15, 1894, XLIII, 507; "Fish, Forests and Politics," *ibid.*, February 2, 1895, XLIV, 81.

2. *Ibid.*, May 6, 1899, LII, 341.

3. "New York Game Protectors," *ibid.*, December 9, 1899, LIII, 469.

4. *Ibid.*

5. "The New York Fish Commission," *ibid.*, December 9, 1899, LIII, 461.

6. Pinchot, *Breaking New Ground*, 145.

7. For a critique of the traditional interpretation of Pinchot as an insensitive utilitarian, see Chapter Three, above, and Reiger, "Gifford Pinchot with Rod and Reel."

8. "The New York Fish Commission," *Forest and Stream*, December 9, 1899, LIII, 461.

9. "The New York Fish Commission," *ibid.*, February 24, 1900, LIV, 141.

10. For a different interpretation of this issue, see Chessman, *Governor Theodore Roosevelt*, 251-52.

11. "The New York Commission," *Forest and Stream*, March 10, 1900, LIV, 181.

12. Roosevelt to Grinnell, March 14, 1900, Roosevelt Papers, Library of Congress, Series 2.

13. Letter of James B. Trefethen to the author, October 23, 1967.

14. Grinnell to Roosevelt, March 17, 1900, Letter Book, 799-800.

15. "The New York Commission," *Forest and Stream*, March 24, 1900, LIV, 221.

16. Roosevelt to Grinnell, March 24, 1900, Roosevelt Papers, Library of Congress, Series 2.

17. Grinnell to Roosevelt, March 26, 1900, Letter Book, 817; Grinnell to Roosevelt, April 26, 1900, *ibid.*, 862; "The New York Commission," *Forest and Stream,* May 5, 1900, LIV, 341.
18. Grinnell to Roosevelt, April 26, 1900, Letter Book, 862.
19. Undated clipping, sometime in early 1901, Boone and Crockett Club File.
20. "The Pollution of Waters," *Forest and Stream,* January 27, 1900, LIV, 61. Early sportsmen's efforts against water pollution are discussed in Chapter Three, above.
21. *The Gun,* undated clipping, Boone and Crockett Club File.
22. Grinnell to Roosevelt, August 29, 1900, Letter Book, 14.
23. Ise, *Our National Park Policy,* 48. Presidents Harrison, Cleveland, and McKinley had all established forest reserves containing millions of acres, but Roosevelt, of course, did much more. By the year 2000, the national forests totaled about 192 million acres.
24. What can be considered the first national wildlife refuge was the "Afognak Forest and Fish-Culture Reserve" (north of Alaska's Kodiak Island) proclaimed by President Harrison in 1892. Besides Harrison, those instrumental in its creation were angler-fish culturist Livingston Stone, George Bird Grinnell, and John W. Noble. See Grinnell to Noble, April 14, 1891, Letter Book, 370; "A Marine Reservation," *Forest and Stream,* April 23, 1891, XXXVI, 265; Grinnell to Noble, April 24, 1891, Letter Book, 385; "Destruction of Seal Life," *Forest and Stream,* April 30, 1891, XXXVI, 285; "Marine Reservations," *ibid.*, 287; "Marine Reservations," *ibid.*, May 21, 1891, XXXVI, 347; "The Reservation of Afognak," *ibid.*, January 12, 1893, XL, 23; Trefethen, *Crusade for Wildlife,* 64-66; and Cart, "The Struggle for Wildlife Protection," 4 and 111-12. The Letter Book citations and *Forest and Stream* editorials reveal that Noble and Grinnell worked closely together to "prepare" the public for the announcement of the reserve. Cart is correct in perceiving that "the language of Harrison's proclamation indicated that the Afognak Reserve was not only the first federal wildlife refuge, but also the first federal 'wilderness area,' anticipating the spirit of the Wilderness Act of 1964 by seventy-two years"; Cart, "The Struggle for Wildlife Protection," 111.
25. Roosevelt to Grinnell, May 5, 1897, Roosevelt Papers, Library of Congress, Series 2.
26. Roosevelt to Grinnell, June 7, 1897, *ibid.*
27. Roosevelt to Grinnell, August 3, 1897, *ibid.*
28. Roosevelt to Grinnell, December 27, 1897, *ibid.* For other evidence of the closeness of this literary partnership and Roosevelt's tendency to follow Grinnell's lead, see Roosevelt to Grinnell, January 30, 1894, Boone and Crockett Club File; Roosevelt to Grinnell, August 2, 1897, Roosevelt Papers, Library of Congress, Series 2; Roosevelt to Grinnell, August 24, 1897, *ibid.*; Roosevelt to Grinnell, August 30, 1897, *ibid.*; Roosevelt to Grinnell, January 8, 1898, *ibid.*; Roosevelt to Grinnell, February 18, 1899, *ibid.*, XV; Roosevelt to Grinnell, February 23, 1900, *ibid.*, Series 2; Grinnell to C. Grant LaFarge, March 19, 1900, Letter Book, 801; Grinnell to Gifford Pinchot, March 13, 1901, *ibid.*, 463; and Grinnell to Madison Grant, June 19, 1901, *ibid.*, 737.
29. *Forest and Stream,* April 15, 1899, LII, 290.

30. William Cronon, "Landscapes of Abundance and Scarcity," in Clyde A. Milner II, *et al.*, eds., *The Oxford History of the American West* (New York, 1994), 612.
31. Quoted in Tober, *Who Owns the Wildlife?*, 249. Emphasis added.
32. For Roosevelt's thinking on this subject and the tremendous influence his actions would have for the later history of the national monuments, see Chapter Three, above; and Rothman, *Preserving Different Pasts,* 68-69.
33. Pinkett, *Gifford Pinchot;* M. Nelson McGeary, *Gifford Pinchot: Forester-Politician* (Princeton, 1960); and Martin L. Fausold, *Gifford Pinchot, Bull Moose Progressive* (Syracuse, 1961).
34. Pinchot, *Breaking New Ground,* particularly 319-26.
35. See Chapter Four, above.
36. Speech at Harvard University, December 14, 1910, *The Works of Theodore Roosevelt* (Memorial Edition), XV, 558.
37. Pinchot, *Breaking New Ground,* 144-45; Pinkett, *Gifford Pinchot,* 34; "The Biltmore Forest," *Forest and Stream,* January 6, 1894, XLII, 1; J. B. Monroe to Grinnell, July 12, 1896, letter in possession of Mrs. John P. Holman, Fairfield, Connecticut; Monroe to Grinnell, December 2, 1896, *ibid.*; Grinnell to Pinchot, November 19, 1897, Letter Book, 164; Grinnell to Pinchot, December 31, 1897, *ibid.*, 301-02; Grinnell to Pinchot, January 15, 1898, *ibid.*, 347; Grinnell, "Opening Up Forest Reserves," *The Forester,* IV (February, 1898), 42-44. Grinnell's admiration for Pinchot is revealed in a letter to his Montana hunting guide, who, on Grinnell's recommendation, was employed by Pinchot several times. Grinnell told his Western friend that he was sorry he could not guide the forester on his next trip, for "I should think [he] would be a charming man to travel with and . . . is certainly one from whom you can learn a great deal"; Grinnell to J. B. Monroe, May 3, 1897, Letter Book, 395.
38. Pinkett, *Gifford Pinchot,* 53-54.
39. Grinnell to Charles Otis, September 25, 1911, Letter Book, 452; Grinnell to C. H. Merriam, January 22, 1920, *ibid.*, 100-01; Grinnell to John P. Holman, April 28, 1919, *ibid.*, 609-10; Grinnell to Arthur L. Clark, December 19, 1923, *ibid.*, 277; author's interview with John P. Holman, March 1, 1969, Fairfield, Connecticut; Grinnell to Charles Sheldon, May 8, 1919, Letter Book, 651.
40. *New York Times,* May 16, 1925; *Washington* [D.C.] *Star,* May 16, 1925. A third medal went to Martha Berry, the educator.
41. For examples of Roosevelt's esteem for Grinnell—besides those already given—see the comments of two famous naturalists: C. Hart Merriam to Grinnell, April 29, 1902, Grinnell File; Merriam, "Roosevelt, the Naturalist," *Science,* LXXV (February 12, 1932), 183; and George Shiras, 3d., to Grinnell, May 2, 1925, Grinnell File.
42. Trefethen to the author, October 23, 1967. Besides his conservation activities, Grinnell was a student of Plains Indian history and culture, and a staunch advocate for the fair treatment of all Native Americans. Because Roosevelt was already committed to his conservation ideas, Grinnell used his influence with the President mainly in an effort to improve the government's treatment of the Indian. Publicly, in *Forest and Stream,* Grinnell described and endorsed each step of Roosevelt's conservation program, but in private discussions with the President, he limited himself to

matters pertaining to Native Americans. Once Roosevelt's chief conservation adviser, Grinnell now became his most trusted consultant on Indian affairs. Among the services he performed for Roosevelt was the settlement in 1902 of a national scandal involving a proposal to lease to cattlemen large sections of the Standing Rock Sioux Reservation in North Dakota; the writing of parts of his 1902 and 1904 annual messages to Congress that dealt with Indians; and the suggestion of Francis E. Leupp for Commissioner of Indian Affairs, the man who filled that office with distinction during Roosevelt's second administration.

For examples of *Forest and Stream*'s support of the Roosevelt-Pinchot conservation program, see "Forest Reserves as Game Refuges," February 8, 1902, LVIII, 101; "Sportsmen in the White House," May 10, 1902, LVIII, 361; "President Roosevelt as a Sportsman," December 5, 1903, LXI, 437; January 30, 1904, LXII, 81; "The President's Message," December 17, 1904, LXIII, 505; "Transfer of Forest Reserves," February 11, 1905, LXIV, 109; "More National Parks," September 9, 1905, LXV, 205; "The Forest Reserves," December 16, 1905, LXV, 485; "The Forest Service," January 26, 1907, LXVIII, 127; and May 23, 1908, LXX, 807.

For the fact that Grinnell limited himself to Indian affairs when talking with the President, see Grinnell to Mrs. G. W. H. Stouch, February 8, 1907, Letter Book, 869. Of course, this does not mean that Grinnell's interest in conservation had lessened. For his later activities in this area, see Madison Grant, *Early History of Glacier National Park Montana* (Washington, D.C., 1919); Trefethen, *Crusade for Wildlife;* Trefethen, *An American Crusade for Wildlife;* and Gerald A. Diettert, *Grinnell's Glacier: George Bird Grinnell and Glacier National Park* (Missoula, Montana, 1992).

For documentation of the "services" mentioned above, which Grinnell performed for Roosevelt in the area of Indian affairs, see C. H. Merriam to Grinnell, February 8, 1902, Grinnell Collection, item no. 206; Grinnell to Merriam, February 19, 1902, Letter Book, 151; Roosevelt to Grinnell, April 28, 1902, Roosevelt Papers, Library of Congress, Series 2; George Kennan to Grinnell, April 28, 1902, Grinnell Collection, item no. 170; Merriam to Grinnell, April 29, 1902, Grinnell File; Grinnell to Merriam, April 30, 1902, Letter Book, 351; Grinnell to S. M. Brosius, April 30, 1902, *ibid.*, 352; Grinnell to Roosevelt, May 1, 1902, *ibid.*, 374; Grinnell to Emerson Hough, May 2, 1902, *ibid.*, 377; Grinnell to Hamlin Garland, May 7, 1902, *ibid.*, 395; "STANDING ROCK AGENCY, FORT YATES, N. DAK. MAY 23, 1902. MEMORANDUM AGREEMENT. Negotiated by GEORGE BIRD GRINNELL. . . ," Grinnell Collection, item no. 549; Grinnell (as Special Confidential Indian Agent) to Secretary of the Interior, May 29, 1902 (Grinnell's report), Grinnell File; Roosevelt to Grinnell, June 13, 1902, Roosevelt Papers, Library of Congress, Series 2; "THE STANDING ROCK INDIANS AND THE GRAZING LEASES" (June, 1902), Grinnell Collection, item no. 206; Grinnell to George B. Cortelyou, October 24, 1902, Letter Book, 575; Willis Fletcher Johnson, ed., *Addresses and Papers of Theodore Roosevelt* (New York, 1909), 97-98; Grinnell to John Pitcher, December 8, 1904, Letter Book, 244; "The President's Message," *Forest and Stream*, December 17, 1904, LXIII, 505; Grinnell to Roosevelt, November 17, 1904, Letter Book, 191-92; Grinnell to F. E. Leupp, November 21, 1904, *ibid.*, 208; Grinnell to Pitcher, December 8, 1904, *ibid.*, 244; and Grinnell to "The President," October 31, 1912, *ibid.*, 467.

For further documentation of Grinnell's role as Roosevelt's chief adviser on Indian matters, see Roosevelt to Grinnell, July 2, 1902, Roosevelt Papers, Library of Congress, Series 2; Grinnell to Roosevelt, July 18, 1902, Letter Book, 422-23; Grinnell to James McLaughlin, July 21, 1902, *ibid.*, 430; Grinnell to Hamlin Garland, November 13, 1902, *ibid.*, 605; Grinnell to J. B. Monroe, January 27, 1903, *ibid.*, 789; Grinnell to Roosevelt, February 5, 1903, *ibid.*, 822; Grinnell to E. Hofer, February 6, 1903, *ibid.*, 828; Roosevelt to Grinnell, February 9, 1903, Roosevelt Papers, Library of Congress, Series 2; Grinnell to Roosevelt, February 14, 1903, Letter Book, 849; Grinnell to William Loeb, Jr., March 2, 1903, *ibid.*, 887; Grinnell to Roosevelt, March 12, 1903, *ibid.*, 909; Grinnell to Roosevelt, March 24, 1903, *ibid.*, 938; Grinnell to Roosevelt, June 3, 1903, *ibid.*, 99; Roosevelt to Grinnell, July 22, 1903, Roosevelt Papers, Library of Congress, Series 2; Roosevelt to Ethan Allen Hitchcock, July 22, 1903, *ibid.*; Grinnell to Roosevelt, August 22, 1903, Letter Book, 175-76; Grinnell to W. A. Jones, August 29, 1903, *ibid.*, 191; Grinnell to Roosevelt, September 14, 1903, *ibid.*, 225-26; Roosevelt to Henry Cabot Lodge, September 30, 1903, Morison and Blum, *Letters of Theodore Roosevelt,* III, 606; Grinnell to Joseph Kipp, October 3, 1903, Letter Book, 285; Grinnell to C. H. Merriam, November 30, 1903, *ibid.*, 406-07; Grinnell to Charles Aubrey (no date: *circa* January 22, 1904), *ibid.*, 494; Grinnell to Monroe, January 29, 1904, *ibid.*, 522; Grinnell to Roosevelt, March 10, 1904, *ibid.*, 675; Grinnell to Merriam, March 12, 1904, *ibid.*, 680; Grinnell to Roosevelt, March 16, 1904, *ibid.*, 687; Grinnell to Roosevelt, March 23, 1904, *ibid.*, 723-24; Grinnell to Roosevelt, July 14, 1904, *ibid.*, 16; Grinnell to Roosevelt, July 19, 1904, *ibid.*, 29; Roosevelt to Hitchcock, July 23, 1904, Morison and Blum, *Letters of Theodore Roosevelt,* IV, 864; Grinnell to Frank Mead, July 25, 1904, Letter Book, 37-38; Grinnell to Roosevelt, July 25, 1904, *ibid.*, 35; Grinnell to Mead, July 28, 1904, *ibid.*, 39-40; Grinnell to F. E. Leupp, August 27, 1904, *ibid.*, 99; Grinnell to Loeb, September 6, 1904, *ibid.*, 109; Grinnell to Lapsley A. McAfee, November 7, 1904, *ibid.*, 142; Grinnell to Roosevelt, November 11, 1904, *ibid.*, 152; Grinnell to Pitcher, November 18, 1904, *ibid.*, 201; Grinnell to Loeb, November 22, 1904, *ibid.*, 212-13; Grinnell to Merriam, May 25, 1905, *ibid.*, 622; Grinnell to Mrs. F. N. Doubleday, June 10, 1905, *ibid.*, 670; Grinnell to Mead, June 23, 1905, *ibid.*, 697; Grinnell to Roosevelt, November 29, 1905, *ibid.*, 965; Grinnell to Joseph M. Dixon, June 21, 1906, *ibid.*, 451; Grinnell to James A. Perrine, June 22, 1906, *ibid.*, 469-70; Grinnell to Monroe, July 2, 1906, *ibid.*, 492; Grinnell to Perrine, July 2, 1906, *ibid.*, 489; and Grinnell to Hofer, July 7, 1906, *ibid.*, 499.

Epilogue
Aldo Leopold and the Continuing Tradition of the Sportsman-Conservationist Ideal

1. Curt Meine, *Aldo Leopold: His Life and Work* (Madison, Wisconsin, 1988), 307.
2. Quoted in *ibid.*
3. *Ibid.*, 526.
4. Roderick Nash, *The Rights of Nature: A History of Environmental Ethics* (Madison, Wisconsin, 1989), 63; quoting Dave Foreman.

5. See the treatment of Leopold in William Cronon, *Nature's Metropolis: Chicago and the Great West* (New York, 1991); Donald Worster, *The Wealth of Nature: Environmental History and the Ecological Imagination* (New York, 1993); and Hal K. Rothman, *The Greening of a Nation? Environmentalism in the United States Since 1945* (Fort Worth, Texas, 1998).

6. Robert Finch, "Introduction: The Delights and Dilemmas of A *Sand County Almanac*," in Leopold, *A Sand County Almanac and Sketches Here and There* (New York, 1989), xv.

7. Leopold, *A Sand County Almanac* (1989 edition), viii, and 224-25.

8. Robert A. McCabe, *Aldo Leopold: The Professor* (Madison, Wisconsin, 1987), 124.

9. *Ibid.*

10. *Ibid.*

11. Nina Leopold Bradley, "How Hunting Affected Aldo Leopold's Thinking and His Commitment to a Land Ethic," in the *Proceedings of the Fourth Annual Governor's Symposium on North American Hunting* (Minnetonka, Minnesota, 1995), 10.

12. *Ibid.*, 11.

13. *Ibid.*; Meine, *Aldo Leopold*, 38.

14. Bradley, "How Hunting . . . ," 13.

15. Leopold, *A Sand County Almanac* (1966 edition), 37.

16. *Ibid.*, 38.

17. *Ibid.*, 120-21.

18. *Ibid.*, 121.

19. *Ibid.*

20. *Ibid.*

21. *Ibid.*

22. *Ibid.*, 121-22.

23. Meine, *Aldo Leopold*, 525.

24. Nash, *Wilderness and the American Mind*, 182.

25. Fox, *John Muir*, 336. For the fact that Fox is wrong about at least three of these individuals, see Altherr and Reiger, "Academic Historians and Hunting," 51-52.

26. Fox, *John Muir*, 336.

27. For a similar statement in his book, see McCabe, *Aldo Leopold*, 124.

28. *Ibid.*

29. *Ibid.*

Annotated Bibliography

Adams, John Quincy. *Life in a New England Town: 1787, 1788. Diary of John Quincy Adams, While a Student in the Office of Theophilus Parsons at Newburyport.* Boston, 1903. Diary published by his grandson, Charles Francis Adams.

Adams, Jr., Robert. "The Oldest Club in America." *Century Magazine,* XXVI (August, 1883), 544-50. On the Schuylkill Fishing Company, founded in Pennsylvania in 1732.

Adams, William R. "Florida Live Oak Farm of John Quincy Adams." *Florida Historical Quarterly,* LI (1972), 129-42.

Allard, Jr., Dean C. "Spencer Fullerton Baird and the U.S. Fish Commission: A Study in the History of American Science." Ph.D. dissertation, George Washington University, 1967.

Allen, Joel A. *The American Bisons, Living and Extinct. Memoirs of the Museum of Comparative Zoology.* IV (1876). Cambridge, Massachusetts, 1876.

———. *Autobiographical Notes and a Bibliography of the Scientific Publications of Joel Asaph Allen.* New York, 1916.

———. "On the Decrease of Birds in the United States." *Penn Monthly* (December, 1876), 931-44. Bound copy in the library of Harvard's Museum of Comparative Zoology. Recommends the formation of societies to protect nongame birds and points out the fallacy of trying to discriminate between "beneficial" and "injurious" birds.

Altherr, Thomas L. "The American Hunter-Naturalist and the Development of the Code of Sportsmanship." *Journal of Sport History,* V (Spring, 1978), 7-22.

———. " 'The Best of All Breathing': Hunting as a Mode of Environmental Perception in American Literature and Thought from James Fenimore Cooper to Norman Mailer." Ph.D. dissertation, Ohio State University, 1976.

———. " 'Chaplain to the Hunters': Thoreau's Ambivalence Toward Hunting." *American Literature,* LVI (October, 1984), 345-61.

———, and John F. Reiger. "Academic Historians and Hunting: A Call for More and Better Scholarship." *Environmental History Review,* XIX (Fall, 1995), 39-56. Part of the discussion is on how historians have misinterpreted Henry David Thoreau and Aldo Leopold.

Altsheler, Brent (comp.). *Natural History Index-Guide: An Index to 3,365 Books and Periodicals in Libraries . . . in All Countries. . . .* New York, 1940. Revised edition of book first published in 1936. Sporting and "scientific" works juxtaposed throughout.

American Angler. New York, 1881-1900.

American Naturalist. Salem, Massachusetts, 1867-1901.

American Sportsman [later *Rod and Gun*]. West Meriden, Connecticut, 1871-1874; and New York, 1874-1877. Merged with *Forest and Stream* in 1877.

American Turf Register and Sporting Magazine. Baltimore and New York, 1829-1844.

Amery, C.F. *Notes on Forestry.* London, 1875. A treatise that influenced Grinnell and others.

Anderson, Charles R. "Thoreau Takes a Pot Shot at *Carolina Sports*." *Georgia Review*, XXII (Fall, 1968), 289-99.

Anonymous. "Game Protectors at Dinner." *New York Times*, May 22, 1894, 4. Describes meeting of New York Association for the Protection of Game, founded in 1844.

————. *The Sportsman's Companion; or, An Essay on Shooting: Illustriously Shewing in What Manner to Fire at Birds of Game, in Various Directions and Situations; And, Directions to Gentlemen for the Treatment and Breaking [of] Their Own Pointers and Spaniels, and the Necessary Precautions to Guard Against Many Accidents That Attend This Pleasant Diversion....* Harrisburg, Pennsylvania, 1948. Originally published in New York in 1783, "By a Gentleman," this reprint contains a Preface, copious Notes, and a Bibliography of important sporting books, all by editor Jan Thornton. It is generally regarded as the first book on sport hunting published in America, and the code of the sportsman is already apparent in its pages.

————. "Sportsman Take Notice." *New York Evening Post*, March 24, 1806. Early statement of what I have called the code of the sportsman, plus the fact that a "New York Sporting Club" had just been formed to make sure the game laws were enforced and the game preserved.

Athearn, Robert G. *Westward the Briton: The Far West, 1865-1900, As Seen by British Sportsmen and Capitalists, Ranchers and Homesteaders, Lords and Ladies.* Lincoln, Nebraska, 1971. First published in 1953. Has a bibliography containing English sporting works on America.

Audubon, John James. *Delineations of American Scenery and Character.* New York, 1970. Reprint of book first published in 1926. Contains a bibliography of Audubon's works and an Introduction by his biographer, Francis Hobart Herrick.

Austin, Elizabeth S., ed. *Frank M. Chapman in Florida: His Journals and Letters.* Gainesville, Florida, 1967.

Bachelder, John B. *Popular Resorts, and How to Reach Them. Combining a Brief Description of the Principal Summer Retreats in the United States, and the Routes of Travel Leading to Them.* Boston, 1874.

Baldwin, Donald N. *The Quiet Revolution: The Grass Roots of Today's Wilderness Preservation Movement.* Boulder, Colorado, 1972. Seeks to prove that sportsman Arthur H. Carhart, and not that other sportsman, Aldo Leopold, was the "Father of the Wilderness Concept." Actually, the idea goes back at least to 1892—with the establishment of the Afognak Forest and Fish-Culture Reserve in Alaska.

Baltzell, E. Digby. *The Protestant Establishment: Aristocracy and Caste in America.* New York, 1966. First published in 1964.

Bancroft, Hubert Howe. *The Book of the Fair: An Historical and Descriptive Presentation of the World's Science, Art, and Industry, as Viewed Through the Columbian Exposition at Chicago in 1893.* This is a reprint, by Bounty Books, of a book apparently published in 1894. Place of publication of original work, or the reprint, is not given. Contains an interesting description of the Boone and Crockett Club exhibit at the fair.

Barber, Joel. *Wild Fowl Decoys.* New York, 1954. First published in 1934. Much on the history of their use.

Barrow, Jr., Mark V. *A Passion for Birds: American Ornithology After Audubon.* Princeton, New Jersey, 1998. Shows the interconnection between sport hunting, ornithology, and bird conservation in the nineteenth century.

Bartlett, Richard A. *Yellowstone: A Wilderness Besieged*. Tucson, Arizona, 1985. A history of the park and the many attacks on its integrity.

Batchelder, Charles F. *An Account of the Nuttall Ornithological Club, 1873 to 1919. Memoirs of the Nuttall Ornithological Club*. No. VIII. Cambridge, Massachusetts, 1937.

Bates, J. Leonard. "Fulfilling American Democracy: The Conservation Movement, 1907 to 1921." *Mississippi Valley Historical Review*, XLIV (June, 1957), 29-57.

Beach, William. *In the Shadow of Mount McKinley*. New York, 1931. Travel and big-game hunting. Introduction by Robert Sterling Yard and Foreword by John Burnham, both important conservationists of a later period.

Bean, Michael J. *The Evolution of National Wildlife Law*. New York, 1983. This is a revised edition of a work first published in 1977.

Beecher, Henry Ward. *Star Papers; or, Experiences of Art and Nature*. New York, 1855. Has chapters called "Trouting," "The Morals of Fishing," etc.

Berkeley, Grantley F. *The English Sportsman in the Western Prairies*. London, 1861. Travel and hunting.

Berryman, Jack W. "The Tenuous Attempts of Americans to 'Catch-Up with John Bull': Specialty Magazines and Sporting Journalism, 1800-1835." *Canadian Journal of History of Sport and Physical Education*, X (May, 1979), 33-61.

[Bethune, George W., ed.] *The Compleat Angler; or, the Contemplative Man's Recreation [1653]. By Izaak Walton and Charles Cotton. With Notes, a Bibliographical Preface, and a Notice of Cotton and his Writings, by the American Editor*. New York, 1847.

Betts, John Rickards. *America's Sporting Heritage: 1850-1950*. Reading, Massachusetts, 1974.

———. "Sporting Journalism in Nineteenth-Century America." *American Quarterly*, V (Spring, 1953), 39-56. On all sports, but much on hunting and fishing.

Bill, Ledyard. *A Winter in Florida; or, Observations on the Soil, Climate, and Products of Our Semi-Tropical State; With Sketches of the Principal Towns and Cities in Eastern Florida. To Which is Added A Brief Historical Summary; Together with Hints to the Tourist, Invalid, and Sportsman*. New York, 1870. First published in 1869. Typical of travel literature for sportsmen.

Biscotti, M. L. (comp.). *American Sporting Book Series*. Madison, Ohio, 1994. An important source for authors and publishing houses of books on both hunting and fishing.

——— (comp.). *A Bibliography of American Sporting Books, 1926-1985*. Far Hills, New Jersey, 1997. A comprehensive updating of John C. Phillips's *American Game Mammals and Birds: A Catalogue of Books, 1582 to 1925*.

Black, John D. *Biological Conservation; With Particular Emphasis on Wildlife*. New York, 1954. Much on the history of wildlife conservation, as well as an excellent annotated bibliography.

Bongartz, Roy. "The Man Who Loved Birds But Shot Them." *New York Times*, February 25, 1973, sect. XI, 1 and 8. On Audubon.

"Boone and Crockett Club File." Formerly at Theodore Roosevelt Birthplace, now at Boone and Crockett Club and University of Montana, both in Missoula. See "Notes" for description of this source, which had never been used before by an academic historian.

Boyle, Robert H. *The Hudson River: A Natural and Unnatural History.* New York, 1969. An important environmental history by a dedicated hunter and angler. Contains much on twentieth-century efforts by fishermen to preserve the river, plus an annotated bibliography.

Bradley, Nina Leopold. "How Hunting Affected Aldo Leopold's Thinking and His Commitment to a Land Ethic." *Proceedings of the Fourth Annual Governor's Symposium on North American Hunting,* 10-13. Minnetonka, Minnesota, 1995.

Branch, E. Douglas. *The Hunting of the Buffalo.* Lincoln, Nebraska, 1962. First published in 1929. Much on hide hunting.

Brander, Michael. *Hunting and Shooting: From Earliest Times to the Present Day.* New York, 1971. Deals with subject on a worldwide basis.

Brewster, William. *The Birds of the Cambridge Region of Massachusetts. Memoirs of the Nuttall Ornithological Club.* No. IV. Cambridge, 1906.

Brinley, Francis. *Life of William T. Porter.* New York, 1860. On an early and important sportsman-conservationist.

Broadbent, Sarah E. (comp.). *Index of Forest and Stream.* Yellowstone, Wyoming, 1996. An index of over 500 references, between 1873 and 1930, to Yellowstone National Park in the pages of *Forest and Stream.* Also contains a valuable Introduction focusing on George Bird Grinnell's key role in developing "the idea of the park's value to the nation."

———. "Sportsmen and the Evolution of the Conservation Idea in Yellowstone: 1882-1894." M.A. thesis, Montana State University, 1997.

Brooks, Paul. *Speaking for Nature: How Literary Naturalists from Henry Thoreau to Rachel Carson Have Shaped America.* Boston, 1980. Includes Roosevelt, Grinnell, and other sportsmen-naturalists.

Brown, John J. *The American Angler's Guide; or, Complete Fisher's Manual, For the United States: Containing the Opinions and Practices of Experienced Anglers of Both Hemispheres. . . .* New York, 1857. First published in 1845.

Bruette, William. *American Duck, Goose, and Brant Shooting.* New York, 1945. First published in 1929. By a later editor of *Forest and Stream.*

Bruns, Henry P. *Angling Books of the Americas.* Atlanta, Georgia, 1975. Much on the history of early fishing books in the United States.

Brusewitz, Gunnar. *Hunting: Hunters, Game, Weapons and Hunting Methods from the Remote Past to the Present Day.* New York, 1969. Translation of work first published in Sweden in 1967. Deals only with Europe. Apparently without seeing its importance to American readers, the author cites the use of wooden duck decoys in Scandinavia in the 1830s as already being a "traditional" method of waterfowl hunting. American writers have always assumed that their early use was unique to North America.

Buchheister, Carl W., and Frank Graham, Jr. "From the Swamps and Back: A Concise and Candid History of the Audubon Movement." *Audubon,* LXXV (January, 1973), 4-45.

Burdick, Jr., Walter E. "Elite in Transition: From Alienation to Manipulation." Ph.D. dissertation, Northern Illinois University, 1969. A study of the elite "mentality," including that of Theodore Roosevelt.

Burnham, John B. "Conservation's Debt to Sportsmen." *North American Review,* CCXXVI (September, 1928), 296-302. An attempt to set the record straight—an excellent historical overview.

———. "The Old Era—and the New." *Bulletin of the American Game Protective [and Propagation] Association,* XIV (January, 1925), 13. On central role of sportsmen in early wildlife conservation.

Burroughs, John. *Camping and Tramping with Roosevelt.* New York, 1970. Reprint of work first published in 1907.

———. *Locusts and Wild Honey.* Boston, 1879. Much on angling and its meaning.

———. "One Duck—A Potomac Sketch." *Scribner's Monthly,* XXI (December, 1880), 245-48. Combines hunting and nature study.

Callahan, J. Kenneth (comp.). *A Dictionary of Sporting Pen Names.* Peterborough, New Hampshire, 1995.

Cameron, Jenks. *The Bureau of Biological Survey: Its History, Activities and Organization.* Baltimore, 1929. Has a wealth of information on early wildlife conservation.

Cantwell, Robert. *Alexander Wilson: Naturalist and Pioneer, A Biography.* Philadelphia and New York, 1961.

Carhart, Arthur H. "Fly and Spinner." *American Forestry,* XXIX (July, 1923), 401-05. A later wilderness proponent, Carhart was also an enthusiastic angler, as this article proves.

———. "Live Game and Forest Recreation." *American Forestry,* XXVI (December, 1920), 723-27. Partly an ode to the joys and benefits of sport hunting.

Cart, Theodore W. "The Federal Fisheries Service, 1871-1940." M.A. thesis, University of North Carolina, 1968.

———. "The Lacey Act: America's First Nationwide Wildlife Statute." *Forest History,* XVII (October, 1973), 4-13.

———. "The Struggle for Wildlife Protection in the United States, 1870-1900: Attitudes and Events Leading to the Lacey Act." Ph.D. dissertation, University of North Carolina, 1971.

Carter, Paul A. *The Spiritual Crisis of the Gilded Age.* DeKalb, Illinois, 1971. Good background material for the changes in social values in the late nineteenth century.

Cartmill, Matt. *A View to a Death in the Morning: Hunting and Nature Through History.* Cambridge, Massachusetts, 1993. An anthropologist, Cartmill claims to be impartial, but his passionate anti-hunting sentiments are obvious, and seem to get in the way of his ability to analyze the subject in depth. For example, he equates hunting with working in a slaughterhouse (p. 230) and sarcastically dismisses Theodore Roosevelt as the "Great White Hunter" (p. 154). Given his apparent preconceptions, it is to be expected that the conservation achievements of American sportsmen are ignored, or disparaged. This book should be contrasted with Paul Shepard's works, two of which are cited in the present bibliography.

Catlin, George. *North American Indians: Being Letters and Notes on their Manners, Customs, and Conditions, Written During Eight Years' Travel Amongst the Wildest Tribes of Indians in North America, 1832-1839.* Philadelphia, 1913. 2 vols. Originally published in London in 1841, as a collection of articles which Catlin had written in the previous decade.

Caton, John Dean. *The Antelope and the Deer of America: A Comprehensive Scientific Treatise Upon the Natural History, Including the Characteristics, Habits, Affinities, and Capacity for Domestication of the Antilocapra, and*

Cervidae of North America. New York, 1877. Written by a sportsman-naturalist.

Catton, Theodore. *Inhabited Wilderness: Indians, Eskimos, and National Parks in Alaska.* Albuquerque, New Mexico, 1997. Good for the central role of sportsmen in Alaskan conservation.

Century Association. *Clarence King Memoirs: The Helmet of Mambrino.* New York, 1904. Mainly reminiscences of King by various people. Includes his hunting exploits.

Chapman, Frank M. *Autobiography of a Bird-Lover.* New York, 1935. First published in 1933.

———. *Camps and Cruises of an Ornithologist.* New York, 1908.

Chessman, G. Wallace. *Governor Theodore Roosevelt: The Albany Apprenticeship,1898-1900.* Cambridge, Massachusetts, 1965.

Chittenden, Hiram Martin. *The Yellowstone National Park.* Cincinnati, 1905. First published in 1895.

Clark, Galen. *Indians of the Yosemite Valley and Vicinity: Their History, Customs and Traditions.* Yosemite Valley, California, 1904. In Introduction W. W. Foote cites Clark's hunting interests.

Clark, Michael D. "American Patricians as Social Critics, 1865-1914." Ph.D. dissertation, University of North Carolina, 1965.

Clepper, Henry, ed. *Leaders of American Conservation.* New York, 1971. Biographical sketches, including their major publications, of well-known conservationists, but many of the nineteenth-century pioneers have been left out.

———, ed. *Origins of American Conservation.* New York, 1966. Articles by various authorities. In "The Conservation Movement: Birth and Infancy," Clepper makes the following, astounding statement: "The rank and file of these [early, private] organizations were ordinary citizens, public-spirited to be sure, but nevertheless not otherwise distinguished." The two organizations he had just been discussing were the Boone and Crockett Club and the American Game Protective [and Propagation] Association, both of which were founded by elite sportsmen and which contained few, if any, "ordinary citizens."

———. *Professional Forestry in the United States.* Baltimore, 1971. Has much on the beginning of forestry.

Cleveland, Grover. *Fishing and Shooting Sketches.* New York, 1906. Contains "The Mission of Sport and Outdoor Life," "The Serene Duck Hunter," and other essays revealing the former President's deep commitment to what I have called the "code of the sportsman."

Cole, Nathan. *The Royal Parks and Gardens of London, Their History and Mode of Embellishment. . . .* London, 1877.

Connett, Eugene V., ed. *Duck Shooting Along the Atlantic Tidewater.* New York, no date. Reprint, by Bonanza Books, of work first published in 1947. Has material on history of sport and commercial hunting extending back into the nineteenth century. The names of some of the contributors are very well known to historians of hunting.

———, ed. *Wildfowling in the Mississippi Flyway.* New York, 1949. Articles by various authorities—has some history.

Coon, Carleton S. *The Story of Man: From the First Human to Primitive Culture and Beyond.* New York, 1962. Revised edition of work first published in 1954. Has some material on meaning of hunting in human history.

Cory, Charles B. *How to Know the Ducks, Geese and Swans of North America.* Boston, 1897.

———. *Hunting and Fishing in Florida, Including a Key to the Water Birds Known to Occur in the State.* New York, 1970. Reprint of book originally published in 1896.

Coues, Elliott. *Handbook of Field and General Ornithology; A Manual of the Structure and Classification of Birds with Instructions for Collecting and Preserving Specimens.* London, 1890. This is a new edition, for a British audience, of certain portions of Coues's *Key to North American Birds,* which first appeared in 1872.

———. "Sketch of North American Ornithology in 1879." *American Naturalist,* XIV (January, 1880), 20-25. Shows difficulty of separating "sport" and "science."

Cox, Thomas R., *et al. This Well-Wooded Land: Americans and Their Forests From Colonial Times to the Present.* Lincoln, Nebraska, 1985.

Cronon, William. "Landscapes of Abundance and Scarcity." In Clyde A. Milner II, *et al.,* eds., *The Oxford History of the American West,* 603-37. New York, 1994. On conservation in the West, with a good "Bibliographic Note."

———. *Nature's Metropolis: Chicago and the Great West.* New York, 1991.

Cumbler, John T. "The Early Making of an Environmental Consciousness: Fish, Fisheries Commissions and the Connecticut River." *Environmental History Review,* XV (Winter, 1991), 73-91.

Cutright, Paul Russell. *Theodore Roosevelt: The Making of a Conservationist.* Urbana, Illinois, 1985.

———. *Theodore Roosevelt the Naturalist.* New York, 1956. Foreword by Fairfield Osborn.

Dall, William Healey. *Spencer Fullerton Baird: A Biography, Including Selections from His Correspondence with Audubon, Agassiz, Dana, and Others.* Philadelphia, 1915.

Danker, Donald F., ed. *Man of the Plains: Recollections of Luther North, 1856-1882.* Lincoln, Nebraska, 1961. The kind of frontiersman with whom elite Easterners such as George Bird Grinnell and Theodore Roosevelt liked to associate.

Davis, John ("One Who is Considered Nobody"). *Essays on Various Subjects, Written for the Amusement of Everybody.* New York, 1835.

Davis, Richard C., ed. *Encyclopedia of American Forest and Conservation History.* 2 vols. New York, 1983. Contains brief articles on Boone and Crockett Club, Grinnell, etc.

——— (comp.). *North American Forest History: A Guide to Archives and Manuscripts in the United States and Canada.* Santa Barbara, 1977. Despite the title, Davis deals with more than just the forests.

Day, Albert M. *North American Waterfowl.* Harrisburg, Pennsylvania, 1949. Much on history of waterfowl conservation, and contains a brief Introduction by duck hunter-conservationist J. N. "Ding" Darling.

DeKay, James E. *Anniversary Address on the Progress of the Natural Sciences in the United States: Delivered Before the Lyceum of Natural History of New York, Feb. 1826.* New York, 1970. Reprint of work originally published in 1826.

Derrydale Press. *A Decade of American Sporting Books and Prints By the Derrydale Press, 1927-1937.* New York, 1937. A bibliography, with an Introduction by the press's founder and president, Eugene V. Connett, III. Among the contributors to Derrydale books are noted conservationists John Burnham and Robert Sterling Yard.

DeSormo, Maitland. *John Bird Burnham: Klondiker, Adirondacker and Eminent Conservationist.* Saranac Lake, New York, 1978. An excellent example of the sportsman-conservationist. He worked with Grinnell on *Forest and Stream,* was commissioner of fish and game for New York State and president of the American Game Protective and Propagation Association, and worked closely with other sportsmen-conservationists like George Shiras, 3d., and E. W. Nelson to protect migratory birds and establish wildfowl refuges.

Dibner, Bern. *Darwin of the Beagle.* New York, 1960. Implies that Darwin's youthful zest for hunting was an important factor in the development of his scientific interests. The same could be said for most American naturalists.

Diettert, Gerald A. *Grinnell's Glacier: George Bird Grinnell and Glacier National Park.* Missoula, Montana, 1992.

Dimock, A. W. *The Book of the Tarpon.* New York, 1911. By an angler who was an early advocate of preserving Florida's Everglades.

Dodge, Richard I. *The Hunting Grounds of the Great West: A Description of the Plains, Game and Indians of the Great North American Desert.* London, 1877. Important account of the commercial slaughter of the southern buffalo herds.

Donlon, Jon G. "Hunting for Leisure: The Social Components and Historic Foundations of American Sport Hunting." Ph.D. dissertation, University of Illinois, 1995.

Dudley, Susan, and David R. Goddard. "Joseph T. Rothrock and Forest Conservation." *Proceedings of the American Philosophical Society,* CXVII (February 16, 1973), 37-50.

Dulles, Foster Rhea. *America Learns to Play: A History of Popular Recreation, 1607-1940.* New York, 1940. Much on hunting and fishing.

Dunlap, Thomas R. *Saving America's Wildlife.* Princeton, New Jersey, 1988. This is not a comprehensive history, as the title implies, but mainly a study of ill-advised state and federal programs to eradicate "varmints" like wolves and coyotes. Advocating an animal-rights position at the start, he disparages the contributions of sportsmen to the overall conservation movement by denying their existence as an elite, self-conscious sub-culture, with a code of ethics that compelled them to become conservationists. Though Dunlap is forced to admit that "the early conservationists were hunters," he sees no significance in that fact, because he claims that these activists cannot be differentiated from "most adult men in that period," who, he believes, were also hunters (p. 178). There is, of course, abundant evidence for just such a differentiation.

――――. "Sport Hunting and Conservation, 1880-1920." *Environmental Review,* XII (Spring, 1988), 51-60. Despite its general title, this article is essentially a critique of one component—he ignores angling—of *American Sportsmen and the Origins of Conservation.* He reveals his lack of detachment when discussing this subject by labeling today's sport hunters a "despised minority," whose days, he hopes, are numbered. For my response, see "John

F. Reiger's Commentary . . ." in *Environmental Review,* XII (Fall, 1988), 94-96.

Dunraven, Earl of. *Hunting in the Yellowstone: On the Trail of the Wapiti with Texas Jack in the Land of Geysers.* Ed. by Horace Kephart. New York, 1917. Originally published in London in 1876. Good description of Yellowstone Park in its early years.

Dupree, A. Hunter. *Science in the Federal Government: A History of Policies and Activities to 1940.* Cambridge, Massachusetts, 1957.

Ehrenfeld, David W. *Biological Conservation.* New York, 1970. Excellent summary of environmental destruction, plus an analysis of how hunting and ecology go together.

Ekirch, Jr., Arthur A. *Man and Nature in America.* Lincoln, Nebraska, 1973. First published in 1963. Mainly a discussion of the various ways in which Americans have perceived the natural environment.

Elliot, Daniel G. *North American Shore Birds: A History of the Snipes, Sandpipers, Plovers and their Allies . . . A Reference Book for the Naturalist, Sportsman and Lover of Birds.* New York, 1895.

————. *The Wild Fowl of the United States and British Possessions; or the Swan, Geese, Ducks, and Mergansers of North America with Accounts of their Habits, Nesting, Migrations and Dispersions, Together with Descriptions of the Adults and Young, and Keys for the Ready Identification of the Species. A Book for the Sportsman, and for Those Desirous of Knowing How to Distinguish These Web-footed Birds and to Learn Their Ways in Their Native Wilds.* New York, 1898. Elliot was often Grinnell's hunting partner at his duck club in Currituck Sound, North Carolina.

Elliott, William. *Carolina Sports, By Land and Water; Including Incidents of Devil Fishing. . . .* Charleston, 1846. The "devil" in the title was a common name for the manta ray.

Elman, Robert. *The Great American Shooting Prints.* New York, 1972. Hunting in America as portrayed by a selection of paintings and lithographs from the 1820s to the present. Elman's accompanying text amounts to a popular history of sport.

Fahl, Ronald J. (comp.). *North American Forest and Conservation History: A Bibliography.* Santa Barbara, 1977.

Farquhar, Francis P., ed. *Up and Down California in 1860-1864: The Journal of William H. Brewer.* New Haven, 1930.

Fausold, Martin L. *Gifford Pinchot, Bull Moose Progressive.* Syracuse, New York, 1961.

Fein, Albert. *Frederick Law Olmsted and the American Environmental Tradition.* New York, 1972.

Fernow, Bernhard E. *A Brief History of Forestry in Europe, the United States and Other Countries.* Toronto, 1907.

Field and Stream [later *The Field, Chicago Field,* and finally *American Field*]. Chicago, 1874-1900. Published in both Chicago and New York after 1881.

Filene, Peter G. "An Obituary for 'The Progressive Movement'." *American Quarterly,* XXII (Spring, 1970), 20-34.

"Fin, Old." "Seth Green as an Angler." *American Angler,* XXVII (July-August, 1897), 178-81.

Finch, Robert. "Introduction: The Delights and Dilemmas of *A Sand County Almanac.*" In Leopold, *A Sand County Almanac and Sketches Here and There,* xv-xxviii. New York, 1989.

Fisher, Albert K. "In Memoriam: George Bird Grinnell." *The Auk,* LVI (January, 1939), 1-12. Summary of his achievements.

Flader, Susan L. *Thinking Like a Mountain: Aldo Leopold and the Evolution of an Ecological Attitude Toward Deer, Wolves and Forests.* Columbia, Missouri, 1974. From the "code of the sportsman" to the "land ethic."

Forbes, James E. "Environmental Deterioration and Declining Species." *Conservationist,* XXV (August-September, 1970), 21-26. This review of eighty-nine endangered species of mammals, birds, and fishes showed that sport hunting and fishing had little or nothing to do with their precarious positions.

Forbush, Edward H. *A History of the Game Birds, Wild-Fowl and Shore Birds of Massachusetts and Adjacent States.* Boston, 1916. Second edition of work originally published in 1912. Much on history of both sport and commercial hunting, plus a section called "The Viewpoint of the [Sport] Hunter, " in which Forbush criticizes the anti-hunting position.

————, and John B. May. *A Natural History of American Birds of Eastern and Central North America.* Boston, 1939. Originally in three volumes, the first of which appeared in 1925.

Forest and Stream. New York, 1873-1911.

Foster, Charles H. W. *Yankee Salmon: The Atlantic Salmon of the Connecticut River.* Needham, Massachusetts, 1991. On the efforts to restore the species, including the first ones, all made by sportsmen.

Fox, Stephen. *John Muir and His Legacy: The American Conservation Movement.* Boston, 1981. A wide-ranging history up to 1975. As Fox's title suggests, he makes great claims for Muir's influence on all aspects of conservation. He does, however, label George Bird Grinnell "the ubiquitous early leader of eastern conservation."

Gard, Wayne. *The Great Buffalo Hunt.* Lincoln, Nebraska, 1971. First published in 1959. Focusing on the years 1871-1883, this work describes the hide hunting that finally wiped out the bison.

Garlick, Theodatus. *A Treatise on the Artificial Propagation of Fish; Also, Directions for the Most Successful Modes of Angling.* Cleveland, 1857.

Gatewood, Willard B. "Theodore Roosevelt: Champion of 'Governmental Aesthetics.' " *Georgia Review,* XXI (1967), 172-83.

Gee, Ernest R. *Early American Sporting Books, 1734-1844: A Few Brief Notes.* New York, 1928.

————. *The Sportsman's Library: Being a Descriptive List of the Most Important Books on Sport.* New York, 1940.

Gerrare, Wirt. "Evolution of Sport with the Gun." *Outing,* XXXVII (September, 1901), 701-06. On European origins of hunting as sport.

Gingrich, Arnold. *The Fishing in Print, A Guided Tour Through Five Centuries of Angling Literature.* New York, 1974. Much on American angling in fresh water.

Giraud, Jr., J. P. *The Birds of Long Island.* New York, 1844.

Glacier National Park. Papers. Glacier National Park Library, West Glacier. Miscellaneous items relating to the reserve's early history, including many papers of George Bird Grinnell, the park's "father."

Goetzmann, William H. *Exploration and Empire: The Explorer and the Scientist in the Winning of the West.* New York, 1966.

————, and Kay Sloan. *Looking Far North: The Harriman Expedition to Alaska, 1899.* New York, 1982.

Gohdes, Clarence, ed. *Hunting in the Old South: Original Narratives of the Hunters.* Baton Rouge, Louisiana, 1967. In addition to his selections, the editor has provided valuable background material.

Goode, George Brown. *American Fishes; A Popular Treatise Upon the Game and Food Fishes of North America, with Especial Reference to Habits and Methods of Capture.* New York, 1888. First published in 1887.

————, ed. *The Smithsonian Institution, 1846-1896: The History of Its First Half Century.* Washington, D. C., 1897.

Goodspeed, Charles Eliot. *Angling in America: Its Early History and Literature.* Boston, 1939. This standard work on the history of freshwater fishing contains an important, annotated bibliography covering the years 1660-1900.

Graham, Jr., Frank. *The Adirondack Park: A Political History.* New York, 1978.

————. *The Audubon Ark: A History of the National Audubon Society.* New York, 1990.

————. *Man's Dominion: The Story of Conservation in America.* New York, 1971.

Grant, Madison. *Early History of Glacier National Park, Montana.* Washington, D.C., 1919.

Gray, Prentiss N., ed. *Records of North American Big Game.* New York, 1932. Contains a list of trophy heads shot by well-known naturalists—published under the auspices of the National Collection of Heads and Horns of the New York Zoological Society.

Green, Seth. *Home Fishing and Home Waters: A Practical Treatise on Fish Culture.* New York, 1888.

————. "Letter from Seth Green: The Trials and Tribulations and Early Experiences of a Practical Fish-Culturist." *Forest and Stream,* II (March 12, 1874), 68.

————, and A. S. Collins. *Trout Culture.* Rochester, New York, 1870.

Grinnell, George Bird. *Alaska, 1899: Essays From the Harriman Expedition.* Seattle, 1995. Contains an essay, "George Bird Grinnell, Pioneer Conservationist," by Polly Burroughs, and another, "The Harriman Expedition in Historical Perspective," by Victoria Wyatt.

————, ed. *American Big Game in Its Haunts.* New York, 1904. Articles on the history and objectives of conservation, including "Theodore Roosevelt," by Grinnell, and "Wilderness Reserves," by Roosevelt.

————. *American Duck Shooting.* New York, 1901. He was an avid waterfowl hunter until the end of his outdoor life.

————. *American Game-Bird Shooting.* New York, 1910. Deals only with upland game.

————, ed. *Audubon Magazine,* I (February 1887-January, 1888).

[————]. "The Biltmore Forest." *Forest and Stream,* XLII (January 6, 1894), I. Explanation of the forestry work on George W. Vanderbilt's estate in western North Carolina.

————, ed. *A Brief History of the Boone and Crockett Club, With Officers, Constitution and List of Members for the Year 1910.* New York, 1910.

[————]. "Charles Hallock." *Forest and Stream,* LXXXVIII (February, 1918), 92.

————. Collection of Journals, Field Notes and Other Materials on the Plains Indians, 1870-1930. Southwest Museum Library, Los Angeles. Also contains some natural history material.

————. "The Crown of the Continent." *Century Magazine*, LXII (September, 1901), 660-72. On the area that later became Glacier National Park.

[————]. "Dr. J. A. Allen." *Forest and Stream*, XCI (October, 1921), 449.

————. "Foreword." *Roosevelt Wild Life Bulletin*, I (1922), 9-10. Comments on Theodore Roosevelt as a naturalist.

————. "Grinnell File." Formerly at the Birdcraft Museum, Connecticut Audubon Society, now at Yale University. See "Notes" for description of this source, which had never been used before by an academic historian.

————, ed. *Hunting at High Altitudes*. New York, 1913. Incorporates Grinnell's *Brief History of the Boone and Crockett Club*, published in book form in 1910.

————. *Jack the Young Ranchman; or, A Boy's Adventures in the Rockies. . . .* New York, 1899. The first of seven volumes in the "Jack" series for boys. As Grinnell's Letter Books prove, these works were based on his own experiences or on the carefully authenticated experiences of friends.

————. "The Last of the Buffalo." *Scribner's Magazine*, XII (September, 1892), 267-86. Perhaps no one has ever surpassed this poetic tribute to the vanished multitudes. The two bison skulls, a bull and cow, that he describes picking up on the prairie "to keep as mementoes of the past" are in the Birdcraft Museum of the Connecticut Audubon Society, Fairfield.

————. Letter Books, August 2, 1886, to October 17, 1929. Formerly at the Connecticut Audubon Society, now at Yale University. See "Notes" for description of this source, which had never been used before by an academic historian.

————. Letters and other papers in the possession of John P. Holman, Fairfield, Connecticut. This material had never been used before by an academic historian.

————. "Memoirs" (other copies called "Memories"), Grinnell File.

————. "Opening Up Forest Reserves." *The Forester*, IV (February, 1898), 42-44.

————. "Othniel Charles Marsh, Paleontologist." In *Leading American Men of Science*, ed. by David Starr Jordan, 283-312. New York, 1910.

[————]. "President Roosevelt as a Sportsman." *Forest and Stream*, LXI (December 5, 1903), 437.

[————]. "The Reservation of Afognak." *Forest and Stream*, XL (January 12, 1893), 23. Brief history of the creation of what was, in fact, the first federal wildlife refuge and first federal "wilderness area."

[————]. "Secretary Noble's Monument." *Forest and Stream*, XL (March 9, 1893), 203. On Noble's conservation achievements.

————. "Sketch of Professor O. C. Marsh." *The Popular Science Monthly*, XIII (1878), 612-17.

[————]. "Sportsmen in the White House." *Forest and Stream*, LVIII (May 10, 1902), 361.

————. *Two Great Scouts and Their Pawnee Battalion*. Cleveland, 1928. On his friends, Luther and Frank North.

[————]. "William Hallett Phillips." *Forest and Stream*, XLVIII (May 15, 1897), 381.

————; Kermit Roosevelt; W. Redmond Cross; and Prentiss N. Gray, eds. *Hunting Trails on Three Continents*. New York, 1933. A Boone and Crockett Club book that contains some history of conservation.

————, and Theodore Roosevelt, eds. *Trail and Camp-Fire*. New York, 1897. Includes a Preface dealing with conservation written by the editors, and an article by Madison Grant on the origins of the New York Zoological Society.

————, and Charles Sheldon, eds. *Hunting and Conservation*. New Haven, 1925. Includes "American Game Protection, A Sketch," and is a key work for documenting the role of sportsmen in wildlife conservation, saving the redwoods, and the establishment of Glacier and Denali National Parks.

Gutermuth, C. R., and Elwood R. Maunder. "Origins of the Natural Resources Council of America: A Personal View." *Forest History*, VXII (January, 1974), 4-17. On later, leading role of sportsmen in conservation and the unfortunate consequences of the "pulling apart of [conservation] organizations" since the 1960s.

Hagedorn, Hermann. *Roosevelt in the Bad Lands*. Boston, 1921. On his ranching experiences.

Haines, Aubrey L. *The Yellowstone Story: A History of Our First National Park*. 2 vols. Yellowstone, Wyoming, 1977. Especially important for his interpretation of how the park was established.

Hallock, Charles. *An Angler's Reminiscences: A Record of Sport, Travel and Adventure; With [an] Autobiography of the Author*. Ed. by Fred E. Pond ("Will Wildwood"). Cincinnati, 1913. Important book in the history of angling and conservation; contains a key essay on the literature of sport fishing.

———— (comp.). *Camp Life in Florida: A Handbook for Sportsmen and Settlers*. New York, 1876. Compilation of articles appearing in *Forest and Stream* and describes the expeditions sent by Hallock to explore the still-wild Lake Okeechobee-Everglades region.

————. *The Fishing Tourist: [An] Angler's Guide and Reference Book*. New York, 1873.

————. *Hallock's American Club List and Sportsman's Glossary*. New York, 1878.

————. *The International Association for Protecting Game and Fish*. New York, 1876. Report of Hallock, the organization's Secretary. This sportsmen's association was initiated by Hallock at a meeting of the American Fish Culturists' Association in 1874, and it included members from British Canada and American "scientists" like Elliott Coues, E. D. Cope, Theodore Gill, and G. B. Goode. Hallock's aim was the establishment of a uniform code of game laws for North America, to be based on isothermal determinants.

————. *The Sportsman's Gazetteer and General Guide. The Game Animals, Birds, and Fishes of North America: Their Habits and Various Methods of Capture. Copious Instructions in Shooting, Fishing, Taxidermy, Woodcraft, Etc. Together with a Glossary, and a Directory to the Principal Game Resorts of the Country; Illustrated with Maps*. New York, 1879. This standard work of the day first appeared in 1877, and even though George Bird Grinnell and others wrote most of it, Hallock took the credit. Contains a "Bibliography for Sportsmen."

Hammond, Samuel H. *Hills, Lakes, and Forest Streams; or, A Tramp in the Chateaugay Woods.* New York, 1854.
————. *Wild Northern Scenes; or, Sporting Adventures with Rifle and the Rod.* New York, 1857.
Hampton, H. Duane. *How the U.S. Cavalry Saved Our National Parks.* Bloomington, Indiana, 1971. He claims that the Army "saved" Yellowstone and later national parks by protecting them from vandals, poachers, forest fires, etc. But the real question is: Who deserves more credit—the soldiers who followed orders or the civilians like Grinnell who got them into the parks in the first place?
————, ed. "With [George Bird] Grinnell in North Park." *Colorado Magazine,* XLVIII (Fall, 1971), 273-98. A hunting account published in *Forest and Stream.*
Hanna, Warren L. *Stars Over Montana: Men Who Made Glacier National Park History.* West Glacier, Montana, 1988. Includes a chapter called "George Bird Grinnell, Father of Glacier National Park."
Harmond, Richard P. "Robert Barnwell Roosevelt and the Early Conservation Movement." *Theodore Roosevelt Association Journal,* XIV (Summer, 1988), 2-11.
Harriman Alaska Expedition [1899]. *Alaska. . . .* Vols. 1 and 2 [14 vols. in all.] New York, 1901. Contributions by George Bird Grinnell, C. Hart Merriam, John Muir, John Burroughs, etc. This important expedition was initiated because of E. H. Harriman's desire to shoot a trophy Alaskan brown bear.
Harris, Harry. "Robert Ridgway with a Bibliography of His Published Writings and Fifty Illustrations." *The Condor,* XXX (January, 1928), 5-118.
Harris, William C. *The Angler's Guide-Book and Tourist's Gazetteer.* New York, 1884. By the editor of *American Angler.*
[————]. "The Fisheries Buildings at the World's Columbian Exposition." *American Angler,* XXII (September, 1893), 407-12. Part I of a series. Contains a description of the contributions of *American Angler* and *Forest and Stream* to the exhibits.
Haskell, William S. *The American Game Protective and Propagation Association: A History.* New York, 1937.
Hawker, Peter. *Instructions to Young Sportsmen, in All That Relates to Guns and Shooting . . . To Which is Added the Hunting and Shooting of North America, With Descriptions of the Animals and Birds . . . Collated . . . by W. T. Porter.* Philadelphia, 1846. Shows the continuing British influence.
Hays, Samuel P. *Beauty, Health, and Permanence: Environmental Politics in the United States, 1955-1985.* New York, 1987. Hays continues to argue, as he did in *Conservation and the Gospel of Efficiency,* that "conservation was an aspect of the history of production that stressed efficiency. . . . " In other words, it had no appreciable aesthetic component. Conversely, "environment[alism]," which arose after 1945, was supposedly "a part of the history of consumption that stressed new aspects of the American standard of living" (p. 13). And despite the obvious continuity in thinking of wildlife conservationists from William Elliott, George Bird Grinnell, and Theodore Roosevelt right through to today's leaders of organizations like Ducks Unlimited and The Wildlife Society, Hays claims that there is a "discontinuity between the earlier conservation and . . . later environmental stages of history . . ." (p. xi).

————. *Conservation and the Gospel of Efficiency: The Progressive Conservation Movement, 1890-1920.* New York, 1969. First published in 1959. Virtually ignores all nongovernmental conservation activity before 1890, and barely mentions wildlife. In Preface to later edition Hays tells the reader that his book has been misinterpreted by many—it is primarily about "political structure" and not conservation.

————. "The Politics of Reform in Municipal Government in the Progressive Era." *Pacific Northwest Quarterly,* LV (October, 1964), 157-69. In this important article Hays seems to have changed his earlier view that "Progressivism" was middle class in origin, at least that aspect of the so-called "movement" that dealt with municipal reform. He now believes that despite the reformers' democratic rhetoric, "the source of support for reform in municipal government did not come from the lower or middle classes, but from the upper class." Of course, the same was true of conservation.

Hedges, Cornelius. "Journal of Judge Cornelius Hedges [Kept on the 1870 Washburn-Doane Expedition]." *Contributions to the Historical Society of Montana . . . ,* V (1904), 370-94.

Heilner, Van Campen. *A Book on Duck Shooting.* New York, 1946. First published in 1939. With a Foreword by Robert Cushman Murphy of the American Museum of Natural History.

Henderson, Robert W. (comp.). *Early American Sport: A Check-List of Books by American and Foreign Authors Published in America Prior to 1860, Including Sporting Songs.* New York, 1953. Revised and enlarged edition of work first published in 1937. Listed chronologically and with brief annotations, this compilation includes all sports, not just hunting and fishing.

Henshall, James A. *Book of the Black Bass, Comprising Its Complete Scientific and Life History, Together with a Practical Treatise on Angling and Fly-Fishing and a Full Description of Tools, Tackle and Implements.* Cincinnati, 1881.

Herbert, Henry William ("Frank Forester"). *American Game in Its Seasons . . . Illustrated from Nature, and on Wood, by the Author.* New York, 1853.

————. *The Complete Manual for Young Sportsmen: With Directions for Handling the Gun, the Rifle, and the Rod; the Art of Shooting on the Wing; the Breaking, Management, and Hunting of the Dog; the Varieties and Habits of Game; River, Lake, and Sea Fishing . . . Prepared for the Instruction and Use of the Youth of America.* New York, 1856.

————. *Frank Forester's Field Sports of the United States and British Provinces of North America.* 2 vols. New York, 1849.

————. *Frank Forester's Fish and Fishing of the United States, and British Provinces of North America.* London, 1849.

Herrick, Francis Hobart. *Audubon the Naturalist: A History of His Life and Times.* 2 vols. New York, 1917.

Hinman, Bob. *The Golden Age of Shotgunning.* New York, 1971. Concentrating on the last thirty years of the nineteenth century, the book discusses both sport and market hunting, as well as the development of shotguns and shotgunning.

Hofstadter, Richard. *The Age of Reform: From Bryan to F.D.R.* New York, 1955. Despite the title, the author ignores a major reform movement—conservation.

————. "Theodore Roosevelt: The Conservative as Progressive." In *The American Political Tradition and the Men Who Made It*, by Richard Hofstadter, 206-37. New York, 1948.

Holder, Charles Frederick, and David Starr Jordan. *Fish Stories, Alleged and Experienced, With a Little History, Natural and Unnatural.* New York, 1909.

Holliday, J. S. "The Politics of John Muir." *Sierra Club Bulletin*, LVII (October- November, 1972), 10-13. By a director of the California Historical Society, this article is typical of the never-ending adulation heaped upon Muir by historians—even if history must be distorted to do so. Holliday goes so far as to suggest that President Harrison set aside the first forest reserve because of Muir's influence!

Holliman, Jennie. *American Sports, 1785-1835.* Durham, North Carolina, 1931. Much on hunting and fishing.

Hornaday, William T. *Camp-Fires in the Canadian Rockies. . . .* New York, 1906. Shows Hornaday as an enthusiastic hunter.

————. *The Extermination of the American Bison; With a Sketch of Its Discovery and Life History. Smithsonian Report (1887)*, Part II, 367-548. Washington, D. C., 1889.

————. *Our Vanishing Wild Life: Its Extermination and Preservation.* New York, 1913.

————. *Thirty Years War for Wild Life: Gains and Losses in the Thankless Task.* New York, 1970. Reprint of work originally published in 1931. It reveals that Hornaday—like Gifford Pinchot in forest conservation—believed that little had occurred before he arrived on the scene. Unfortunately, many historians have accepted their claims.

————. *Two Years in the Jungle: The Experiences of a Hunter and Naturalist in India, Ceylon, The Malay Peninsula and Borneo.* New York, 1886. Though he later attacked hunters because he believed they failed to live up to his own interpretation of the code of the sportsman, Hornaday here describes the utter joy of hunting.

————. *Wild-Life Conservation in Theory and Practice.* New York, 1972. Reprint of work originally published in 1914.

Hough, Emerson. *Getting a Wrong Start: A Truthful Autobiography.* New York, 1915. Particularly good for a picture of the inner workings of *Forest and Stream*.

Hunt, William S. *Frank Forester [Henry William Herbert]; A Tragedy in Exile.* Newark, New Jersey, 1933. A good biography, based on extensive research, and containing a "Chronology of [Herbert's] Writings."

Huntington, Dwight W. *Our Big Game: A Book for Sportsmen and Nature Lovers.* New York, 1904. Much on sportsmen's clubs and private game parks and preserves.

————. *Our Feathered Game: A Handbook of the North American Game Birds.* New York, 1903. By a sportsman-naturalist, this work contains a recommendation for a "state park" in the Everglades to save that region's bird life. This suggestion antedates by forty-four years the establishment of Everglades National Park and is the earliest such proposal the writer has found.

Huth, Hans. *Nature and the American: Three Centuries of Changing Attitudes.* Lincoln, Nebraska, 1972. Originally published in 1957.

————. "Yosemite: The Story of an Idea." *Sierra Club Bulletin,* XXXIII (1948), 46-78. Limited to earliest history of what became Yosemite National Park. Contains Introduction by David R. Brower of the Sierra Club claiming—erroneously—that Yosemite, and not Yellowstone, was the first national park.

Iddings, Joseph P. "Memorial of Arnold Hague." *Bulletin of the Geological Society of America,* XXIX (1918), 35-48.

Ingersoll, Ernest. "A History of the Audubon Movement." *Forest and Stream,* LXXXII (March 14, 1914, and March 28, 1914), 339-40 and 406-07.

Irving, Washington. *The Sketch Book of Geoffrey Crayon, Gent.* No. VII. New York, 1820. Contains "The Angler," 29-49.

————. *A Tour on the Prairies.* Ed. by John F. McDermott. Norman, Oklahoma, 1956. First published in 1835. Lots of hunting.

Ise, John. *Our National Park Policy: A Critical History.* Baltimore, 1961.

————. *The United States Forest Policy.* New York, 1972. Reprint of work originally published in 1920. A history of federal activities in forest conservation.

Isenberg, Andrew C. "The Returns of the Bison: Nostalgia, Profit, and Preservation." *Environmental History,* II (April, 1997), 179-196. Claims that there is no continuity between "nineteenth-century motivations for wildlife preservation [and] . . . late-twentieth century concerns" (p. 193), but the thinking, and efforts, of sportsmen through the years prove him wrong.

Ives, Edward D. *George Magoon and the Down East Game War: History, Folklore, and the Law.* Urbana, Illinois, 1988. An interesting study of how this notorious Maine poacher became a folk hero to those fighting the efforts of elite sportsmen to enforce game laws.

Jackson, Clarence S. *Picture Maker of the Old West: William H. Jackson.* New York, 1947.

Jackson, John B. *American Space—the Centennial Years: 1865-1876.* New York, 1972. Describes and analyzes the environmental changes taking place in those years.

Jackson, W. Turrentine. "The Creation of Yellowstone National Park." *Mississippi Valley Historical Review,* XXIX (September, 1942), 187-206.

Jackson, William H. *Time Exposure: The Autobiography of William Henry Jackson.* New York, 1940.

————, and Howard R. Driggs. *The Pioneer Photographer: Rocky Mountain Adventures with a Camera.* Yonkers-on-Hudson, New York, 1929.

Jacoby, Karl H. "Class and Environmental History: Lessons from 'The War in the Adirondacks'." *Environmental History,* II (July, 1997), 324-42. An interesting article on this important, often ignored, aspect of conservation history.

————. "The Recreation of Nature: A Social and Environmental History of American Conservation, 1872-1919." Ph.D. dissertation, Yale University, 1997.

Jaher, Frederic Cople, ed. *The Rich, the Well-Born, and the Powerful: Elites and Upper Classes in History.* Urbana, Illinois, 1974. Contains an article on New York high society in the late nineteenth century.

Johnson, Robert Underwood. *Remembered Yesterdays.* Boston, 1923.

Jordan, David Starr. *Science Sketches.* Chicago, 1888. Includes his reminiscences of boyhood fishing experiences.

————, and Barton Warren Evermann. *American Food and Game Fishes. A Popular Account of All the Species Found in America North of the Equator, With Keys for Ready Identification, Life Histories and Methods of Capture.* New York, 1902.

Judd, David W., ed. *Life and Writings of Frank Forester (Henry William Herbert).* 2 vols. New York, 1882.

Judd, Richard W. *Common Lands, Common People: The Origins of Conservation in Northern New England.* Cambridge, Massachusetts, 1997.

Kaplan, Moise N. *Big Game Anglers' Paradise: A Complete, Non-Technical Narrative Treatise on Salt Water Gamefishes and Angling in Florida and Elsewhere.* New York, 1937. Contains "Philosophy of Angling," a section tracing the appeal, and benefits, of angling from ancient times to the modern period.

Kellam, Amine. "The Cobb's Island Story." *Virginia Cavalcade,* XXIII (Spring, 1974), 18-27. History of famous Eastern Shore waterfowl and shore-bird shooting resort of last century.

Kellert, Stephen R. "Hunting in America." Unpublished consultant report done for the Science Museum of Minnesota exhibit, "The Hunt." March, 1985.

Kester, Jesse Y. ("A Gentleman of Philadelphia County"). *The American Shooter's Manual.* Philadelphia, 1827.

Keyser, Charles S. *Fairmount Park: Sketches of Its Scenery, Waters, and History.* Philadelphia, 1872. Evidently first published in 1871. By a pioneer in the city-park movement, this work contains a section on "The State in Schuylkill," which reflects the author's tremendous affection for angling, although he never actually says he is a fisherman.

Kimball, David and Jim. *The Market Hunter.* Minneapolis, Minnesota, 1969. Popular history of this infamous breed, with some important insights into the meaning of hunting in contemporary society and its relationship to ecology and conservation.

Klinko, Donald W. "Antebellum American Sporting Magazines and the Development of a Sportsmen's Ethic." Ph.D. dissertation, Washington State University, 1986.

Kohlsaat, H. H. "The Greatest Game Market in the World." *Saturday Evening Post,* CXCVI (April 26, 1924), 72. On Chicago market of nineteenth century.

Kortright, Francis H. *The Ducks, Geese and Swans of North America: A Vade Mecum for the Naturalist and the Sportsman.* Harrisburg, Pennsylvania, 1960. First published in 1942. Long the leading work of its kind, it was compiled by an amateur naturalist and duck hunter from Toronto, Canada. Includes an Introduction by Aldo Leopold.

Kranz, Marvin W. "Pioneering in Conservation: A History of the Conservation Movement in New York State, 1865-1903." Ph.D. dissertation, Syracuse University, 1961.

Krider, John. *Krider's Sporting Anecdotes, Illustrative of the Habits of Certain Varieties of American Game.* New York, 1966. Reprint of book originally published in 1853. One of the more notable items in this work is the fact that many sportsmen were already aware that the ingestion by waterfowl of spent lead pellets (on shooting grounds) caused lead poisoning and paralysis.

Lacey, John F. "Let Us Save the Birds: Speech of Hon. John F. Lacey, in the House of Representatives." *Recreation,* XIII (July, 1900), 33-35. Here he proclaims himself a hunter and a follower of the code of the sportsman.

Langford, Nathaniel Pitt. *The Discovery of Yellowstone Park: Journal of the Washburn Expedition to the Yellowstone and Firehole Rivers in the Year 1870.* Lincoln, Nebraska, 1972. Reprint, with Foreword by Aubrey L. Haines, of book originally published in 1905.

Lanman, Charles. *Adventures of an Angler in Canada, Nova Scotia and the United States.* London, 1848.

[————]. *Letters From a Landscape Painter.* Boston, 1845. Contains angling.

Lapham, Increase A. *Wisconsin: Its Geography and Topography, History, Geology, and Mineralogy: Together With Brief Sketches of Its Antiquities, Natural History, Soil, Productions, Population, and Government.* Milwaukee, 1846; first published in 1844. At one point, Lapham states: "For the scientific naturalist, the sportsman and the angler, Wisconsin affords a very interesting and highly attractive field."

Laycock, George. *The Alien Animals: The Story of Imported Wildlife.* Garden City, New York, 1966. History of successes, such as the ringneck pheasant, and disasters, such as the carp. The latter, of course, far outnumber the former.

————. *The Sign of the Flying Goose: The Story of Our National Wildlife Refuges.* Garden City, New York, 1973. Originally published in 1965. Much history.

Leffingwell, William Bruce. *The Art of Wing Shooting: A Practical Treatise on the Use of the Shot-Gun, Illustrating, By Sketches and Easy Reading, How to Become an Expert Shot . . . Also Treating of the Habits and Resorts of Game Birds and Water Fowl. . . .* New York, 1967. Reprint of work first published in 1894.

————. *Wild Fowl Shooting. Containing Scientific and Practical Descriptions of Wild Fowl: Their Resorts, Habits, Flights and the Most Successful Method of Hunting Them.* Chicago, 1888.

Leopold, A. Starker. "The Essence of Hunting." *National Wildlife,* X (October- November, 1972), 38-40. By an eminent ecologist, Aldo Leopold's son, this article probes the deeper meaning of hunting. It also points out that the bulk of the wildlife-conservation bill is paid by sportsmen.

Leopold, Aldo. *Game Management.* New York, 1933. Much on history and meaning of hunting and wildlife conservation.

————. *A Sand County Almanac; With Other Essays on Conservation from Round River.* New York, 1966. *A Sand County Almanac* first appeared in 1949 and *Round River* in 1953. In many ways, these two works together represent the highest expression ever achieved of the environmental responsibilities inherent in the code of the sportsman.

————. *A Sand County Almanac and Sketches Here and There.* New York, 1989. Has some different material from the 1966 edition.

Lewis, Elisha J. *The American Sportsman: Containing Hints to Sportsmen, Notes on Shooting, and the Habits of the Game Birds and Wild Fowl of America.* Philadelphia, 1863. Originally published, under a different title, in 1851.

Long, Joseph W. *American Wild-Fowl Shooting. Describing the Haunts, Habits, and Methods of Shooting Wild Fowl, Particularly Those of the Western States of America. With Instructions Concerning Guns, Blinds, Boats, and Decoys; The Training of Water-Retrievers, Etc.* New York, 1874.

Long, William J. *Northern Trails: Some Studies of Animal Life in the Far North.* Boston, 1905. By the leading "nature faker"—as Roosevelt called those whose works reeked with anthropomorphism.

Lorbiecki, Marybeth. *Aldo Leopold: A Fierce Green Fire.* Helena, Montana, 1996.

Lowenthal, David. *George Perkins Marsh: Versatile Vermonter.* New York, 1958.

Ludlow, William. *Report of a Reconnaissance from Carroll, Montana Territory, on the Upper Missouri, to the Yellowstone National Park, and Return, Made in the Summer of 1875.* Washington, D.C., 1876.

———. *Report of a Reconnaissance of the Black Hills of Dakota, Made in the Summer of 1874.* Washington, D.C., 1875.

Lund, Thomas A. *American Wildlife Law.* Berkeley and Los Angeles, 1980.

Lutts, Ralph H. *The Nature Fakers: Wildlife, Science and Sentiment.* Golden, Colorado, 1990. On the efforts of Theodore Roosevelt, John Burroughs, and others to maintain what they believed were strict scientific standards in discussing the lives of wild animals and birds.

(The reader is advised that I have alphabetized Mc as if it were spelled Mac.)

McCabe, Robert A. *Aldo Leopold: The Professor.* Madison, Wisconsin, 1987.

McClane, A. J., ed. *McClane's New Standard Fishing Encyclopedia and International Angling Guide.* New York, 1974. Revised edition of book first published in 1965. Has excellent section entitled "Literature of Angling."

McCormick, Richard L. "The Discovery that Business Corrupts Politics: A Reappraisal of the Origins of Progressivism." *American Historical Review,* 48 (April, 1981), 247-74.

McDonald, John. *The Origins of Angling.* Garden City, New York, 1963. Combined with a new printing of *The Treatise of Fishing with an Angle* (1496)—the first published essay on sport fishing—this work concludes that angling owes a large debt to hunting. Important early literature on both hunting and fishing is cited.

McEvoy, Arthur F. *The Fisherman's Problem: Ecology and Law in the California Fisheries, 1850-1980.* Cambridge, England, 1986. Some discussion of sport fishing.

McGeary, M. Nelson. *Gifford Pinchot: Forester-Politician.* Princeton, 1960.

McHenry, Robert, ed. *A Documentary History of Conservation in America.* New York, 1972.

McHugh, Tom. *The Time of the Buffalo.* New York, 1972. Much on the commercial slaughter of the nineteenth century.

McIlhenny, Edward Avery. *The Wild Turkey and Its Hunting.* Garden City, New York, 1914. Compiled by a sportsman-naturalist who did much to save the snowy egret from extinction.

Mackey, Jr., William J. *American Bird Decoys.* New York, no date. Reprint, by Bonanza Books, of work first published in 1965. Contains a chapter on American decoys as folk art by Quintina Colio.

Main, Jackson T. "History of the Conservation of Wild Life in Wisconsin." M.A. thesis, University of Wisconsin, 1940.

Manchester, Herbert. *Four Centuries of Sport in America, 1490-1890.* New York, 1968. First published in 1931. All sports, but stresses hunting and fishing. Contains important "List of Sources."

Mann, William M. *Wild Animals In and Out of the Zoo.* New York, 1930. Vol. VI of Smithsonian Scientific Series. New York, 1930 and 1934. Contains information on the establishment of the National Zoological Park, particularly the roles of Senator George F. Edmunds and William T. Hornaday, both sportsmen.

Marcham, Frederick G., ed. *Louis Agassiz Fuertes and the Singular Beauty of Birds*. New York, 1971.

Marks, Stuart A. *Southern Hunting in Black and White: Nature, History, and Ritual in a Carolina Community*. Princeton, New Jersey, 1991.

Marsh, George Perkins. *Man and Nature; or, Physical Geography as Modified by Human Action*. New York, 1864.

————. *Report, Made Under Authority of the Legislature of Vermont, on the Artificial Propagation of Fish*. Burlington, 1857.

Mather, Fred. *Men I Have Fished With: Sketches of Character and Incident with Rod and Gun, From Childhood to Manhood; From the Killing of Little Fishes and Birds to a Buffalo Hunt*. New York, 1897. By a leading fish culturist.

————. *Modern Fishculture in Fresh and Salt Water*. New York, 1900. Has some history of the subject.

————. *My Angling Friends: Being a Second Series of Sketches of Men I Have Fished With*. New York, 1901. Includes Chester A. Arthur, Charles Hallock, and Thaddeus Norris.

————. "Progress in Fish-Culture." *Century Magazine*, XXVII (April, 1884), 900-13. A history.

Matthiessen, Peter. *Wildlife in America*. New York, 1987. First published in 1959.

Mayer, Alfred M., ed. *Sport with Gun and Rod in American Woods and Waters*. 2 vols. Edinburgh, Scotland, 1884. First published in New York in 1883. With a few exceptions, this is a collection of articles originally appearing in *Century Magazine*. Among the contributors are George Bird Grinnell, Thaddeus Norris, John Burroughs, and Charles E. Whitehead.

Meine, Curt. *Aldo Leopold: His Life and Work*. Madison, Wisconsin, 1988.

Menna, Larry K., ed. *The Origins of Modern Sports, 1820-1840*. Vol. 2 of *Sports in North America, A Documentary History*. Gulf Breeze, Florida, 1995.

Merriam, C. Hart. *A Review of the Birds of Connecticut*. New Haven, 1877. Grinnell contributed to this work.

————. "Roosevelt, the Naturalist." *Science*, LXXV (February 12, 1932), 181-83.

Merritt, H. Clay. *The Shadow of a Gun*. Chicago, 1904. The classic, book-length account of nineteenth-century market hunting by one of the most successful commercial gunners and game merchants of the Middle West. Contains many examples of hatred between sportsmen and market hunters.

Mershon, William B. (comp.). *The Passenger Pigeon*. New York, 1907.

————. *Recollections of My Fifty Years Hunting and Fishing*. Boston, 1923.

Migel, J. Michael, ed. *The Stream Conservation Handbook*. New York, 1974. Contributions by various authorities revealing the continuing efforts of sportsmen-naturalists to preserve both their sport and the environment that produces it.

Mighetto, Lisa. *Wild Animals and American Environmental Ethics*. Tucson, Arizona, 1991. Like many historians before her, she ignores the contributions of sport fishermen to conservation and focuses on hunters, whose only concern, she believes, was "the availability of future targets" (p. 41). Hunting, for her, has been a facile experience, with no special relationship between the hunter and the hunted, with no rights accorded to the latter; the "code of the sportsman" simply did not exist as far as she is concerned.

Miller, Char, ed. *American Forests: Nature, Culture, and Politics.* Lawrence, Kansas, 1997. Contains several essays on the history of forest conservation before 1901.

――――. *Gifford Pinchot: The Evolution of an American Conservationist—Two Essays.* Milford, Pennsylvania, 1992. The first essay is entitled "Before the Divide: John Muir, Gifford Pinchot, and the Early Conservation Movement," and the second is called "The Greening of Gifford Pinchot."

――――. "Keeper of His Conscience? Pinchot, Roosevelt, and the Politics of Conservation." In Natalie A. Naylor, *et al.*, eds., *Theodore Roosevelt: Many-Sided American*, 231-44. Interlaken, New York, 1992. On the thinking of these two men in regard to the decision to dam Hetch Hetchy Valley in Yosemite National Park.

Milne, Lorus J. and Margery. *The Balance of Nature.* New York, 1960. Excellent study of the ecology of native wildlife and the impact of alien species.

Mitchell, John G. "A Man Called Bird." *Audubon*, LXXXIX (March, 1987), 81-104. On George Bird Grinnell, who is described on the title page of the article as a "Sportsman, Scientist, Publisher, Companion of Custer and T.R., Friend of the Cheyenne Indians, Pioneer American Conservationist, [and] Father of the Audubon Movement." This was the 100th anniversary issue; the first *Audubon Magazine* was published and edited by Grinnell, and appeared in February, 1887.

Mitchell, Lee Clark. *Witnesses to a Vanishing America: The Nineteenth-Century Response.* Princeton, 1981. On the meaning of a passing frontier to, among others, Grinnell and Roosevelt.

Morison, Elting E., and John M. Blum, eds. *The Letters of Theodore Roosevelt.* 8 vols. Cambridge, Massachusetts, 1951-54.

Mowrey, George E. *The Progressive Era, 1900-20: The Reform Persuasion.* Washington, D. C., 1972. Earlier versions of this pamphlet were published in 1958 and 1964. An interpretation of "Progressivism," as well as a survey of the literature.

Murphy, John Mortimer. *American Game Bird Shooting.* New York, 1882.

Murphy, Robert Cushman. *Fish-Shape Paumanok: Nature and Man on Long Island [New York].* Philadelphia, 1964. An environmental history.

Murphy, Robert W. *Wild Sanctuaries: Our National Wildlife Refuges—A Heritage Restored.* New York, 1968. Has material on market hunting of various species.

Murray, William H. H. *Adventures in the Wilderness; or, Camp-Life in the Adirondacks.* Syracuse, New York, 1970. New edition—edited by William K. Verner and with Introduction and Notes by Warder H. Cadbury—of work originally published in 1869.

Nash, Roderick, ed. *American Environmentalism: Readings in the History of Conservation.* New York, 1990. Third edition of a book first published in 1968. Includes Nash's thesis on "Conservation as Anxiety," plus a "Selected Bibliography," with annotations, that concentrates on the history of the conservation movement.

————. *The Rights of Nature: A History of Environmental Ethics.* Madison, Wisconsin, 1989. Nothing on sporting ethics or on the fact that sportsmen were the first Americans to grant wildlife "rights"—like the right to breed unmolested.

————. *Wilderness and the American Mind.* New Haven, 1982. Third edition, with updated bibliographical essay, of book first published in 1967.

New York Association for the Protection of Game. Papers. Manuscripts and History Division, New York State Library (Albany). Miscellaneous items pertaining to a conservation organization founded in 1844.

New York Public Library. *List of Works in the New York Public Library on Sport in General, and on Shooting in Particular.* Reprint from library *Bulletin,* VII (May and June, 1903).

New York Zoological Society. *First Annual Report of the New York Zoological Society.* New York, 1897. Has some history of the organization, and lists its leaders. The organization grew out of the efforts of big-game hunters in the Boone and Crockett Club, their main purpose being the preservation of big-game animals.

————. *New York Zoological Society—New York Zoological Park, New York Aquarium, [and] Department of Tropical Research—A Presentation of the Aims and Achievements of a Great Institution.* New York, 1937. Copy in New York Public Library. Contains some history.

Norris, Thaddeus. *The American Angler's Book: Embracing the Natural History of Sporting Fish, and the Art of Taking Them. With Instructions in Fly-Fishing, Fly-Making, and Rod-Making; And Directions for Fish-Breeding. . . .* Philadelphia, 1865 [?]. First published in 1864.

————. *American Fish-Culture, Embracing All the Details of Artificial Breeding and Rearing of Trout, the Culture of Salmon, Shad and Other Fishes.* Philadelphia, 1868. Cites the practice of marking salmon to trace their migrations, a fact that should not be surprising since Izaak Walton also mentions it in his *Compleat Angler,* first published in 1653!

Olson, Sherry H. *The Depletion Myth: A History of Railroad Use of Timber.* Cambridge, Massachusetts, 1971.

O'Neill, Eugene J. "Parks and Forest Conservation in New York, 1850-1920." Ed.D. dissertation, Columbia University, 1963.

Orr, Jr., Oliver H. *Saving American Birds: T. Gilbert Pearson and the Founding of the Audubon Movement.* Gainesville, 1992.

Ortega Y Gasset, José. *Meditations on Hunting.* New York, 1972. Originally published in Madrid in 1943. By Spain's leading twentieth-century philosopher, this brilliant work contains a wealth of insights into anthropology and ecology. Ortega claims that hunting attunes one to the natural environment, and that photographing game is not a substitute for hunting it.

Orvis, Charles F., and A. Nelson Cheney (comps.). *Fishing With the Fly: Sketches by Lovers of the Art, With Illustrations of Standard Flies Collected by Charles F. Orvis and A. Nelson Cheney.* Manchester, Vermont, 1883. Contributions by Charles Hallock, Seth Green, Robert Barnwell Roosevelt, and other well-known anglers.

Osborn, Henry Fairfield. *The American Museum of Natural History: Its Origin, Its History, [and] the Growth of Its Departments to December 31, 1909.* New

York, 1911.

―――. *Impressions of Great Naturalists: Reminiscences of Darwin, Huxley, Balfour, Cope and Others.* New York, 1924. The "others" include Theodore Roosevelt and John Burroughs.

Palmer, Theodore S. (comp.). *Chronology and Index of the More Important Events in American Game Protection, 1776-1911.* U.S. Biological Survey Bulletin No. 41. Washington, D.C., 1912.

―――― (comp.). *Digest of Game Laws for 1901.* U.S. Biological Survey Bulletin No. 16. Washington, D.C., 1901.

―――. *Hunting Licenses: Their History, Objects, and Limitations.* U.S. Biological Survey Bulletin No. 19. Washington, D.C., 1904.

―――. *Legislation for the Protection of Birds Other than Game Birds.* U. S. Biological Survey Bulletin No. 12. Washington, D.C., 1900.

―――. "Lest We Forget." *Bulletin of the American Game Protective [and Propagation] Association,* XIV (January, 1925), 11-12 and 19. Greatest expert on history of wildlife legislation gives brief biographies of five key figures in history of wildlife conservation: "Frank Forester"; Royal Phelps (who with Charles E. Whitehead, another member of the N.Y. Association for the Protection of Game, achieved a crucial legal precedent when they won a case against a New York City game dealer, Joseph H. Racey, for illegal possession of quail); Charles Hallock; George Bird Grinnell; and Theodore Roosevelt. All five men were sportsmen.

―――. *National Reservations for the Protection of Wildlife.* U.S. Biological Survey Circular No. 87. Washington, D.C., 1912.

―――. *Private Game Preserves and Their Future in the United States.* U.S. Biological Survey Circular No. 72. Washington, D.C., 1910.

―――. *A Review of Economic Ornithology in the United States.* Reprint of a publication [1899?] of the Bureau of Biological Survey, U.S. Department of Agriculture, in the New York Public Library.

Parkman, Francis. "The Forests of the White Mountains." *Garden and Forest,* I (February 29, 1888), 2.

―――. *The Oregon Trail: Sketches of Prairie and Rocky-Mountain Life.* Boston, 1872. First appeared in 1847.

Paxson, Frederic L. "The Rise of Sport." *Mississippi Valley Historical Review,* IV (September, 1917), 143-68. Has information on George Bird Grinnell, the history of the Boone and Crockett Club, changing attitudes toward hunting, etc.

Pearson, T. Gilbert. *Adventures in Bird Protection: An Autobiography . . . With an Introduction by Frank M. Chapman.* New York, 1937.

―――. *Fifty Years of Bird Protection in the United States.* New York, 1933.

Penick, Jr., James. "The Progressives and the Environment: Three Themes from the First Conservation Movement." In Lewis L. Gould, ed., *The Progressive Era,* 115-31. Syracuse, New York,1974. Suggests the central role of patricians in conservation during the "Progressive" period, and has some interesting comments concerning John Muir.

―――. Review of Harold T. Pinkett's *Gifford Pinchot* (1970). *Pacific Northwest Quarterly,* LXII (October, 1971), 141. Criticizes Pinkett because "the functional relationship between Pinchot's social class and his profession is not explored, although forestry in the Progressive era is an example of patrician reform, and the profession is peculiarly dependent on the support of the upper class. But other historians have also avoided this problem."

————. Review of Robert V. Hine's *American West—An Interpretative History* (1973). *Journal of the West,* XIII (April, 1974), 113-14. Contains a good criticism of the "fashion" of splitting environmental groups into "conservationists" and "preservationists," with the latter seen as pure and everyone else as tainted.

Persons, Stow. *The Decline of American Gentility.* New York, 1973. Contains important insights regarding the social and intellectual milieu from which many conservationists came.

Petersen, Eugene T. *Conservation of Michigan's Natural Resources.* Lansing, 1960.

————. "The History of Wild Life Conservation in Michigan, 1859-1921." Ph.D. dissertation, University of Michigan, 1953.

Peterson, Jon A. "The Origins of the Comprehensive City Planning Ideal in the United States, 1840-1911." Ph.D. dissertation, Harvard University, 1967. Discusses the idea that the origins of city parks can be traced back to the hunting preserves of royalty.

Phillips, John C. (comp.). *American Game Mammals and Birds: A Catalogue of Books, 1582 to 1925.* Boston, 1930. Over 600 pages long, this annotated bibliography of works on hunting, natural history, and conservation is a must for all students of these subjects. It has now been updated by M. L. Biscotti.

————. *The American Wild Fowlers: A Brief History of the Association, 1927-1931.* A pamphlet, with no date or place of publication, in the possession of John P. Holman, Fairfield, Connecticut. Good for later waterfowl-conservation efforts of sportsmen like Phillips, Charles Sheldon, and George Bird Grinnell.

————. *Boy Journals, 1887-1892.* Cambridge, Massachusetts, 1915. Has a chapter on early recollections of hunting.

————. *Migratory Bird Protection in North America: The History of Control by the United States Federal Government and a Sketch of the Treaty with Great Britain.* Cambridge, Massachusetts, 1934.

————. *A Natural History of the Ducks.* 4 vols. Boston, 1922-26. A massive work by the noted sportsman-naturalist.

————. "Naturalists, Nature Lovers, and Sportsmen." *The Auk,* XLVIII (January, 1931), 40-46. Shows how the groups overlap. Among the more notable items in this article is an attack on "the appalling threat of oil" which is "killing countless thousands of our finest . . . marine ducks, loons, auks, grebes and gulls."

————, ed. *Shooting Journal of George Henry Mackay, 1865-1922.* Cambridge, Massachusetts, 1929. Cites William Dutcher, founder of the National Association of Audubon Societies, as a sportsman, and includes a bibliography of Mackay's contributions to *The Auk.*

————. *Shooting-Stands of Eastern Massachusetts.* Cambridge, Massachusetts, 1929. On waterfowling.

Pinchot, Gifford. *Biltmore Forest, the Property of Mr. George W. Vanderbilt: An Account of its Treatment, and the Results of the First Year's Work.* New York, 1970. Reprint of work originally published in 1893.

————. *Breaking New Ground.* New York, 1947.

————. *The Fight for Conservation.* New York, 1910.

―――――. "How Conservation Began in the United States." *Agricultural History,* XI (October, 1937), 255-65. The opening line is "Conservation grew out of forestry, as many of you know."

―――――. "How the National Forests Were Won." *American Forests and Forest Life,* XXXVI (1930), 615-19, and 674.

―――――. *Just Fishing Talk.* New York, 1936. Reminiscences of angling, including that boyhood fishing trip to the Adirondacks that "not improbably . . . had much to do with making me a forester." For the importance of this book in understanding Pinchot, see Reiger, "Gifford Pinchot With Rod and Reel."

―――――. Papers. Manuscript Division, U.S. Library of Congress.

―――――. "Roosevelt's Part in Forestry." *Journal of Forestry,* XVIII (February, 1919), 122-24.

Pinkett, Harold T. *Gifford Pinchot: Private and Public Forester.* Urbana, Illinois, 1970.

Pisani, Donald J. "Fish Culture and the Dawn of Concern Over Water Pollution in the United States." *Environmental Review,* VIII (1984), 117-31.

Posewitz, Jim. *Beyond Fair Chase: The Ethic and Tradition of Hunting.* Billings, Montana, 1994.

Prewitt, Wiley C., Jr. " 'The Best of All Breathing': Hunting and Environmental Change in Mississippi, 1900-1980." M.A. thesis, University of Mississippi, 1991.

Proctor, Nicholas W. "Bathed in Blood: Hunting in the Antebellum South." Ph.D. dissertation, Emory University, 1998.

Prouty, Lorenzo. *Fish: Their Habits and Haunts and the Methods of Catching Them, Together with Fishing as a Recreation.* Boston, 1883.

Putnam, Carleton. *Theodore Roosevelt: The Formative Years, 1858-1886.* New York, 1958.

Radford, Harry V. *Adirondack Murray: A Biographical Appreciation.* New York, 1905. Includes a list of Murray's published works.

Rakestraw, Lawrence. "Conservation Historiography: An Assessment." *Pacific Historical Review,* XLI (August, 1972), 271-88. Traces historical "trends" in the writing of the history of conservation, and offers his own important reinterpretation of the supposed "preservation" versus "conservation" split.

―――――. Review of Henry Clepper's *Professional Forestry in the United States* (1971), in *Pacific Historical Review,* XLII (February, 1973), 118. Asserts that Gifford Pinchot had an interest in aesthetic conservation.

―――――. Review of *Man's Dominion* (1971), by Frank Graham, Jr., in *Forest History,* XVI (April, 1972), 31-32. Reinterpretation of the supposed "preservation" versus "conservation" clash, particularly as it has been applied to Gifford Pinchot. Rakestraw observes that Pinchot has been judged "by his rhetoric, rather than by his actions."

Raymond, George B. (comp.). *Catalogue of Books on Angling, Shooting, Field Sports, Natural History, the Dog, Gun, Horse, Racing, and Kindred Subjects.* New York, 1904.

Recreation. New York, 1894-1901.

Reeves, Jr., John H. "The History and Development of Wildlife Conservation in Virginia: A Critical Review." Ph.D. dissertation, Virginia Polytechnic Institution, 1960.

Reeves, Thomas C. "President Arthur in Yellowstone National Park." *Montana, the Magazine of Western History*, XIX (July, 1969), 18-29. Mentions Arthur's angling, as well as that of Senator George G. Vest, who was in the President's party.

Reid, [Thomas] Mayne. *The Hunter's Feast; or, Conversations Around the Campfire*. New York, 1856. Reid inspired countless boys—George Bird Grinnell and Theodore Roosevelt among them—to seek the same adventures described in his many books. The one cited here is noteworthy, as it contains an account of a hunting trip Reid took with Audubon.

Reiger, George W. *Profiles in Saltwater Angling: A History of the Sport—Its People and Places, Tackle and Techniques*. Englewood Cliffs, New Jersey, 1973. A popular history of saltwater sport fishing. Includes a bibliography.

Reiger, John F. "A Dedication to the Memory of George Bird Grinnell, 1849-1938." *Arizona and the West*, XXI (Spring, 1979), 1-4.

———. "George Bird Grinnell." *National Wildlife*, XI (February-March, 1973), 12-13.

———. *"Gifford Pinchot with Rod and Reel"/"Trading Places: From Historian to Environmental Activist"—Two Essays in Conservation History*. Milford, Pennsylvania, 1994. The second essay argues that the author's background as an "environmental historian" gave him perspective during his five-year term as Executive Director of the Connecticut Audubon Society.

———. "John Burroughs." *National Wildlife*, XIV (December-January, 1976), 48-49.

———. "John F. Reiger's Commentary on Thomas R. Dunlap's Article, 'Sport Hunting and Conservation, 1880-1920'," *Environmental Review*, XII (Fall, 1988), 94-96. Also see Altherr and Reiger, "Academic Historians and Hunting."

———. "The Merging of Sport, Art, and Conservation in Late Nineteenth-Century America." In William V. Mealy and Peter Friederici, eds., *Value in American Wildlife Art: Proceedings of the 1992 Forum*, 44-51. Jamestown, New York, 1992. From a conference at the Roger Tory Peterson Institute of Natural History.

———. " 'Part of My Life . . . Part of My Identity': Hunting, Fishing, and the Development of Jimmy Carter's Conservation Ethic." *Journal of Sport History*, XX (Spring, 1993), 43-47. On how the "code of the sportsman" influenced a later president to make conservation a major thrust of his administration.

———, ed. (and commentator). *The Passing of the Great West: Selected Papers of George Bird Grinnell*. Norman, Oklahoma, 1985. First published in 1972. Based on Grinnell's previously unpublished "Memoirs," which trace his life from 1849 to 1883, this work blends his words with the editor's commentary to paint a picture of the "Wild West's" last years.

———, ed. "Sailing in South Florida Waters in the Early 1880s." Parts I and II. *Tequesta*, XXXI (1971), 43-66 and XXXII (1972), 58-78. Description of extended hunting-fishing trip taken by sportsman-naturalist James A. Henshall. The account originally appeared in *Forest and Stream*.

———, ed. "With Grinnell and Custer in the Black Hills." *Discovery: The Magazine of the Yale Peabody Museum of Natural History*, XX (1987), 16-21. From a diary Grinnell kept on the 1874 Custer expedition, this account describes his scientific collecting and his relationship with the General.

Remsburg, John E. and George J. *Charley Reynolds: Soldier, Hunter, Scout and Guide*. Kansas City, Missouri, 1931. A close friend of Grinnell's before he was killed at the Little Bighorn in 1876.

Reynolds, Charles B. (comp.). *The Game Laws in Brief. Laws of the United States and Canada, Relating to Game and Fish Seasons. For the Guidance of Sportsmen and Anglers*. New York, 1896. Published by *Forest and Stream*.

Riley, Glenda. *Women and Nature: Saving the "Wild" West*. Lincoln, Nebraska, 1999.

Riling, Ray (comp.). *Guns and Shooting: A Selected Chronological Bibliography*. . . . New York and Toronto, 1951. The chronology is from 1420 to 1950 and includes European, English, and American works.

Robbins, Roy M. *Our Landed Heritage: The Public Domain, 1776-1936*. Lincoln, Nebraska, 1962. First published in 1942.

Robinson, Donald H. *Through the Years in Glacier National Park: An Administrative History*. West Glacier, Montana, 1967. First published in 1960. Contains material on Grinnell's effort to establish the park.

Rodgers III, Andrew Denny. *Bernhard Eduard Fernow: A Story of North American Forestry*. New York, 1968. Reprint of work first published in 1951.

Roe, Frank Gilbert. *The North American Buffalo: A Critical Study of the Species in Its Wild State*. Toronto, 1951.

Rogers, Daniel T. "In Search of Progressivism." *Reviews in American History*, 10 (December, 1982), 113-32.

Roosevelt, Robert Barnwell. *Florida and the Game Water-Birds of the Atlantic Coast and the Lakes of the United States. With a Full Account of the Sporting Along Our Seashores and Inland Waters, and Remarks on Breech-Loaders and Hammerless Guns*. New York, 1884.

———. *Game Fish of the Northern States of America, and British Provinces*. New York, 1862.

———. *Superior Fishing; or, the Striped Bass, Trout, and Black Bass of the Northern States*. . . . New York, 1865.

———, and Seth Green [order of authors' names on title page—in reverse order on spine]. *Fish Hatching, and Fish Catching*. Rochester, New York, 1879.

Roosevelt, Theodore. "Big Game Disappearing in the West." *The Forum*, XV (August, 1893), 767-74. Includes hunting experiences of Clarence King.

———. *Hunting Trips of a Ranchman: Sketches of Sport on the Northern Cattle Plains*. Upper Saddle River, New Jersey, 1970. Reprint of work first published in 1885.

———. "My Life as a Naturalist: With a Presentation of Various First-Hand Data on the Life Histories and Habits of the Big Game Animals of Africa." *American Museum Journal* (later *Natural History*), XVIII (May, 1918), 320-50.

———. Papers. Houghton Library, Harvard University.

———. Papers. Manuscript Division, U.S. Library of Congress.

———. *Ranch Life and the Hunting-Trail*. New York, 1969. Reprint of work first published in 1888.

———. *Theodore Roosevelt: An Autobiography*. New York, 1913.

———. *Theodore Roosevelt's Diaries of Boyhood and Youth*. New York, 1928. No editor cited.

————. *Works.* Memorial Edition. 24 vols. New York, 1923-26.

————. *Works.* National Edition. 20 vols. New York, 1926.

————, and George Bird Grinnell, eds. *American Big-Game Hunting.* New York, 1901. First published in 1893. Includes articles on the conservation needs of the nation, written by the editors.

————, and George Bird Grinnell, eds. *Hunting in Many Lands.* New York, 1895. Includes material on conservation written by the editors.

————; T. S. Van Dyke; D. G. Elliot; and A. J. Stone. *The Deer Family.* New York, 1902.

Rothman, Hal K. *The Greening of a Nation? Environmentalism in the United States Since 1945.* Fort Worth, Texas, 1998.

————. *Preserving Different Pasts: The American National Monuments.* Urbana, Illinois, 1989.

Rothrock, Joseph T. *Vacation Cruising in Chesapeake and Delaware Bays.* Philadelphia, 1884. Describes himself as a hunter and believer in the code of the sportsman.

Runte, Alfred. *National Parks: The American Experience.* Lincoln, Nebraska, 1997. Third edition of a work first published in 1979.

Sargent, D. A., *et al. Athletic Sports.* New York, 1897. Has section entitled "Country Clubs and Hunt Clubs in America," showing that the former grew out of the latter.

Sargent, Shirley. "Galen Clark—Mr. Yosemite." In *Yosemite: Saga of a Century, 1864-1964,* published by the Yosemite Natural History Association, 19-20. Oakhurst, California, 1964.

————. *Galen Clark, Yosemite Guardian.* San Francisco, 1964.

Saveth, Edward N. "The American Patrician Class: A Field for Research." *American Quarterly,* XV (Summer, 1963), 235-52.

Schenck, Carl A. *The Biltmore Story: Recollections of the Beginnings of Forestry in the United States.* St. Paul, Minnesota, 1955. Ed. by Ovid Butler. Contains reference to his establishing a "deer park" at Biltmore "to get acquainted with the feeding and breeding habits of the native Virginia [white-tailed] deer."

Schmitt, Peter J. *Back to Nature: The Arcadian Myth in Urban America.* New York, 1969. Schmitt dates the "back to nature" craze from around the turn of the century to shortly after World War I, when in fact it was already in high gear by the 1870s—at least among thousands of sportsmen.

Schorger, A. W. *The Passenger Pigeon: Its Natural History and Extinction.* Norman, Oklahoma, 1973. First published in 1955.

Schrepfer, Susan R. *The Fight to Save the Redwoods: A History of Environmental Reform, 1917-1978.* Madison, Wisconsin, 1983. Despite the claim of some historians, sportsmen were often as interested in aesthetic conservation as utilitarian conservation, as shown by the efforts of Madison Grant and William Kent to "save the redwoods."

Schuchert, Charles, and Clara Mae LeVene. *O. C. Marsh, Pioneer in Paleontology.* New Haven, 1940. Yale sportsman-scientist under whom Grinnell received his Ph.D. in 1880.

Schullery, Paul. *American Fly-Fishing: A History.* New York, 1987.

————. "A Partnership in Conservation: Theodore Roosevelt and Yellowstone [National Park]." *Montana, the Magazine of Western History,* XXVIII (July, 1978), 2-15. On Roosevelt's first conservation fight.

———. *Royal Coachman: The Lore and Legends of Fly-Fishing.* New York, 1999.

———. *Searching for Yellowstone: Ecology and Wonder in the Last Wilderness.* New York, 1997. Much on the early history of the park.

———. "Theodore Roosevelt: The Scandal of the Hunter as Nature Lover." In Natalie A. Naylor, *et al.*, eds., *Theodore Roosevelt: Many-Sided American*, 221-30. Interlaken, New York, 1992. An important article on the "emotional messiness" exhibited by some scholars when discussing hunting, a kind of self-righteous indignation that "trivializes something of great significance."

Schurz, Carl. "Reminiscences of a Long Life." *McClure's Magazine*, XXVI (November and December, 1905), 6, 14, and 170-71. Cites his youthful interest in hunting and shooting. The pages given here refer to only part of a much longer article.

Schwerdt, C. F. G. R. (comp.). *The Schwerdt Collection: Catalogue of the Renowned Collection of Books, Manuscripts, Prints, and Drawings Relating to Hunting, Hawking and Shooting Formed by the Late C. F. G. R. Schwerdt. . . .* London, 1939 and 1946. Published in six "Portions": 1-4 published in 1939 and 5-6 in 1946. Bound in one volume in New York Public Library. Some American items, but useful mainly for Old World antecedents of sport.

Scott, Genio C. *Fishing in American Waters.* New York, 1875. First published in 1869.

Seccombe, Joseph. *A Discourse Utter'd in Part at Ammauskeeg-Falls in the Fishing Season, 1739.* Barre, Massachusetts, 1971. Reprint, with an Introduction by C. K. Shipton, of a work originally published in Boston in 1743. This sermon on the benefits of angling is generally regarded as the first work on sport fishing to be published in America.

Selmeier, Lewis W. "First Camera on the Yellowstone—A Century Ago. . . . " *Montana, the Magazine of Western History*, XXII (Summer, 1972), 42-53. On William H. Jackson.

Seton, Grace Gallatin. *Nimrod's Wife.* New York, 1907. "Nimrod" is Ernest Thompson Seton.

Shaw, S. M., ed. *A Centennial Offering, Being a Brief History of Cooperstown with a Biographical Sketch of J. F. Cooper, by Hon. Isaac N. Arnold, Together with other Interesting Local Facts and Data.* Cooperstown, New York, 1886. Cites fact that Cooper was very fond of fishing and hunting in his youth.

Sheldon, Charles. *The Wilderness of Denali: Explorations of a Hunter-Naturalist in Northern Alaska.* New York, 1960. First published in 1930, it contains an Introduction by C. Hart Merriam and deals with the Mount McKinley region, which was set aside as a national park largely through Sheldon's efforts.

Shepard, Paul. *The Others: How Animals Made Us Human.* Washington, D.C., 1996. Should be contrasted with Cartmill's anti-hunting work, for Shepard argues that hunting has always been an excellent way of involving oneself intensely with the lives of wild animals. To approach them from an animal "rights" position and the "precept of untouchability" results, he asserts, in nothing more than our "spectatorship" (p. 6) at the edge of nature. Interestingly, George Bird Grinnell and Aldo Leopold influenced his thinking.

———. *The Tender Carnivore and the Sacred Game.* New York, 1973. Argues that modern humans' most cherished qualities and abilities are the result of their hunter-gatherer past.

Shields, George Oliver, ed. *American Game Fishes: Their Habits, Habitat, and Peculiarities; How, When, and Where to Angle for Them.* Chicago and New York, 1892. Papers by a number of authorities.

————, ed. *The Big Game of North America: Its Habits, Habitat, Haunts, and Characteristics; How, When, and Where to Hunt It. . . .* Chicago and New York, 1890. Papers by a number of authorities.

————. *Hunting in the Great West: Hunting and Fishing by Mountain and Stream.* Chicago, 1883. Contains an Introduction by Nicholas Rowe, editor of *American Field* (later name of *Field and Stream*), emphasizing the code of the sportsman. Later, Shields edited *Recreation,* a popular sportsman's periodical.

Shiras, George, 3d. *Hunting Wild Life with Camera and Flashlight: A Record of Sixty-Five Years' Visits to the Woods and Waters of North America.* 2 vols. Washington, D.C., 1936. First published in 1935. By a leading sportsman-conservationist and pioneer wildlife photographer.

Shoemaker, Carl D. *The Stories Behind the Organization of the National Wildlife Federation and Its Early Struggles for Survival.* Washington, D.C., 1960.

Slotkin, Richard. *The Fatal Environment: The Myth of the Frontier in the Age of Industrialization, 1800-1890.* Norman, Oklahoma, 1998. First published in 1985.

Smallwood, William M. *Natural History and the American Mind.* New York, 1967. First published in 1941.

Smith, Charles D. "The Appalachian National Park Movement, 1885-1901." *North Carolina Historical Review,* XXXVII (January, 1960), 38-65.

Smith, Henry Nash. *Virgin Land: The American West as Symbol and Myth.* New York, 1957. First published in 1950.

Smith, Jerome V. C. *Natural History of the Fishes of Massachusetts, Embracing a Practical Essay on Angling.* Boston, 1833.

The Spirit of the Times. New York, 1831-1861.

Sprague, Marshall. *A Gallery of Dudes.* Boston, 1966. On British, Continental, and East-coast "dudes" who went West and what they found.

Stange, Mary Zeiss. *Woman the Hunter.* Boston, 1997.

Steen, Harold K., ed. *The Origins of the National Forests: A Centennial Symposium.* Durham, North Carolina, 1992.

Sterling, Keir B., *et al.,* eds. *Biographical Dictionary of American and Canadian Naturalists and Environmentalists.* Westport, Connecticut, 1997.

————. *Last of the Naturalists: The Career of C. Hart Merriam.* New York, 1974.

Stimson, Henry L. *My Vacations.* New York [?], 1949. Privately printed. Describes travel and hunting in area that became Glacier National Park. Also cites the hunting activities of Gifford Pinchot.

Stoddard, S. R. *The Adirondacks.* Glens Falls, New York, 1893 [?]. 1894 (24th) edition of guidebook first published in 1874. Copyright year of this edition is 1893.

Stone, Livingston. *Domesticated Trout. How to Breed and Grow Them.* Charlestown, New Hampshire, 1877. First published in 1872. Includes "Books on Fish Culture" and an account from an earlier work describing tagging of salmon to learn about their life histories.

————. "The Early Days of Fish Culture in the United States." *American Angler,* XXVIII (November, 1898), 217-24.

Strout, Cushing. *The American Image of the Old World*. New York, 1963. Has much on the Anglophilia of the upper class in the late nineteenth century.
Swift, Ernest F. *A Conservation Saga*. Washington, D.C., 1967. Some material on former wildlife abundance, plus an analysis of the conservation philosophy.
———. *The Public's Land: Our Heritage and Opportunity*. Washington, D.C., 1963.
Terrie, Philip G. *Forever Wild: A Cultural History of Wilderness in the Adirondacks*. Syracuse, 1994. A good example of both the anti-hunting and anti-upper-class bias possessed by some academic historians, who disparage, or understate, the conservation efforts of gentlemen sportsmen. For example, despite *Forest and Stream*'s leadership in Adirondack forest preservation, he attacks the paper's editors for supposedly being more interested in saving deer than in protecting forests, so that "the gentlemanly *art of killing* [emphasis added] the white-tailed deer" could continue (pp. 73-74).
Thoreau, Henry David. *Cape Cod*. New York, 1951. Dudley C. Lunt's edition of book first published in 1865.
———. *The Concord and the Merrimack*. New York, 1954. Dudley C. Lunt's edition of *A Week on the Concord and Merrimack Rivers*, published by Thoreau in 1849.
———. *The Maine Woods*. New York, 1950. Dudley C. Lunt's edition of book first published in 1864.
———. *Walden, or Life in the Woods*. New York, 1942. First published in 1854.
Tober, James A. *Who Owns the Wildlife? The Political Economy of Conservation in Nineteenth-Century America*. Westport, Connecticut, 1981.
Tomsich, John. *A Genteel Endeavor: American Culture and Politics in the Gilded Age*. Palo Alto, California, 1971.
Townsend, Charles H. *Guide to the New York Aquarium*. New York, 1929. Contains an outline history of this institution, founded by sportsmen-naturalists.
Trefethen, James B. *An American Crusade for Wildlife*. New York, 1975. A rewriting, and updating, of his 1961 book.
———. *Crusade for Wildlife: Highlights in Conservation Progress*. Harrisburg, Pennsylvania, 1961. Mainly a history of the Boone and Crockett Club, this work traces the development of wildlife conservation—conceived in its broadest sense—through the 1950s. Almost every individual cited was a sportsman.
True, Webster P. *The Smithsonian Institution*. Vol. 1 of the Smithsonian Scientific Series. New York, 1929 and 1934. On origins of National Zoo, U.S. Fish Commission, etc.
Udall, Stewart L. *The Quiet Crisis*. New York, 1967. First published in 1963. General history of Americans' impact on the natural environment and the rise of the conservation movement.
U.S. Cartridge Company. *Where to Hunt American Game*. Lowell, Massachusetts, 1898. State-by-state survey.
U.S. Commission of Fish and Fisheries. *Report on the Condition of the Sea Fisheries of the South Coast of New England in 1871 and 1872*. Washington, D.C., 1873.

U.S. Department of the Interior, Fish and Wildlife Service, and U.S. Department of Commerce, Bureau of the Census. *1991 National Survey of Fishing, Hunting, and Wildlife-Associated Recreation.* Washington, D.C., 1993.

U.S. Department of the Interior. *Waterfowl Tomorrow.* Washington, D.C., 1964. Contains articles by many authorities on the management of ducks and geese, including "Waterfowl and the Hunter," which is partly an analysis of why people hunt.

Van Brocklin, Ralph M. "The Movement for the Conservation of Natural Resources in the United States Before 1901." Ph.D. dissertation, University of Michigan, 1952.

Van Dyke, Henry. *Fisherman's Luck, and Some Other Uncertain Things.* New York, 1905. First published in 1899. Van Dyke's work is notable for portraying the aesthetic quality of angling.

———. *Little Rivers.* New York, 1900. First published in 1895.

Van Winkle, William Mitchell (comp.). *Henry William Herbert ["Frank Forester"]: A Bibliography of His Writings, 1832-1858.* Portland, Maine, 1936.

Wallace, E. R. *Descriptive Guide to the Adirondacks. . . .* New York, 1878. Apparently first published in 1872. Emphasizes that the region is a paradise for sportsmen and calls for the creation of a great state park in its mountains.

Walsh, Harry M. *The Outlaw Gunner.* Cambridge, Maryland, 1971. A popular history of commercial waterfowl hunting in the Chesapeake Bay region.

Ward, George B., III. "Bloodbrothers in the Wilderness: The Sport Hunter and the Buckskin Hunter in the Preservation of the American Wilderness Experience." Ph.D. dissertation, University of Texas, 1980.

Ward, Rowland. *The English Angler in Florida, With Some Descriptive Notes of the Game Animals and Birds.* London, 1898.

———. *The Sportsman's Handbook to Collecting, Preserving, and Setting-Up Trophies and Specimens, Together with a Guide to the Hunting Grounds of the World.* London, 1911. First published in 1880.

Warren, Louis S. *The Hunter's Game: Poachers and Conservationists in Twentieth-Century America.* New Haven, Connecticut, 1997.

Waterman, Charles F. *Fishing in America.* New York, 1975. A popular history, from pre-Columbian times to the years just before publication.

———. *Hunting in America.* New York, 1973. A popular history, from pre-Columbian times to the years just before publication.

Webb, William E. *Buffalo Land: An Authentic Account of the Discoveries, Adventures, and Mishaps of a Scientific and Sporting Party in the Wild West.* Philadelphia, 1872. Note the juxtaposition of terms in the title.

Welker, Robert Henry. *Birds and Men: American Birds in Science, Art, Literature, and Conservation, 1800-1900.* New York, 1966. First published in 1955.

Westwood, Thomas T., and Thomas Satchell (comps.). *Bibliotheca Piscatoria: A Catalogue of Books on Angling, The Fisheries and Fish-Culture, With Bibliographical Notes and an Appendix of Citations Touching on Angling and Fishing from Old English Authors.* London, 1883. First appeared in 1861. Works in all languages and includes some American items.

Wetzell, Charles M. (comp.). *American Fishing Books; A Bibliography From the Earliest Times Up to 1948, Together with a History of Angling and Angling*

Literature in America. Newark, Delaware, 1950. Particularly good for the history of *Forest and Stream.*

Whipple, Gurth. *Fifty Years of Conservation in New York State, 1885-1935.* Syracuse, 1935.

White, G. Edward. *The Eastern Establishment and the Western Experience: The West of Frederic Remington, Theodore Roosevelt, and Owen Wister.* New Haven, 1968.

White, Jr., Lynn. "The Historical Roots of Our Ecological Crisis." *Science,* CLV (March 10, 1967), 1203-07. The classic statement on the negative impact of the Judeo-Christian tradition.

Whitehead, Charles E. *Wild Sports in the South; or, The Camp-Fires of the Everglades.* New York, 1860.

Whitney, Caspar; George Bird Grinnell; and Owen Wister. *Musk-Ox, Bison, Sheep and Goat.* New York, 1904. Hunting and natural history.

Whitney, Gordon G. *From Coastal Wilderness to Fruited Plain: A History of Environmental Change in Temperate North America, 1500 to the Present.* New York, 1994.

Wiebe, Robert H. "The Progressive Years, 1900-1917." In *The Reinterpretaion of American History and Culture,* ed. by William H. Cartwright and Richard L. Watson, Jr., 425-42. Washington, D.C., 1973. Discussion of the history of the writing of history of the so-called "Progressive" period.

———. *The Search for Order, 1877-1920.* New York, 1967. Both a synthesis and a thought-provoking interpretation.

"Wildwood, Will" (Frederick E. Pond), ed. *Frank Forester's Sporting Scenes and Characters.* 2 vols. Philadelphia, 1881.

Williston, S. W. "The American Antelope." *American Naturalist,* II (October, 1877), 599-603. Typical of many articles in this journal that assume that hunting is an integral part of natural history study.

Wilson, Alexander. *Wilson's American Ornithology, With Notes by Jardine: To Which is Added A Synopsis of American Birds, Including Those Described By Bonaparte, Audubon, Nuttall, and Richardson; By T. M. Brewer.* New York, 1970. Reprint of the one-volume 1840 edition. This work originally appeared in nine volumes, beginning in 1808.

Woodbury, Robert. "William Kent: Progressive Gadfly, 1864-1928." Ph.D. dissertation, Yale University, 1967. Kent was a noted conservationist and enthusiastic hunter.

Worster, Donald. *The Wealth of Nature: Environmental History and the Ecological Imagination.* New York, 1993.

Yates, Norris W. *William T. Porter and the Spirit of the Times. . . .* Baton Rouge, Louisiana, 1957. Study of a well-known sportsman and periodical of the pre-Civil War period.

Yellowstone National Park. Papers. Yellowstone National Park Library, Mammoth Hot Springs. Miscellaneous items relating to the reserve's early history, including some correspondence of Grinnell, Hague, and Superintendent Anderson.

Index